1 & 2
Chronicles

UNDERSTANDING THE BIBLE
COMMENTARY SERIES

GENERAL EDITORS

W. Ward Gasque

Robert L. Hubbard Jr.

Robert K. Johnston

1 & 2
Chronicles

Louis C. Jonker

BakerBooks
a division of Baker Publishing Group
Grand Rapids, Michigan

© 2013 by Louis C. Jonker

Published by Baker Books
a division of Baker Publishing Group
P.O. Box 6287, Grand Rapids, MI 49516-6287
www.bakerbooks.com

Printed in the United States of America

Library of Congress Cataloging-in-Publication Data
Jonker, Louis C.
    1 & 2 Chronicles / Louis C. Jonker.
        pages cm. — (Understanding the Bible commentary series)
    Includes index.
    ISBN 978-0-8010-4825-8 (pbk.)
    1. Bible. Chronicles—Commentaries. I. Title. II. Title: First and Second Chronicles.
BS1345.53.J66 2013
222′.607—dc23   2013015982

13   14   15   16   17   18   19   7   6   5   4   3   2   1

Contents

Foreword

As an ancient document, the Old Testament often seems something quite foreign to modern men and women. Opening its pages may feel, to the modern reader, like traversing a kind of literary time warp into a whole other world. In that world sisters and brothers marry, long hair mysteriously makes men superhuman, and temple altars daily smell of savory burning flesh and sweet incense. There, desert bushes burn but leave no ashes, water gushes from rocks, and cities fall because people march around them. A different world, indeed!

Even God, the Old Testament's main character, seems a stranger compared to his more familiar New Testament counterpart. Sometimes the divine is portrayed as a loving father and faithful friend, someone who rescues people from their greatest dangers or generously rewards them for heroic deeds. At other times, however, God resembles more a cruel despot, one furious at human failures, raving against enemies, and bloodthirsty for revenge. Thus, skittish about the Old Testament's diverse portrayal of God, some readers carefully select which portions of the text to study, or they avoid the Old Testament altogether.

The purpose of this commentary series is to help readers navigate this strange and sometimes forbidding literary and spiritual terrain. Its goal is to break down the barriers between the ancient and modern worlds so that the power and meaning of these biblical texts become transparent to contemporary readers. How is this to be done? And what sets this series apart from others currently on the market?

This commentary series will bypass several popular approaches to biblical interpretation. It will not follow a *precritical* approach that interprets the text without reference to recent scholarly conversations. Such a commentary contents itself with offering little more than a paraphrase of the text with occasional supplements from archeology, word studies, and classical theology. It mistakenly believes that there have been few insights into the Bible since Calvin or Luther. Nor will this series pursue an *anticritical* approach whose preoccupation is to defend the Bible against its detractors, especially scholarly ones. Such a commentary has little space left to move beyond showing why the Bible's critics are wrong to explaining what the biblical text means. The result is a paucity of vibrant biblical theology. Again, this series finds inadequate a *critical* approach that seeks to understand the text apart from belief in the meaning it conveys. Though modern readers have been taught to be discerning, they do not want to live in the "desert of criticism" either.

Instead, as its editors, we have sought to align this series with what has been labeled *believing criticism*. This approach marries probing, reflective interpretation of the text to loyal biblical devotion and warm Christian affection. Our contributors tackle the task of interpretation using the full range of critical methodologies and practices. Yet they do so as people of faith who hold the text in the highest regard. The commentators in this series use criticism to bring the message of the biblical texts vividly to life so the minds of modern readers may be illumined and their faith deepened.

The authors in this series combine a firm commitment to modern scholarship with a similar commitment to the Bible's full authority for Christians. They bring to the task the highest technical skills, warm theological commitment, and rich insight from their various communities. In so doing, they hope to enrich the life of the academy as well as the life of the church.

Part of the richness of this commentary series derives from its authors' breadth of experience and ecclesial background. As editors, we have consciously brought together a diverse group of scholars in terms of age, gender, denominational affiliation, and race. We make no claim that they represent the full expression of the people of God, but they do bring fresh, broad perspectives to the interpretive task. But though this series has sought out diversity among its contributors, they also reflect a commitment to a common center. These commentators write as "believing critics"—scholars who desire to speak for church and academy, for academy and church. As editors, we offer this series in devotion to God and for the enrichment of God's people.

ROBERT L. HUBBARD JR.
ROBERT K. JOHNSTON
Editors

Preface

To start writing a commentary on a biblical book is analogous to embarking on a long journey. Not only is the actual writing a tedious process that spans a number of years, but the commentary-to-be also becomes a travel companion in one's academic work that shapes one's perspectives, narrows one's focus, and provides one with unexpected joys (and pains). The writing of a commentary also draws one into a journey with those who were responsible for the authoring and editing of the biblical book in ancient times, into their world, their struggles of faith, their hopes. But the commentary-to-be also creates an awareness of a journey with those scholars and people of faith who will read this publication, who will engage with what has been written in it, and who will (hopefully) be enlightened by it.

On this journey I had many other trusted and appreciated companions. I thank Bob Hubbard for inviting me to do this commentary, as well as for his valuable comments and feedback during the years. I also have great appreciation for James Korsmo's input as responsible editor at Baker Books for the finalization of the manuscript. He and his editorial team did a formidable job. I am furthermore privileged to be part of a guild of Chronicles scholars who show remarkable collegiality, cooperation, and engagement with one another. Two good friends and able scholars, Gary Knoppers and Ehud Ben Zvi, should be mentioned by name. I am grateful to have had in this project the support of my colleagues in the Discipline Group Old and New Testament and the Faculty of Theology in Stellenbosch, and I hereby express my gratitude toward this institution for study leave granted, as well as for financial support. My home-away-from-home is Tübingen, Germany, where I have spent many a month over the past four years to finish this manuscript. Erhard Blum always was a hospitable host in the Protestant Faculty there, and he therefore deserves my appreciation. Without the generous financial support of the Alexander von Humboldt Stiftung (Bonn, Germany) these visits—and therefore this commentary—would never have materialized.

My wife, Anita, and sons, Johannes and Cornelius, were not only understanding and supportive companions in the journey toward the finalization of this commentary. They are also the best companions in the journey of life.

Last, but not least, Edwin Hees deserves a great word of thanks for his editing of my language use and style.

I dedicate this commentary to all my undergraduate and postgraduate students in Stellenbosch who had to listen to many lectures and talks on Chronicles over the past years. Your engagement with and enthusiasm for this project meant a lot to me.

STELLENBOSCH, DECEMBER 2011

Abbreviations

AB	Anchor Bible
ABG	Arbeiten zur Bibel und ihrer Geschichte
ABR	*Australian Biblical Review*
ACCS	Ancient Christian Commentary on Scripture
AcT	*Acta Theologica*
A.D.	anno Domini
ADPV	Abhandlungen des Deutschen Palästina-Vereins
AOTC	Abingdon Old Testament Commentaries
BBB	Bonner Biblische Beiträge
BBR	*Bulletin for Biblical Research*
B.C.	before Christ
Bib	*Biblica*
BibInt	*Biblical Interpretation*
BKAT	Biblischer Kommentar Altes Testament
BN	*Biblische Notizen*
BWANT	Beiträge zur Wissenschaft vom Alten und Neuen Testament
ca.	circa
CBQ	*Catholic Biblical Quarterly*
CH	*Church History*
cf.	*confer*, compare
CurBS	*Currents in Research: Biblical Studies*
e.g.	*exempli gratia*, for example
FAT	Forschungen zum Alten Testament
HCOT	Historical Commentary on the Old Testament
HTR	*Harvard Theological Review*
i.e.	*id est*, that is
JBL	*Journal of Biblical Literature*
JNSL	*Journal of Northwest Semitic Languages*
JSOT	*Journal for the Study of the Old Testament*
JSOTSup	Journal for the Study of the Old Testament: Supplement Series
LHBOTS	Library of Hebrew Bible / Old Testament Studies
LXX	Septuagint
MT	Masoretic Text

NIV	New International Version
NIVAC	New International Version Application Commentary
NRSV	New Revised Standard Version
OTE	*Old Testament Essays*
p(p).	page(s)
RB	*Revue biblique*
RevExp	*Review and Expositor*
SJOT	*Scandinavian Journal of the Old Testament*
SSN	Studia semitica neerlandica
TOTC	Tyndale Old Testament Commentaries
TQ	*Theologische Quartalschrift*
TSHB	Textpragmatische Studien der Hebräischen Bibel
vol(s).	volume(s)
VT	*Vetus Testamentum*
WBC	Word Biblical Commentary
ZAH	*Zeitschrift für Althebräistik*
ZAW	*Zeitschrift für die alttestamentliche Wissenschaft*

Introduction

For a long time Chronicles studies were the Cinderella of biblical scholarship.[1] Because many saw this book as just some sort of duplication of the histories presented in Joshua, Judges, Samuel, and Kings, no effort was made to analyze Chronicles in its own right. The old tradition started by the Septuagint[2] of calling this book Paraleipomenon ("Of the omitted/remaining things")[3] did not help to gain attention for Chronicles either! This name suggested that Chronicles offered only a few additions to the "real history" preserved in the so-called Deuteronomistic History.

Recently, however, Chronicles studies have boomed at a remarkable rate. The last quarter of the twentieth century saw the advent of many studies in the form of books, commentaries, and scholarly articles. In the past decade and a half, particularly, a new wave of Chronicles commentaries has emerged, ranging from the technical and scholarly[4] to more popular presentations aimed at laypeople and preachers.[5]

The present commentary forms part of this recent development in Chronicles scholarship. The intention is, however, to glean from the current discussions on Chronicles in such a way that modern readers will understand the message and theology of this book. This commentary also aims at relating other disciplines and interests (such as insights from social-identity theory) to recent exegetical scholarship on this fascinating biblical book in order to show what the implications of Chronicles are for readers living in the twenty-first century.

Overview of the History of Interpretation of Chronicles

Readers of Chronicles have long noted that we are in a fortunate position when we study this book.[6] Whereas the literary history of the Hebrew Bible/Old Testament books is mostly very intricate, vague, and uncertain, and only informed theories can be formulated with reference to the sources of which these biblical books made use, the situation is totally different when it comes to Chronicles. When Chronicles was composed and included in the biblical collection of authoritative scriptures, the writer(s)/composer(s) did not omit or supersede their sources. We know that the writer(s) of Chronicles made use mainly of (probably earlier versions of) Joshua, Judges, Samuel, and Kings (as part of a collection spanning Joshua to Kings referred to as the Deuteronomistic History or Early Prophets) in writing and compiling this book. Comparison has therefore been the main scholarly activity when it comes to the analysis of Chronicles: the version of Israelite history presented in Chronicles is compared to that of the Deuteronomistic History.[7]

However, comparisons can be made for different purposes. In what follows I identify three prominent lines of interpretation: the historical value, nature, and rhetoric of Chronicles, respectively.

In early Chronicles scholarship (during the nineteenth and twentieth centuries but also continuing in some studies until today) these two versions of Israelite history were compared in order to judge their relative *historical value*. The question asked was, which of these two blocks of history writing offered the most reliable account of past events? Inevitably this early heuristic angle on the analysis of Chronicles revealed more about the conventions of interpretation of the nineteenth and early twentieth centuries than about the time of Chronicles. Under the influence of positivism and historicism, biblical scholars regarded these texts as reflections of past events, resulting in Chronicles being judged as an inadequate version of those events. Some early scholars depicted Chronicles as midrash, a well-known Jewish form of interpretation where, out of respect for tradition, Jewish interpreters latched onto an earlier transmitted text, but then elaborated on the particular text in very creative ways. Others emphasized that Chronicles was written long after the events and therefore could not be expected to present a reliable picture of past events.

Already in early scholarship, but particularly after archeological evidence (both material and epigraphic) increasingly became available, other scholars emphasized the historical superiority of Chronicles over the Deuteronomistic History. Certain details mentioned in Chronicles but not in Samuel-Kings were confirmed by archeological excavations (such as the reference to the Siloam tunnel in 2 Chron. 32:30). Together with the increasing archeological evidence, scholars also started gaining more knowledge about historical geography. This newfound knowledge confirmed data in Chronicles in many instances. These developments in scholarship turned the tide of argumentation in favor of the historical reliability of Chronicles. However, although the argument was the opposite, the quest in this phase (or part) of Chronicles scholarship remained the same, namely, the historical authenticity of the book's account.

Whereas the quest for the historical value of Chronicles can be described as a first line of interpretation in the history of scholarship, a second line is constituted by those studies investigating the *nature* of Chronicles. The question What is Chronicles? is central in these studies. Since the first quarter of the twentieth century, scholars—under the influence of the disillusionment with "objective history"—started qualifying the view that Chronicles could be read as history. Increasingly, it was acknowledged that this book contains history-with-a-purpose. That Chronicles narrates the history of Judah (and Israel) does not necessarily mean that the writer(s) had a historical interest. History can (as we know from many examples in our own age and context) be utilized for different purposes. One prominent theory in this regard comes from scholars who regard Chronicles as theology. According to this view (in all its variety), the writer(s) of Chronicles wanted to convey a particular theology that shows continuity with the past (embodied in the fact that history forms the basis of the book) to an audience whose changed circumstances required innovation and adaptation. The main focus in the interpretation of Chronicles from this heuristic angle was the differences between Chronicles and the Deuteronomistic History. Differences and changes, so scholars interpreting from this perspective argued, are indications of the unique theology of Chronicles.

Other scholars attempt different answers to the question What is Chronicles? Some advanced the opinion that Chronicles presents a very early form of commentary or exegesis. According to this view, the writer(s) of Chronicles presented to their audience an exposition of earlier influential, or even authoritative, sources.[8] Still others emphasize the literary character of Chronicles, categorizing the genre of Chronicles as historiography.[9] According to this view, the main emphasis in Chronicles interpretation should be to analyze the literary makeup and quality of the book in order to establish how the past is utilized in a new narrative construction. Related to these last-mentioned studies are also those contributions that discuss the position of Chronicles in the history of composition of the biblical canon. These studies investigate the process of canonical development by focusing on how different blocks of literature interpret one another. In this regard, with a fairly late date normally associated with its final composition, Chronicles is considered to be of special importance. Some even argue that Chronicles was especially composed to conclude the Hebrew Bible canon.[10]

A third line of interpretation emerged from those studies emphasizing the literary nature of Chronicles. In the last quarter of the twentieth century *rhetorical studies* of Chronicles became more prominent.[11] Taking their cue from the different views on the literary nature of Chronicles, scholars focused on the intention of this book. The central question became What did Chronicles want to achieve? The peculiar literary formation of this book was now interpreted as an indication that Chronicles was an attempt to bolster certain ideological and/or theological positions (e.g., the position of the Levites in the Second Temple cultic community). The presentation of figures of the past in Chronicles was no longer seen as a reflection of past realities, but rather as idealization serving particular rhetorical purposes in a new present (the time of origin of Chronicles). Inevitable, therefore, in these interpretations are certain informed presuppositions about the sociohistorical (particularly, socioreligious and sociopolitical) circumstances within which the book originated.

In line with these rhetorical studies of Chronicles, the issue of identity negotiation has been introduced into Chronicles research recently.[12] This position proceeds from the presupposition that these texts also serve or function as part of an active process of identity negotiation in the postexilic restoration period. This position does not imply that Chronicles is a reflection of a formulated and closed identity of the postexilic Judahite community.[13] It rather emphasizes that the very construction and composition of Chronicles were part of a dynamic process of identity negotiation during this period.

This position will also form a prominent lens for my analysis in this commentary and will be described in fuller detail below.

Content, Structure, and Genre

Anybody who has read through Chronicles knows that this book contains a retelling of the history of God's people. However, the reader would also probably be surprised that the retelling actually starts with Adam! Although Chronicles made use mainly of (probably earlier forms of) Samuel and Kings as sources for the retelling of history, it becomes clear from the start of this book that the final composition of the book presents the history of God's people within the universal framework of the story of humanity. The family lists in the first nine chapters (1 Chron. 1–9) of Chronicles therefore construct the broad familial horizon within which the rest of the retold history should be understood.

After the family lists there are elaborate sections on King David (1 Chron. 10–29) and his son, King Solomon (2 Chron. 1–9). It becomes clear through a reading of these sections that Chronicles particularly wanted to emphasize the lives of these two kings. It will become clear in the commentary that the presentation of these two kings in Chronicles, when compared to that in Samuel and Kings, shows interesting differences from those books, emphasizing certain aspects of their respective reigns.

King Solomon's history is followed by the history of God's people
during the time of the divided kingdom (2 Chron. 10–36). Up until this
point I have deliberately used the neutral term "God's people" to refer
to Judah/Israel, because Chronicles' presentation focuses mainly on the
southern kingdom, Judah. When one compares Chronicles to Samuel-
Kings, one gets the impression that the northern kingdom, Israel, was
largely ignored by Chronicles.[14] Although Israel and kings from the northern kingdom are not completely absent from Chronicles, Chronicles
clearly presents the kings of Judah as the royal line running from David
and Solomon, and the people of Judah as being God's chosen people.
The term "All-Israel" is often employed to refer to God's people.

Whereas Chronicles' retelling of history starts with Adam in
1 Chronicles 1:1, it ends with the proclamation of the Persian emperor,
Cyrus, which allowed the Judahite exiles to return to Jerusalem and to
rebuild their temple (2 Chron. 36:22–23).[15] Apart from this section indicating that the book was finalized after the return from exile, it also extends
the presentation of Kings to include the end of the exile.

The time span covered by Chronicles' retelling of the past (although
fairly cursory) is therefore from Adam until the return from exile. The
four sections of Chronicles (which will also form the main frame of this
commentary) can be outlined as follows:

1 Chron. 1:1–9:44	from the beginning: family lists
1 Chron. 10:1–29:30	David's reign
2 Chron. 1:1–9:31	Solomon's reign
2 Chron. 10:1–36:23	from Rehoboam to Cyrus

It is already clear from the presentation of the contents of Chronicles that we have different genres in this book. Although one would be
able to describe the whole book as historiography, such a categorization
of the book's genre would be too broad to cover the variety of forms
present in Chronicles.

The book starts with nine chapters of *name lists* and *genealogies*. Although the majority of modern readers would not find these lists
and genealogies particularly interesting, they form an important part of
Chronicles' final construction. These lists and genealogies, which are
not uncommon in different parts of the Old Testament (particularly the
Pentateuch), and even appear in the New Testament as well (see in the
Gospels of Matthew and Luke), give the reader a glimpse of how the ancient writer(s) saw society: how it was structured, who was influential and
important, and so forth. Many studies on these genealogies compare the

family lists with those in Ezra-Nehemiah, as well as in the Pentateuch, in order to determine how the generations of old were related to one another, but also to determine from the differing versions what particular emphasis each of these Old Testament texts wanted to convey. In this commentary the genealogies will be discussed from the perspective of social-identity theory in order to determine whether they contributed to the rhetoric of identity negotiation during the Persian era.

Most of Chronicles consists of *narratives*. The retelling of Judah's past is done mainly through the medium of stories. These narratives are mostly taken over from the sources that the writer(s) of Chronicles made use of, namely, (probably earlier forms of) Samuel and Kings. These narratives were then adapted, reconstructed, and added to, according to the purpose that the writer(s) wanted to achieve. In this commentary the dynamic mode of communication of the past by means of narratives will be taken seriously.

Apart from genealogies and narratives, other less frequent genre types also occur, for example, a *letter* (Elijah's letter in 2 Chron. 21:12–15) and a quotation from an *edict* (of Cyrus in 2 Chron. 36:22–23), various *prayers*, and *speeches*.[16] However, these elements are built into the narratives that form the broad framework of Chronicles.

Establishing the genre of a specific piece of literature such as Chronicles is important, not only in order to present an adequate description of the literary form of a text, but also to determine its rhetorical mode. Different genres evoke different responses from an audience. Attention to the genre of Chronicles will therefore be an important aspect of our approach to understand the rhetoric of the book.

"The Chronicler": Authorship and Historical Setting

In the discussion up to now I have employed the vague and neutral term "writer(s)" to refer to the authorship of Chronicles. This was done deliberately in anticipation of this section. Who wrote Chronicles? Should we look for one hand behind this text, or should we envision a collective authorship? Or should we also consider the possibility that multiple authors wrote and composed the book over a period of time?

According to an old Jewish rabbinic tradition, Ezra wrote the majority of Chronicles and Nehemiah finished it.[17] This view indicated, on the one hand, that the book was regarded as very late and that it probably formed the closing phase of the Hebrew Bible's origin. On the other hand, this view confirmed the authority of the book by associating a prominent person from the past with it and thus arguing in favor of its canonicity.

Many variations on this view have occurred through the ages: some argued for an earlier date for Chronicles, making Ezra one of the final editors of the book; others turned the argument around and made the writer(s) of Chronicles also the author(s) of Ezra-Nehemiah.

It becomes clear from this very broad overview of earlier views that the relationship between Chronicles and Ezra-Nehemiah is determinative in advancing theories about the authorship of both these books. A special section will be dedicated to this specific issue below.

Presently the majority of Chronicles scholars agree that the writer(s) of Chronicles remain(s) anonymous. The textual evidence (both biblical and extrabiblical) does not allow us to be more specific. It is also not possible to determine whether one person was responsible for the book (although highly unlikely), or whether collective authorship should be assumed. At this stage, then, I will substitute the neutral designation "writer(s)" with the term "Chronicler." When I use the term "Chronicler" in this commentary, I am referring to the writer(s)/editor(s) of the books of Chronicles. Although the term refers to a masculine individual, it functions as a collective for all those hands that contributed to the formation of Chronicles.[18] The term "Chronistic writer(s)/editor(s)" will occasionally be used as a synonym for "Chronicler." "Chronistic" refers to Chronicles, then, and not to a so-called Chronistic history, which would include the book of Ezra-Nehemiah.

Can we say anything more about the authorship of Chronicles apart from giving the writer(s) the name "Chronicler"? From the content of Chronicles we can at least venture the following description of the Chronicler.[19] He was particularly interested in the Davidic dynasty, the temple in Jerusalem, its clergy, and its cult. Chronicles leaves the impression that he had inside knowledge about those institutions and could therefore probably have been a member of the temple staff or at least part of the literate cultic leadership in Jerusalem.[20] The Chronicler's portrayal of the Levites in Chronicles is very special, which provides an argument for regarding the Chronicler as one of the Levitical priesthood.[21] The issues reflected in the book convince me that the Chronicler must have been an inhabitant of the postexilic Persian province of Yehud.

The historical setting of the book forms an important part of our investigation, not so much for the sake of determining the history of the book and the author, but particularly in order to determine the rhetorical mode of the communication included in the book. I will mainly deal with the rhetorical aspect of the book in this commentary. It is my opinion that the rhetoric of any literary work cannot be determined in generic isolation. It is only when a literary work is viewed against the background and in the context of its supposed circumstances of origin that its rhetorical thrust can be determined.

The ending of Chronicles is an indication that the book could not have been concluded before the release of the exiles during the reign of Cyrus of Persia. The other end of the time spectrum is normally determined with reference to the description of King David in the apocryphal (or deuterocanonical) book of the Wisdom of Sirach, which leaves the impression that it presupposes the Chronicler's description of this king. Since Sirach's date is normally determined as 200–180 B.C., this would form a cutoff point on this side of the time spectrum. Within these approximately three and a half centuries the Chronicler wrote and finalized his book.

But can we be more specific? In my estimation the middle of the fourth century B.C. (the late Persian era) could be a likely time of composition—at least, before the invasion of the Hellenistic leader Alexander the Great in 322 B.C. Although some argue for a dating well into the Hellenistic era, there is in my view insufficient reflection of that time period in the book. I do not deny that the final touches to the book could have been made in the Hellenistic era, but Chronicles is suffused with the atmosphere of the late Persian era.

The significance of the late Persian era lies particularly in the geographical area of Judah (including Jerusalem) more or less forming the Persian province of Yehud. Views diverge on when exactly the province of Yehud was proclaimed. From the time of Cyrus (who released the exiles in 538 B.C.) Judah probably constituted a so-called *medinah* (or province) for the purposes of tax collection and tribute payments. The province might have been subject to another province to the north, namely, Samaria. However, this cannot be confirmed. We do not have information on the early organization of this province until the time of Artaxerxes I of Persia (465 B.C.). It seems from material evidence (e.g., the appearance of the name Yehud on coins and changes in the appearance of seals that were used on official documents) that the province Yehud was granted a more formal status sometime in the second half of the fifth century B.C. Some scholars hold that the phase in Judah before the more formal proclamation of the province was characterized by a drive toward continuity with the exilic, and even preexilic, past. The new phase, however, reveals more evidence that a greater self-consciousness, or even new identity, was emerging.[22]

It is very important to consider the socioreligious context of this era here. The situation was radically different from what it had been in the preexilic and exilic phases. Before the Babylonian exile, which was

largely initiated in 586 B.C. with the fall of Jerusalem, the Davidic monarchy and the temple of Solomon in Jerusalem formed the foundation
of the prevalent theology in the kingdom of Judah. These institutions
were destroyed by the exile, leaving a disillusioned people who sensed the
precariousness of their position and the vulnerability of their theological
convictions. During the exile parts of the Jewish community in Babylon
started reflecting on why they lost their promised land. Within this context the so-called Deuteronomic theology became more prominent—a
theology that emphasized the Torah of Yahweh, which was handed to the
people by Moses. This reflection on their plight as exiles was the context
within which the Deuteronomistic History originated in which the past
was scrutinized through the lens of Deuteronomic theology. Some prophetic voices comforted the people with the message that Yahweh would
again reinstitute the Davidic kingship. However, certain voices (such as
that of Deutero-Isaiah) also emphasized that Yahweh would bring a new
dispensation. In this view the Persian ruler Cyrus is even presented as
a sort of messiah, as the anointed of Yahweh who will bring about the
restoration of God's people.

The restoration after the exile (which was initiated with Cyrus's
edict promulgated in 538 B.C.) strengthened the idea of a new beginning. But what would this new dispensation be like? What if the Davidic
kingship was not resurrected? What if the cult of Yahweh was seen as
just one among many? These difficult questions necessitated deep theological reflection.

The socioreligious circumstances of the Persian era gave a higher
profile to these questions. Although the Persian policy of the time should
not be overexaggerated or equated with a modern-day understanding of
freedom of speech and religion, it is well known that the Persian leaders
since Cyrus adopted a strategy whereby local cults were tolerated in the
various provinces of the empire. Local shrines (like the rebuilt temple in
Jerusalem—the so-called Second Temple) were allowed and could even
be erected or rebuilt with imperial financial assistance.[23] A prerequisite,
however, was that these provinces should remain loyal to the empire
in terms of tributes and military campaigns. The communities within
which Chronicles probably originated were heirs to this socioreligious
context. But they were also heirs to a sociopolitical environment where
they remained subservient to the Persian Empire and did not have the
luxury of independence under a Davidic monarchy.

An issue that is often underestimated in Chronicles studies is the
influence of the international situation of the time on the origin of writings such as Chronicles. The majority of Chronicles studies tend to focus

so much on the situation in Yehud and Jerusalem that the international context of the time is barely taken into consideration. It is my opinion, along with a few prominent scholars who also advocate this point, that the cultic community in Jerusalem and the literati among them were well acquainted with the power struggles between (particularly) Persia and Greece (and also Egypt, which was almost always in some way involved in the international troubles of the day) as well as with the ideologies that prevailed in the wider international arena.[24] One should of course be well acquainted with the situation in Jerusalem when interpreting Chronicles. However, I am of the opinion that very interesting nuances will be missed if the book is not also situated in its wider international contexts.

The battles between Greece and Persia were legendary, and famous classical writers such as Herodotus wrote extensively on this history. When studying the classical sources on the wars between Greece and Persia, and how Egypt was often involved, one should of course also remember that these writings are tendentious historiography that cannot be taken at face value. Careful and responsible study of the classical extrabiblical sources is needed to help us understand this fascinating period in history.[25]

The Relationship between Chronicles and Ezra-Nehemiah

When the books of Chronicles, Ezra, and Nehemiah are read simply on a literary level, one could be persuaded that there is some chronological order in the history they present. First comes Chronicles with its description up to the point where the Persian emperor promulgated the return of the exiles to their own country. It is exactly at this point where Ezra takes up the narrative line to continue with a description of the history of the restoration after the exile (among other things the rebuilding of the Jerusalem temple). Nehemiah then joins in to continue the description of postexilic events.

For quite a long time these three books were regarded as part of the same literary work, a so-called Chronistic history, originating from the same author(s). Apart from the continuous narrative line, those in favor of such a unity advanced mainly four arguments to prove their theory: (1) an analysis of linguistic evidence shows that Chronicles and Ezra-Nehemiah[26] stem from the same time and region; (2) 2 Chronicles 36:22–23 and Ezra 1:1–3a present the same quotation from the Cyrus edict (although the Chronicles version is shorter); (3) the extrabiblical book 1 Esdras includes sections from both Chronicles and Ezra-Nehemiah; and (4) there are remarkable agreements in terms of theological perspective in Chronicles and Ezra-Nehemiah.

However, not one of the above arguments could be considered definitive. Linguistic similarities do not necessarily prove common authorship; other reasons than a single literary work could be offered as an explanation for the doublet at the end of Chronicles and the beginning of Ezra; 1 Esdras (which originated later than both Chronicles and Ezra-Nehemiah) could have included sections from different earlier literary works; and there are also remarkable theological differences between Chronicles and Ezra-Nehemiah, for example, in terms of the attitude toward mixed marriages, the early history of Israel, the position of the northern kingdom and the definition of "Israel," the notion of immediate retribution, the role of cultic officials, and the emphasis on the Davidic monarchy.[27]

Much more nuanced views on the connections between these two literary works are nowadays presented. A major consensus has grown over the past decades that Chronicles should definitely be considered as a separate literary composition from Ezra-Nehemiah and should be dated later than Ezra-Nehemiah. This does not exclude the possibility—on account of the long process of growth of both these literary works—that literary and theological influences could have run in both directions.

For the purpose of this commentary, however, I agree with other recent commentators that the interpretation of Chronicles should be undertaken in its own right, particularly in comparison to the Deuteronomistic source texts, and should not be forced through the Ezra-Nehemiah lens.[28] I do not, therefore, subscribe to the notion of a Chronistic history here. The term "Chronicler" is also reserved here to refer to the author(s)/editor(s) of Chronicles and should not be taken to refer to a presumed Chronistic historian.

The Chronicler's Sources, Composition, and Canonical Position

The Chronicler made use of the Deuteronomistic History (particularly Samuel and Kings) in his reinterpretation of Israelite history. The repetition of huge blocks of text from Samuel-Kings in Chronicles probably contributed to the early tradition of regarding the latter as contributing only a "few remaining things." The repetition also led to the view that we are very fortunate to have the main source texts of Chronicles available. The method of comparison therefore remains important for my interpretation of Chronicles.

However, caution should also be exercised. Although we have those source texts available, we should remember that they also underwent a history of growth and composition. Differences between Chronicles and Samuel-Kings should therefore not immediately be attributed to a difference in theology or ideology without considering the possibility that the Chronicler could have made use of an earlier version of the source texts than those that we are working from. Every comparison of Chronicles with Samuel-Kings should therefore first determine (by consulting the ancient manuscript traditions and translations) whether the source text differed from the text of Samuel and Kings extant today and whether Chronicles agreed with an older or different tradition of the source text.[29] This activity is of course a very technical enterprise, which will not be undertaken in this commentary. However, we will have to rely on those specialized studies that can provide the necessary information.[30]

Did the Chronicler make use of sources other than the Deuteronomistic History? The readers of Chronicles would know that some of the genealogies are taken over from Pentateuchal traditions, that some psalms are quoted (e.g., Ps. 105:1–15 in 1 Chron. 16:8–22), and that certain cultic rituals or reform measures in Chronicles are also referred to in other parts of the Pentateuchal traditions. One even gets the impression that the Chronicler made use of some prophetic texts, such as Jeremiah (see 2 Chron. 36:12, 22).[31] I will deal with his usage of other sources when we encounter them.

The most prominent aspect of the Chronicler's use of his sources is that he had the courage to adapt, reinterpret, and even merge different traditions.

However, since we may assume that Chronicles was finalized over a long period of time (probably a century or more), we should recognize that the book underwent further growth by means of editing and additional composition processes. There are different views about the extent to which the variety of literary material in Chronicles should be attributed to the Chronicler's creative usage of sources or to further processes of editing and composition. Some hold that the early form of Chronicles underwent a few different consecutive processes of redaction, each editor working from a different ideological perspective.[32] This would then result in different layers of editing accumulating on proto-Chronicles. Others would rather work with a model that suggests that certain blocks of literary material were added at consecutive phases and that the diverse materials found in Chronicles should rather be attributed to these blocks and not to further layers of redaction. Whatever the case, the very peculiar method of the Chronicler's working with his sources is often underestimated or neglected in these theories.

Another important issue in the long process of transmission of Chronicles is its position in the biblical canon. Without going into all the intricacies of the formation of the biblical canon, I note that Chronicles has been included in the Hebrew Bible canon as part of the Ketubim (or Writings), the third part of the Jewish canon. There are, however, two different Hebrew textual traditions. One tradition opens the Writings with Chronicles, the other closes the Writings with Chronicles.[33] The one closing the Writings with Chronicles is also preserved in the critical editions of the Hebrew Bible normally used by students and scholars. That is, Chronicles concludes the Jewish canon, placed after Ezra-Nehemiah. Along with probably betraying something of the relatively late origin of Chronicles, this position also means the Hebrew Bible ends on the very hopeful note of the announced return.[34] It also gives Cyrus, the Persian emperor, the last say in the Hebrew Bible!

The attentive reader would of course have noticed that Chronicles does not occupy this last position in the NIV Old Testament. It rather follows Kings and comes before Ezra-Nehemiah. The reason for this peculiarity is that the old Greek translation of the Hebrew Bible (the Septuagint), which dates back to approximately the second to first centuries B.C., shifted Chronicles to a position that would make more chronological and thematic sense to the reader. Since Chronicles is also dealing with the historical reconstruction of Israel's past, it was placed right after the other historical books. And because the content of Chronicles precedes that of Ezra-Nehemiah, the latter book was also moved into a new position, following right after Chronicles. One could, of course, see nothing more in this position than an attempt at achieving a more logical order in the Septuagint's adaptation. However, one should also consider what implications this would hold for the interpretation of Chronicles.

The Chronicler's Method

The Chronicler had the courage to adapt, reinterpret, and even merge different traditions into a new literary work. An interesting aspect of Chronicles is that we can pick up traces of all the prominent Pentateuchal traditions (mainly from the Priestly, Levitical, and Deuteronomic strands) in the book. This led to a variety of theories about the composition of the book. However, an emerging consensus, one with which I concur, is that the representation of various theological nuances in Chronicles could be attributed to a deliberate attempt of the Chronicler to merge different traditions into an overarching perspective.

One prominent theme that often forms the basis of theories about different redactional phases is the distinction between priests and Levites. We know from other parts of the Hebrew Bible that there was a long-standing rivalry between different factions within the priesthood. We certainly find both pro-Priestly and pro-Levitical nuances in Chronicles. Furthermore, in some cases the Chronicler seems to rely heavily on the Priestly Pentateuchal laws, and in other cases he seems to latch onto certain Deuteronomic traditions.

However, one does not necessarily have to revert to redactional theories to explain this peculiarity of the Chronicler's method.[35] The Chronicler, very much situated in the sociohistorical context of the late Persian era, was heir to different authoritative traditions from the past. He drew on all those traditions to come to a new understanding of his own time. Interacting with a variety of traditions, he was participating in a process of new identity formation. However, because this interpretation of the peculiar method adopted in Chronicles forms such an important presupposition in our presentation in this commentary, the next subsection must deal with it in more depth.

Chronicles as "Reforming History"

Investigation into the rhetorical strategy of Chronicles is becoming a more prominent feature of recent studies. The crucial question is, What did the Chronicler want to achieve with his reinterpretation and merging of different older traditions?

The designation "reforming history" could be applied to Chronicles.[36] The ambiguity of this designation is intentional. It indicates that Chronicles is simultaneously an attempt to reformulate and sanitize the older traditions about the past, as well as an attempt to reformulate the identity of God's people in the changed sociohistorical circumstances of the late Persian era.

Times have changed since the existence of the preexilic kingdom of Judah. Provincial existence under Persian imperial rule was much different from being an independent monarchy with its own cult. This does not mean, however, that the past was simply left behind and that a new beginning was made. In order to understand who they were, it was absolutely necessary for the postexilic writers to latch onto the historical traditions about the past. However, since their reality had changed so much, everything from the past could not simply be continued. The past had to be retold and rewritten in order to be useful in the new dispensation. In order to situate themselves in the new sociopolitical and socioreligious circumstances, and to get clarity on where they were heading from there, the writers made use of the past traditions but adapted them to their needs.[37]

The designation "reforming history" that I use to describe Chronicles is therefore not primarily a genre indication. It rather is an attempt to describe the intention or purpose of this work and to characterize its hermeneutical dynamics. The description of Chronicles as reforming history indicates that it was intended to form a unique bridge between past and present. The Chronicler wanted to reflect on the new present (and future), but in continuity with past traditions. And the perspective of the Chronicler went even further back than the Deuteronomists. Not only Israel's past was involved in this historical construction—the Chronicler even situates his retelling within the history of humanity (going all the way back to Adam).

It is within this context that Chronicles can also be interpreted as a bold attempt to take part in the process of social-identity negotiation during this period. The formal proclamation of the Persian province Yehud initiated a new phase of reflection among the Yehudites on their own identity. The new sociopolitical circumstances prompted them to reflect on what their status was as a nation within the changed political dispensation. And the new socioreligious conditions let them reflect on what their relationship was with their god, Yahweh, given that other religions had equal status during this time.

When speaking about "identity," however, we should be clear about what we mean. Developments in the fields of social-identity theory and social-categorization theory have taught us that identity is not merely an issue of personal psychology or genetics.[38] Identity is always a social and dynamic process. Identities constantly develop over time, reacting to changed and changing circumstances in the social environment. Identity is not something like a building that can be constructed according to a preconceived plan and then be finished by a certain date. Identity is rather something very complex, always in flux, always being negotiated in interaction with social phenomena of the environment.[39]

This understanding emphasizes that not only individuals but also groups have identities. Many different factors contribute to group members associating with one another on the basis of an idealized prototype. This prototype of who they want to be then naturally leads to the categorization of others as part of the group (in-group) or not part of the group (out-group). In the field of social psychology (within which social-identity theory and social-categorization theory are formulated) many studies nowadays seek explanations for the (sometimes very sad and tragic) social relations between groups (be they ideological, ethnic, religious, etc.) in our own time.

Also with regard to our understanding of Chronicles, social-psychological distinctions can potentially be very useful. They can, for example, sensitize us to those subtle ways in which the Chronicler depicted the relationship between rival priestly groups in the Persian period. Or they may shed some interesting light on the numerous additions of neighboring nations to the royal narratives. Or they may help us to understand why some foreign monarchs (e.g., Neco from Egypt and Cyrus from Persia) are portrayed in a very favorable light by the Chronicler.

This does not, however, mean that these texts in Chronicles are documentations of completed identity-formation processes. Social psychology teaches us that texts are rather part of these processes themselves. To apply this understanding to our study of Chronicles, then, Chronicles should not be seen as a fossilized self-understanding of the Judahite community in the Persian era—as if we can read off from the texts what the identity of this community was. It rather should be studied with the awareness that these texts wanted to do something, wanted to move an audience to a specific understanding of themselves in their changed circumstances. Chronicles, and the way in which it interacted with handed-down authoritative traditions (historical and legal), should be studied as a witness to identity formation in process, not at an end.

Practically, this means that we will have to be on the lookout for those themes that seem to be prominent in the Chronicler's narrative, for the relationships the Chronicler constructs between characters (individuals and groups) in his retelling of the past, and for the way in which the older traditions are engaged (by being quoted, changed, omitted, added to, etc.).

Although this will be done best in the commentary, I will here take a brief look at certain important thematic complexes.

Thematic Complexes in Chronicles

Any attempt to find a common thematic thread for Chronicles would be reductive. The book is simply too diversified to be encapsulated under one rubric. The following theological themes are therefore not an attempt to impose a systematization on the materials of Chronicles but an initial exploration of the thematic fibers that make up the multicolored tapestry we find in Chronicles.

Kingship is an important institution, according to the Chronicler. Apart from the plotline of the major part of the book revolving around the theme of royal succession, the Chronicler relates the kings of Judah particularly to God's actions. It becomes clear from many of the royal narratives that Yahweh sustains his people by acting through the kings. When the kings seek Yahweh during their respective reigns, they can count on Yahweh supporting and sustaining them.[40]

It is manifestly clear that for the Chronicler this close link between kingship and Yahweh's actions is limited to the Davidic line of kings who reigned in Judah. The northern kings are often neglected or ignored, and the kingdom of Israel is mentioned only when its history impinges on that of Judah.

David and Solomon receive special treatment by the Chronicler as the model of kingship expected in their own day under Persian rule. This emphasis, together with the very interesting portrayals of foreign kings (Neco of Egypt and Cyrus of Persia) as servants of Yahweh, could have been part of a subtle polemic in the direction of the Persian rulers (probably the provincial governors) during the time when God's people had no king of their own. With this subtle reconstruction of their monarchical history, the writers would have emphasized for all those "political ears" of their time that good rulers seek Yahweh and that bad rulers should expect some sort of punishment.

Although a close relationship between the Davidic kings and Yahweh forms the basis of the Chronicler's description, these kings are not idealized or romanticized. They are shown as fallible and frail human beings who can reign only through Yahweh's power. A comparison of the Chronicler's portrayals of these kings with the Deuteronomistic versions produces interesting results in this regard. The changes the Chronicler made to the histories of Asa, Jehoshaphat, Hezekiah, and Josiah are good examples. Although these kings are also evaluated as good kings like in the Deuteronomistic History, finer details of the Chronicler's additions/changes to their histories show that they did not always fully trust in Yahweh.

Another important issue for the Chronicler was who belonged to *Israel*. The northern kings and their kingdom were viewed as illegitimate by the Chronicler. Some earlier studies therefore also suggested that there is an anti-Samaritan sentiment in the book. However, a close reading reveals that the Chronicler did not limit his definition of God's people to those living in Judah. He often uses the concept of All-Israel and gives clear indications that the northern inhabitants were also considered to be part of this identity and that they belonged to the same cultic community that was centered in Jerusalem. This was of course different from the Deuteronomist's description, which tells of rival sanctuaries in the northern kingdom. However, the Chronicler—like the older history—reminds the reader that those from the north were actually "blood family" (see the genealogies in 1 Chron. 1–9).

If the reader remembers that Chronicles originated in the postexilic period, this understanding of Israel becomes interesting on two levels. (1) We know that the northern kingdom, Israel, was exiled and its capital, Samaria, destroyed by the Assyrians long before Judah was (the fall of Samaria is normally dated 722 B.C.). Although Judah still existed as an independent monarchy until the fall of Jerusalem (586 B.C.), Israel had already disappeared as an independent state from the political scene in the last quarter of the eighth century B.C. The postexilic era, with returning exiles originating from the former states of Israel *and* Judah, was an interesting stage in the reamalgamation of these two peoples (who both belonged to the united kingdom under David and Solomon). Furthermore, since not all inhabitants of Israel and Judah were taken into exile, the returning exiles had to integrate into a society of Israelites and Judahites who existed alongside one another and who did not experience the exile. One may assume that tension between the "remainees" and the "returnees" would have developed in this period. (2) We know from Persian sources that Samaria to the north of Judah was administered by the Persians as a separate province. Archeology also reveals that during this time Samaria was much more affluent and rich in resources than Jerusalem.[41] It is therefore significant that the Chronicler denies the north any political power but nevertheless includes the northern tribes in the All-Israel that he is constructing. It seems that the religious and ethnic relationship with the north, and not so much the political relationship (which might have rendered Yehud in a bad light), forms the Chronicler's point of departure.

The Chronicler indicates a close relationship between the royal rulers of Israel and their *temple and worship*. In many instances the kings are intimately involved in cultic matters (e.g., David's bringing of the ark to Jerusalem; Solomon's building of the temple; the cultic reforms of Asa, Jehoshaphat, Joash, Hezekiah, and Josiah; the celebration of Passover by Hezekiah and Josiah, etc.). Ensuring true worship of Yahweh at the central sanctuary in Jerusalem belongs to the core responsibilities of the kings of Judah. This close connection of Davidic monarchs with the temple and worship sharply contrasts with the picture in the Deuteronomistic History, where the focus is much more on political and military matters.

In this context it is also worthwhile to trace the Chronicler's portrayal of the *Levites*. The Levites occupied a subservient position in the priesthood for a long time in the cult of Judah. The Chronicler's depiction is interesting insofar as it allocates to the Levites a position that is not inferior to that of the other sections of the priesthood. In some contexts (e.g., in the portrayal of the Passover celebrations during Hezekiah's and Josiah's reigns) the Levites are even elevated to being fit to perform the cultic rituals.

Readers of Chronicles will surely notice how prominent *prophetic figures* are in this book. The peculiarity of this, however, is twofold: (1) quite a number of previously unknown prophets are introduced by the Chronicler,[42] in addition to the occasional mention of the known writing prophets Isaiah (2 Chron. 26:22; 32:20, 32) and Jeremiah (2 Chron. 35:25; 36:12, 21, 22); and (2) radical changes were made to the portrayal of those few prophetic figures whom we encounter in both the Deuteronomistic History and Chronicles.[43] Interpreters are fascinated by this peculiarity, particularly because some argue that the classic phenomenon of prophecy had already ceased before Chronicles was written.[44]

Theology of Chronicles

In the many discussions about a fitting designation to describe the Chronicler, some suggest that the Chronicler was a theologian.[45] Although other designations (such as historian, exegete, author) are equally valid, there are good reasons for calling the Chronicler a theologian. It is clear from Chronicles that, although the theme of this work is the history of Judah, the approach and perspective of the writer is theological. The following theological lines (which in some cases are a continuation of theological themes already present in Samuel-Kings, but in other cases are new) can be identified in the book:

First, *Yahweh is a god who engages human reality and human history.* Yahweh's actions can be observed in the lives of Judah's kings, in military encounters with other nations, and in cultic rituals. The power of Yahweh can be seen in the positive outcomes of battles, in the healing of kings, and in the obedience of foreign kings to his command. However, his power is also manifested in the death or sickness of kings and in military defeat. Yahweh's engagement with reality also renders the kings of Judah, but also of neighboring nations and empires, as instruments in his hand. The Chronicler shows that kings have only relative power: the flow of history is not in their hands but in Yahweh's. Yahweh's power is acted out in the realm of history.

Second, the Chronicler portrays *Yahweh as a god of new beginnings.* The tone of Chronicles is neither pessimistic nor fatalistic. Chron- icles differs from some (more or less contemporary) apocalyptic literature in which no hope can be found in this reality. The Chronicler does not envision a supernatural reality as the basis of hope; he rather interprets events of the past as hopeful signs for the future. One prominent example is the way in which the Chronicler depicts the exile in 2 Chronicles 36. Unlike the Deuteronomistic writers, the Chronicler describes the exile as a fulfillment of a sabbath period of seventy years. And the return from exile through Cyrus's edict is seen as a fulfillment of the prophecy of Jeremiah. Yahweh starts anew with his people. The new sociopolitical dispensation is not a sign of failure for Yehud but is a new beginning under Yahweh's guidance.

A third theological line that runs through Chronicles is the central *importance of the sanctuary* in Jerusalem. The temple building under Solomon forms the focal point of the historical description. For the Chronicler the past can be divided into a period "before the temple building" and another "after the temple building." Observance of the temple service therefore forms an integral part of this theological theme. The Chronicler dedicates much space in his work to a careful division of labor among the different temple personnel. The celebration of the Passover is also closely connected to this theme. The terminology used in Josiah's Passover narrative even suggests that the temple was complete only after the right celebration of the Passover during his reign.

A fourth theological line is the very clear opposition between *obedience and disobedience*. The Chronicler has taken over the Deuteronomic understanding of faithfulness bringing reward and well-being, and unfaithfulness leading to punishment and ill-being. The Chronicler employs this opposition in a unique way. Some refer to the Chronicler's usage of this notion as an ideology of immediate retribution.[46] That means that, unlike the Deuteronomistic History, the Chronicler indicates that the effects of (dis)obedience already materialize within the lifetime of the individual and do not accumulate to the next generations.[47] Although this issue is not central to the Chronicler's theology as some interpreters suggest, it is certainly a prominent theme. We clearly see, for example, that certain terms are closely associated with obedience, such as "to seek Yahweh" or "to rely upon Yahweh." The outcome of this seeking of and relying on Yahweh is often associated with "to be successful," "to prosper," "to have peace," or "to experience rest/peace." This is particularly epitomized in King Solomon, "the man of rest," whose name is closely associated with the word for "peace" (1 Chron. 22:7–10).[48]

Closely related to the previous theme is the notion of *Torah*. The cultic rituals and temple service, but also the personal obedience required of kings, are often motivated with the reference "as written in the Law of Moses" (e.g., 2 Chron. 23:18). In this reference we observe a move toward acknowledging the authoritative status of those scriptures handed down through previous generations. The Yahwistic religion is still characterized by cultic rituals, but it also involves interpretation and application of the scriptures.

A theological theme already mentioned, *peace*, needs to be treated separately. Terminological patterns in Chronicles show that peace, rest, and quietness form the ultimate theological ideal for the writer. In this respect, the description of Solomon's reign is telling. Solomon conducted no wars or battles, his name is related to the theme of peace, and he builds the "house of rest" in Jerusalem. But also other kings' reigns are characterized by rest and quietness, particularly the reigns of those kings who were obedient to Yahweh. The Chronicler thereby suggests that Yahweh is the ultimate giver of peace, rest, and quietness and that these values should be pursued in future.

The Message of Chronicles

Why would modern-day Jews and Christians read Chronicles? What would appeal to them, and how would this appeal be different from that of other Hebrew Bible books?

Anyone who understands the dynamics of interpretation knows that the context of the reader also inevitably contributes to the process of understanding. The relevance of Chronicles is, therefore, at least co-determined by the context of the modern-day reader(s) of the book. However, one should of course be very aware that identification with the data in the text can occur too easily and too hastily. Questions such as Who is All-Israel in our context? Where is the New Jerusalem? and Whose cultic community can be associated with the Chronicler's community? should be answered very carefully. It is certainly possible to draw interpretive analogies between the text of Chronicles and modern-day societies in transition.

These analogies should be developed in a sophisticated and circumspect way, though. We should be aware of the correspondences between Chronicles and our circumstances, but particularly also of the dissimilarities. This can, in my opinion, be done best by studying seriously both the particular literary dynamics of Chronicles and the historical circumstances of its origin and early interpretations. Only by engaging thoroughly with these dimensions of Chronicles may we venture into exploring the message of this fascinating book for our own circumstances.

Any reader who experiences, or has experienced, times of societal change knows that such times tend to prompt new processes of reflection. Those processes often concern social identity ("Who are we supposed to be in the new dispensation? With whom should we be in alliance, and whom should we oppose?") and religious identity ("What should we believe? How should we differentiate ourselves from others who believe differently?"). The new world order that started developing from the last decade of the twentieth century has seen the crumbling and disappearance of old international tensions and power constellations (e.g., between the Communist world and the West). The ripple effect of this development was widespread—from the fall of the Berlin Wall in Germany to the end of apartheid in South Africa. The former tensions have now been replaced by new constellations, by a world order dominated by the tension between the Islamic-Arab world and the Christian-oriented West, as well as by the emergence of new economic powers such as China that dominate the world economy. Some even speak of the new world order as a "clash of civilizations."

The appeal for a greater appreciation of diversity is strong in the new world order, and understandably so. We realize that new oppositions do not bring solutions. What is needed in our world is rather the ability to navigate between extreme views, between the local and the global, between the past and the present.

Does the book of Chronicles have a message in these circumstances? Chronicles is a reinterpretation of older historiographical traditions in new, changed sociopolitical and socioreligious circumstances, and it offers the modern-day reader fascinating insights into how one could engage with similar circumstances in our own time. The following are significant in this regard.

First, Chronicles teaches us that history is important. We should realize that we cannot, and should not, sever our ties with the past. However, Chronicles indicates that changed circumstances bring new perspectives on the past. The Chronicler even shows that one could take the courage to reinterpret the past for the sake of the present.

Second, the Chronicler shows that believers do not subscribe to the contingency of history. History, and therefore also the continuation of the past into the present and future, can and should be interpreted theologically. The existence of faith communities and nations is not simply a function of fate. For believers there is more than meets the eye in the past, present, and future.

Third, Chronicles shows us that it is inevitable and vital for faith communities during periods of socioreligious change to reflect on who they are within the new dispensation. Differently from other writings from the time (e.g., Ezra-Nehemiah), Chronicles emphasizes inclusiveness instead of opposition and tension. The Chronicler shows how a faith community can situate itself in a context of religious diversity. Yahwism is neither reduced to a colorless manifestation of Persian imperial religion nor propagated as an exclusivist position over against other religions.

And fourth, Chronicles teaches us that Yahweh is a universal God. By starting the historical construction with Adam and by ending his history with Cyrus, the Persian emperor speaking on behalf of Yahweh, the Chronicler shows that Yahweh's power is universal and not limited to the boundaries of Yehud and All-Israel. In this respect, Chronicles shows similarities with some other biblical writings (such as Jonah).

Notes

1. In this commentary the term "Chronicles" indicates a singular entity. The term will refer to the literary work also called the biblical books of Chronicles. It is used in the singular form here, since these biblical books, according to Jewish tradition, in fact form a singular literary work that was later divided into two biblical books by the Septuagint translators. Although the term "Chronicles" in itself refers to more than one chronicle, a singular verb will always be used with it, referring to the one collection of chronicles.

2. The Septuagint (LXX) translation of Chronicles dates back to approximately the second or first century B.C.

3. See G. N. Knoppers and P. B. Harvey Jr., "Omitted and Remaining Matters: On the Names Given to the Book of Chronicles in Antiquity," *JBL* 121 (2002), pp. 227–43.

4. See, e.g., P. B. Dirksen, *1 Chronicles* (HCOT; Leuven: Peeters, 2005); R. W. Klein, *1 Chronicles: A Commentary* (Hermeneia; Minneapolis: Fortress, 2006); G. N. Knoppers, *1 Chronicles 1–9* (AB 12; New York: Doubleday, 2003); G. N. Knoppers, *1 Chronicles 10–29* (AB 12A; New York: Doubleday, 2004); T. Willi, *1. Chronik* (BKAT 24; Neukirchen-Vluyn: Neukirchener Verlag, forthcoming).

5. See, e.g., M. J. Boda, *1 and 2 Chronicles* (Cornerstone Biblical Commentary; Carol Stream, IL: Tyndale, 2010); J. M. Hicks, *1 and 2 Chronicles* (College Press NIV Commentary; Joplin, MO: College Press, 2001); J. Jarick, *1 Chronicles* (Readings; London: Sheffield Academic Press, 2002); J. Jarick, *2 Chronicles* (Readings; Sheffield: Sheffield Phoenix, 2007); S. L. McKenzie, *1–2 Chronicles* (AOTC; Nashville: Abingdon, 2004); S. S. Tuell, *First and Second Chronicles* (Interpretation; Louisville: John Knox, 2001).

6. In this section I rely heavily on the discussion in T. Willi, "Zwei Jahrzehnte Forschung an Chronik und Esra-Nehemia," *Theologische Rundschau* 67 (2002), pp. 61–104, as well as on the introductions to recent scholarly commentaries such as Knoppers, *1 Chronicles 1–9*; and Klein, *1 Chronicles*. See also

S. Japhet, "The Historical Reliability of Chronicles: The History of the Problem and Its Place in Biblical Research," *JSOT* 33 (1985), pp. 83–107; R. K. Duke, "Recent Research in Chronicles," *Currents in Biblical Research* 8 (2009), pp. 10–50.

7. Chronicles scholars often find it useful to compile synopses, that is, comparisons of the Chronicles texts with those of the Pentateuch and particularly of Samuel-Kings in parallel columns so that one can easily see where they agree and disagree. See, e.g., a critical synopsis of the Hebrew texts in J. Kegler and M. Augustin, *Synopse zum chronistischen Geschichtswerk* (Frankfurt: Peter Lang, 1984); a German version in J. Kegler and M. Augustin, *Deutsche Synopse zum chronistischen Geschichtswerk* (Frankfurt: Peter Lang, 1993); and an English version in J. C. Endres et al., eds., *Chronicles and Its Synoptic Parallels in Samuel, Kings, and Related Biblical Texts* (Collegeville, MN: Liturgical Press, 1998). Readers of this commentary would probably find the latter study the most useful. It takes the NRSV as its point of departure and adheres to the paragraph divisions suggested by the United Bible Societies.

8. The notion of "rewritten Bible" is applied to Chronicles by some commentators. See, e.g., the discussion in Knoppers, *1 Chronicles 1–9*, pp. 129–34. Although some argue that this category, which has been identified in a number of Qumran materials, is suitable to describe the Chronicler's usage of earlier sources, it does not cover all the distinctive characteristics of Chronicles.

9. See E. Ben Zvi's "Shifting the Gaze: Historiographic Constraints in Chronicles and Their Implications" and "The Chronicler as a Historian: Building Texts," both in E. Ben Zvi, *History, Literature, and Theology in the Book of Chronicles* (London: Equinox, 2006), pp. 78–99, 100–116; E. Blum, "Historiographie oder Dichtung? Zur Eigenart alttestamentlicher Geschichtsüberlieferungen," in *Das Alte Testament—ein Geschichtsbuch? Beiträge des Symposiums "Das Alte Testament und die Kultur der Moderne" anlässlich des 100. Geburtstags Gerhard von Rads (1901–1971) Heidelberg 18.–21. Oktober 2001* (ed. E. Blum and C. Hardmeier; Münster: LIT, 2005); K. G. Hoglund, "The Chronicler as Historian: A Comparativist Perspective," in *The Chronicler as Historian* (ed. M. P. Graham; JSOTSup 238; Sheffield: Sheffield Academic Press, 1997), pp. 19–29; I. Kalimi, "Was the Chronicler a Historian?" in *The Chronicler as Historian*, pp. 73–89; I. Kalimi, *An Ancient Israelite Historian: Studies in the Chronicler, His Time, Place, and Writing* (SSN 46; Assen: Van Gorcum, 2005).

10. See G. Steins, *Die Chronik als kanonisches Abschlussphänomen: Studien zur Entstehung und Theologie von 1/2 Chronik* (BBB 93; Weinheim: Beltz Athenäum, 1995).

11. See, e.g., R. K. Duke, *The Persuasive Appeal of the Chronicler* (Sheffield: Sheffield Academic Press, 1990).

12. See J. E. Dyck, "The Ideology of Identity in Chronicles," in *Ethnicity and the Bible* (ed. M. G. Brett; Leiden: Brill, 1996), pp. 89–116; J. E. Dyck, *The Theocratic Ideology of the Chronicler* (Leiden: Brill, 1998); A. Siedlecki, "Foreigners, Warfare, and Judahite Identity in Chronicles," in *The Chronicler as Author* (ed. M. P. Graham and S. L. McKenzie; Sheffield: Sheffield Academic Press, 1999), pp. 229–66. See also my own contributions in the following publications: "The

Rhetorics of Finding a New Identity in a Multi-cultural and Multi-religious Society," *Verbum et Ecclesia* 24 (2004), pp. 396–416; "The Cushites in the Chronicler's Version of Asa's Reign: A Secondary Audience in Chronicles?" *OTE* 19 (2006), pp. 863–81; "The Exile as Sabbath Rest: The Chronicler's Interpretation of the Exile," *OTE* 20 (2007), pp. 702–19; "Refocusing the Battle Accounts of the Kings: Identity Formation in the Books of Chronicles," in *Behutsamens Lesen: Alttestamentliche Exegese im interdisziplinären Methodendiskurs* (ed. S. Lubs; Leipzig: Evangelische Verlagsanstalt, 2007), pp. 245–74; "Reforming History: The Hermeneutical Significance of the Books of Chronicles," *VT* 57 (2007), pp. 21–44; "The Chronicler's Portrayal of Solomon as the King of Peace within the Context of the International Peace Discourses of the Persian era," *OTE* 21 (2008), pp. 653–69; "The Chronicler and the Prophets: Who Were His Authoritative Sources?" *SJOT* 22 (2008), pp. 271–92; "Who Constitutes Society? Yehud's Self-understanding in the Late Persian Era as Reflected in the Books of Chronicles," *JBL* 127 (2008), pp. 707–28; "The Disappearing Nehushtan: The Chronicler's Reinterpretation of Hezekiah's Reformation Measures," in *From Ebla to Stellenbosch: Syro-Palestinian Religions and the Hebrew Bible* (ed. I. Cornelius and L. C. Jonker; ADPV 37; Wiesbaden: Harrassowitz, 2008), pp. 116–40; "Textual Identities in the Books of Chronicles: The Case of Jehoram's History," in *Community Identity in Judean Historiography: Biblical and Comparative Perspectives* (ed. G. N. Knoppers and K. Ristau; Winona Lake, IN: Eisenbrauns, 2009), pp. 197–218.

13. In this commentary I make a distinction between "Judahite" (referring to the geographical area or inhabitants of the preexilic kingdom of Judah) and "Yehudite" (referring to the provincial existence under Persian rule). I avoid the term "Jewish," which is starting to emerge in the postexilic era, since this term is not necessarily related to either the geographical area or the provincial manifestation. However, I occasionally use this term when referring to people of Jewish descent who lived in the Mesopotamian or Egyptian areas.

14. See E. Ben Zvi, "The Secession of the Northern Kingdom in Chronicles: Accepted 'Facts' and New Meanings," in *History, Literature, and Theology in the Book of Chronicles* (London: Equinox, 2006), pp. 117–43.

15. These last two verses of Chronicles are (with small differences) also included in the first part of the book of Ezra.

16. See M. A. Throntveit, *When Kings Speak: Royal Speech and Royal Prayer in Chronicles* (Atlanta: Scholars Press, 1987); E. Ben Zvi, "When the Foreign Monarch Speaks," in *The Chronicler as Author*, pp. 209–28.

17. Babylonian Talmud, tractate *Baba Bathra* 15a. Interestingly enough, a few twentieth-century scholars, such as W. F. Albright and J. Bright, returned to this traditional view on the authorship of Chronicles. However, the majority of Chronicles scholars no longer accept this position.

18. According to what we know about the sociocultural conventions of biblical times, it would be unlikely that female hands contributed to this book. Education and literacy were available to males, but probably not to females. The pronoun "he" will therefore be used throughout this commentary as a reference to the Chronicler.

19. See the short but excellent summary in Klein, *1 Chronicles*, pp. 16–17.

20. Levin, although not unwilling to accept the position that the Chronicler should be sought among the literati of Jerusalem, comes to the conclusion (after his investigations into the forms contained in the genealogies in 1 Chron. 1–9) that the intended audience of Chronicles was rather largely agrarian and clan based and should be sought among "the peoples of the land." See Y. Levin, "Who Was the Chronicler's Audience? A Hint from His Genealogies," *JBL* 122 (2003), pp. 229–45; Y. Levin, "From Lists to History: Chronological Aspects of the Chronicler's Genealogies," *JBL* 123 (2004), pp. 601–36.

21. See G. N. Knoppers, "Hierodules, Priests, or Janitors? The Levites in Chronicles and the History of the Israelite Priesthood," *JBL* 118 (1999), pp. 49–72.

22. See, e.g., T. Willi, *Juda-Jehud-Israel: Studien zum Selbstverständnis des Judentums in persischer Zeit* (FAT 12; Tübingen: Mohr Siebeck, 1995); as well as my discussion and application of his work in L. C. Jonker, *Reflections of King Josiah in Chronicles: Late Stages of the Josiah Reception in 2 Chr 34f.* (Textpragmatische Studien zur Literatur- und Kulturgeschichte der Hebräischen Bibel 2; Gütersloh: Gütersloher Verlag, 2003), pp. 73–82.

23. See R. Lux, "Der zweite Tempel von Jerusalem—ein persisches oder prophetisches Projekt?" in *Das Alte Testament—ein Geschichtsbuch? Geschichtsschreibung oder Geschichtsüberlieferung im antiken Israel* (ed. U. Becker and J. van Oorschot; Leipzig: Evangelische Verlagsanstalt, 2005), pp. 145–72.

24. See, e.g., G. N. Knoppers, "Greek Historiography and the Chronicler's History: A Reexamination," *JBL* 122 (2003), pp. 627–50. I elaborate on this point in "Cushites in the Chronicler's Version" and "Chronicler's Portrayal of Solomon."

25. I rely particularly on the following studies, which offer thorough scholarship on the dynamics of the Persian period: P. Briant, *From Cyrus to Alexander: A History of the Persian Empire* (Winona Lake, IN: Eisenbrauns, 2002); E. Gerstenberger, *Israel in der Perserzeit: 5. und 4. Jahrhundert v. Chr.* (Stuttgart: Kohlhammer, 2005); L. L. Grabbe, *A History of the Jews and Judaism in the Second Temple Period* (London: T&T Clark, 2004); J. Wiesehöfer, *Das antike Persien* (Düsseldorf: Albatros, 2005); J. Wiesehöfer, *Das frühe Persien: Geschichte eines antiken Weltreichs* (2nd ed.; Munich: Beck, 2006).

26. Since it is not the task of this commentary to go into the intricacies of Ezra-Nehemiah scholarship, I merely bring to the attention of the reader that Ezra and Nehemiah are considered to be part of one (albeit composite) literary work. The reader may consult the Ezra-Nehemiah commentary by Leslie Allen in the Understanding the Bible Commentary Series for further information.

27. See, e.g., in this regard Klein, *1 Chronicles*, pp. 8–10.

28. See, e.g., in this regard Knoppers, *1 Chronicles 1–9*, pp. 96–100.

29. Another possibility that is considered—although not generally accepted in Chronicles scholarship—is that Chronicles did not make use of the Deuteronomistic History but that they both utilized (albeit in somewhat different ways) a common source text. See particularly A. G. Auld, "What If the Chronicler Did Use the Deuteronomistic History?" *BibInt* 8 (2000), pp. 137–50.

30. See, e.g., in this regard Knoppers, *1 Chronicles 1–9*, pp. 52–65.

31. See, e.g., Jonker, "Chronicler and the Prophets," pp. 271–92.

32. One prominent scholar who suggested three stages in the redaction of Chronicles is F. M. Cross, "A Reconstruction of the Judean Restoration," *JBL* 94 (1975), pp. 4–18.

33. I have already referred to the view of Steins (see note 10 above), who thinks that Chronicles was especially composed to occupy this closing position in the Hebrew Bible canon.

34. This conclusion of Chronicles might intend to offer a literary parallel to the release of Jehoiachin in Babylon with which 2 Kings ends.

35. See Knoppers, *1 Chronicles 1–9*, pp. 90–93; and Jonker, "Reforming History," pp. 21–44.

36. I base this section particularly on two of my earlier publications: Jonker, "Reforming History," pp. 21–44; and Jonker, "Textual Identities," pp. 197–218.

37. See the views of S. Japhet, *I and II Chronicles* (London: SCM, 1993), p. 49; and Knoppers, *1 Chronicles 1–9*, pp. 133–34.

38. For secondary literature on these social disciplines, see the bibliographies in Jonker, "Reforming History"; and Jonker, "Textual Identities."

39. See J. L. Berquist, "Constructions of Identity in Postcolonial Yehud," in *Judah and the Judeans in the Persian Period* (ed. O. Lipschits and M. Oeming; Winona Lake, IN: Eisenbrauns, 2006), pp. 53–66. Berquist discusses different models of dealing with the issue of identity, emphasizing the complexity of the endeavor.

40. See W. Riley, *King and Cultus in Chronicles: Worship and the Reinterpretation of History* (Sheffield: Sheffield Academic Press, 1993).

41. See G. N. Knoppers, "Revisiting the Samarian Question in the Persian Period," in *Judah and the Judeans in the Persian Period*, pp. 265–89.

42. Iddo (2 Chron. 9:29; 12:15; 13:22), Oded (15:8; 28:9), Hanani (16:7, 10), Jehu (19:2), Jahaziel (20:14), Eliezer (20:37), and Zechariah (24:20), as well as a number of anonymous or minor prophets (20:20, 25; 29:25; 33:18–19).

43. Samuel (1 Chron. 6:28; 9:22; 11:3; 26:28; 29:29; 2 Chron. 35:18), Nathan (1 Chron. 29:29; 2 Chron. 9:29; 29:25), Gad (1 Chron. 29:29; 2 Chron. 29:25), Ahijah the Shilonite (2 Chron. 9:29), Shemaiah (2 Chron. 12), and Elijah (2 Chron. 21).

44. See, e.g., the following more recent studies: P. Beentjes, "Prophets in the Book of Chronicles," in *The Elusive Prophet: The Prophet as a Historical Person, Literary Character, and Anonymous Artist*, ed. J. C. De Moor (Leiden: Brill, 2001), pp. 45–53; J. Blenkinsopp, "'We Pay No Heed to Heavenly Voices': The 'End of Prophecy' and the Formation of the Canon," in *Treasures Old and New: Essays in the Theology of the Pentateuch* (ed. J. Blenkinsopp; Grand Rapids: Eerdmans, 2004), pp. 192–207; E. S. Gerstenberger, "Prophetie in den Chronikbüchern: Jahwes Wort in zweierlei Gestalt?" in *Schriftprophetie: FS für Jörg Jeremias zum 65. Geburtstag* (ed. F. Hartenstein et al.; Neukirchen-Vluyn: Neukirchener Verlag, 2004), pp. 351–67; A. Hanspach, *Inspirierte Interpreten: Das Prophetenverständnis der Chronikbücher und sein Ort in der Religion und Literatur zur Zeit des zweiten Tempels* (St. Ottilien: EOS, 2000); Jonker, "Chronicler and the Prophets."

45. See M. P. Graham et al., eds., *The Chronicler as Theologian: Essays in Honor of Ralph W. Klein* (JSOTSup 371; London: T&T Clark, 2003).

46. See particularly S. Japhet, *The Ideology of the Book of Chronicles and Its Place in Biblical Thought* (Frankfurt: Peter Lang, 1989), pp. 150–89. See also B. E. Kelly, *Retribution and Eschatology in Chronicles* (JSOTSup 211; Sheffield: Sheffield Academic Press, 1996).

47. Although the Chronicler reflects an understanding of immediate/individual retribution, he is still drenched in corporate thinking—which was characteristic of societies of those days—when negotiating a new identity for All-Israel.

48. Some scholars rightly point out that these constructions are similar to what we find in some (traditional) wisdom literature in the Old Testament. Although the link with wisdom theology is clear in Chronicles, the Chronicler employed the theme of obedience/disobedience in a unique way. See also I. Gabriel, *Friede über Israel: Eine Untersuchung zur Friedenstheologie in Chronik i 10–ii 36* (Klosterneuburg: Österreichisches Katholisches Bibelwerk, 1990); Jonker, "Chronicler's Portrayal of Solomon"; A. Ruffing, *Jahwekrieg als Weltmetapher: Studien zu Jahwekriegstexten des chronistischen Sondergutes* (Stuttgart: Katholisches Bibelwerk, 1992).

§1 Let's Start at the Beginning
(1 Chron. 1:1–9:44)

When the Chronicler started writing his version of the history of God's people, he started at the very beginning: Adam! It is surprising that this history, unlike the Deuteronomistic version, situates the history of God's people within the history of humankind.

On the one hand, this is already an indication of the Chronicler's universalist or inclusivist approach (which is also echoed in the closing of the book in 2 Chron. 36:22–23, where Cyrus, the Persian emperor, is described as the great liberator of God's people). To start right at the beginning suggests that God's people are part of a wider humanity. Interestingly, Luke opens his gospel with a similar wide perspective, introducing Jesus of Nazareth as God's very own son and therefore a universal savior (Luke 3:23–38). He, too, traces Jesus's lineage—by means of a detailed genealogy—all the way back to Adam, a different version from that in Matthew 1:1–17. The similarity may reflect Luke's familiarity with Chronicles, although we cannot be sure.

On the other hand, the interesting start to Chronicles is also an indication that the Chronicler wanted to take as his point of departure the transmitted traditions of old, particularly those preserved in what is called the Pentateuch or Torah (the first five books of the Hebrew Bible). One may assume that these traditions were available to the Chronicler in a fairly stabilized form and that he—so to speak—wanted to summarize these traditions to form the point of entry for his reconstruction of the history of Israel. The genealogies included in 1 Chronicles 1–9 go back mainly to the so-called Priestly traditions, a strand of literary and redactional work that forms the backbone of the Pentateuch.

Genealogies were not uncommon either in Mesopotamia or in Greece. Although the practice is not widespread, there are other examples of literature from the Mediterranean world that introduce a narration of history with a genealogy.

Genealogies are also not uncommon in (even modern-day) oral cultures. Such genealogies are mainly of two types, namely, segmented (or horizontal) genealogies and linear (or vertical) genealogies. The first type normally depicts (like the branches of a tree) the breadth of one family by listing all the descendants of every generation. The second depicts (like a rope) the depth of a family by listing one generation after another, tracing the line of descent from only one person in every generation to another. These genealogies normally have the function of conveying the pedigree, hierarchy, and status of a specific group or nation. Anthropological studies show that these genealogies do not normally have a historical intention, but rather serve social, judicial, or religious purposes, legitimating certain claims concerning these spheres of society.

Anyone reading the genealogies of Chronicles against the background of other Hebrew scriptures would notice that these lists are strongly selective in their portrayals. We find both segmented and linear forms in the first nine chapters of Chronicles, portraying the ancient past from Adam, the first human, through to David, the first king (according to the Chronicler's reconstruction). The genealogies jump around in history, dwelling mainly on the Abrahamic ancestors and the Davidic reign, but also including the postexilic community in the genealogy of 1 Chronicles 9. The Chronicler simply skipped certain periods considered very important by other biblical writers, such as the time of the desert wanderings and the era of the judges.

Given such an approach, one should also not expect to find accurate genealogical information of a historical kind here. (The heading of the NIV before 1 Chron. 1:1, namely, "Historical Records," might therefore be somewhat misleading.) Clearly, these chapters certainly served a thoroughly theological (versus purely historical) function. The Chronicler wanted to emphasize the continuity of the postexilic community with the Israel of the past. It is likewise clear that the postexilic community is portrayed as a continuation of the cultic community of the Judahite kingdom. The significance of Jerusalem and the temple community of the preexilic period continues after the exile. The Davidic royal line—which is clearly linked with the patriarchal (Abraham and Jacob-Israel) and universal (Adam) past—is extended into the postexilic era (albeit in another form).

The strong indication of continuity with the past emphasizes Yahweh's faithfulness. It becomes clear from the genealogies that the Chronicler considered the history from Adam to David to be authored by Yahweh, the God of Israel. This theological emphasis would have readily found an audience in the changed socioreligious and sociopolitical circumstances of the Persian era. Those living in Yehud would be comforted to hear that Yahweh is steering history.

The focus in the Chronicler's genealogies is clearly on Judah, Levi, and Benjamin. These references are closely associated with the preexilic southern kingdom, Judah. The Chronicler goes to great lengths to show that the postexilic community is grounded in the kingdom (and particularly the cult) of Judah, but he often employs the term "All-Israel" when he describes it. What becomes clear from the genealogies is that the Chronicler did not exclude the northern tribes from his definition of All-Israel. However, the golden line of divine election is manifested by Judah, the Jerusalemite cult, and the Davidic kingship.

The issue of postexilic identity was high on the agenda of the Chronicler. At a time when God's people were still settling into a new religious-cultic and political dispensation, reflection on who they were in these circumstances became necessary. And they did this in continuity with the past but also in serious engagement with their new present.

The genealogies in 1 Chronicles 1–9 are creatively structured to emphasize where the continuities with the past lie. These nine chapters comprise seven genealogical units. The first (1:1–54) and the last (9:2–34) correspond, indicating as an outer ring the peoples of the world and the inhabitants of Persian-period Jerusalem. A narrower ring correlates Judah (2:3–4:23) and Benjamin (8:1–40), who receive much of the genealogical attention. Another circle parallels the Transjordanian tribes (4:24–5:26) with the northern tribes (7:1–40), acknowledging in this way the inclusion of these regions in the definition of All-Israel. The central nexus of this structure is, then, the genealogies of the tribe of Levi (6:1–81), emphasizing the special position of the Levites in the Chronicler's view.

I will use a structure that differs somewhat from the one suggested above (to correlate with the NIV pericope divisions), but the above description shows that the genealogies were certainly not a haphazard collection of family lists. Rather, they were an artful construction of genealogical material to help their first readers negotiate an identity within the social, cultic, and theological landscape of the postexilic community.

§1.1 From Adam to Abraham (1 Chron. 1:1–27)

The Chronicler's family lists start with Adam (1:1) and swiftly continue from there to Abram (1:27). If there was ever an abridged version of some Pentateuchal genealogical traditions, this is it! These twenty-seven verses quickly run through at least three genealogies contained in Genesis 5, 10, and 11. This first of the Chronicler's genealogies utilizes both linear and segmented forms in its summary of the Genesis traditions.

The intention of the Chronicler's construction is clear, namely, to emphasize the Semite lineage over against the Japhethite and Hamite lineages. The family line running from Adam to Abram goes through the Semite family, which is emphasized by the recapitulation in 1:24–27.

1:1–4 / In the first three verses the Chronicler clearly used Genesis 5 as a source (which is normally attributed to the Priestly tradition). There the compiler of the genealogy was meticulous in providing the ages of all persons, even indicating how old they were when they died. The Chronicler merely picks up the "headings" of the Genesis list, resulting in a list of ten names, starting with **Adam** and ending with **Noah**. He compresses that full presentation into three verses. If we had no access to the genealogy in Genesis 5, we would probably not have known that these people were each actually the sons of the previously mentioned person.

The form of the first three verses is linear. Only one person per generation is mentioned. First Chronicles 1:4, however, mentions the three sons of Noah, namely, **Shem, Ham and Japheth,** in that order. Here the linear presentation pauses for the first time to dwell on the descendants of Noah.

The order of the names of Noah's sons is the same as in Genesis 5:32, from where the Chronicler took his cue to go over into a segmented form. First Chronicles 1:4, therefore, introduces the threefold genealogical segments that follow (1:5–7, 8–16, 17–23).

1:5–7 / These verses present the seven **sons of Japheth.** Two of them, **Gomer** and **Javan,** are singled out by also listing their descendants.

These verses are copied exactly from Genesis 10:2–4 (also attributed to the Priestly writers). There the genealogy of Noah's sons starts with Japheth, continues with Ham, and ends with Shem. The order of presentation is thus the opposite from that in 1 Chronicles 1:4 but in reality makes the same point. Both the Chronicler and Genesis 10 agree that the Semites are clearly the focal point of their interest.

1:8–16 / The descendants of **Ham** are mentioned here. Again, this is an exact quotation from Genesis 10:6–20, although the Chronicler omitted Genesis 10:9–12, 19–20 from his source. Four sons of Ham are mentioned in 1 Chronicles 1:8. The descendants of three of these are then listed in 1:9–10 (**Cush**), 1:11–12 (**Mizraim**), and 1:13–16 (**Canaan**) respectively. As in Genesis 10, no genealogy for **Put** is provided.

The names mentioned here are probably references to geographical and/or socioethnic entities. Cush is normally associated with the area of modern-day Ethiopia in northeastern Africa, Mizraim is Egypt, and Put is probably Libya in north Africa. On the basis of these geographical indications, the Hamites have been associated with dark-skinned Africans, and many atrocities of history (e.g., the biblical justification of slavery in America and apartheid in South Africa) can be traced back to this interpretation (together with the so-called curse of Ham in Gen. 9:18–27). However, Canaan (which we know was not in Africa) is also mentioned in this list (in Genesis as well as in Chronicles), indicating that there must have been another criterion for grouping these specific nations together. Some scholars observe that the Hamite list includes those mighty settled nations that built cities and abandoned their seminomadic existence. (The Japhethites represent the maritime peoples around and in the Mediterranean, and the Semites the seminomadic peoples of the Levant.) The text, for example, includes **Nimrod,** who is associated in Genesis 10:9–12 (a part that the Chronicler left out) with places such as Babel and Nineveh. The Chronicler's omission of these verses, as well as Genesis 10:19, probably shows that he had a different intention than the Priestly writers who compiled Genesis 10. There the genealogy likely intended to describe the socioeconomic landscape from a Semite point of view. In Chronicles the genealogy is again employed to cast the spotlight on the Semites, but now for the purpose of situating the Davidic lineage in that context.

1:17–23 / The descendants of **Shem** are now listed. Again, the Chronicler quoted from his source in Genesis 10:21–32. However, a few differences from the source text can be noted.

First, the Chronicler leaves out the problematic Genesis 10:21, which probably has the function of resuming Genesis 10:1 there.

Second, 1 Chronicles 1:17 in the Hebrew text is a shortened version of Genesis 10:22–23. The sons of Aram are included in Genesis, but they are left out in the Hebrew text of Chronicles. This part probably dropped out of the text during the long manuscript transmission process. The NIV therefore includes this phrase on account of some Septuagint manuscript evidence (see the footnote there).

Third, the Chronicler omits the closing verses of the source genealogy (Gen. 10:30–32). In their place he substitutes a section from another genealogy.

The Semite genealogy is also a combination of linear and segmented forms. Two sons of Shem—Arphaxad and Aram—are singled out. For Aram, four descendants are listed. The descendants of Arphaxad, however, are presented in a more intricate way. Two generations following Arphaxad are mentioned in 1:18, namely, Shelah and Eber. Two sons of the latter are then named in 1:19, namely, Peleg and Joktan. In 1:20–23 a total of thirteen sons of Joktan are mentioned. This more complicated presentation is an exact quotation from Genesis 10:24–29.

1:24–27 / In these verses the Chronicler suddenly reverts to the same linear pattern that we saw in 1:1–3. He presents another version of the Semite lineage, one that corresponds with the version in the previous section (1:17–23) starting with Shem and continuing through Arphaxad, Shelah, Eber, and Peleg. The latter version continues the line through Joktan, whereas the line here continues through Peleg and his descendants. In the deviation from the previous Semite genealogy, the Chronicler is quoting from another source, namely, Genesis 11:10–32 (again associated with the Priestly tradition). The Chronicler (as in 1:1–3) merely picks up the first name in each subsection of his source text, but follows the order precisely.

The mention of Abram at the end of this Semite line seems to be the reason that the Chronicler included this version. Abram (who can be traced through Peleg, but not through Joktan) forms the culmination of this first section of the Chronicler's genealogies. The next section clarifies why this was so important.

There is, however, a very interesting addition to the name of Abram in the Chronicler's account (1:27), compared to the version in Genesis 11:27. The NIV presents this addition between parentheses: (that is, Abraham). Readers familiar with the patriarchal narratives in Genesis know that the name change from Abram to Abraham was quite significant.

The changed name is closely associated with the covenant relationship initiated by Yahweh with this ancestor, as well as with the promise of a great nation. The name Abraham in fact means "father of many nations" (see Gen. 17:5). This addition in Chronicles might indicate that the Chronicler understood his cultic community to be in continuity with the covenant community of the patriarch, Abraham.

The Chronicler opted not to include the conclusion of the Genesis 11 genealogy, probably because the information presented there about Abram's father, Terah, was irrelevant for the new literary context at the start of Chronicles.

Additional Notes §1.1

1:1–27 / Three specific studies have been dedicated to 1 Chron. 1–9. See (in chronological order) M. Kartveit, *Motive und Schichten der Landtheologie in I Chronik 1–9* (Stockholm: Almqvist & Wiksell, 1989); M. Oeming, *Das wahre Israel: Die "genealogische Vorhalle" 1 Chronik 1–9* (BWANT 128; Stuttgart: Kohlhammer, 1990); J. T. Sparks, *The Chronicler's Genealogies: Towards an Understanding of 1 Chronicles 1–9* (Leiden: Brill, 2008). Whereas Kartveit primarily tracks the literary growth of this section in Chronicles, as well as how the ancient geography was described in this literature, Oeming's work gives more prominence to the so-called kerygma of the genealogies. Sparks focuses on the literary form, identifying an elaborate chiastic pattern in the genealogies.

1:1 / T. Willi finds it very significant that Chronicles starts with **Adam**. He rightly indicates that Israel is from the start embedded in a relational humanity and that Chronicles should be understood as an "Adam book." See T. Willi, "Innovation aus Tradition: Die chronistischen Bürgerlisten Israel 1 Chr 1–9 im Focus von 1 Chr 9," in *"Sieben Augen auf einem Stein" (Sach 3,9): Studien zur Literatur des Zweiten Tempels; Festschrift für Ina Willi-Plein zum 65. Geburtstag* (ed. F. Hartenstein; Neukirchen-Vluyn: Neukirchener Verlag, 2007), pp. 405–18 (esp. 410). See also G. N. Knoppers, "Shem, Ham, and Japheth: The Universal and the Particular in the Genealogy of Nations," in *The Chronicler as Theologian: Essays in Honor of Ralph W. Klein* (ed. M. P. Graham; JSOTSup 371; London: T&T Clark, 2003), pp. 13–31.

1:4 / The attentive reader will notice that a footnote at 1:4 in the NIV indicates that the words **the sons of Noah** are not in the Hebrew text. The Septuagint, the Greek translation of the Hebrew, however, contains these words, probably to avoid any confusion at this point. Someone unfamiliar with those names may mistakenly think that these three names in 1:4 are also presented in a linear form. The reading of the Septuagint text draws attention to these three persons actually being the sons of the last-mentioned person, Noah. See Dirksen, *1 Chronicles*, p. 39.

1:7 / The two place names **Elishah** and **Tarshish** (which is also mentioned in Jonah), as well as the groups of people **the Kittim and the Rodanim,** are associated with the ancient maritime world—a reference made explicit in Gen. 10:7 but omitted by the Chronicler. See Klein, *1 Chronicles*, p. 65.

1:27 / The phrase **Abram (that is . . .)** might be an addition by a later hand. The original Hebrew text probably just had Abraham (like the Septuagint). A later reader probably felt uncomfortable that the patriarch was called by his covenant name here, understandably so in light of the source text in Gen. 11:26, which has "Abram." It might also be the Chronicler's way to make the transition from those texts in Genesis that use Abram to those using the covenant name Abraham. From 1 Chron. 1:28 only the latter is used. See Dirksen, *1 Chronicles*, p. 40; Knoppers, *1 Chronicles 1–9*, p. 278.

§1.2 Abraham's Descendants (1 Chron. 1:28–2:2)

The previous section ended with Abraham, so this section dwells on Abraham's descendants. The Chronicler hastens from Adam and Noah to Abraham, narrowing his focus all the time to get to the specific part of the family that he wants to portray, namely, the tribe of Judah (see next section).

This section starts with a heading in 1:28, introducing the two sons of Abraham, Isaac and Ishmael. First Chronicles 1:29–31 contains the genealogy of Ishmael, while 1:32–33 presents the descendants of Abraham through Keturah. After an introduction (1:34), 1:35–2:2 takes the Isaac lineage further, presenting first the descendants of Esau (1:35–54) and then of Israel (2:1–2). Israel, of course, refers to Jacob—a custom that the Chronicler followed throughout (apart from 16:13, 17, where he quotes from two psalms).

The order of the presentation of these genealogies is significant. It is a well-known practice in these family lists to present the most important person or lineage last (as we saw with Shem in the previous section). In the headings the tendency is often the opposite. There the focal element often comes first (as we saw with Shem, Ham, and Japheth in 1:4). Here the situation is the same. Although 1:28 presents Abraham's sons in the order Isaac-Ishmael, the genealogies are presented in the opposite order. The focus is clearly on Isaac's descendants. The presentation of Isaac's lineage follows the same pattern (apart from the heading in 1:34 not following the pattern seen with Shem and Isaac). The presentation of Esau's lineage comes first, and then the focus shifts to Israel. Some scholars argue that this ordering was a deliberate but subtle polemic against the Edomites (who were closely associated with Esau). Whether this reflects a preexilic reality or rather a postexilic situation where the successor of Edom was probably another Persian province, Idumea, cannot be determined here. What we can say for sure is that the emphasis is not on Esau.

1:28 / Whereas Adam stood at the head of the previous section, with Abram concluding it, this section now opens with **Abraham,** and it will be concluded with Israel in 2:1–2. Only the names of the two sons, **Isaac and Ishmael,** are mentioned, without any elaboration on the colorful history of these two boys presented in the Genesis account. One may assume that these narratives were known to the Chronicler's audience.

1:29–31 / This subsection starts with a phrase containing the well-known Hebrew technical term normally translated **descendants.** It indicates the offspring of **Ishmael.** Besides the **firstborn Nebaioth,** eleven other sons of Ishmael are named. This is clearly a quotation from Genesis 25:12–16, where the lineage of Ishmael is indicated. Interestingly enough, the Chronicler omits any mention of "Sarah's maid-servant, Hagar the Egyptian," who is mentioned in Genesis 25:12 as the one who bore Ishmael to Abraham.

1:32–33 / This subsection focuses on **the sons born to Keturah** and ends with the phrase **all these were descendants of Keturah.** Altogether six sons of Keturah are mentioned. Two of them, **Jokshan** and **Midian,** are then singled out, and their descendants are also mentioned.

What is very interesting in this part is Keturah's being presented as the family head, not unlike the way in which Abraham is presented in 1:28. This might be an indication that the Chronicler definitely wanted to contrast this part of the family with the favorite lineage of Isaac. The genealogy of Keturah functions on the same level as that of Ishmael, preparing the way for the climax in the next section, where Isaac's descendants will be listed.

Another interesting aspect of the inclusion of Keturah in 1:32 is the description the Chronicler gives her, namely, **Abraham's concubine.** First Chronicles 1:32–33 clearly quotes from Genesis 25:1–4. However, in Genesis 25:1 Keturah is explicitly called the "wife" of Abraham. The Chronicler probably called her "Abraham's concubine" in order to make it clear that these descendants rank lower in importance than the main lineage of Isaac. The Chronicler probably took his cue from Genesis 25:6, which indicates that, after Abraham gave all he had to Isaac (25:5), "he gave gifts to the sons of his concubines" (the same word is used here as in 1 Chron. 1:32), and that "he sent them away from his son Isaac to the land of the east."

1:34 / After having established in the previous subsections that the descendants of neither Ishmael nor Keturah were the focal point, the genealogy can now continue from **Abraham** to **Isaac** and through him to his two sons **Esau and Israel.** The verb form ("he fathered"—in the NIV

was the father of) emphasizes that the line runs from Abraham to Isaac, and not through Ishmael and Keturah. The Chronicler uses "Israel" for "Jacob" throughout. Since the Chronicler's great concern is to help negotiate the social identity of All-Israel in the late Persian era, this is understandable. He wanted to emphasize that the origin of this people goes back to the covenant bearer, whose name was changed from Jacob to Israel.

1:35–54 / The genealogy of **Esau** starts in 1:35. It is clear that this list is an abridged version of Genesis 36:1–19. Apart from **Eliphaz** and **Reuel**, three other sons of Esau are mentioned. This differs slightly from Genesis 36:10, which features only the first two. For each of these two sons, the Chronicler lists a few sons, again with slight differences from the source texts in Genesis 36. One small variation is the inclusion of **Timna** in 1 Chronicles 1:36 as an offspring of Eliphaz. According to Genesis 36:12 (which the Chronicler excludes), Timna was a concubine of Eliphaz, who bore him the son **Amalek**. The NIV's translation **by Timna: Amalek** follows the Septuagint reading of this verse.

From 1:38, however, a new lineage, namely, that of **Seir**, is taken up. This segmented genealogy, which continues through 1:42, is not related in any way to Esau in the Chronicler's version. From Genesis 36:8–9, however, it becomes clear that Seir is a geographical designation of the area where Esau settled. The lineage of Seir presented here is therefore implicitly connected to Esau. For each of the seven descendants of Seir the Chronicler describes a branch, again quoting from Genesis 36:20–28.

The next verses (1:43–54) offer a section that is strictly speaking not a genealogy but rather a name list of Edomite **kings** (1:43–51a) and **chiefs** (1:51b–54), filled in with some narrative details. This section, a slightly adapted quotation from Genesis 36:31–43, opens with the telling remark (which the Chronicler took over from the source text) that these **kings . . . reigned in Edom before any Israelite king reigned.** It is clear that the implicit connection with Esau occurs through the mentioning of Edom, the area closely associated with the descendants of Esau. Through this implicit relationship these "kings" and "chiefs" are taken up into the genealogy of Esau.

The late Persian context could have influenced the Chronicler to give prominence to Edom through Esau. We will encounter the Edomites again in later sections of Chronicles (see particularly 2 Chron. 21 and 25), and I will then comment on their prominence. For now, we should consider that the presentation of Edom might be another indication that the Chronicler wanted to help negotiate the social identity of the

Yehudite community here. The positioning of Esau, Seir, and Edom is therefore significant. The Chronicler provided an elaborate genealogy for this group (by quoting extensively from his source text in Gen. 36). However, Esau is still discussed before Isaac, which indicates that the Chronicler's sympathy does not lie with Edom but rather with Isaac and Israel. One could perhaps say (with A. Siedlecki, "Foreigners, Warfare, and Judahite Identity in Chronicles," in *The Chronicler as Author* [ed. M. P. Graham and S. L. McKenzie; Sheffield: Sheffield Academic Press, 1999], pp. 229–66) that Israel is defining itself "at its margins" here.

The change from "kings" (1:43) to "chiefs" (1:51b) is interesting, as if the writer wanted to suggest that, since David came to the throne, the Edomite kings have been demoted to chiefs. The suggestion is that the Israelite monarchs by some unstated standard outrank the Edomite ones and, hence, are more deserving of focus here.

2:1–2 / In these two verses we encounter the other segment of Isaac's genealogy, namely, that of his son **Israel** (i.e., Jacob). These verses, naming the twelve sons of Jacob, actually form the introduction to all the genealogies that follow (2:3–9:1a). As Hicks (*1 and 2 Chronicles*, p. 77) puts it, these two verses are "the hinge that swings the door" between a presentation of "world history" and the presentation of "Israelite history."

In comparison to the scope of the Esau genealogy, it is remarkable that so much attention is given to the sons of Israel. This confirms the point made earlier that they are actually the destination toward which the Chronicler's whole genealogical construction has been pointing.

We find similar lists of Jacob's sons in Genesis 35:23–26 and Exodus 1:2–4. The Chronicler's list provides only the twelve names (so also Exod. 1) and does not mention the respective mothers (as does Gen. 35). The Exodus version moves **Joseph** to the narrative part following the name list, indicating that he was already in Egypt when the other eleven brothers came there. Chronicles positions Joseph with **Benjamin** (as does Gen. 35:24) and groups the name **Dan** with Joseph and Benjamin. In the Genesis and Exodus versions, by contrast, Dan is placed together with **Naphtali**. Klein (*1 Chronicles*, p. 80) theorizes that the Chronicler's positioning of Dan just before Joseph (the seventh position) might be an indication of his importance, or might form the transition between the children of Leah and those of Rachel (with Dan being the first son attributable legally to the latter).

The Chronicler does not keep to the order and content of the present list of **the sons of Israel** when he compiles the genealogies of these sons in the subsequent sections. No lineages are offered for **Zebulun** and

Dan. Joseph does not receive separate treatment, although his two sons, Manasseh and Ephraim (who are not mentioned by name in 2:1–2), are placed in the compilation that follows. The order in which these sons receive attention in the lists that follow is **Judah, Simeon, Reuben, Gad, Levi, Issachar, Benjamin, Naphtali,** and **Asher,** with a section focusing on Benjamin again at the end of the compilation. **Manasseh** and **Ephraim** are then inserted in 1 Chronicles 5 and 1 Chronicles 7. This change of order is an indication that the overall construction of the Chronicler's genealogies was deliberate. Whereas the present list approximately follows the source text to expound the familial relationships, the overall genealogical constructions emphasize importance and prominence.

Additional Notes §1.2

1:29–31 / The Hebrew term *toledoth* in 1:29 is a very well-known technical term that occurs at strategic junctions in the narratives in Genesis (2:4; 5:1; 6:9; 10:1; 11:10; 25:12; 36:1; 37:2) and Exodus (6:16; 28:10). The Chronicler took over the term in 1:29 from his source text Gen. 25:12. Because the term is used in 1 Chron. 1:29 with the third-person plural suffix, it could also have been taken from Gen. 25:13, where the word occurs with the suffix. See Knoppers, *1 Chronicles 1–9,* p. 278. The Chronicler's striking omission of prominent women is discussed by Labahn and Ben Zvi, who come to the conclusion that, although the genealogies "reflected and reinforced the main construction of family and family roles in a traditional ancient near eastern society," many references "indicated to the early (and predominantly male) readers of the book that ideologically construed gender expectations may and have been transgressed in the past and with good results. By implication, these references suggested to the readers that gender (and ethnic) boundaries can and even should be transgressed on occasion, with divine blessing, and resulting in divine blessing" (A. Labahn and E. Ben Zvi, "Observations on Women in the Genealogies of 1 Chronicles 1–9," *Bib* 84 [2003], pp. 457–78, at p. 478). This interpretation would support the observation that the Chronicler took an inclusivist stance. However, Labahn and Ben Zvi fail to give a satisfying explanation for why the Chronicler omitted Sarah and Hagar.

1:32 / Labahn and Ben Zvi interpret the Chronicler's inclusion of the concubine **Keturah** as head of a sublineage very positively. It is doubtful, however, whether this positive appraisal is appropriate. These authors have not noticed that the very mention of Keturah as head of a lineage relegates her to a part of the family that does not really matter to the Chronicler, because the male hero Isaac forms the focus. Because of their neglect to consult the source texts in Genesis ("Observations on Women," 463n18), they did not notice that the change of a wife into a "concubine" was deliberate. This change alludes to another part in the Gen. 25 text where it is made clear that Isaac, and not the sons of Abraham's concubines, carries the covenantal line.

1:43–54 / E. Assis sees an anti-Edomite ideology in action here (E. Assis, "From Adam to Esau and Israel: An Anti-Edomite Ideology in 1 Chronicles 1," *VT* 56 [2006], pp. 287–302). This could be a plausible theory if Lipschits is correct in his assessment of the developments in the southern and southwestern areas during the late Persian era. According to him, "the Negev, the Hebron Mountains, and the southern and central Shephelah were separated from the province of Judah. These areas became the center of another national-territorial unit: Idumea" (O. Lipschits, *The Fall and Rise of Jerusalem* [Winona Lake, IN: Eisenbrauns, 2005], p. 149). That the southeastern border of Yehud (in the direction of Edom) was a contested area is evident in the system of fortresses erected in this area by the Persians at the end of the fifth to the beginning of the fourth centuries B.C. The Chronicler's treatment of Edom might then well be a reflection that a polemic against Yehud's southern neighbors was still continuing in those days. We know that the Idumean population consisted of various ethnic minorities during this period, including also some Judahites (see A. Kloner and I. Stern, "Idumea in the Late Persian Period [Fourth Century B.C.]," in *Judah and the Judeans in the Fourth Century B.C.E.* [ed. O. Lipschits et al.; Winona Lake, IN: Eisenbrauns, 2007], pp. 139–44). This might be the reason that the Chronicler portrays Edom as part of the family but also separate from the covenant bearers.

§1.3 Focus on Judah and His Famous Descendants (1 Chron. 2:3–4:23)

Whereas the Chronicler merely introduced the twelve sons of Israel by name in the last two verses of the previous section (2:1–2), the sections that follow each focus on one of these sons. First Chronicles 2:3–4:23 focuses particularly on the descendants of Judah. The reader familiar with Israelite history would know the presentation of the Deuteronomistic History that the united Israel under David and Solomon comprised twelve tribes, each originating from one of the sons of Jacob/Israel. The genealogies presented by the Chronicler should therefore not be read as the family lists of a few individuals, but rather as a kind of social-identity map. The presentations of the Chronicler promote the influence and extent of these different sections of society but also shape their supposed interrelationships.

It is no coincidence that the discussion of Judah in the present section is the most extensive of all the Chronicler's genealogical presentations. Embedded in this section are the genealogies of the most famous of Judah's descendents, namely, David (3:1–9) and Solomon (3:10–24), the latter containing a list of all Judah's kings and leaders beyond the exile. The final construction of the genealogies (whether they originally formed part of Chronicles or were later added to form an integral part of Chronicles) already paves the way for the focal point in the narrative parts of the book, namely, the ideal historical period under David (1 Chron. 10–29) and Solomon (2 Chron. 1–9).

Judah's genealogy is introduced in two subsections (1 Chron. 2:3–55 and 4:1–23), surrounding the sections dedicated to David and Solomon. Whether they compose a chiastic structure, as some commentators suggest, is not clear. Such structures are often in the eyes of the beholder. However, there is no doubt that the embedding of David's and Solomon's descendants within the broader family of Judah was particularly significant to the Chronicler. The ancient readers of Chronicles would not have missed the message here!

2:3–4 / These verses introduce the five **sons of Judah**, the first three, **Er, Onan and Shelah**, being the sons of the **Canaanite woman, the daughter of Shua**, whom Judah took as his wife, and **Perez and Zerah** being the twin sons of **Tamar, Judah's daughter-in-law**. Behind this short summary of Judah's sons is, of course, the very enigmatic narrative in Genesis 38. It tells the story—amid the narrative of the highly exemplary other son of Israel, Joseph (Gen. 37–50)—of this ancestor who fathered twin brothers from his daughter-in-law, Tamar. This happened after the ancestor did not satisfy her legal rights, and she thus disguised herself as a prostitute to claim those rights. An anticlimax in the patriarchal history, one would say! Surprisingly enough, this very Judah is the father of the lineage under discussion in this central part of the Chronicler's genealogies. It is quite telling that the golden line of Israelite covenantal history does not shy away from the dubious characters. Father Jacob/ Israel was, of course, another example.

All five "sons of Judah" are mentioned in the Genesis 38 narrative. The Chronicler took over some small elements of this narrative, such as the statement that the first three sons were born to Judah from "a Canaanite woman, the daughter of Shua" (1 Chron. 2:3a), as well as the sad death of Er by the hand of **the LORD** (2:3b). Like Genesis 38:7, the Chronicler does not elaborate on what Er did wrong.

Interestingly enough, the Chronicler does not tell us anything more about Onan, whose wickedness is described in full color in Genesis 38:8–10. He did not want to fulfill his brotherly duty after the death of his older brother to procreate with his brother's widow, Tamar. So he spilled his semen on the ground every time he lay with her. This was considered to be wicked in the eyes of the Lord, and the Lord also killed him. The Chronicler deals with this dark patch in Judah's history by merely mentioning Onan in 1 Chron. 2:3, but not providing any comments or genealogy for him.

2:5 / The three sons of Judah whose genealogies are presented— Er and Onan had no children—are Perez, Zerah, and Shelah (in that order). **Perez** is obviously the main figure, being mentioned first in this verse, forming a heading for the extensive segmented genealogy of Perez in 2:9–4:20. Zerah's genealogy follows next (2:6–7), but Shelah's is postponed until after the discussion of Perez's descendants (4:21–23). This short introduction to Perez's genealogy has parallels in Genesis 46:12b and Numbers 26:21.

2:6–8 / Five sons of **Zerah** are now listed in 2:6. Although these names might have been taken from 1 Kings 4:31, the latter text is not parallel. First Kings 4 praises the wisdom of Solomon, indicating that he was wiser than **Ethan** the Ezrahite as well as **Heman, Calcol and Darda,** the sons of Mahol. No indication is given in 1 Kings 4 that these figures were in any way related to the Judah lineage running through Perez and Zerah. The mentioning of Ethan and Heman in the present text should, however, not be seen as a coincidence. This is probably a good example of genealogical fluidity. Certain elements of one lineage can be taken up into another lineage in order to make some connection between the two. Ethan and Heman are prominent descendants of Levi (see 1 Chron. 6 as well as 15:19) who acted as temple musicians in the sanctuary in Jerusalem. According to 1 Chronicles 6:31–32 David appointed them for this duty. Whether the Ethan and Heman mentioned in 2:6 are the same persons as those mentioned later in the Levite genealogy cannot be determined. However, since these names are used very rarely in the Hebrew Bible, the similarity remains conspicuous. By adopting these names in the Judahite genealogy, the Chronicler could have intended to connect the Levites with the Judahites (from whose lineage David would come). This would have given some status to these cultic staff and would confirm our suspicion that the Chronicler himself might have had links with the Levites.

Carmi, mentioned in 2:7, is not related explicitly to one of the sons of Zerah. The Chronicler took over a piece of the narrative of Joshua 7 by reminding the reader of the transgression of **Achar** (the name may be either a scribal error for "Achan" or a wordplay on the Hebrew verb "to bring trouble"). He was the one who **brought trouble on Israel by violating the ban on taking devoted things.** Some commentators already see in this reference an indication of the Chronicler's so-called theology of immediate retribution. However, one should remember that this information is taken over from Joshua 7 and is therefore not unique to the Chronicler. The selection of this reference to Achar instead of others might be significant because of its allusion to cultic transgression, an issue that the Chronicler considered in a serious light.

One **son of Ethan** is mentioned, namely, **Azariah.** It is difficult to reconcile the information of 1 Chronicles 6:41–42 with this verse, since the son of Ethan indicated there is called Adaiah (which is unlikely to be confused with the name Azariah).

2:9 / The Perez line is taken up again and traced through **Hezron,** indicating the three sons of Hezron, **Jerahmeel, Ram and Caleb.** These sons are dealt with in the next subsections.

2:10–17 / This subsection deals with the descendants of **Ram**. The first part of the genealogy is in linear form, tracing the lineage through Jesse. A parallel to this family list can be found in the genealogy attached to the book of Ruth. In Ruth 4:18–22 the same lineage is given, running from Perez through Hezron and Ram to Jesse and David. It is not certain who borrowed from whom in this case. It might be that the attachment to Ruth was made after the example of Chronicles, or that they both incorporated a preexisting genealogy.

A comparison with the genealogy in Ruth 4 also shows two interesting additions and a variant spelling for **Salmon** (Hebrew Salma, taken as Salmon by the NIV, with support from the Septuagint). **Nahshon** is described in 1 Chronicles 2:10 as **the leader of the people of Judah.** The Chronicler probably added the comment on account of Numbers 1:16, which lists Nahshon, the son of Amminadab (mentioned in Num. 1:7), among the leaders of the people (with the same Hebrew term as here). The other addition to the information in Ruth is the segmented description given of Jesse's children. Whereas Ruth 4:22 merely mentions David as the (only important) son of Jesse, the Chronicler elaborates on Jesse's lineage, mentioning seven sons (with David being the seventh) and two daughters. Interestingly enough, he extends the family tree by providing information on the descendants of these two daughters—something that is uncommon in Hebrew Bible practice. The information about the two daughters' descendants could draw on references in 2 Samuel (2:18; 17:25). Some of the names of Jesse's sons (**Eliab, Abinadab,** and **Shimea** = Shammah in 1 Sam. 16:9) go back to the narrative in 1 Samuel 16. The other names (**Nethanel, Raddai,** and **Ozem**) are not mentioned there, although it mentions that Jesse let seven sons pass before Samuel. David would accordingly have been the eighth child of Jesse. That the Chronicler made him the seventh son is telling, since the seventh position in lineages is often reserved for persons of significance. We do not know who was substituted in the seventh position, since 1 Samuel 16 narrates only the first three sons in chronological order.

2:18–20 / The lineage of **Caleb** in this subsection has no parallel in the Hebrew Bible (apart perhaps from 2:2, which has parallels in Exodus). Whether the Chronicler used an unknown source or whether this was his own creation, we cannot say for sure. (Another section on Caleb follows in 2:42–50a.)

One figure who might be significant here is **Bezalel**. In three texts in Exodus (31:2; 35:30; 38:22) he is the one whom Moses appointed to build the tabernacle. This might be another attempt of the Chronicler to tie the sanctuary tradition to the Judahite/Davidic line. In the late Persian era, when the status of the Second Temple still had to be consolidated, such a link would have been very valuable.

2:21–24 / This subsection jumps back to **Hezron,** indicating his descendants from a later marriage. This later marriage was to **the daughter of Makir the father of Gilead.** Scholars agree that this phrase probably voices a territorial claim. According to Numbers 32:39–41 Moses gave Gilead to Makir. Makir is there called a son of Manasseh. **Jair,** who is presented as a grandson of Hezron here, is also mentioned in Numbers 32:39–41, also as a son of Manasseh. Since we do not have any other parallel for the information in the Chronicler's genealogy, I suggest that the Chronicler made creative use of this earlier tradition of Makir and Jair to establish a link between the lineage of the Judahites and Manasseh and also to voice Judah's territorial claim on (parts of) Gilead in the Transjordanian area. Within the late Persian period, when this area probably formed part of another Persian province, such a claim would indicate that the Persian administration did not enforce strict boundaries between provinces. The Chronicler, writing from a Judahite perspective, utilizes this context to indicate that the Transjordan was also under the influence of Jerusalem.

2:25–41 / This subsection deals with the descendants of **Jerahmeel the firstborn of Hezron.** No parallel to this genealogy exists in the Hebrew Bible, so it is particularly difficult to situate these figures. The concluding formula in 2:33, **these were the descendants of Jerahmeel,** creates the impression that the list ends at that point. From 2:34 onward, however, we find an elaboration on the lineage of **Sheshan,** who is mentioned in 2:31 as the son of **Ishi.**

2:42–50a / This second section deals with the descendants of **Caleb.** There are no resemblances between the two Calebite genealogies, leaving the impression that two different Caleb genealogies might be confused here. The only connection is that in 2:42 Caleb is called **the brother of Jerahmeel,** who is associated (in 2:9, 25) with the lineage of Hezron (who is not explicitly mentioned in this particular subsection).

Scholars observe that many of the names mentioned in this genealogy are place names and/or geographical names, mainly situated in the southern part of Judah, with **Hebron** forming one of the geographical focal points. As we will see in 3:1–9, Hebron was the initial capital from where David consolidated his reign over Israel. This particular genealogy prepares the way on a literary level for the description of Israel's great king, but it might possibly be another territorial claim for the Persian-period Yehud.

2:50b–55 / First Chronicles 2:19 states that **Hur** was born from the marriage of Caleb and Ephrath. Here, in 2:50b, Hur is called **the firstborn of Ephrathah**, obviously an echo of the previous occurrence. However, this cross-reference creates a difficulty, since 2:20 indicates that Hur became the father of Uri, who became the father of Bezalel. The Hur genealogy provided in this subsection seems not to relate to the one mentioned earlier. We also do not have any parallel to this particular family list in the Hebrew Bible.

Again, as in the previous subsection, many of the names can be associated with place names and/or geographical names. However, a concentration in one area cannot be observed here. We also know very little of the groups behind the many gentilica (names of nations) included in this list. However, the mentioning of Ephrathah might be an allusion to Bethlehem, the town of David's origin.

3:1–9 / We finally come to the long-awaited focus of this particular Judahite genealogy, David's and Solomon's descendants.

With the mention of **Hebron** and **Jerusalem**, the presentation of the descendants of **David** simultaneously becomes a short overview of the phases in his reign. He first established his kingship from Hebron and later moved his capital to Jerusalem, which he captured from the Jebusites (see 11:4). For **seven years and six months** he reigned in Hebron, and in Jerusalem for **thirty-three years**. This information correlates with 2 Samuel 5:5 except for one slight difference: there David's territory is called "all Israel and Judah."

The **six sons** who were **born to him in Hebron** are listed in 3:1b–3. All six had different mothers. The Chronicler found this information in 2 Samuel 3:2–5 (although **Daniel** is called Kileab there). Two of these sons are better known from the Deuteronomistic History: **Absalom** killed his brother **Amnon** after the latter raped their half-sister **Tamar** (2 Sam. 13); Absalom once conspired to become king in Hebron (2 Sam. 15); and sadly he was killed by Joab, David's military leader (2 Sam. 18). **Adonijah the son of Haggith** is also well known from the Deuteronomistic History (1 Kgs. 1–2) as the son who tried to usurp his father's reign at the end of David's life, an attempt that was foiled by **Bathsheba** and led to **Solomon** becoming king.

In Jerusalem David fathered a total of fourteen children. **Four of** those are the sons of Bathshua, also known as Bathsheba (the NIV follows the Vulgate's translation at this point). The incident with Bathsheba in 2 Samuel 11 is not mentioned here or anywhere else in Chronicles. In 2 Samuel 11:3 she is called the daughter of Eliam; here she is the **daughter of Ammiel**. Although these four sons are also mentioned in 2 Samuel 5:14, they are not indicated to be Bathsheba's sons there. In both 2 Samuel 5 and 1 Chronicles 3 Solomon is mentioned in the fourth position. Second Samuel 12:24 mentions, however, that Solomon was the first surviving son (and thus the oldest) of David and Bathsheba. This has led commentators to assume that the order in 2 Samuel and 1 Chronicles is not the order of birth. Another possibility would be that the comment in 2 Samuel 12:24 tried to establish Solomon's position over against his older brothers.

Nine other sons and one daughter, Tamar, are mentioned, being born from other mothers. We find parallels to the Jerusalemite descendants of David in 2 Samuel 5:13–16. There, however, only seven additional sons are mentioned, eliminating the first mention of **Eliphelet** as well as **Nogah** (see Additional Note on 3:6–8). Another parallel to this Jerusalemite genealogy found later in 1 Chronicles 14:3–7 lists thirteen sons in total (four plus nine), with minor spelling differences for some of the names. The second list may be an indication that the same hand compiled these different parts of Chronicles. Tamar is, however, not mentioned in 1 Chronicles 14, probably on account of her being female.

3:10–24 / The next subsection presents the genealogy of **Solomon**, David's chosen son, who became king after him. The first part (3:10–14) follows a linear pattern, listing all the kings of Judah up to **Josiah**. In this construction Josiah descends by a direct line from Solomon, who stands at the beginning of this list. This foreshadows the narrative arc drawn in Chronicles from Solomon to Josiah.

There are no variations in order in this first part of the genealogy compared to the descriptions we find in the books of Kings.

From Josiah onward the genealogy changes into a segmented format, highlighting one specific person in each generation. Four sons of Josiah are indicated, namely, **Johanan, Jehoiakim, Zedekiah**, and **Shallum**. According to 2 Kings 23:31–35 and 24:17 Josiah had three sons, namely, Jehoahaz, Eliakim (whose name was changed to Jehoiakim), and Zedekiah. On the basis of Jeremiah 22:11 Shallum is identified with Jehoahaz. The reason for the inclusion of Johanan in this list remains unclear. We know from both Kings and Chronicles that the order of the kings in the final years of Judah was Shallum/Jehoahaz; Jehoiakim/Eliakim; **Jehoiachin/ Jeconiah** (the **son** of Jehoiakim—3:16); and finally Zedekiah. Although

Jehoiachin also had a son called Zedekiah (3:16), the last king is explicitly indicated in 2 Kings 24:17 as the uncle of Jehoiachin.

Commentators point out that Josiah is here portrayed as the end of an era. From the books of Kings we know that he was the last king not to have been taken into exile. Shallum was taken to Egypt, where he died, while the other three remaining rulers were all exiled to Babylon. An accurate count of the generations from Adam to Josiah brings the number to forty-nine. The fiftieth generation, according to the Chronicler's construction, went into exile. Since we know that the fiftieth year was considered to be a Jubilee year (Lev. 25) after seven periods of seven years have elapsed, the count of generations may also be an indication that seven full cycles of generations have passed before the exile came. In this interpretation, the exile is then associated with the (positive) outcome of the Jubilee year—as with the interpretation given in 2 Chronicles 36:20–21 of the exile as sabbath rest for the land.

The Chronicler signals the beginning of the exilic period in this genealogy when he calls Jehoiachin **the captive** (1 Chron. 3:17). The lineage from him runs through **Pedaiah, Zerubbabel, Hananiah, Shecaniah, Shemaiah, Neariah,** and **Elioenai,** extending across the exilic period into the time of the postexilic restoration. Information about when exactly and in which sectors of society all the people mentioned in this part of the genealogy were active is not accessible to the modern-day interpreter. However, on the basis of smaller details in the text one may assume that some of them could have lived in the Chronicler's time (i.e., in the first half of the fourth century B.C.).

One could say that this particular genealogy becomes the bridge between the historical period of the kingdom of Judah and the reality of Yehud during the Chronicler's own time. This genealogy, in particular, reflects the Chronicler's awareness of continuity. The Chronicler portrays postexilic reality as a continuation of the kingdom of Judah under David's lineage. The theological significance of this should not be underestimated. The faithfulness of Yahweh, who proclaimed the house of David as rulers over Judah, persists despite the interruption of the exile. However, the social identity being fostered here should also not be overlooked. By means of this genealogical interface between two eras, the postexilic community (or at least the part that is the Chronicler's origins) is claiming its rightful place in a new dispensation. One could ask at this stage whether this material was intended only for an inner-Jerusalemite audience (which was certainly the primary audience) or whether it also has polemical overtones directed against the Persian rulership (a point that will be discussed in greater detail later in this commentary, for example, in our discussion of Asa's history in 2 Chron. 14).

4:1–20 / In this subsection the Chronicler returns to the head of the genealogy under discussion from 2:3 onward, namely, **Judah.** First Chronicles 4:1 is a brief, linear summary of the genealogies presented in 2:2–55, although the lineage presented here differs from the earlier presentation. The names in this subsection create the impression of a haphazard compilation of names mentioned earlier in the Judahite genealogy. The literary effect is that of comprehensiveness. We do not find any parallel to this specific genealogy in any other part of the Hebrew Bible. It might well be, then, that the Chronicler created this amalgam in order to sandwich the Davidic and Solomonic family lists (discussed in the previous subsections) into the genealogy of Judah.

This subsection features the first narrative section in Chronicles (4:9–10), the story of **Jabez.** This also marks the first appearance of the term **God of Israel** in Chronicles. This little narrative is unrelated to anything in the genealogical context in which it stands. Apparently, the Chronicler intends it to give a glimpse of the vulnerable existence of the Judahites in the time of restoration. He indicates that Jabez is **named** by **his mother.** Elsewhere in the Hebrew Bible, names are often a wordplay on some circumstance surrounding the birth of a child (a practice still found in some traditional African cultures). In this case, a play of Hebrew consonants relates the name to a painful birth (the name is formed from the Hebrew root *'abats*, while the noun *'atsab* refers to pain). The little narrative immediately continues with a prayer of Jabez addressed to "the God of Israel." He asks that God will indeed **bless** him (1) by enlarging his **territory**; (2) by letting his (God's) **hand** be with him; and (3) by keeping him **from harm.** He specifically petitions for God's blessing **so that** he **will be free from pain.** In the latter phrase, the consonant-play of the naming is employed again, leaving the impression that Jabez's prayer was intended as an escape from the sad destiny implied by his name.

The context of the genealogies, as well as Chronicles as a whole, should guide the interpretation of this little narrative. Here we glimpse the process of identity negotiation of an Israel that has endured the hardship of the exile and the postexilic restoration but that is experiencing a new beginning under Persian imperial rule. Within this context the Chronicler wants to remind his contemporaries of the hardships of the past but also of what the right religious and cultic attitudes should be in their present and future. Specifically, they need to rely fully on "the God of Israel." As we will see, the theme of seeking and relying on God forms a very prominent theme throughout Chronicles. Any forgetfulness of their own limitations, and any attempt at becoming self-reliant, will lead to destruction at the hands of their enemies. Even when Jabez's prayer is answered (as 4:10 indicates), he is still called Jabez, the one who was born "in pain." The identity of this people being described in these genealogies should not be rooted in their troubled past, but rather in reliance on "the God of Israel" in the future.

This interpretation opposes the use of this little narrative in isolation for advocating an individualistic, prosperity theology. The narrative should rather be interpreted within the context of the collective social-identity negotiation that we witness in these texts.

4:21–23 / The previous sections follow the genealogy of Judah, son of Israel, particularly through the lineage of Perez (2:5) and his son Hezron (2:9–4:20). Apart from a brief genealogy of Zerah (2:6–8), we do not hear much about the rest of Judah's children. We have already seen that Er and Onan had no descendants. The very extensive genealogy of Judah now concludes with the short but informative family list of the remaining brother of Judah's five children, **Shelah**. We do not find any parallel for this genealogy elsewhere in the Hebrew Bible, and many of the names—some again indicating places—remain unknown to us.

One striking feature of this final family list is again the explication of relationships with neighboring areas and peoples. In the phrase **who ruled in Moab** (4:22), the Hebrew verb also means "became husband." The majority of commentators and translations therefore translates this phrase "who married into Moab." Many scholars take the next phrase **and Jashubi Lehem** (so the Septuagint and Vulgate) to mean "and they returned to Lehem," the latter name an abbreviation of Bethlehem. Since the book Ezra-Nehemiah is so strongly opposed to mixed marriages, this relationship, as well as all the others where the Chronicler highlights foreign associations, is telling. Part of the Chronicler's self-understanding of All-Israel is the diversity included in this social group as well as the close interrelationships (both familial and in terms of land) with their neighbors. The kind of social identity being negotiated here seems to be inclusive and accommodating, rather than defensive.

Additional Notes §1.3

2:3–4:23 / Another parallel to this genealogy of **Judah** can be found in Numbers 26:19–22. The latter section, which forms part of the Priestly writing's indication of the Israelites who came out of Egypt, mentions that **Er** and **Onan** died in Canaan (Num. 26:19). G. Snyman's study asks, "Who would have used an ideological construct of Israel and an inclusive genealogy for Judah in early days of Persian Yehud? Who would have benefited from the use of the story of Israel, or at least, from a new look at the story of the kings of Judah?" He concludes that the main beneficiaries of the Chronicler's work would have been people in power. Possibly they negotiated a deal with Persia: they agreed to serve the Persian king following their own local customs in exchange for Persian restoration of their privileges. "In this way," says Snyman, "a solidarity would have been created between the local elite and the Persian representatives" (Snyman, "Possible World of Text Production," pp. 32–60, at p. 58). See also Knoppers, "Intermarriage, Social Complexity, and Ethnic Diversity," pp. 15–30.

2:7 / This verse contains the first occurrence of a Hebrew verb (*ma'al*; NIV **violating**) that recurs twelve times in Chronicles. The recurring word underscores a prominent theme of the Chronicler, namely, the transgressions of the past. See Klein, *1 Chronicles*, p. 93.

2:24 / Whether this verse is connected to the previous verses that offer another elaboration on the genealogy of **Hezron** is uncertain. Furthermore, the place name **Caleb Ephrathah** is not attested elsewhere. Some scholars, therefore, suggest, in line with variant readings from the Septuagint and Vulgate, that the verse should read: "After the death of Hezron, Caleb went to Ephrathah." The continuation of the sentence would then mean that Caleb had a son **Ashhur** with the late Hezron's wife, Ephrathah (who is called Ephrath in 2:19, but Ephrathah in 2:50). But no commentator provides a final answer to this textual problem. See H. G. M. Williamson, *1 and 2 Chronicles* (New Century Bible Commentary; Grand Rapids: Eerdmans, 1982), p. 53.

2:34 / The remark **Sheshan had no sons—only daughters** creates a difficulty for relating this person to the one mentioned in 2:31. There Sheshan, the son of Ishi, is said to have had a son called Ahlai. The rabbis attempted to solve this problem by speculating that this son had died in the meantime and that Sheshan then had only daughters left. The only reasonable explanation would be that these two genealogies (2:25–33 and 2:34–41) came from different traditions and therefore preserved these conflicting reports. See Dirksen, *1 Chronicles*, pp. 55–56.

3:4–5 / I. Kalimi ("View of Jerusalem," pp. 556–62) investigates all the occurrences of **Jerusalem** in the Chronicler's genealogies. Jerusalem occurs three times in the genealogies: here in the list of David's descendants, in the Levite genealogy in 1 Chron. 6, and in the concluding section about the postexilic inhabitants of the city in 1 Chron. 9. Kalimi concludes: "The repetitive information mentioning that the Temple was built in Jerusalem may be stressed to point out the unique holiness of the Chronicler's own Jerusalem" (p. 561).

3:6–8 / In comparison with 2 Sam. 5:15–16 the names in this section show some peculiarities. First, the name **Elishama** occurs twice (1 Chron. 3:6, 8). The first of these may well be a variant spelling of **Elishua**, the spelling used in

2 Sam. 5:15 and 1 Chron. 14:5 (also followed by NIV). Second, the name **Eliphe-let** occurs twice (1 Chron. 3:6, 8), whereas it is mentioned only once in 1 Sam. 5:16. Third, the name **Nogah** (also 1 Chron. 14:6) does not occur in 1 Sam. 5. A text-critical way to harmonize the two texts is to say that the first occurrence of Eliphelet and the following word, Nogah, were erroneously duplicated in the Chronicler's list, resulting in nine sons instead of seven. That the version with nine sons is also preserved in 1 Chron. 14:5–7 is an indication that the writer made the changes in 3:6–8 deliberately. One explanation for this deliberate change flows from the observation that, of the total of nineteen sons of **David** (six in Hebron and thirteen in Jerusalem), nine come before Solomon and nine after him. This arrangement would give Solomon, the son who became king after his father, David, died, the central position in this genealogy. See Klein, *1 Chronicles*, p. 116.

3:19 / **Zerubbabel** is well known from other parts of the Hebrew Bible, namely, Ezra, Nehemiah, and Haggai. In all those cases, however, he is called the son of Shealtiel (even in the genealogies included in Matt. 1 and Luke 3), while in Chronicles he is a son of **Pedaiah** (who, according to 3:17, was a brother of Shealtiel). Perhaps the early death of Shealtiel led to Zerubbabel being raised by Pedaiah, or maybe there were two persons called Zerubbabel. At present, we do not have enough evidence to settle this conclusively. See Knoppers, *1 Chronicles 1–9*, pp. 328–29.

4:21–23 / This final genealogy mentions two professions, namely, **linen workers** and **potters**. Knoppers is probably right: the terms may be a reflection of the Chronicler's time rather than of monarchic Israel. The Hebrew word for "linen" is found in late sources. Knoppers observes that "the Persian period witnessed a growing interest in the organization and development of certain professions. Indeed, this was a period in which markets and international trade flourished. Although craftsmen could be organized in groups and families, there is no clear evidence for the rise of professional guilds with their own constitutions and officials before the fifth century B.C.E." (*1 Chronicles 1–9*, p. 351). Klein (*1 Chronicles*, p. 142) is convinced that **worked for the king** (4:23) refers not to the great king of Persia but rather to one of the Davidic kings in monarchic times. However, if Knoppers is right, one could perhaps also suggest that this final remark about service to "the king" extended this genealogy of **Shelah** into the present era of the Chronicler, showing how people of Judahite/Israelite origin were contributing to the imperial economy. The interesting remark in 4:22, **these records are from ancient times**, is probably a metacomment by the Chronicler himself, a side note that was probably not meant to be incorporated in the text!

§1.4 Simeon's Descendants (1 Chron. 4:24–43)

In the previous section (2:3–4:23) we dealt with Judah, the first son of Israel. We now come to a second son of Israel, Simeon. This genealogy not only gives a list of descendants but also elaborates on the areas in which they settled as well as on the confrontations they had in the process of settlement. Although the focus of the Chronicler's genealogies is very much on Judah, Benjamin, and Levi, Simeon's genealogy is still fairly comprehensive. The reason might be that the tribe of Simeon is also closely associated with Judah (Simeon was absorbed into Judah long before the Chronicler's time). The genealogy intends to reflect the preexilic existence, when Simeon was still a separate tribe, but also to state the situation in the Chronicler's time.

4:24–27 / Although we also have references to the descendants of **Simeon** in texts such as Genesis 46:10 and Exodus 6:15, the Chronicler probably made use of Numbers 26:12–14 in his compilation here. The only difference is that Jakin is replaced by **Jarib.**

What follows in 4:25–27 is not attested elsewhere and was either taken from an unknown source or was the Chronicler's own creation. First Chronicles 4:27 probably hints in the direction of the absorption of Simeon into Judah, when the Chronicler indicates that **Shimei** was the only one of these descendants who had numerous children. The others did not multiply as much as **the people of Judah.**

4:28–33a / From 4:28 onward we find a list of names of places where the Simeonites had settled. The Chronicler took over this list (with minor differences) from Joshua 19:1–9, where it is explicitly stated that the portion of land allotted to the Simeonites came from the territory of Judah. The close connection between Simeon and Judah is confirmed in this territorial indication. However, the Chronicler's portrayal emphasizes the separate status of the Simeonites. These cities and villages probably lay to the south of Judah's territory, surrounding one of the major centers in this area, namely, **Beersheba.** We do not know the precise location of the other towns mentioned. However, we could assume that they were in the vicinity of the main town, Beersheba. One theory as to why the Chronicler emphasized the separate status of this southern region is that he wanted to emphasize the south in counterbalance to the Deuteronomistic History, which is more focused on the northern regions.

The temporal remark in 4:31, **these were their towns until the reign of David,** seems to indicate that these towns ceased to be in Simeonite possession when **David** started reigning. This might be the case, although there are indications that the Simeonite character of the southern region extended into the monarchic period. This temporal remark is, however, not attested in the Joshua 19 list and could be considered to come from the Chronicler's hand. Should that be the case, it confirms the Chronicler's view on how influential a watershed the reign of David was in history.

4:33b–38 / The last phrase in 4:33 introduces another name list with the words **and they kept a genealogical record.** This list concludes in 4:38 with the indication that **the men listed . . . were leaders of their clans** (here probably referring to the heads of the different families). Whereas the previous subsection contained geographical indications, the Chronicler is now turning his attention to the leadership in the "clans."

The names mentioned here are not known to us from any other source. Either the Chronicler used an unknown source or this list is a creation of the Chronicler himself.

At the end of this list the Chronicler indicates that—under the leadership of these family heads—the **families** (or ancestral houses, the next kinship unit in a tribe) **increased greatly.** This remark is in contrast with 4:27, where the writer states that the Simeonites "did not become as numerous as the people of Judah."

4:39–43 / The writer dedicates the final section in the Simeonite genealogy to some remarks about campaigns that were undertaken to expand their geographical area. Two expansions are mentioned. First, a campaign in the direction of **Gedor** to gain new **pasture for their flocks** is described here. This happened, according to the Chronicler, **in the days of Hezekiah king of Judah.** The Simeonites attacked the **dwellings** (literally "tents") of **the Hamites** (suggested from 4:40), as well as **the Meunites,** imposing the ban on them, that is, **completely** destroying them. Although we have clear indications of who were regarded as Hamites (see the commentary on 1:8–16), it is not clear here to which group(s) and time period the Chronicler refers. The Meunites appear again in 2 Chronicles 20:1 and 26:7, but their identity remains a mystery. What is important about this campaign is that the attackers found a **land** that was **spacious,**

peaceful and quiet. This seems to be a foreshadowing of a theme that is prominent in Chronicles as a whole, namely, the ideal of having quietness, rest, and peace. This theme is present in the Chronicler's presentation of Solomon, but at this stage it is only important to take note that the Hebrew term translated "peaceful" occurs in prominent positions in the description of the Judahite kingdom (2 Chron. 14:1, 5; 20:30; 23:21).

A second geographical expansion is mentioned in 2:42–43, indicating that some **Simeonites** went to **the hill country of Seir** and **killed . . . the Amalekites who had escaped.** Seir is closely linked to the Edomites (see commentary on 1:35–54), who occupied land to the south and southeast of Judah. The Amalekites mentioned here are also related to them, as the writer made clear in the genealogy (where Amalek is indicated to be a grandson of Esau in 1:35–36).

In both descriptions of the two campaigns the Chronicler remarks that the Simeonites live there **to this day** (2:41, 43). Whether this is a reference to the time of the Chronicler or to the time of the sources that he used is unclear. Given the close association of Judah and Simeon, it seems likely that the genealogical description given here makes certain claims of land for Judah.

Additional Notes §1.4

4:28 / The verb **lived** used in this verse and the related word in Hebrew used in 4:33 (translated "settlements") suggest that the Simeonites were settled in this area. The source used by the Chronicler, namely, Joshua 19:1–9, mentions that Simeon had their "inheritance" in the area of Judah. This is in line with the Deuteronomistic understanding of the promised land being legally allotted to the different tribes. The Chronicler does not use the term "inheritance," however. He was probably insinuating that the Simeonites were settled on Judahite land but the land still belonged to Judah.

4:33b / The verb translated **kept a genealogical record** (alternatively "took a census") is quite prominent in Chronicles. It occurs exclusively in Ezra-Nehemiah and Chronicles. Fifteen of its twenty occurrences are in Chronicles (1 Chron. 4:33; 5:1, 7, 17; 7:5, 7, 9, 40; 9:1, 22; 2 Chron. 12:15; 31:16, 17, 18, 19). It refers to the act of enrolling oneself or being enrolled in a genealogy (by means of a census). It is interesting that in Chronicles this verb is never used in connection with the tribes of Judah, Levi, and Benjamin (see P. C. Beentjes, "Identity and Community in the Book of Chronicles: The Role and Meaning of the Verb *Jahas*," *ZAH* 12 [1999], pp. 233–37). The account of David's census in 1 Chron. 21 comes to mind here, since Joab refused to count Levi and Benjamin in the census (see commentary on 1 Chron. 21).

§1.5 Descendants of Reuben, Gad, and the Half-Tribe of Manasseh (1 Chron. 5:1–26)

Whereas the previous genealogy covered the area south of Judah, the Chronicler now moves to the Transjordanian tribes to the east of Judah. Two of Israel's sons mentioned in 2:1–2 are particularly associated with these tribes, namely, Reuben (5:1–10) and Gad (5:11–17). However, from 5:18 the half-tribe of Manasseh is also mentioned together with these other tribes. The last subsection of this particular genealogy (5:23–26) deals explicitly with the descendants of Manasseh.

Our current knowledge of these tribes confirms that they, like the Simeonites, had probably disappeared as separately identifiable groups by the time of the Chronicler. Their inclusion again could be interpreted as part of the Chronicler's strategy to help define an inclusive All-Israel. On the one hand, the Judahite writer probably made some claims on the former tribal areas by reminding his readers that those dissolved tribes were once part of the family. On the other hand, readers who had a historical memory of being part of those tribes would find comfort in their existence still being in the mind of the writer.

5:1–2 / The genealogy of **Reuben** is introduced here with the phrase **the sons of Reuben the firstborn of Israel** but is then immediately interrupted with an explanatory note about the position of Reuben over against **Judah**. Although all Hebrew Bible traditions agree that Reuben was Jacob's firstborn, there is no uncertainty about why he fell from favor and did not receive the blessing associated with the firstborn. First Chronicles 5:1 reminds the reader of the incident in Genesis 35:22 in which Reuben had sexual intercourse with Bilhah, Jacob's concubine—an act described in Chronicles with the statement that **he defiled his father's marriage bed**. The wording probably comes from Genesis 49:4, where Jacob, in his final blessings to his sons, indicates that Reuben will not excel, and why: "for you went up onto your father's bed, onto my couch and defiled it." The Chronicler also reminds the reader of the incident narrated in Genesis 48, where Jacob blessed Ephraim and Manasseh (in that order of preference), the sons of **Joseph**. The transgression of Reuben led to the blessing of the firstborn passing to Joseph's sons. This is the reason, says the Chronicler, that Reuben is **not listed in the genealogical record in accordance with his birthright.** Again, the prominent position of Judah is confirmed (in 5:2), although the reader is reminded that **the rights of the firstborn belonged to Joseph**—a reference by which the Chronicler acknowledges the valid rights of the inhabitants of the former northern kingdom (closely associated with Ephraim). The respective rights of Judah and Joseph are, however, not put in opposition here.

5:3–10 / After the interruption of 5:1–2, the Chronicler returns to the **Reuben** genealogy by repeating the phrase **the sons of Reuben the firstborn of Israel.** The basic list of Reubenite descendants in 5:3 has parallels in Genesis 46:9; Exodus 6:14; and Numbers 26:5–6 (although more limited information is provided in Genesis, Exodus, and Chronicles than in Numbers).

In 1 Chronicles 5:4–10 we find the lineage of **Joel.** The position of this genealogy (with its associated narrative information) implies that Joel belongs to the **Reubenites.** However, this link is never made explicit. The only connection is that **Beerah** is called **a leader of the Reubenites** in 5:6. First Chronicles 5:4–10 remains detached from the surrounding genealogies, and no parallels can be found in the Hebrew Bible for the names included here.

First Chronicles 5:9 indicates the geographical area occupied by this group of people: **up to the edge of the desert that extends to the Euphrates River.** This is echoed in the indication in 5:10: **the entire region east of Gilead.** Two reasons for the expansion eastward are provided: on the one hand, their **livestock . . . increased** (5:9), but on the other hand, **they waged war against the Hagrites** (5:10), who apparently lived in the Transjordanian territory and were expelled by this conquest.

First Chronicles 5:10 provides the first reference to **Saul** in Chronicles. However, his connection with the Reubenites and their chronology cannot be determined from the text. Other biblical texts record Saul as a Benjaminite (e.g., 1 Sam. 9:21).

5:11–17 / The next subsection concerns another son of Israel, **Gad.** First Chronicles 5:11 indicates that the **Gadites lived next to them** (i.e., the Reubenites) in the Transjordanian territory. The references to **Bashan** (an area from the Yarmuk River to Mount Hermon in the north) in 5:11 and 5:16 suggest that the Gadites' territory was probably more to the north of the Reubenites. The tradition associating the Gadites with Bashan is also present in other Hebrew Bible texts (e.g., Num. 32:33).

Although Genesis 46:16 and Numbers 26:15–18 report on the descendants of Gad, none of these correlate with the information provided in this subsection of Chronicles. The names mentioned here are therefore not in agreement with other traditions about the Gadites. This probably reflects the dynamic fluctuations of the tribes' size and extent at different points in history.

In 1 Chronicles 5:17 a temporal comment relates the entering in the genealogical records of the Gadites to the reigns of Jotham king of Judah and Jeroboam king of Israel. Commentators normally indicate that the taking of a joint census by Judahite and Israelite kings would have been unlikely. This reference is, therefore, normally taken to mean that the official record of the Gadites was compiled when Jotham reigned in Judah and when Jeroboam II reigned in Israel, and not during a joint census.

What makes this reference remarkable is that the Chronicler eliminated all correlating dates from his version of the divided kingdom in 2 Chronicles 10–36. Whereas the Deuteronomistic History often correlates the reigns of southern and northern kings, the Chronicler avoids this practice in order to emphasize the Judahite perspective. Here, however, the correlating temporal indication is preserved—probably because this genealogical section deals with eastern tribes, who belonged to the northern kingdom.

5:18–22 / This subsection, which has a narrative (versus genealogical) tone to it, groups the **Reubenites, Gadites,** and **the half-tribe of Manasseh** together to describe their success in warfare against the **Hagrites** and other groups. The strife with the Hagrites is picked up from the reference in 5:10. This subsection already acts as a prelude to some of the battle accounts that will play such a prominent role in the Chronicler's version of (particularly) the history during the divided kingdom. One good example is the account of King Asa's reign (2 Chron. 14–16). The subsection under discussion here shares many motifs with that type of account, one being the cry to God in battle, which results in a victory over the enemies. The emphasis that **the battle was God's** also occurs in other passages in Chronicles.

5:23–24 / Whereas the previous subsection grouped together the **half-tribe of Manasseh** with the Reubenites and Gadites, this subsection now deals specifically with "the half-tribe of Manasseh." First Chronicles 5:23 indicates the geographical area they occupied on the northern border of Israel, that is, just to the south of **Mount Hermon.** First Chronicles 5:24 provides the names of **the heads of their families.** This list of names has no parallels in other Hebrew Bible books.

5:25–26 / Whereas 5:18–22 recalled the victories of **the Reubenites, the Gadites and the half-tribe of Manasseh** on account of their calling to God, this subsection emphasizes the opposite, namely, their unfaithfulness. First Chronicles 5:26 clarifies that **they** in 5:25 again refers to this joint group. They **were unfaithful to the God of their fathers** (an expression that occurs twenty-seven times in Chronicles) and were therefore punished with exile through the Assyrians. Their unfaithfulness is that they **prostituted themselves to the gods of the peoples of the land,** an expression used only once again—in 2 Chronicles 21:11, in connection with the transgressions during King Jehoram's reign. However, the reversal of the fate of a king or a group on account of their unfaithfulness is also attested in other Chronicles narratives, with the account of King Asa's reign in 2 Chronicles 14–16 probably the best example.

The punishment of exile is ascribed to **Pul king of Assyria,** which is another name for **Tiglath-Pileser** III, but the Chronicler makes clear that this king is only an agent of **the God of Israel.** God **stirred up the spirit** of this king to take Israel into exile (symbolized by the geographical indications in 5:26, all in the region of the Tigris River).

The expression **to this day** emphasizes here that the Chronicler is describing the conditions of his own present day.

Additional Notes §1.5

5:10 / The **Hagrites** are probably associated with Hagar, of whom we read in the Abraham narrative (Gen. 16, 21), although this is nowhere made explicit. A reference in Ps. 83:6 creates an association between "Edom and the Ishmaelites" and "Moab and the Hagrites." One would have expected to find the Hagrites in Ishmael's genealogy. However, 1 Chron. 5:10 does not claim that they were part of the Reubenites. The Reubenites "waged war against the Hagrites" (5:19).

5:17 / Here we get the second occurrence of the technical term translated by the NIV as **entered in the genealogical records** (see Additional Note on 4:33b).

5:25 / The term often used by the Chronicler to indicate transgressions of the past occurs here for the second time (see Additional Note on 2:7).

5:26 / The verb used here with **the God of Israel** as subject, "to stir up the spirit of X," occurs in a few instances in Chronicles, the most dramatic example being the spirit of Cyrus, the Persian king, being stirred by God to let the Israelite exiles return to their land (2 Chron. 36:22).

§1.6 Focus on Levi (1 Chron. 6:1–81)

The introduction to 1 Chronicles 1–9 pointed out a ring structure in these genealogies whose centerpiece is the present section. That the genealogy of Levi occupies such a central place in the Chronicler's presentation should not escape the specific attention of the reader. Not only does it function centrally in the genealogical literary construction; it also functions centrally in the ideological framework with which the Chronicler probably worked. The whole Jerusalemite cult—with all its officials and institutions—was based on Levitical descent. The prominence of this genealogy, therefore, from the start signals the reader that the Chronicler is working from a cultic perspective. The cult forms a central notion in the identity construction he is negotiating here. Whoever wants to understand himself or herself as part of All-Israel should also be embedded in the cultic community.

The Levitical genealogy is closely related in the literary structure to the genealogies of Judah and Benjamin. The community identity that the Chronicler fosters rests solidly upon these three pillars.

This long chapter covers different aspects related to the lineage of Levi. Levi, being one of the twelve sons of Israel mentioned in 2:1–2, is credited with being the ancestor who delivered to Israel its priestly lineage. The very extensive genealogy therefore starts with the family list of the high priests who served in Jerusalem (6:1–15). Then a more general genealogy of the Levites is presented (6:16–30), followed by a list of those who were appointed as singers in the sanctuary in Jerusalem (6:31–48). A short section returns to the high priestly lineage (6:49–53), before the final section provides an elaborate description of the cities and land allotted to the priests and Levites (6:54–81).

6:1–15 / The family list starts with the presentation of three **sons of Levi**, namely, **Gershon, Kohath and Merari**. Although this section explicitly mentions only one person who **served as priest** (6:10), some scholars are of the opinion that it lists the names of the so-called main priests or high priests who served in Jerusalem, tracing their ancestry back to one specific son of Levi, namely, Kohath. Others see this merely as a list of priests (not necessarily high priests, although some who were named in the list were high priests).

The first part of this genealogy is segmented, taking the priestly line from Kohath (6:2) through **Amram** (6:3a) to **Aaron** (6:3b). From **Eleazar** (6:4), the son of Aaron, the presentation becomes linear, running to **Jehozadak** (6:15), who comes last in the lineage. The change from the segmented style to the linear form after 6:3 emphasizes the leading position of Aaron, who, according to the Priestly tradition in the Pentateuch, was the founding father of the Israelite priesthood.

One of the well-known figures mentioned is **Zadok** (6:8, and again in 6:12, but probably referring to different persons). Both the Deuteronomistic History and Chronicles indicate that Zadok played a major role in the Jerusalem cult during the reigns of David and Solomon (e.g., 2 Sam. 15 and 1 Kgs. 1–2). Another prominent figure is **Hilkiah** (6:13), the priest who recovered the Book of the Law of the Lord during the temple restoration in the time of King Josiah (2 Kgs. 22–23 || 2 Chron. 34–35). Interestingly enough, Hilkiah is the only priest referred to as a "high priest" (*hakkohen haggadol*) in the Hebrew Bible (2 Kgs. 22:4 || 2 Chron. 34:9).

A peculiarity of this list is that several priests who feature prominently in the narratives in Kings and Chronicles do not appear here: Amariah (2 Chron. 19:11), Jehoiada (2 Kgs. 11–12 || 2 Chron. 22–24), Azariah (2 Chron. 26:17, 20), and Uriah (2 Kgs. 16:10, 11, 15, 16). Some scholars (see those listed in Additional Note on 6:31–48) attribute the omission of some names to scribal error.

Although this genealogy is mainly in list form, the Chronicler inserted two explanatory remarks. In 6:10 **Azariah** is specified as the one **who served as priest in the temple Solomon built in Jerusalem.** It is generally accepted that this comment should actually be moved back to 6:9, where another Azariah is mentioned, who was more likely to be the contemporary of Solomon.

Another remark refers to the end of the preexilic priesthood: 6:15 mentions that **Jehozadak was deported when the Lord sent Judah and Jerusalem into exile by the hand of Nebuchadnezzar.** This comment is interesting, not only because it is the first time that the Judahite exile is mentioned in Chronicles, but also because it signifies the termination of the priestly lineage with the exile. The exile is attributed to the action of "the Lord," who used the Babylonian king, Nebuchadnezzar, as his instrument.

6:16–30 / In 6:16 the same **sons of Levi** featured in the previous subsection are reintroduced. Whereas the previous list mainly focused on the lineage of **Kohath,** here more exposure is given to other descendants of the family. This subsection is normally interpreted as the genealogy of the "regular Levites" (according to Klein) or "nonpriestly line" (according to Hicks), in contrast to the priestly lineage presented in the previous subsection. The distinction in usage of "Levite" in a generic, tribal sense and in a more specific sense referring to a particular part of the priesthood should, therefore, be kept in mind here.

First Chronicles 6:16 functions as an introduction to this genealogy, with 6:17–19 as a segmented version of the descendants of each of Levi's sons. A next, smaller subsection opens with the remark (6:19b) that **these are the clans of the Levites listed according to their fathers.** In 6:20–21 a linear presentation of the Gershonites is offered, followed by a section on the Kohathites (6:22–28), with a concluding section on the Merarites (6:29–30).

The attentive reader will notice that there are some differences between the Levite genealogy provided here and the one in the previous section, illustrating the fluid character of this type of literature. One striking feature of the present list is that **Samuel** is included in the Levite lineage, as part of the Kohathites (6:27–28). According to 1 Samuel 1:1, though, he originated from the tribe of Ephraim. However, his dedication to the sanctuary makes his inclusion in the Levite genealogy, closely associated with the priesthood, not improbable. This may be the Chronicler's way of bestowing a very high honor on an Ephraimite who made it into the priestly ranks.

6:31–48 / This subsection starts with a comment (6:31–33a) that the people listed here played a significant role in the musical service at the sanctuary in **Jerusalem. David** appointed them to **minister . . . with music,** first **before the tabernacle, the Tent of Meeting,** and later in the **temple of the** Lord that was built in Jerusalem by **Solomon.** It also explicitly specifies that David gave them this function **after the ark came to rest there.**

The temple musicians are then listed according to the two lineages of **Kohathites** (6:33–43)—one line running to **Heman** (6:33–38), the other to **Asaph** (6:39–43)—and the lineage of the **Merarites** (6:44–47), running up to **Ethan.**

A striking feature of this genealogy is its format. Here we see the so-called ascending, linear form, where the genealogy is traced backward into the past. Heman (starting in 6:33) is traced backward through **Levi** to **Israel** (6:38), while Asaph and Ethan are traced back to Levi (6:43 and 6:47, respectively).

This subsection clarifies two things about the temple musicians associated with Heman, Asaph, and Ethan. The Chronicler, first, presents them as closely associated with the priestly lineage of Levi and, second, as already commissioned by David even before the temple in Jerusalem was built. By linking the cult singers so closely with both the ancestor Israel and the ideal King David, this writing firmly establishes their status. This might be an indication of how these temple musicians were regarded in the Chronicler's days or, even more likely, of how the Chronicler wanted society to regard the musicians.

6:49–53 / In this brief section the reader is returned to the list of priests already presented in the first part of the Levitical genealogy (6:3b–8 in particular). Recent studies normally reckon the present subsection to be an excerpt from the longer list provided earlier in this chapter. Some small differences have to be noted, however.

First, this subsection is introduced with a short narrative description of the functions of **Aaron and his descendants**. Together with the last verse of the previous subsection (6:48), it could be seen as a kind of narrative glue the Chronicler uses to join the different genealogical sections. It explains that they **presented offerings on the altar of burnt offerings and on the altar of incense**, doing the work related to **the Most Holy Place** in order to make **atonement for Israel** and in order to fulfill the commandments of God, which were delivered to them through **Moses**. This introduction establishes a close connection between the Aaronites, the temple service, the cultic function of "making atonement for Israel," and the Torah, associated with Moses. Second, one should observe that the writer changed the format of this excerpt from the longer list slightly, making it more compact. And third, one should also take note that the present, shorter version of **the descendants of Aaron** stops with **Ahimaaz**, the son of **Zadok**, taking the reader chronologically only into the time of David.

Why repeat the priestly genealogy? On the one hand, the repetition results in the genealogy of the temple musicians being enveloped by, and therefore tied to, the Levitical priestly families (Knoppers, *1 Chronicles 1–9*, p. 428). On the other hand, the present formulation, which stops in the time of David, situates the following section on the allocation of cities to the Levites in the time of this monarch. It thereby changes the Deuteronomistic version's scheduling of this event in the time of Joshua (Klein, *1 Chronicles*, p. 213). Both of these suggested functions, therefore, emphasize the integration of this brief excerpt into the broader genealogical construction.

6:54–81 / The last subsection in the Levitical genealogy reviews the cities in which the priestly families lived. The list shows a close association with the narrative text in Joshua 21, which reports the allotment of dwelling places to the Levites during the conquest of the land. However, the Chronicler made interesting changes in the order of the material in Joshua 21.

After a general introduction to the list of Levitical cities in 1 Chronicles 6:54a, the Chronicler first offers a detailed list of the places given to **the descendants of Aaron who were from the Kohathite clan** in 6:54b–60. Although this material is also present in Joshua 21 (in Josh. 21:10–19), the Chronicler shifted it earlier in his presentation. The Chronicler justified this shift with the following comment: **because the first lot was for them.** By first presenting the Aaronite cities, the Chronicler has given prominence to this part of the Levitical lineage, emphasizing the status of the Aaronites within the priesthood.

After the extensive description of Aaronite cities there are three short summaries of the towns given to **Kohath's descendants** (6:61), **the descendants of Gershon** (6:62), and **the descendants of Merari** (6:63). Since according to Joshua 21 the Levitical tribe did not receive their own tribal land, the Chronicler attributed city names belonging to other tribes to these sublineages. The Kohathites receive cities from **half the tribe of Manasseh;** the Gershonites receive cities from **the tribes of Issachar, Asher and Naphtali, and from the part of the tribe of Manasseh that is in Bashan;** and the Merarites received cities from **the tribes of Reuben, Gad and Zebulun.** This summary section is then closed with a concluding remark in 6:64, mentioning in a general statement that **the Israelites gave the Levites these towns and their pasturelands.**

First Chronicles 6:65 opens another section with detailed information about the cities that were given to the three parts of the Levitical family. Here the order of presentation returns to the order of Joshua 21. First Chronicles 6:66–70 is a detailed description of the **Kohathite** cities, 6:71–76 of the **Gershonite** cities, and 6:77–81 of the **Merarite** cities.

A well-attested tradition in the Hebrew Bible is that of the cities of refuge. All the Pentateuchal legal traditions indicate that there should be six cities in different tribes that could act as places of refuge for those accused of unintentional murder ("homicide" or "manslaughter" in modern terminology). That tradition is preserved in Joshua 21, where the cities of refuge are always mentioned first in the list of cities given to that particular tribe. In all cases (Bezer, Hebron, Shechem, Golan, Kedesh, and Ramoth Gilead) these cities are explicitly designated as cities of refuge. Although the Chronicler has kept the tradition of listing these cities at the beginning of those particular lists, only **Hebron** (in 6:57) and **Shechem** (in 6:67) are explicitly called **a city of refuge**. Why the other cities lack the designation cannot be determined for sure.

Additional Notes §1.6

6:8 / This is the only instance in the Hebrew Bible where the influential priestly figure, **Zadok**, is embedded in a genealogy. Therefore, some scholars argue that this whole list is actually an artificial construction to provide the Zadokites with a genealogy. The paucity of evidence on Zadok, however, warns us not to draw too bold conclusions. Some argue, instead, that the Zadokites became an important part of the priesthood only after the exile and that this genealogical embedding was an attempt to increase the group's influence in the postexilic era. This issue will be discussed further when we come to another enigmatic section in the book, namely, 1 Chron. 23–27. For more detailed scholarly discussions on Zadok, as well as the different factions and groups among the Israelite priesthood, see, e.g., Hunt, *Missing Priests*; Schaper, *Priester und Leviten im achämenidischen Juda*.

6:31–48 / The history of the temple musician families has been a much-debated topic in biblical scholarship, particularly since the publication of the seminal article by H. Gese, "Zur Geschichte der Kultsänger am zweiten Tempel," in *Vom Sinai zum Zion: Alttestamentliche Beiträge zur biblischen Theologie* (Munich: Kaiser, 1974), pp. 147–58. Gese proposed four stages in the development of the traditions around the cult singers. He places the subsection in 1 Chron. 6 in his phase 3b, that is, material added to Chronicles after the substantial completion of the book. Although the study by Gese sheds valuable light on the development of the Levitical cult singer families, more recent studies (e.g., Klein, *1 Chronicles*, pp. 348–49) tend to modify Gese's argument with reference to two aspects: (1) textual investigation proves that the situation is even more complex in Chronicles than reflected in Gese's stages; and (2) explanations of this complexity other than literary-critical constructions are sought, with scholars proposing, rather, that a diversity of traditions were available and that one should not necessarily think of consecutive and linear historical progression. One could, then, also see the Chronicler's final composition as a toleration of this diversity. These newer studies caution us to think less in terms of linear, progressive development and more in terms of a complexity of traditions. Some studies examine the peculiarity that the prominent cult singer names, **Asaph, Heman, Ethan,** and **Jeduthun,** also appear in some of the Psalm headings. For an overview of this correlation of biblical materials, see Jonker, "Revisiting the Psalm Heading," pp. 102–22; Jonker, "Another Look at the Psalm Heading," pp. 65–85. Since Levitical names occur exclusively in headings of psalms in books 1–3 of the Psalter, I argue that some Levites were probably responsible for starting a cultic hymnbook shortly after the exile. The addition of these names served two purposes: (1) to attempt an amalgamation of different preexilic traditions of psalm collections and (2) to claim a more prominent position for the Levites in the Second Temple cult. These headings may therefore be seen as Levitical propaganda.

§1.7 Descendants of Issachar, Benjamin, Naphtali, Manasseh, Ephraim, and Asher (1 Chron. 7:1–40)

In §1.4 and §1.5 the Chronicler included the southern and eastern (Transjordanian) tribes in his genealogical constructions. There, although the Chronicler's focus is very much on Judah, Levi, and Benjamin in his overall construction, he also included Simeon, Reuben, Gad, and Manasseh in his genealogies, probably to strengthen the inclusivity of his definition of All-Israel.

The next section of the Chronicler's genealogy takes the reader northward to focus on those tribes traditionally considered to be part of the northern kingdom, Israel. Their link with the ancestor, Israel, is of course clear, since this next section (like the previous one) is closely linked to 2:1–2, where the writer listed the sons of Israel. However, the overall construction does not strictly keep to the list of sons provided in 2:1–2. Dan and Zebulun are left out (although some see faint traces of a Dan genealogy in 2:12), and Joseph is replaced by his two sons Ephraim and Manasseh. Dan might have been omitted for a theological reason, namely, on account of its detestable cult referred to in Judges 18:30–31 and 1 Kings 12:29. But these explanations do not account for Zebulun's omission. The simplest solution might be to remember that the northernmost tribes apparently left very scanty records, probably because they were always the first in the line of fire during Assyrian onslaughts, which came from the northeast.

Clearly, the Chronicler makes selective use of materials that are now at our disposal in the Hebrew Bible (mostly from Gen. 46 and Num. 26). From some he quotes selectively, while of others he makes no use at all, such as sections in Numbers 26 and Joshua 16–19 dealing with the tribes under discussion.

The style of the majority of genealogies provided here (with the exclusion of those of Ephraim and Manasseh) is different from what we have seen thus far in the Chronicler's genealogies. For example, the inclusion of the numbers of "fighting men" in the different families reminds scholars of military census lists, of which we have some biblical examples.

7:1–5 / This subsection deals with the descendants of **Issachar,** tracing his lineage through **Tola, Uzzi,** and **Izrahiah.** The Chronicler probably obtained his information from texts such as Genesis 46:13 and Numbers 26:23–25. The specific statistics in 1 Chronicles 7:2, 4, 5 leave the impression of a military census list, which the Chronicler projected to a time **during the reign of David.**

7:6–12 / **Benjamin** receives separate treatment in the next genealogical section (8:1–40), but this subsection also deals with his descendants. (Interestingly enough, the two versions of Benjamin's genealogy differ significantly.) Commentators normally credit the inclusion of Benjamin at this position to the sources of which the Chronicler probably made use. Specifically, Genesis 46 and Numbers 26 discuss Benjamin at this position. Benjamin's lineage is traced through **three sons,** namely, **Bela, Beker and Jediael.** In each case the number of **fighting men** is given.

7:13 / A very brief genealogy of **Naphtali** is provided in this verse, probably taking its information from Genesis 46:24–25 and Numbers 26:48–50.

7:14–19 / This subsection presents a genealogy of **Manasseh,** coming before the genealogy of his younger brother, Ephraim, which follows. The half-tribe of Manasseh was already included in §1.5. In that list the writer indicated that the geographical area occupied by the half-tribe was east of the Jordan River (Transjordan). In this presentation some of the references (e.g., **Zelophehad, Abiezer, Mahlah, Shemida, Shechem,** and **Likhi**) are associated with the Manassite area lying on the western side of the Jordan, although some other references (e.g., **Makir** and **Gilead**) still refer to the Transjordanian area. However, the broad geographical outline of the Chronicler's genealogical construction (although not without deviations) becomes more apparent now. He started in Judah and moved to the south and southeast with Simeon. From there he moved northward on the Transjordanian side with Reuben, Gad, and the half-tribe of Manasseh. He then discussed Levi, which is distributed over the whole land, and continued with the northern tribes Issachar and Naphtali. Now he is moving southward again on the western side of the

Jordan with his discussions of Manasseh, Ephraim, and Asher, until he arrives back in the south with Benjamin.

The Manasseh genealogy is a very confusing literary construction that is difficult to reconcile with the biblical source material (mainly Num. 26:29–34), probably witnessing to a complex process of textual transmission. For example, in 1 Chronicles 7:15 **Maacah** is indicated to be Makir's sister, but in 7:16 to be his **wife**. Furthermore, 7:15 mentions that Zelophehad was the second, although no first child is mentioned. (The NIV partly solved this textual problem by translating "the second" as **another descendant**.) Many attempts have been made to rearrange the materials in this genealogy or to substitute some information from other biblical source texts. However, all these attempts remain speculative, and we cannot explain exactly why this genealogy has taken on such a difficult shape. It is not always clear whether the confusion was already present in the Chronicler's source material, whether the Chronicler was responsible for some rearrangements, or whether these confusions were the result of processes of transmission after the Chronicler's work.

One reference that should not be overlooked in the complexity of this genealogy is the indication that **Makir**, Manasseh's son, was born from **his Aramean concubine**. Again, the Chronicler does not shy away from mentioning that the lineage of All-Israel includes people (mainly women) of foreign descent. Therefore, in contrast to, for example, Ezra-Nehemiah, the Chronicler shows an inclusivist stance with respect to foreigners being included in his definition of All-Israel.

7:20–29 / The descendants of Manasseh's younger brother, **Ephraim**, are now presented. The genealogy starts off with a linear presentation of his descendants up to **Ezer and Elead** (7:20–21a). But then **misfortune** strikes (7:21b–23). The latter two sons were killed by **the native-born men of Gath** during a livestock raid. This probably hints at hostile relationships between the Ephraimites and some of the local inhabitants (i.e., peoples who had already occupied the land before the invasion of Israel from Egypt). After mourning the deceased, Ephraim and his wife started a new lineage, of whom three names are mentioned: **Beriah, Sheerah,** and **Rephah**. To Sheerah, a daughter, is attributed the building of certain cities (7:24)—the only instance in the Hebrew Bible where a female is indicated in the role of city builder. This unusual attribution compares to the function as head of a lineage associated with Keturah in 1:32.

The prominence of the last member of the Ephraimite tribe indicated here, namely, **Joshua,** should not be overlooked. That the genealogy ends with him emphasizes his position as the one who led the people of Israel into the promised land.

Although 7:28–29 stands at the end of the Ephraimite genealogy, the remark at the end of 7:29, **the descendants of Joseph son of Israel lived in these towns,** probably forms the conclusion not only to Ephraim but also to Manasseh (the other son of Joseph). These verses provide a list of towns occupied by the descendants of the sons of Joseph.

7:30–40 / Another son of Israel, **Asher,** is now presented. The five children of Asher, the sons **Imnah, Ishvah, Ishvi,** and **Beriah** and the daughter **Serah** (7:30), are also mentioned in the parallel texts in Genesis 46:17 and Numbers 26:44–46 (although Ishvah was—probably erroneously—left out of the list). Also the children of Beriah, **Heber and Malkiel** (1 Chron. 7:31), are mentioned in those parallel texts. However, the further descendants mentioned in 7:32–39 are not attested elsewhere in the Hebrew Bible.

The conclusion to the Asherite genealogy in 7:40 with mention of **the number of men ready for battle** indicates again that the writer probably took the data from a military census list.

Additional Note §1.7

7:12–13 / The Chronicler left out Dan and Zebulun from his genealogical lists. However, some scholars see in 7:12 a faint trace of what could have been the lineage of Dan. The argument goes that the text was damaged in some way at this point, resulting in 7:12 becoming fragmentary and corrupt (and 7:13 abbreviated to the minimum). First Chronicles 7:12 does not link well with the previous or next subsections. See Knoppers, *1 Chronicles 1–9*, pp. 453–54; Klein, *1 Chronicles*, pp. 222–23.

§1.8 Focus on Benjamin (1 Chron. 8:1–9:1a)

We now come to the discussion of the final son of Israel (see 2:1–2), namely, Benjamin. The Chronicler's genealogical construction emphasizes the lineages of Judah, Levi, and Benjamin. Whereas Judah occupied the initial position and Levi the middle position, Benjamin now closes the genealogical discussion of the sons of Israel. The significance of Judah lies in this being the tribe of King David. Levi is emphasized in order to focus on that tribe's connection with the cult and the temple. Benjamin, however, is the other tribe that supported David in his kingship, and its geographical territory enclosed Jerusalem.

As part of the genealogies of the northern tribes, a section on Benjamin was already present in 7:6–12, but there are significant differences between that genealogy and the one presented here. The present genealogy has a very elusive structure, leading scholars to see different subsections here (see Additional Note on 8:1–40). The most we can say is that this genealogy presents the reader with a fairly unstructured indication of (particularly) the places where the Benjaminites were settled. (Note that the abbreviated form used by the NIV, "Benjamites," does not give good expression to the Hebrew form of the name, and this commentary therefore uses the full form "Benjaminites.")

A special section at the end (8:33–40) connects the lineage of Benjamin to Saul, who will feature later in the book (in a separate genealogy in 9:39–44, but also in a narrative in 1 Chron. 10).

8:1–2 / These verses indicate that **Benjamin was the father** of five sons: **Bela, Ashbel, Aharah, Nohah,** and **Rapha.** At least three other versions of this line of descent are found in the Hebrew Bible. According to Genesis 46:21, Benjamin had ten children (of whom only Bela and Ashbel also occur in 1 Chron. 8:1–2). Numbers 26:38–39 gives descendants of Benjamin (again sharing only Bela and Ashbel with 1 Chron. 8:1–2). The version in 7:6 states that Benjamin had three children, namely, Bela, Beker, and Jediael (this time sharing only Bela with 8:1–2). The only point that can be established from this information is that the Chronicler surely worked eclectically with his sources!

8:3–7 / The descendants of **Bela** are now listed in 8:3–5. Although parallel texts occur in Numbers 26:40 and 1 Chronicles 7:7, these three texts differ totally in terms of the names offered. It seems as if 8:7 repeats the genealogy of Bela in some way. However, it is difficult to find a satisfying explanation for 8:6 since the reference to **Ehud** does not link to any of the previous information. The NIV mentions in a footnote to 8:3 one of the solutions suggested, namely, that **Gera, Abihud** should rather be read as "Gera the father of Ehud." Such an emendation will then provide a link to 8:6, where Ehud is mentioned.

8:8–14 / The genealogy of **Shaharaim** provided in this section is unparalleled in the Hebrew Bible and also does not bear any relationship with the lineage of Benjamin presented here. Like other genealogies in the Chronicler's construction, this list provides information on the subject group's geographical settlement patterns. In this respect the mention of **Moab** (8:8) and **Aijalon** (8:13) seems to be important. We know from the book of Ruth that Ruth, an ancestress of King David, came from Moab. Aijalon was one of the Levitical cities according to Joshua 21:24 and 1 Chronicles 6:69.

8:15–28 / This list of names is also unparalleled in the Hebrew Bible. It can be linked to the previous list through the name **Elpaal** (8:18), which probably functions as a catchword of some sort. First Chronicles 8:28 states that these **heads of families** resided in **Jerusalem.**

8:29–32 / This brief section introduces some people who were probably of Benjaminite descent but settled around **Gibeon.** Some scholars relate this town to Saul (whose lineage is provided in the next subsection). Interestingly, Gibeon is also mentioned later in Chronicles as the place where the tabernacle rested before it was brought to Jerusalem (1 Chron. 16:39; 21:29; 2 Chron. 1:3).

8:33–40 / This subsection is actually a continuation of the genealogy provided in 8:29–32, since it traces the lineage of Jeiel through **Ner** and **Kish** to **Saul.** This lineage will be taken up again in 9:35–44, a section exclusively dedicated to the genealogy of Saul. It closes in 8:40 with the remark **all these were the descendants of Benjamin.** With this remark an arc is completed from 8:1, where the Chronicler opened the Benjaminite genealogy.

9:1a / With the comment **all Israel was listed in the genealogies recorded in the book of the kings of Israel,** the Chronicler now comes to the end of the great genealogical construction that opened in 1:1 with Adam but commenced its prime focus in 2:1–2 with the sons of Israel. First Chronicles 2–8 lays out a very elaborate genealogical social-identity map of All-Israel, which is pertinently mentioned in this final pen stripe on his map. The social-identity map includes many names of numerous tribes and families; it also includes the names of geographical areas and cities. In presenting all this information the Chronicler contributes to the process of the self-definition of All-Israel in the late Persian time. This map not only shows the contours of the All-Israel that the Chronicler has in mind (with Judah, Levi, and Benjamin forming the elevations, and the other tribes the lower landscape). It also sketches the breadth or extent of the Chronicler's concept of All-Israel: all those tribes in the Transjordan, the very south, and the very north are included in his definition. Using language from social-identity theory here, we may describe the Chronicler's effort in the genealogies as the development of the prototype of what All-Israel entails.

Additional Notes §1.8

8:1–40 / Because this genealogy has a very elusive structure, commentators offer different delimitations of the subsections. Knoppers divides it into five sections: 8:1–7; 8:8–12; 8:13–28; 8:29–40; 9:1 (*1 Chronicles 1–9*, p. 474). Both Klein and McKenzie also work with five sections, which they divide as follows: 8:1–7; 8:8–14; 8:15–28; 8:29–32; 8:33–40 (Klein, *1 Chronicles*, pp. 244–45; McKenzie, *1–2 Chronicles*, p. 105). First Chronicles 9:1 is then taken as the opening of the next genealogy. Dirksen works with two main sections, 8:1–32 and 8:33–40, but subdivides the first into a structure similar to that of Knoppers: 8:1–7; 8:8–12; 8:13–28; 8:29–32 (Dirksen, *1 Chronicles*, pp. 131–32). Attempts to harmonize the information internally, as well as with reference to other biblical sources, have not been satisfactory thus far.

9:1a / Some scholars speculate about the identity of the source **the book of the kings of Israel**. Was this a single source? And what was its content? Yet it seems unlikely that this comment would refer to one specific source, since the Chronicler certainly takes his information from different traditions in the Pentateuch and the Deuteronomistic History. Some suggest that the phrase should have the words "and Judah" appended from the following phrase in 9:1b (as in the Septuagint, Vulgate, and Targum), as do later references (2 Chron. 27:7; 35:27; 36:8). However, if "and Judah" is taken with this reference, the sentence in 1 Chron. 9:1b would be without an explicit subject. That sentence would then suggest that All-Israel was taken into exile to Babylon—a description that does not fit the Chronicler's narrative. It seems best to leave open the possibility that the Chronicler might have had another unknown source available, probably containing a compilation of various materials from the Pentateuch and the Deuteronomistic history. See Klein, *1 Chronicles*, p. 265; Knoppers, *1 Chronicles 1–9*, pp. 479–80.

§1.9 Jerusalem's Inhabitants and Cultic Officials (1 Chron. 9:1b–34)

After the Chronicler's presentation of the great Israelite genealogy in 1 Chronicles 2–8, we now come to the time of the Chronicler himself. He bridges the gap from the downfall of Judah and Jerusalem to the resettlement in the land in two brief sentences (9:1b–2). Judah's exile—"because of their unfaithfulness"—is acknowledged, but he does not dwell on this sad time in Israelite history. He quickly continues to indicate those who have resettled in the land (9:2).

The focus of the resettlement immediately shifts from "their own towns" (9:2) to "Jerusalem" (9:3) and its inhabitants in the postexilic age. It particularly features the prominent presence of "priests, Levites, and temple servants."

In the overall narrative construction of Chronicles, this section actually forms the end of the chronological line. The Chronicler started with Adam and continued through the lineages of the sons of Israel, ending with a description of those who lived and worked in Jerusalem after the exile. Then in 1 Chronicles 10 the Chronicler starts recapping the history of Israel in fuller detail, taking it chronologically from the time of Saul (1 Chron. 10) to the proclamation of Cyrus (2 Chron. 36:22–23)—that is, to the point when the return from exile started. Apart from 1 Chronicles 3:17–24, the present subsection is the only one taking the Chronicler's story chronologically into the postexilic era. Could it be that the Chronicler actually wished the information included in this subsection to form the context within which his whole construction was to be understood? If so, this would be a powerful literary tool that lets the reader understand that the following retelling of Israel's history is actually done with the hope that it will have a bearing on the postexilic present (and future).

This subsection mainly contains information on the cultic officials in Jerusalem as well as their respective functions. Whether this chapter provides a factual account of the postexilic cultic community or whether this was an idealistic indication of how the Chronicler wanted the cult to be organized, we will never know for sure. However, the status attributed to the different functionaries in this list forms the backdrop against which the final composition of Chronicles should be read.

Structurally, 9:1b–2 bridges the gap from the beginning of the exile to the resettlement; 9:3–9 introduces Jerusalem as the center of the resettlement, listing the inhabitants of the city; 9:10–13 concentrates on the priests; while 9:14–34 deals with the Levites, not only listing a number of names but also indicating the various functions they performed.

9:1b–2 / First Chronicles 6:15 already referred to the Judahite exile. The Chronicler returns to that point in history, indicating that this happened on account of Judah's **unfaithfulness** (*ma'alah*). This concept plays an important role in the Chronicler's theology. We have already seen in 1 Chronicles 2:7 (the sin of Achar) and 5:25 (the transgression of the half-tribe of Manasseh) that the Chronicler used the related verb (*ma'al*) to indicate the kind of conduct that is not acceptable within the understanding of the Lord's will. The use of this concept at this point in Chronicles anticipates many of the narratives of the kings of Judah that the Chronicler will (re)tell.

First Chronicles 9:2 lists four groups of people who were **the first to resettle on their own property in their own towns**, namely, **some Israelites, priests, Levites and temple servants**. This verse still speaks of different "towns," although the next verse focuses attention on Jerusalem. First Chronicles 9:2 is parallel to the introduction to a similar list in Nehemiah 11 (see Additional Note on 9:2–18). However, unlike our text, in Nehemiah 11:3 a distinction is made between the leaders of the province, who lived in Jerusalem (Neh. 11:3a), and those groups of people who dwelled in the towns of Judah (Neh. 11:3b). Indeed, Nehemiah distinguishes five groups who lived in the towns of Judah: Israelites, priests, Levites, temple servants, and descendants of Solomon's servants. The latter group does not appear in Chronicles. The technical term for "temple servants" (*nethinim*) occurs in Chronicles only here (in contrast to Ezra-Nehemiah, where it occurs fifteen times). These servants are not mentioned again in the subsection, in contrast to Nehemiah 11:21, which contains more information on where they lived and who was in charge of them. This might be an indication of a decline in their status by the time of the Chronicler.

9:3–9 / First Chronicles 9:3 introduces the section that describes the lay Israelites (i.e., the first group mentioned in the previous verse) who lived in **Jerusalem**. They are defined as people from the tribes of **Judah, Benjamin, Ephraim**, and **Manasseh**. (The names Ephraim and Manasseh are absent from the parallel text in Neh. 11:4.) The following verses then list the descendants of Judah and Benjamin, but no descendants for Ephraim and Manasseh. The emphasis on Judah and Benjamin is understandable in the light of the southern perspective of the Chronicler. The inclusion of Ephraim and Manasseh in this heading (regardless of whether this inclusion was already present in the source text that the Chronicler used or whether the Chronicler himself added them) signifies an attempt to define the cultic community in Jerusalem inclusively. That understanding of All-Israel, one evident in the construction of the genealogies of 1 Chronicles 2–8, shapes the content here.

First Chronicles 9:4–6 lists the descendants of **Judah,** while 9:7–9 provides the names of the Benjaminites. Although these lists are paralleled in Nehemiah 11:4–9, the content of these two versions differs remarkably. The reason might be the Chronicler's agenda to portray these tribes in a very special way.

9:10–13 / This subsection deals with the **priests,** the second group mentioned in 9:2. It is remarkable that the section dedicated to them is much shorter than the extensive description of the Levites and their functions that follows in the next subsection. These verses on the priests are paralleled in Nehemiah 11:10–14. Given the central function of the priests in the temple cult, one would have expected a more elaborate description.

Whether the numbers of people given here should be taken literally is debatable. Although implausible, the numbers give an indication of the importance the Chronicler accords certain groups over against others. In this respect it is particularly noteworthy that the number of priests indicated here is **1,760,** in contrast to the parallel text in Nehemiah, which mentions 1,192 in total (indicated in three separate numbers). The number of lay Israelites mentioned in 1 Chronicles 9:3–9 is 690 for the Judahites and 956 for the Benjaminites. The next subsection, on the Levites, provides only the number of gatekeepers. If the Chronicler intended these numbers to emphasize the relative status of the different groups, he still considered the priests to be very important in Jerusalem—despite the short section given to them here.

9:14–34 / The very elaborate subsection on the **Levites** can be subdivided into a general introduction to the Levitical lineage (9:14–16), a description of the **gatekeepers** and their functions (9:17–27), a description of other functions performed by Levites (9:28–32), an introduction to the **musicians** (9:33), and a conclusion to the section on the Levites (9:34).

The general introduction is paralleled in Nehemiah 11:15–18. Although there are some similarities between these two lists, they differ considerably. Two peculiarities of this general list are striking. First, it includes the **Asaph** lineage (1 Chron. 9:15). We know from previous genealogies that the writer closely associated the Asaphites with the temple musicians. The singers are listed separately in 9:33, although no specific names are mentioned there. Ezra 2:41 and Nehemiah 7:44 make a clear distinction between Levites and singers, but 1 Chronicles 9:15 presents the musician lineage as part of the general Levitical lineage. These different views might be attributed to the history of development of the Levitical families, which indicates that the Asaphites were not originally considered Levites. Chronicles would then reflect a later stage than Ezra 2 and Nehemiah 7. Second, although the inhabitants of Jerusalem are described here, 1 Chronicles 9:16 mentions that **Berekiah . . . lived in the villages of the Netophathites.** According to Nehemiah 12:28 these villages must have been very close to Jerusalem. The Netophathites are associated with Judah in 1 Chronicles 2:54.

The gatekeepers are also mentioned in Nehemiah 11:19, but only there in Nehemiah. In contrast, Chronicles includes an elaborate section on them, a section that is unparalleled in biblical literature. The description takes this history of the gatekeepers back into the desert period (1 Chron. 9:19–21). However, their history is also explicitly tied to **David** (9:22), that is, it says that they **had been assigned to their positions of trust by David and Samuel the seer.** Since Samuel died before the reign of David started, rather than indicate contemporaneity, the statement instead legitimizes the gatekeepers' function by relating them to royal (David) and prophetic (Samuel) ancestors.

First Chronicles 9:19 mentions the **Korahites** within the context of gatekeepers, although we know that elsewhere (e.g., in 2 Chron. 20:19 as well as in some Psalm headings) they are associated with the singers.

First Chronicles 9:28 indicates that **some of them** (i.e., the gatekeepers) were also assigned other functions in the sanctuary. Some were to **take charge of the articles used in the temple service** (9:28), while others had **to take care of the furnishings and all the other articles of the sanctuary,** as well as of the stocks of ingredients used in the offerings (9:29). Still others, **some of the priests,** were responsible for **mixing the spices** (9:30), and others for **baking the offering bread** (9:31) and **preparing for every Sabbath the bread set out on the table** (9:32). This description creates the impression of a well-organized cultic service in the postexilic sanctuary in Jerusalem.

Although commentators are not unanimous in their opinions on which section is in fact concluded by the last verse (9:34), it is likely that it closes the section starting in 9:3. In 9:3 the writer emphasized that what follows is a list of people living in **Jerusalem.** First Chronicles 9:34 repeats this geographical indication, forming an inclusio around 9:3–34. In this way the Chronicler succeeds in emphasizing for the reader that the cult of All-Israel is centered in Jerusalem and that priests and Levites play an important role in the cultic organization, depending for their legitimacy on "David the king" and "Samuel the seer."

Additional Note §1.9

9:2–18 / Knoppers (*1 Chronicles 1–9*, pp. 509–11) is of the opinion that the relationship of this section to Neh. 11:3–19 is overstated by many scholars. He sees "more differences between the two lists than there are parallels" (p. 510). Some scholars presuppose that both Neh. 11 and 1 Chron. 9 made use (in different ways) of a common source. Others see 1 Chron. 9 as a later addition to Chronicles. Still others regard 1 Chron. 9 as an original part of Chronicles, but one that depends on Neh. 11—a situation that is also reversed by some, so that Neh. 11 is made dependent on 1 Chron. 9. Knoppers indicates that all these theories have largely overlooked the Septuagint version of Neh. 11. After comparing both versions of Nehemiah with one another, as well as with the two versions (Masoretic Text and Septuagint) of 1 Chron. 9, he concludes that both writers made use of an earlier text but then also took the liberty of contextualizing and supplementing this text to suit their own respective interests. Klein (*1 Chronicles*, pp. 263–65) disagrees, claiming that Knoppers misjudged the significance of the minuses (i.e., those sections which are not present) in the Septuagint of Nehemiah. Klein argues that "these minuses in Nehemiah do not represent an earlier or superior text, but are the result of textual damage" (i.e., various transmission errors). This technical argument between the two commentators shows that it is not always clear-cut what source materials—and particularly which stage of development in those materials—the Chronicler used. It cautions the reader not to make too bold conclusions about the differences between biblical texts.

§1.10 Saul's Descendants (1 Chron. 9:35–44)

After the description of the inhabitants of postexilic Jerusalem in the previous section, the last few verses of this chapter jump back to Saul. Commentators are in agreement that the Chronicler (or those responsible for the final composition) probably included the genealogy of Saul here in order to lead into the narrative section starting with the death of Saul in 1 Chronicles 10.

In 8:29–32 and 8:33–40 we already encountered a genealogy of Saul. Apart from 8:39–40, the rest of those sections are reproduced here (with only minor changes). The writer probably added the last two verses of 1 Chronicles 8 for the purpose of concluding the Benjaminite context within which Saul features. In the case of 9:35–44 the different literary context did not necessitate that the addition be taken over here.

9:35 / Some see a link between Saul's family and the place Gibeon (as in 8:29–32). This geographical reference will be revisited in the narratives that follow in Chronicles.

9:39–40 / Although Saul's son, Jonathan, is mentioned here, the extensive narratives about David's friendship with Jonathan that we encounter in 1 Samuel 18–2 Samuel 1 are not included in the Chronicler's construction. Also David's special relationship with Mephibosheth (here called Merib-Baal), reported in 2 Samuel 4 and 2 Samuel 21, is absent from the Chronicler's version. This may be the Chronicler's way of differentiating clearly between the kingship of Saul and that of David.

Additional Note §1.10

9:41 / The name Ahaz is normally supplied in translations at the end of this verse, although this name does not appear in the Hebrew text. On the basis of 1 Chron. 8:35 (supported by the Septuagint, Vulgate, and Peshitta versions of 9:41) we may assume that the name erroneously fell away in the process of textual transmission. See Klein, *1 Chronicles*, p. 262; Knoppers, *1 Chronicles 10–29*, p. 516.

Summary of §1

Read from the point of view of social-identity theory, the Chronicler's grand construction, the genealogical introduction (1 Chron. 1–9), yields the following observations:

a. The Chronicler situates his description of the history of Israel within the context of humanity in general, starting his genealogical description with Adam in 1:1. This emphasizes that, although the focus is very much on the identity of Israel in this literature, this particular identity is understood within a universalistic framework. That this literature has the historical conditions in the Persian Empire as backdrop probably codetermined this perspective. Israel's identity is thereby embedded in the broader sociopolitical and socioreligious landscape of the time. Another reason for this universalistic framework might be that the Chronicler understands All-Israel to be the fulfillment (or, at least, the continuation) of the patriarchal history in which Yahweh's promise that all the nations of the earth will be blessed is so prominent.

b. The conclusion to 1 Chronicles 8 emphasizes that the Chronicler's interest is to help define the concept All-Israel. He uses this term to describe the community in Jerusalem who returned from exile. He develops his prototype of what this community should entail and who should be included in this understanding.

c. Although the Chronicler's emphasis is very much on Judah, Benjamin, and Levi in the genealogies, he does not exclude the tribes that used to live in the southern, eastern (Transjordanian), and northern areas. His understanding of All-Israel includes those tribes that formerly belonged to the northern kingdom of Israel. By showing that these tribes are all descendants from their ancestor Israel, the Chronicler includes them in his prototype of All-Israel. However, with the genealogical differentiations he also ventures into describing the relationships among these tribes. The ideology of the Chronicler is inclusivist, but that does not inhibit him from giving his view on the power relations among and status of the different groups. In the language of social-identity theory this can be called a process of intragroup categorization.

d. His definition of the All-Israel community is closely related to the lineage of Judah, particularly the royal line of David and Solomon. However, his definition of All-Israel is not a political one.

e. He also emphasizes the close connection between All-Israel and the cultic community (particularly the Levite lineage), thereby interpreting All-Israel first and foremost as a cultic community. The self-understanding of All-Israel is therefore closely connected to Jerusalem, and particularly to the temple in Jerusalem.

f. Does all this have any theological bearing? It might be clear enough to the reader that these genealogies could have significance from a social-identity perspective, but what do these name lists contribute theologically to the message of Chronicles (particularly in light of the name of Yahweh occurring rarely in 1 Chron. 1–9)? The Chronicler certainly knew that his readers (ancient and modern) would have had a good knowledge of other authoritative writings. The genealogies are therefore not presented in a vacuum. They rather function as icons into the rich theologies presented in other scriptures. At least three important theological strands are in the background here. First, the Chronicler's presentation of the genealogies puts All-Israel right in the middle of covenant history. Even if the name of Yahweh does not feature regularly in 1 Chronicles 1–9, the Chronicler strongly suggests with these sections that All-Israel's existence is the result of Yahweh's covenant promise to the patriarchs. Second, the focus of the genealogies on Judah (particularly David and Solomon) would have reminded the readers of the book about the unconditional promise Yahweh made to David through Nathan his prophet (2 Sam. 7). The strong theological conviction that David's house is the divinely elected line of kingship stands in the background here. And, finally, the strong focus on Jerusalem and the cultic staff (the Levites in particular) would recall Zion and the temple of Solomon. The temple on Zion—so was the belief—was the dwelling place on earth of Yahweh and his name.

Even before the Chronicler starts his historical narrative in 1 Chronicles 10, the genealogies prepare the way for a deeply theological understanding of the book. But these name lists also emphasize that theological understanding cannot be isolated from the social-identity processes that we also witness here. Yahweh is working in and through the sociopolitical and socioreligious existence of All-Israel.

§2 David, the First King (1 Chron. 10:1–29:30)

After the genealogical introduction in the previous chapters, the Chronicler's history resumes with the golden age in Israel's history, namely, the reign of David, followed by the reign of his son Solomon (described in 2 Chron. 1–9). It is clear from the literary construction that the writer's focus is very much on this period. Not only do the histories of David and Solomon in total take up about a third of the length of the book, but they also show indications of careful selection of source materials and deliberate construction. This is intended to portray the reigns of David and Solomon as epitomizing the manifestation of royalty at its finest.

The time of David and Solomon in the preexilic history of Israel was, of course, the period of the united kingdom (ca. 1004–926 b.c.). We know from archeological excavations that after the establishment of the kingdom, particularly under David, it went through a phase of economic prosperity and geographical expansion. Never again in its entire history did Israel have control over such a vast area. It was also in this period, according to the Deuteronomistic version of history, that Jerusalem was established as the capital (after David had reigned from Hebron for seven years) and that the illustrious temple was built there. But the success of the united kingdom took its toll. Particularly under Solomon's reign, the dissatisfaction with the high taxes and hard labor that were required of the Israelites started growing—so much so that the united kingdom split into two monarchies at the end of Solomon's reign. Two kingdoms arose: the kingdom of Judah, associated with two of the southern tribes and the royal line of David, and the kingdom of Israel, with its support base among the northern tribes and its capital in Samaria.

When the Deuteronomists looked back on this history, they did not hesitate to point out the sins, rebellion, disunity, foreign influence, and idolatry that characterized the united kingdom and led to its downfall. However, the Chronicler's portrayal of its two kings is very different. Except for two minor incidents, all the dark episodes in the lives of David and Solomon are eliminated. It is clear that the Chronicler intended to present a picture of these kings as unblemished, highlighting their association with Jerusalem, temple building, and the establishment of peace and tranquility. The reader of Chronicles should therefore be attentive not only to what the Chronicler took from his source materials but also to what information he omitted, adapted, or added. Through careful comparisons with the Samuel-Kings materials we can find interesting and significant differences that can help us to gain a better understanding of the unique perspective that the Chronicler wanted to offer on the past.

The reader of this commentary might ask why I call David the first king in the heading. We know from 1–2 Samuel that Saul was the first king, anointed by Samuel, who ruled from Gibeah and Mizpah. We also know of the dark years of Saul's reign, when he felt threatened by David, until he was killed and David took over as king. A careful comparison of this material with the version in Chronicles, however, shows that the Chronicler omitted almost the entire history of Saul's reign. Only the narrative of Saul's death was preserved in 1 Chronicles 10. The Chronicler's very selective use of the source materials from 1–2 Samuel convinces the reader that the actual first king was David. Saul's death signifies the start of David's glorious reign.

The Chronicler's version of David's history (1 Chron. 10–29) can be divided into ten subsections. The first episode (10:1–14) is the narrative of Saul's death, which cleared the way for David to become king. The second episode (11:1–12:40) describes the anointing of David at Hebron. The third episode marks one of David's triumphs, namely, the bringing of the ark of the covenant to Jerusalem (13:1–16:43). This is followed by the announcement (17:1–27) that a house will be built for Yahweh in Jerusalem. The association of David with the temple also means that his lineage (literally "house") will be in continuity with the promise of a temple in Jerusalem. The fifth section (18:1–20:8) narrates a number of David's battles. However, the Chronicler's insinuation is that these battles established peace and tranquility for Israel. The sixth section (21:1–22:1) tells of David's census, but its climax is the theophanic revelation that the threshing floor of Araunah the Jebusite will be the site where the temple will be built. In the next section (22:2–19) David orders Solomon to build the temple, since he himself has too much blood on his hands. An elaborate section (23:1–27:34) subsequently describes the organization of David's officials—mainly cultic but also secular staff. The penultimate episode (28:1–29:25) presents David's final arrangements for the building of the temple and his transfer of the kingship to his son Solomon. The last section (29:26–30) then concludes the Chronicler's narrative about David's reign.

§2.1 Saul's Death and the Start of David's Reign (1 Chron. 10:1–14)

The Chronicler's portrayal of Saul deviates significantly from the source text in 1 Samuel 31. The narrative about Saul's death is the only remaining part of the elaborate description of this king's life in the Deuteronomist's version. The reader might wonder why the Chronicler chose to present Saul's story in this truncated way. In my opinion, this presentation is entirely related to the way in which the Benjaminites feature in Chronicles. Saul was a prominent member of the Benjaminite tribe (as seen in the genealogy of 1 Chron. 8:33–40). This association might be the key to understanding the Chronicler's portrayal of Saul. After my detailed discussion of the text, I will come back to this issue at the end of this section.

A few other passing references to Saul are included in Chronicles, namely, in 1 Chronicles 11:2; 12:1, 2, 19 (twice), 23, 29 (twice); 13:3; 15:29; 17:13; and 26:28. It will enrich our understanding of the narrative in this particular section if we also take note of some of the subtleties of these other references.

In 11:2 All-Israel addresses David at Hebron, indicating that they have regarded him as their military leader for some time already, "even while Saul was king." This is the first time that Saul is called "king" in Chronicles. However, one should take note that this comment does not form part of the Chronicler's own material but was rather taken over from 2 Samuel 5:2.

In 12:1–2 we find an introduction to "the men who came to David at Ziklag." The temporal indication situates this episode during the time "while he was banished from the presence of Saul son of Kish." This remark occurs in the Chronicler's own material and shows that the Chronicler presupposed knowledge of the Deuteronomistic account of Saul's strained relationship with David (although the Chronicler omitted this from his own narrative construction). The Chronicler continues to identify those men who came to David as "kinsmen of Saul from the tribe of Benjamin," specifying that they could shoot arrows and sling stones with both hands. The latter remark, which occurs a few times in the Hebrew Bible, is an ironic wordplay on the etymology of the name Benjamin, which means "son of the right hand." This was an allusion to the Benjaminites' military reputation, the prime example of which occurs in Judges 3–4, where Ehud, a left-handed Benjaminite, killed Eglon, the Moabite king. It is thus quite significant when the Chronicler indicates (in his own material) that these valiant warriors from Saul's men joined forces with David.

In 1 Chronicles 13:3 the Chronicler offers his account of the bringing of the ark of the covenant to Jerusalem. In the Chronicler's version David addresses his men saying that they should bring the ark to Jerusalem, "for we did not inquire of it during the reign of Saul." The verb used here is *darash* ("to inquire/seek")—a verb that occurs prominently in Chronicles and is typical of the Chronicler's theology. The ultimate goal of All-Israel should be to seek Yahweh, because then they will experience rest and peace. This comment therefore suggests at this point, with a clear relationship to the Chronicler's addition in 10:13–14, that the era of Saul's reign was not a time in which Yahweh was sought. The bringing of the ark to Jerusalem in David's time expresses this new devotion.

The last reference to Saul occurs in 1 Chronicles 26:28. It indicates that the "dedicated things" from "Samuel the seer" and "Saul son of Kish," together with those of Abner and Joab, were placed in the care of David's treasurers. This section belongs to the Chronicler's own writing. Apart from the genealogies, this is probably the only reference in Chronicles that reflects a positive image of Saul, indicating that he contributed to the "dedicated things." However, the comment that they were put in the care of David's officials is certainly an indication of the transfer of power to David.

These references to Saul in Chronicles will now form the literary backdrop against which to discuss Saul's death narrative. There are three sections in this text: 10:1–7 narrates the death of Saul and his house, 10:8–12 concentrates on the benevolent acts of the people of Jabesh Gilead, and 10:13–14 provides a theological interpretation of Saul's death.

10:1–7 / This section tells of Saul's death in a battle with the Philistines. In verse 6 the Chronicler inserted a phrase into the source text, 1 Samuel 31:6, after having omitted some other information from the same text. First Samuel 31:6 reads: "So Saul and his three sons and his armor-bearer and all his men died together that same day." The Chronicler omitted reference to the armor-bearer and all his men, as well as the temporal reference "that same day." He furthermore supplied another finite verb (**died**) at the end of the verse and inserted the expression **and his whole house** as the subject of this verb.

In verse 7 the Chronicler changed "the men of Israel" (my translation) of the source text into "every person in Israel" (my translation—an expression that emphasizes the collective), a change that correlates with a similar modification in 10:1. Although this change could merely be of a literary nature, Dirksen sees here an attempt by the writer "to denote the totality of Israel more forcibly" (*1 Chronicles*, p. 163).

10:8–12 / The next section opens with the temporal indication **the next day,** which was taken over from the source text. The Chronicler took over 1 Samuel 31:8 unchanged, but eliminated the word "three," the number of Saul's sons according to the Samuel text—an omission that was probably necessitated by the Chronicler mentioning four sons of Saul in 1 Chronicles 8:33 and 9:39. This omission seems strange, however, since the mention of three sons was not a problem for the Chronicler in 10:6, where he retained the reference.

Whereas 1 Samuel 31:9 reads, "They cut off his head and stripped off his armor," 1 Chronicles 10:9 mentions that the Philistines **stripped him and took his head and his armor,** thus omitting the explicit reference to the cutting-off of Saul's head. The Samuel version then indicates that the Philistines, after having spread the good news of Saul's death "in the temple of their idols and among their people," took his armor to "the temple of the Ashtoreths," while his body was fastened to the wall of Beth Shan. No indication is given in Samuel of what happened to Saul's head. The Chronicler's version differs significantly at this point. Apart from indicating that the news was spread **among their idols** (10:9) and that the armor was taken to **the temple of their gods** (10:10), instead of to "the temple of the Ashtoreths" (1 Sam. 31:10), the Chronicler mentions that Saul's head was **hung up . . . in the temple of Dagon** (instead of "his body to the wall of Beth Shan" as in 1 Sam. 31:10). Although the Chronicler did not mention explicitly the cutting-off of Saul's head, that act is implied here. With this change the Chronicler solved the mystery remaining in 1 Samuel 31 about what happened to Saul's head, since it does not play any further role in that narrative. However, this change in Chronicles also emphasizes the humiliation and mockery accompanying the death of Saul—a humiliation at the hands of the Philistines.

After 10:11 mentions that **all the inhabitants of Jabesh Gilead** ("the people of Jabesh Gilead" in 1 Sam. 31:11) heard of what happened to Saul at the hands of the Philistines, 1 Chronicles 10:12 reports that their **valiant men** took **the bodies of Saul and his sons** to Jabesh. The indication in 1 Samuel 31:12 about the valiant men of Jabesh Gilead journeying "through the night" was omitted, and obviously also the reference to "the wall of Beth Shan," which is not part of the Chronicler's version. First Samuel 31:12 also indicates that the bodies of Saul and his sons were cremated there. This detail was left out by the Chronicler. In the next-to-last sentence of 1 Chronicles 10:12 the Chronicler then merges the information provided in the first two sentences of 1 Samuel 31:13 into one sentence, changing the "tamarisk" of 1 Samuel for some unknown reason into an **oak.**

10:13–14 / The last two verses are the Chronicler's own material, since the information is not attested in 1 Samuel 31 (MT or LXX). It is clear that the Chronicler wanted to give a theological interpretation to Saul's death. According to 10:13, Saul died **because he was unfaithful to the** LORD (literally "because of his unfaithfulness in which he has acted unfaithfully against Yahweh")—the noun and verb are from the root *ma'al*, which we have already seen is one of the Chronicler's favorite theological terms. This unfaithfulness is then defined in two statements: on the one hand, **he did not keep the word of the** LORD, while on the other hand, Saul **consulted a medium for guidance, and did not inquire of the** LORD. The ironic wordplay between "Saul" (*sha'ul*) and "to consult" (*lish'ol*), and also the use of the verb "seek" (*darash*), which occurs prominently in the Chronicler's own material elsewhere in the book, are strong indications of the writer's theological evaluation of Saul. Saul not only disobeyed the word he had from Yahweh but also sought divine guidance from elsewhere.

First Chronicles 10:14 continues with the statement that **the** LORD **put him to death** (Hebrew: "he put him to death"). There is general agreement among exegetes that the unidentified subject of the Hebrew verb is Yahweh. The next sentence, which has the same subject (**the** LORD . . . **turned the kingdom over to David son of Jesse**), shows that the Chronicler understood the transfer of the kingship from Saul to David as an act of Yahweh. It is noteworthy that Saul is never called "king" in this narrative, although this last verse suggests that he was in charge of the kingdom.

Let us now come back to the question, Why did the Chronicler choose to portray Saul's history in this way? In the introduction to this section I suggested that this might be related to the way in which Benjamin features in Chronicles. It seems that Saul's history is not narrated for its own sake (as in the Deuteronomistic version) but that the Chronicler rather makes it an element within a Benjamin discourse.

The Chronicler's portrayal of Benjamin is very ambiguous. The genealogies provide a positive portrayal of Benjamin, on a par with the tribe of Judah. However, in other instances, of which the Saul narrative is a prominent example, Benjamin is cast in a negative light. The distribution of the name Benjamin in Chronicles is also instructive. An overwhelming majority of occurrences of Benjaminite terminology in Chronicles belong to the writer's own material. It seems therefore that, although Benjamin is equally prominent in Chronicles and the Deuteronomistic History, the Chronicler presents Benjamin on his own terms. Furthermore, the term Benjamin occurs in all parts of Chronicles, that is, in the histories of David and Solomon (1 Chron. 10–29 and 2 Chron. 1–9, respectively) as well as the history of Judah's kings (2 Chron. 10–36). It is particularly interesting that Benjamin occurs almost exclusively (with the exception of five occurrences in the Rehoboam narrative) in the narratives about those kings who were evaluated positively by the Chronicler (namely, David, Asa, Jehoshaphat, Amaziah, Hezekiah, and Josiah). Another significant statistic is that Benjamin occurs ten times in the expression "Judah and Benjamin" in the contexts of the narratives about Rehoboam (2 Chron. 11:1, 3, 12, 23), Asa (15:2, 8, 9), Amaziah (25:5), Hezekiah (31:1), and Josiah (34:9). In seven of these ten cases the expression is introduced by the same element that is used in the term "All-Israel," namely, *kol*—thus "All Judah and Benjamin."

What do all these ambiguous statistics and terminological patterns tell us about Benjamin and the Saul narrative in 1 Chronicles 10? We might find some clues in the respective histories of the tribes of Judah and Benjamin. It is probably well known among readers of this commentary that the tribe of Judah, as part of the kingdom of Judah, was taken into exile by the Babylonians after the latter conquered Jerusalem in 586 B.C. Jerusalem with its temple and royal palace was destroyed, and a dismal village remained in its stead during the years of the exile. What might not be so well known among readers, however, is that the tribe of Benjamin was much less affected by the exile. We read in 2 Kings 25:22–26 that the Babylonians appointed Gedaliah as governor over those who remained behind in Judah. Gedaliah had his seat in Mizpah, a Benjaminite town. We know from archeological records (such as seal impressions) that Mizpah remained the administrative center during the exile until Jerusalem was reestablished sometime in the fifth century B.C. Furthermore, the earlier history of Benjamin might also be significant here. When the united kingdom divided into the kingdoms of Judah and Israel after Solomon's reign, it seems that the tribe of Benjamin, which had its land in the border region between the two (even bordering or including, as some texts suggest, Jerusalem), was divided in its loyalty. Although the tribe was traditionally associated with the northern tribes, we know from 1 Kings 12:21 that at least a part of Benjamin's warriors supported Rehoboam, the king of Judah. Therefore, Benjamin could be considered as part of both Israel and Judah.

This historical background helps us to better understand the Chronicler's portrayal of Benjamin. The Chronicler, writing from the reestablished center of political and cultic power in the postexilic era, had great difficulty with Benjamin. On the one hand, as a staunch supporter of the Second Temple in Jerusalem, the Chronicler did not want to give any credit to Benjamin. In the more relaxed Persian imperial context the Benjaminites could potentially try to resuscitate their political-administrative role (in Mizpah) or their cultic influence (particularly in Gibeon, where the tabernacle was kept before David brought it to Jerusalem and where Solomon still worshiped). This the Chronicler wanted to prevent at all costs, since he wanted to claim those powers exclusively for Jerusalem. Downplaying the role of Saul fits well into this context. The only statements that the Chronicler wanted to make about this Benjaminite were that he failed because he did not seek Yahweh and that Yahweh himself removed him and gave the kingship to David.

However, the Chronicler also needed Benjamin! For the establishment of an All-Israel identity in the late Persian period, the Chronicler needed to emphasize the close relationship between the north and the south again (without, of course, conceding any political-administrative or cultic influence to the north). Benjamin, with its mixed history, proved to be quite important in this regard. The Chronicler therefore uses "All Judah and Benjamin" almost as a synonym for "All-Israel." Benjamin was the key to the Chronicler's construction of an All-Israel identity.

The Chronicler's version of Saul's history, therefore, becomes a function of a larger discourse. Some commentators interpret Saul's history in 1 Chronicles 10 as the dark foil against which the bright star of David would arise. Although there is some truth in this interpretation, one should remember that the contrast between Saul and David already features in the Deuteronomistic source materials. That element is not new here. What is unique, however, in the Chronicler's use of the Saul narrative is the larger discourse about Benjamin within which this history is embedded.

Additional Notes §2.1

10:1–14 / The Septuagint of 1 Sam. 31 shows that the Chronicler's source material for 1 Chron. 10 probably did not differ significantly from the

Masoretic Text of 1 Sam. 31. Ho's theory that 1 Sam. 31 and 1 Chron. 10 made use of a common source, with 1 Chron. 10 closer to the original, cannot be accepted. See C. Y. S. Ho, "Conjectures and Refutations: Is 1 Samuel xxxi 1–13 Really the Source of 1 Chronicles x 1–12?" *VT* 45 (1995), pp. 82–106.

10:9–10 / According to Frevel, references to female gods were systematically omitted by the Chronicler. See C. Frevel, "Die Elimination der Göttin aus dem Weltbild des Chronisten," *ZAW* 103 (1991), pp. 263–71.

10:13–14 / That 10:14 says that the LORD put Saul to death is quite significant for the Chronicler's understanding of kingship. Knoppers rightly emphasizes that there is one significant difference between Samuel's and the Chronicler's presentation of the monarchy. In Samuel the monarchy as such is still controversial. For the Chronicler, however, the issue is not the institution of monarchy but rather the failure of Saul and his sons (Knoppers, *1 Chronicles 10–29*, pp. 528–29).

§2.2 All-Israel Anoints David at Hebron
(1 Chron. 11:1–12:40)

Whereas the previous narrative about Saul formed the introduction to the Chronicler's description of David's kingship, the next section narrates David's actual anointing and coronation as king and the consolidation of his military power. It is quite clear that the Chronicler wanted to get to this point in his historical description as swiftly as possible. For that reason he skips over some events that are considered important in the Deuteronomistic History (see 2 Sam. 1–4), for example, the interim reign of Ish-Bosheth.

Some commentators see a ring structure in this section. According to this view, 1 Chronicles 11:1–9, which tells that All-Israel came to Hebron to crown David, and 12:38–40, which narrates the actual coronation and celebration of David, form the outer circle of this narrative. Included in this circle then are subsections describing the support that David gathered at Hebron (11:10–47 and 12:23–37), at Ziklag (12:1–7 and 12:19–22), and at the stronghold in the desert (12:8–15 and 12:16–18). However, there are also some good arguments why different delimitations can be made. In my division of the subsections I take as the point of departure the different place names or geographical locations that feature in these verses. First Chronicles 11:1–3 is situated in Hebron. In 11:4–9 the location moves to Jebus, which was captured to become the City of David. First Chronicles 11:10–47 contains indications of different military groups who supported David; there is some confusion about the location where this happened. First Chronicles 12:1–7 and 12:19–22 indicate the men who joined forces with David at Ziklag, the section in between (12:8–18) has the desert stronghold as setting, and 12:23–40 is again located in Hebron.

11:1–3 / The Chronicler used the material in 2 Samuel 5:1–3 to compile the introduction to the David narrative. The location is Hebron, from where **David** reigned for the first few years of his kingship. Whereas the source text indicates that "the tribes of Israel came to David," the Chronicler made slight changes to both the verb and subject. He substituted "the tribes of Israel" (clearly associated with the northern part of the kingdom) with **all Israel**—a clear indication again of the Chronicler's intention to define an all-inclusive community here. The verb was changed from "came" to **came together** (literally "gathered"). This verb is used at various important occasions in Chronicles, often in connection with cultic gatherings or the tribes of Judah and Benjamin (e.g., 1 Chron. 13:2; 2 Chron. 15:9, 10; 18:5; 20:4; 23:2; 24:5; 25:5; 32:4, 6). The Chronicler presents this event, the anointment of David as king over All-Israel, as the first in the row of significant events that shaped the past.

Some small changes were made in 1 Chronicles 11:2 compared to the source text in 2 Samuel 5:2. The first of these hints at the Chronicler's underplaying of Saul's kingship over Israel again. Whereas the source text has "while Saul was king over us," Chronicles has **while Saul was king,** omitting the words "over us." Furthermore, the same verse quotes the words of Yahweh, which indicate that David is to be a **shepherd** and a **ruler.** Whereas the source text refers to "the LORD," Chronicles states **the LORD your God.** This emphasizes the close relationship between Yahweh and David.

Another addition in 11:3 puts further emphasis on the relationship between Yahweh and David. To the source text's statement "and they anointed David king over Israel" (2 Sam. 5:3) the Chronicler added the words **as the LORD had promised through Samuel.** This addition indicates that the Chronicler knew the source texts (where Samuel's involvement is elaborately narrated) and also introduces a prophetic figure for the first time. As elsewhere in Chronicles, the prophet acts here as explicator of Yahweh's involvement in the royal history. This role of prophets is a prominent feature of the book and will be discussed more fully in a later section of this commentary.

The information about David's reign in 2 Samuel 5:4–5 is not present at this point in the Chronicler's construction. A similar summary is given near the end of the Chronicler's David narrative in 1 Chronicles 29:27, but that text was probably taken over from the version in 1 Kings 2:11. Since the Samuel text from Qumran (4QSam^a) also did not contain this information, one could assume that the Chronicler made use of a source text without the information.

11:4–9 / The setting now changes to **Jerusalem.** Although the Chronicler made use of his source text 2 Samuel 5:6–10 here, he made some significant changes to it. The first change is in line with the use of the concept All-Israel. Whereas the source text indicates that "the king and his men" went up to Jerusalem to capture the city from the Jebusites, Chronicles mentions that **David and all the Israelites** went up. The same

Hebrew concept as the one above is used here. The taking of Jerusalem is indicated to be a national event and not merely the endeavor of a few men together with David.

The Chronicler furthermore (and differently from the source text) comments on Jerusalem parenthetically: **Jerusalem, that is, Jebus.** This is one of only three places in the Old Testament where the name Jebus occurs (the others are Josh. 18:28 and Judg. 19:10). The connection with Jebus and the Jebusite land is quite significant. First Chronicles 21 indicates that the temple was built on the threshing floor of Araunah the Jebusite. Although the argument will be presented more fully below in the discussion of 1 Chronicles 21, I note here that the explication of Jebus might be the way in which the Chronicler claimed that David's city and the temple were established in neutral terrain between Judah and Benjamin.

Another significant change in Chronicles is the omission of the mocking remark of the Jebusites (in 2 Sam. 5:6) that David will never be able to conquer the city, since "even the blind and the lame can ward you off." According to the source text, David then challenges his men to use the "water shaft" (Hebrew *tsinnor*) to reach the blind and the lame. Second Samuel 5:8 furthermore provides an etiological indication: "That is why they say: 'The blind and the lame will not enter the palace.'" There is no certainty among commentators what these comments in 2 Samuel mean. The difficulty of the passage might be the reason why the Chronicler also simplified the Jebusites' mocking of David by not mentioning the blind and the lame. However, it is also possible that these references could have cast a shadow over David, and that that might have been the reason for the Chronicler's omission.

The Chronicler also changed David's challenge to his men to use the water shaft to conquer the city into an explanation of Joab's prominence as commander-in-chief of David's army. Although **Joab** is not mentioned in the source text in 2 Samuel 5, the Chronicler used the first part of the challenge, **whoever leads the attack on the Jebusites,** and then changed the second part into **will become commander-in-chief.** Joab, who is also mentioned in 1 Chronicles 21 in connection with David's census, was first to attack, and **he received the command.** The Chronicler also adds to his source text when he mentions in 11:8 that **Joab restored the rest of the city.** It is clear that the Chronicler wanted to give a prominent place to Joab as the king's commander in his reconstruction of the Davidic history.

11:10–47 / This section lists the military support that David got from different groupings, as well as some of their heroic deeds. It is clear from the content that the section was probably composed from different anecdotes and lists to form a composite record of David's support. But this was already present in the source text, 2 Samuel 23:8–39, which the Chronicler took over with only minor changes.

The composite nature of this literature probably explains the confusion about the location(s) where all this happened. First Chronicles 11:13 mentions that **Eleazar,** one of David's **mighty men,** was at his side **at Pas Dammim when the Philistines gathered there for battle.** This location, which the Chronicler added to his source text, is unknown to us, but one may assume that it was in the Philistine area. In 11:15 (‖ 2 Sam. 23:13) another location is given, namely, **the cave of Adullam,** but the next verse mentions **the stronghold** (‖ 2 Sam. 23:14), which was probably near **Bethlehem.** For the rest of the chapter there is no specific indication of place.

First Chronicles 11:10 and 11:11 start with similar phrases, namely, **these were the chiefs of David's mighty men,** and **this is the list of David's mighty men.** In Hebrew these phrases are exactly the same except for the change from "chiefs" to "list." The same phrase (again, with the exception of one word) also occurs in the source text in 2 Samuel 23:8: "these are the names of David's mighty men." It seems, therefore, that the Chronicler used the beginning of this section from his source text, but then added information (the rest of 11:10), only to resume again his quotation from the source text with the phrases in 11:11. The four pieces of information added by the Chronicler in 11:10 are very important for his ideology. Again **all Israel** was involved here, and they **gave his kingship strong support** in order **to extend it over the whole land** so that it could happen **as the Lord has promised.** One could say that this verse summarizes in a nutshell all the important themes that the Chronicler wanted to advance in his work.

In the next verses (11:11–14) the information was taken over from the source text with minor changes to the numbers as well as the omission of the name of one of David's heroes (see Additional Note on 11:10–14).

With the change of location in 11:15 another group of **three of the thirty chiefs** is introduced in 11:15–19, together with their heroic deed of risking their lives to draw water for David **from the well near the gate of Bethlehem.** When David realized that he had risked the lives of his warriors, he refused to drink the water and rather **poured it out before the Lord** (information taken over from the source text). Some commentators suggest that this might have been a libation offering by David. However, it seems more likely that David considered the water to be the **blood of his men** (11:19) and that it therefore had to be poured out upon the ground (as ordered in Lev. 17:10–13 and Deut. 12:23–25, for blood contains life).

In the next verses (1 Chron. 11:20–25) two further warriors are introduced, namely, **Abishai the brother of Joab** and **Benaiah son of Jehoiada.** The Chronicler again took the information about these two warriors' deeds from the source text in 2 Samuel 23:18–23. It is not clear how these two figures fit into the threesomes of heroes indicated in the text. However, the confusion was not caused by the Chronicler's reworking, since it already occurs in the source text.

After the introduction of Abishai and Benaiah follows a long list (11:26–47) of David's **mighty men.** First Chronicles 11:26–41a was taken over with minor changes from the source text in 2 Samuel 23:24–39, but 1 Chronicles 11:41b–47 is the Chronicler's additions (probably from a source unknown to us). The point made by this long list of military supporters is that David drew support from all tribal areas and that he should be seen as the king of All-Israel.

12:1–40 / The whole of 1 Chronicles 12 consists of the Chronicler's own material (or, at least, is quoted from a source or sources unknown to us).

12:1–7 and 12:19–22 / These sections are situated in Ziklag. First Chronicles 12:1–2 forms an introduction to the first list. It indicates again that the Chronicler presupposed his readers to have knowledge of the tension between Saul and David. He furthermore indicates that **the warriors** who **came to David at Ziklag** included **kinsmen of Saul from the tribe of Benjamin.** This remark consolidated support for David even from the ranks of Saul's men. The Benjaminites, as we saw in an earlier discussion, were renowned as warriors. They are described here as **armed with bows and were able to shoot arrows or to sling stones right-handed or left-handed.** First Chronicles 12:3–7 then contains the names of these Benjaminite warriors who supported David.

First Chronicles 12:19–22 again has **Ziklag** as setting. This time the Chronicler indicates that **men of Manasseh** joined forces with David **when he went with the Philistines to fight against Saul.** First Chronicles 12:22 forms a conclusion indicating that **day after day men came to help David** and that his army grew until it was **a great army, like the army of God.** The latter expression emphasizes the immense size of David's army. However, it also adds a theological dimension to David's forces, as Klein indicates: "The human and divine participation in David's military adventures is emphasized by comparing the human troops with an army of God" (*1 Chronicles,* p. 321).

12:8–18 / First Chronicles 12:8 now moves the scene to David's **stronghold in the desert.** First Chronicles 12:8–15 indicates those **Gadites who defected to David** to pledge their support for him. First Chronicles 12:16–18 then deals with **other** Benjaminites **and some men from Judah,** who also came to David at the "stronghold." This scene again emphasizes the divine support for David in a dramatic way. David challenged these men, demanding to know why they came: **If you have come to me in peace, to help me,** or **if you have come to betray me to my enemies.** A very strong statement of support then came from **Amasai, chief of the Thirty,** after **the Spirit came upon** him. The Hebrew term used here can also be translated "the Spirit clothed him," an expression that signifies, according to Klein, "someone who speaks with prophetic authority" (*1 Chronicles*, p. 319). Although the Hebrew text does not mention that "the Spirit" was Yahweh's, one may assume this from the context. In the exclamation uttered by the Spirit-clothed Amasai, the theme of peace is very prominent (unfortunately, this is translated **success** in the NIV): **Peace, peace to you, and peace to those who help you, for your God will help you** (my translation). This first prophetlike utterance in Chronicles already introduces a prominent theological theme of the Chronicler, namely, that Yahweh's involvement in the royal history of his people brings peace. This also occurs in further passages.

12:23–40 / The setting of these verses is back in Hebron. First, in 12:23–38a **the men armed for battle who came to David at Hebron** are listed. Their purpose was **to turn Saul's kingdom over to him, as the LORD had said.** This introduction links back to the remark at the end of the Saul narrative, namely, 1 Chronicles 10:13–14 (the Chronicler's own material), which indicates that Yahweh was responsible for turning over the kingdom from Saul to David. The names listed here represent more or less the same tribal communities listed in the genealogies of 1 Chronicles 2–9: **men of Judah** (12:24), **men of Simeon** (12:25), **men of Levi** (12:26–28), **men of Benjamin** (12:29), **men of Ephraim** (12:30), **men of half the tribe of Manasseh** (12:31), **men of Issachar** (12:32), **men of Zebulun** (12:33), **men of Naphtali** (12:34), **men of Dan** (12:35), **men of Asher** (12:36), and **from east of the Jordan, men of Reuben, Gad and the half-tribe of Manasseh** (12:37). It is clear that the writer wanted to present a version of David's support similar to that given in the genealogies: All-Israel supported this king!

After the list is presented, the discussion proceeds in 12:38 with the indication that they all **came to Hebron** with one intention, namely, **fully determined to make David king over all Israel.** The section then concludes with a description of the huge festivities in Hebron in celebration of David's being anointed as king over All-Israel (see again 11:1–3). The supplies mentioned speak of affluence and generosity, and the concluding phrase is telling: **for there was joy in Israel.** The theme of joy, closely related to peace, rest, and quietness, is another prominent topic in Chronicles (see commentary on 1 Chron. 15–16). The Chronicler does not mention here that the festivities had any religious or ritual element to them. This was probably deliberate, since with no sanctuary at Hebron, such an indication would have been a blemish on David's association with the cult in Jerusalem.

With the consolidation of support of All-Israel for David in 1 Chronicles 11–12, the Chronicler is now free to narrate the most significant event in David's reign, namely, the bringing of the ark of the covenant to Jerusalem (1 Chron. 13–16).

Additional Notes §2.2

11:4–9 / Scholars emphasize the difficulty of accepting the chronological order of events presented in Chronicles. It is highly unlikely that Jerusalem could have been conquered during the enthronement, as suggested by the sequence of events in the Chronicler's text. The Chronicler's presentation furthermore does not quite correlate with the indication that David reigned from Hebron for seven years (as also attested in 1 Chron. 29:27). Knoppers reminds us, however, that the writer probably did not place the conquering of Jerusalem here in the narrative for chronological reasons. He is rather applying to the figure of David an epic-heroic topos that is well established in ancient Near Eastern historiography, in which the most significant actions of the king are mentioned right at the outset of their reigns. Knoppers therefore calls this "an excellent example of achronological historiography" (*1 Chronicles 10–29*, p. 545). Since the Chronicler reorganized his source material from 2 Sam. 5:7–23:7, he has also brought the capturing of Jebus and the lists of mighty men following in 1 Chron. 11:10 together. Dirksen is of the opinion that this is done to establish a direct link between David's kingship and the capture of Jerusalem (*1 Chronicles*, p. 159). Manfred Oeming offers an interesting explanation for why the Chronicler omitted the reference to the blind and the lame here. Second Sam. 5:8 contains David's comment that the men had to use the "water shaft" (Hebrew *tsinnor*) to reach the blind and lame. Oeming suggests that the Hebrew term might be a euphemistic reference to the genitals and that David's challenge to his men was to mutilate the blind and the lame. Oeming states that the Chronicler understood this reference all too well and therefore could not see his way clear to reusing this information. See M. Oeming, "Die Eroberung Jerusalems durch David in deuteronomistischer und chronistischer Darstellung (II Sam 5,6–9 und I Chron 11,4–8)," *ZAW* 106 (1994), pp. 404–20.

11:10–14 / In the first list of chiefs of David's mighty men, two names are listed together with some anecdotes about their heroics. These two are Jashobeam and Eleazar. Second Sam. 23:8 refers to the first person as "Josheb-Basshebeth," however. The second name is the same in 2 Sam. 23:9, but a third name is also mentioned there, namely, "Shammah" in 2 Sam. 23:11. The name in 2 Sam. 23:8 is uncertain, since some Septuagint manuscripts suggest "Ish-Bosheth" instead of "Josheb-Basshebeth." If there had been any uncertainty in the Chronicler's time about the right name, one could suggest that the Chronicler deliberately chose another name in order not to make any association with Ish-Bosheth (whose presence is eliminated by the Chronicler). That Shammah is omitted by the Chronicler might be related to the elimination of 2 Sam. 23:10b–12 in the source text. Making the kind of reading error that often occurred during the copying of manuscripts in ancient times, the Chronicler's eye might have skipped from "the LORD brought about a great victory" in 23:10 to exactly the same Hebrew phrase at the end of 23:12. The information in between these phrases, which contains the mention of Shammah, was thus accidentally omitted.

12:23–38a / The large numbers of troops indicated in this section have been the topic of heated discussions among commentators. Some propose that the Hebrew word for "thousand" should rather be understood as a military unit. Although this proposal would make the numbers more realistic, it is unlikely that the word would have this meaning. Klein concludes that the high numbers are primarily theological and provide another example of the Chronicler's All-Israel agenda (*1 Chronicles*, pp. 315–16).

§2.3 David Brings the Ark to Jerusalem (1 Chron. 13:1–16:43)

The four chapters under discussion in this section are often taken as a unit traditionally referred to as the "ark narrative." Although there are different scholarly views on the existence of such an ark narrative and its divisions (see Additional Note on 13:1–16:43), the contents of these chapters deal mainly with the bringing of the ark of the covenant to Jerusalem. The exception is 1 Chronicles 14 (taken over from the source text), which deals with seemingly unrelated matters.

The Chronicler made extensive use again of source material known from other biblical records. Second Samuel 5:11–25 forms the basis for 1 Chronicles 14:1–16 (with 14:17 being the Chronicler's own material). The Chronicler furthermore used 2 Samuel 6:1–23, but in a very peculiar way. The Chronicler used 2 Samuel 6:1–11 in 1 Chronicles 13:5–14. In doing so he swapped around the sequence of 2 Samuel, starting with the material from 2 Samuel 6 in 1 Chronicles 13 and then following it up with material from 2 Samuel 5 in 1 Chronicles 14. The rest of 2 Samuel 6 was used at 1 Chronicles 15:25–16:3 (|| 2 Sam. 6:12–19a) and in 1 Chronicles 16:43 (|| 2 Sam. 6:19b–20a). Some small sections of the source material in 2 Samuel 5–6 were omitted, namely, 2 Samuel 6:12a and 6:20b–23, which have no parallel in Chronicles.

The Chronicler furthermore made use of material paralleled in the book of Psalms. Psalm 105:1–15 was used in 1 Chronicles 16:8–22; Psalm 96:1b–13a in 1 Chronicles 16:23–33; and Psalm 106:1b, 47–48 in 1 Chronicles 16:34–36. These sections from Psalms were then merged into one work of praise and thanksgiving on the occasion of the bringing of the ark into Jerusalem.

The Chronicler also added some of his own material (or, alternatively, quoted from sources not known to us) in 13:1–4; 14:17; and 15:1–24.

The macrostructure of this section can be described as follows: 13:1–14 deals with the first, unsuccessful attempt to bring the ark of the covenant to Jerusalem; 14:1–17 narrates various other activities in and around Jerusalem; and 15:1–16:43 presents the narrative of the successful bringing of the ark to Jerusalem as well as its installation there and the organization of the cultic officials for its service.

13:1–4 / The narrative starts with an introduction undoubtedly from the Chronicler's own hand (although 13:1 might already be an adaptation of 2 Sam. 6:1; see commentary on 13:5–7). It shows **David taking the initiative to consult with his military staff and addressing the whole assembly of Israel.** The prominence of the Hebrew word *kol,* "all," in these introductory verses (used five times) is in line with the Chronicler's interest in involving All-Israel in all the watershed events of David's kingship. It was also "the whole assembly" who **agreed to do this, because it seemed right to all the people.** This confirmation followed after David addressed "the whole assembly," hoping that his request would be **good to** the people and **the will of the** Lord **our God.** If there was approval, David wanted to **send word . . . throughout the territories of Israel** (literally "in all [*kol*] the lands of Israel") as well as **to the priests and Levites** to be part of this momentous occasion. The core of David's call comes in 13:3: **Let us bring the ark of our God back to us.** The motivation provided uses another of the Chronicler's theme words, *darash* ("seek"): **We did not inquire of** (*darash*) **it during the reign of Saul.** In Chronicles the "seeking" of Yahweh is the prerequisite of having rest and peace. Here, in David's words, it is ambiguous whether the "seeking of the ark" or the "seeking of Yahweh" is meant. Both are grammatically possible. In line with the usage in the rest of Chronicles we may assume that the bringing of the ark to Jerusalem was interpreted by David as the "seeking of Yahweh." First Chronicles 13:4 then states that **the whole assembly** and **all the people** (both expressions with *kol*) approved of David's request. However, in the next section we will see that the first attempt to bring the ark to Jerusalem was not successful. The ambiguity of 13:3 will then become significant. And the interpretation of the failure by David (in 15:13) again uses the verb "to seek": "We did not inquire of him about how to do it in the prescribed way." Is the suggestion in 13:3, then, that David (with "all the people's" approval) sought the ark for his own political benefit rather than to seek Yahweh?

This introduction, stemming from the Chronicler's own hand, sets the theological context within which he wants the reader to interpret the bringing of the ark to Jerusalem. This is not just a cultic ritual or a political event, but rather manifests the "seeking of Yahweh." It is furthermore an event that will confirm that David's reign is a total break with the past under Saul.

13:5–7 / It is important to note that no information on the location of the ark has been supplied up to this point in Chronicles. We know from the Deuteronomistic History (1 Sam. 4–6) that there was a whole prehistory to the ark's location in **Kiriath Jearim**. The Chronicler totally omitted this prehistory, probably taking for granted the reader's knowledge of how the ark was captured by the Philistines and, after inflicting some misfortunes on those enemies, eventually returned to Kiriath Jearim.

The Chronicler made use of source material in 2 Samuel 6:1–4 but made some significant changes to it. Second Samuel 6:1 might already have been paralleled in 1 Chronicles 13:1 (with similar references to great numbers of military staff). However, the Hebrew verb in 2 Samuel 6:1 (*'asaf*, "to gather") is also paralleled at the beginning of 1 Chronicles 13:5 (although the latter uses the verb *qahal*, "to assemble"). Whereas 2 Samuel 6:2 indicates that "he and all his men" set out to fetch the ark, the Chronicler uses his favorite expression in 1 Chronicles 13:5 again, saying that **David assembled all the Israelites.** The inclusive attitude of the Chronicler is again made explicit. It is further strengthened by the geographical indications that the Chronicler supplies: All-Israel had to be assembled **from the Shihor River in Egypt to Lebo Hamath.** (In 2 Sam. 6:2 David's company sets out, in contrast, from Baalah of Judah.) The two indicators signify the southernmost and northernmost areas, signaling that All-Israel came from everywhere to join the process of bringing the ark to Jerusalem. The actual area constituting the Persian province of Yehud was considerably smaller than the Chronicler's grandiose portrait, which recalls the extent of the Davidic-Solomonic empire. The ideal image of the land from the past aims to show how inclusive was Israel's participation in the event.

First Chronicles 13:6 closely follows the source text (2 Sam. 6:2) but additionally identifies **Baalah of Judah** as **Kiriath Jearim.** According to Joshua 15:9, Kiriath Jearim was situated in Judahite territory, but Joshua 18:14 locates it on the border between the tribal area of Benjamin and Jerusalem. The rivalry between the Benjaminites and Judahites within Yehud might have been the background to this ambiguity about where the place was situated (cf. 1 Chron. 10, 21). The moving of the ark to Jerusalem would signify that this city is the actual center of Yahweh worship, which should be closely identified with the province of Yehud (i.e., what's left of ancient Judah) but also with All-Israel (hence, the mention of Benjaminite Kiriath Jearim).

The parallel of 1 Chronicles 13:7 in 2 Samuel 6:3–4 supplies more detailed information, but the Chronicler follows the basic information of the Samuel text.

13:8–14 / These verses were carefully taken over from the source text in 2 Samuel 6:5–11 with only minor changes. "The whole house of Israel" in 2 Samuel 6:5 was changed into the now familiar phrase **all the Israelites,** two of the musical instruments were changed in 13:8 (probably reflecting the Chronicler's own time), and the **threshing floor** in 13:9 was changed to that of **Kidon** (instead of "Nacon" in 2 Sam. 6:6). The reason for the latter change remains a mystery to commentators. Another small change, which reflects again the Chronicler's theology, was made in 1 Chronicles 13:10. The source text, 2 Samuel 6:7, mentions that "Uzzah," after having touched the ark when the oxen stumbled, was "struck" by God and "he died there beside the ark of God." The latter phrase is clearly meant as locative. The Chronicler, however, changed the phrase into **so he died there before God.** This small change strengthens the theological nature of what was happening there. **Uzzah's** deed was clearly a transgression of the border between human decision making and divine presence. Although some commentators see here the Chronicler's theology of immediate retribution in action, one should remember that this immediate death of Uzzah is not a unique element of the Chronicler's version; it already occurs in the source text. However, the Chronicler's small change identifies the death of Uzzah as an exemplar of what might happen if the symbolic significance of the ark is not acknowledged and when humans trespass into divine territory.

According to both the Chronicler's version and the source text's (1 Chron. 13:13–14 ‖ 2 Sam. 6:10–11), the ark was then taken **to the house of Obed-Edom,** where it remained for **three months.** During this time **his household and everything he had** experienced the Lord's blessing. This stands in sharp contrast to the disastrous results described in 1 Samuel 4–6 every time the ark was brought to a Philistine location. Although the death of Uzzah was an expensive lesson to learn along the way, these blessings on Obed-Edom and his household and possessions at least signified that the ark was "on the right way" and that its presence was still of great benefit.

14:1–17 / Before the Chronicler comes to the renewed attempt to bring the ark to Jerusalem (starting in 1 Chron. 15:1), there is a detour in the narrative. I have already discussed the difficulty involved in fitting 1 Chronicles 14 into the narrative logic of the Chronicler's broader construction. Although there might be good (compositional-historical) reasons to transpose this chapter to another position, the effect of the present form of the text is twofold. It provides an interlude during which the reader may digest the significance of the previous episode and also prepares the way for the successful bringing of the ark to Jerusalem. This two-stage construction can also be seen in two other related and significant events. Later in the David-Solomon narrative, the Chronicler deliberately describes David's reign as a time of preparation for the building of the temple under Solomon. Similarly, in the history of the kings of Judah, the Passover celebrations scheduled during Hezekiah's reign (stage one) are postponed until the time of Josiah (stage two). The Chronicler thereby closely associated these three themes: the ark of the covenant, the temple, and the Passover celebration.

The Chronicler uses 2 Samuel 5:11–25 as the source text for this interlude without making great changes. The first two verses narrate how **Hiram king of Tyre** came to support David's plan to build a palace, which is interpreted by David as confirmation of his kingship and his kingdom. First Chronicles 14:3–7 lists the names of more children who were born to David **in Jerusalem.**

First Chronicles 14:8–16 describes the raids David conducted against the Philistines, not deviating significantly from the source text in 2 Samuel 5:17–25. However, in 1 Chronicles 14:17 the Chronicler adds his own interpretation of the significance of those events. They confirm that **David's fame spread throughout every land.** His dealings with the Philistines exemplify his military power and therefore confirm that **the Lord made all the nations fear him.** These closing remarks append to the descriptions of the Deuteronomistic source text the Chronicler's own ideological agenda, namely, to show David as the ideal king.

15:1–16:43 / The Chronicler now narrates the renewed and this time successful attempt to bring the ark to Jerusalem (15:1–16:43; cf. 2 Sam. 6:19–20a as source material). The actual bringing of the ark to Jerusalem comprises only a small part of the narrative (1 Chron. 15:25–16:3; cf. 2 Sam. 6:12–19a). The remainder of 1 Chronicles 15–16 features descriptions of David's preparations as well as the appointment of clergy and other staff to minister before the ark.

The Chronicler's use of source material is quite interesting here. He apparently uses quotations from 2 Samuel 6 to bracket the whole episode of the actual ark procession in 1 Chronicles 15:25–16:3 (cf. 2 Sam. 6:12–19a) and the conclusion in 16:43 (cf. 2 Sam. 6:19b–20a).

Quotations from 2 Samuel 6 enclose three other sections: first, in 1 Chronicles 16:4–7 (without biblical parallel), the appointment of singers to praise Yahweh before the ark; second, a song of praise sung by the Levites (composed from three excerpts from the Psalter); and third, 16:37–42 (again, without biblical parallel), the appointment of additional singers, as well as priests and gatekeepers, for the ministry at the tabernacle at Gibeon.

The part of the narrative preceding the Chronicler's creative use of source materials (15:1–24) is mainly dedicated to the Levites and Levitical responsibilities.

15:1–3 / The Chronicler now ties up the loose ends of the previous sections. The conquest of Jebus to become the **City of David** now acquires new significance, and Hiram's assistance in constructing a palace for David (mentioned in 14:1) forms the backdrop for the preparation of **a place for the ark.** Also, 15:2 probably alludes to the first, aborted attempt to bring the ark to Jerusalem, the time that Yahweh struck Uzzah dead. The idea of bringing the ark to Jerusalem was not the heart of the problem, but rather the irreverent or illegitimate touching of the ark was. David therefore announces that **no one but the Levites may carry the ark of God.** The election of "the Levites" for this purpose goes back to Pentateuchal prescriptions (Num. 4:15 and Deut. 10:8), but it also signifies the Chronicler's high regard for the Levites. They are assigned this duty on account of their status, and they therefore occupy a special position within the Jerusalem cult, at least in the Chronicler's view.

The remark in 1 Chronicles 15:3 that **David assembled all Israel in Jerusalem** links back with similar terminology to the first attempt (13:5). Again, All-Israel is involved. However, the Chronicler this time adds that the ark had to be brought **to the place he had prepared for it.** Both the word "place" (Hebrew *maqom*) and the word "prepared" (from the Hebrew verbal root *kun*) are significant here. The Chronicler often uses *maqom* (following the example of his Deuteronomistic source texts) to refer to places of cultic significance. The verb "prepare," which can also be translated "complete" or "finalize," is used at important junctions in Chronicles. I will postpone full discussion of this aspect until the Josiah narrative in 2 Chronicles 35, where this verb is used for the last time in Chronicles (2 Chron. 35:20), at the end of the Passover celebration. However, I need to point out here that this verb ties together the themes of ark, temple, and Passover and relates these institutions to the peace and tranquility that flow from seeking Yahweh. We witness here how the Chronicler is slowly weaving a tapestry, making use of different themes and terminology as his colored threads of wool, in order to negotiate the identity of All-Israel.

15:4–15 / This section starts with David calling together **the descendants of Aaron and the Levites** (15:4). This phrase not only introduces

the name list of Levitical family leaders (15:5–10) but also anticipates
the further arrangements made (15:11–15). First Chronicles 15:5–10
follows a strict pattern of supplying the (Levitical) familial connection,
the name of the leader, and the number of accompanying relatives. The
family division found here is not attested elsewhere in the Old Testament,
although the lines of **Kohath, Merari,** and **Gershon** are traditionally
associated with the Levites.

First Chronicles 15:11 indicates that **David** addressed these Levitical leaders as well as **Zadok and Abiathar the priests.** David's words
in 15:12–13 are again full of theologically significant terminology. **The
heads of the Levitical families** are ordered to consecrate themselves for
the task of bringing **up the ark of the LORD, the God of Israel.** The
consecration of priests and Levites plays a significant role in the rest of
Chronicles, with the celebration of the Passover during Hezekiah's reign
probably the climax of this theme. In the narrative about Hezekiah's
Passover it is indicated that there were not enough consecrated priests
available to celebrate the Passover on the fourteenth day of the first month
and that it had to be postponed to the fourteenth of the second month.
First Chronicles 15:12 furthermore mentions the verb *kun* ("prepare,
complete, finalize") again in connection with the **place** to which the ark
had to be transferred. First Chronicles 15:13 continues with a motivation,
still in David's direct speech, explaining why the Levites had to bring the
ark. It was because they **did not bring it up the first time that the LORD
our God broke out in anger against us.** The problem is specified that
we (i.e., David, together with All-Israel) **did not inquire** (*darash*) **of him
about how to do it in the prescribed way.** The suggestion is, of course,
that this inquiry has now been made and that God indicated that the
Levites were to be the right carriers of the ark.

First Chronicles 15:14–15 then indicates that **the priests and Levites
consecrated themselves** and that **the Levites carried the ark of God with
poles on their shoulders.** That this transfer was now done in accordance
with Yahweh's will is confirmed by the statement that the carrying of the
ark took place **as Moses had commanded in accordance with the word
of the LORD.** The consecration of the Levitical carriers, as well as the
way in which they carried the ark, is related to obedience to the Torah of
Yahweh (which is suggested in the expression "the word of the LORD").

15:16–24 / Now that preparations have been made for bringing
the ark to Jerusalem and installing it in the "place" that David "prepared"
for it, further appointments of cultic staff can take place. **The leaders
of the Levites** are commanded by David **to appoint their brothers as**

singers to sing joyful songs, accompanied by musical instruments. The successful bringing of the ark to Jerusalem will introduce joy to the cultic community and All-Israel. The theme of joy forms another significant marker of the Chronicler's theology. First Chronicles 15:17 indicates that the Levites fulfilled their task, and the names of the appointed Levitical musicians are listed in 15:17–24.

15:25–16:3 / This section now forms the climax of the so-called ark narrative with the actual bringing of the ark from the house of Obed-Edom to Jerusalem. The Chronicler made use of his source text in 2 Samuel 6:12b–19a again, following it less strictly than he did with some previous sections and making some significant changes. For example, in 1 Chronicles 15:25–29 he changed some of the perfect tense verbs of his source text into participles to emphasize ongoing action.

Whereas 2 Samuel 6:12a indicates that David was informed about the blessings that the Lord had bestowed on Obed-Edom's house since the ark came there, this information is omitted in 1 Chronicles 15:25. Instead, the Chronicler's text immediately mentions that **David and the elders of Israel and the commanders of units of a thousand** (compared to just "David" in the source text) went to fetch the ark. The inclusive portrayal of the event is again clear in the Chronicler's version. Whereas the ark is called "the ark of God" in 2 Samuel 6:12b, the Chronicler refers to it as **the ark of the covenant of the Lord.** This is the first place in Chronicles that the ark is called this. Klein remarks in this regard: "Only now, as the account of the last stage of the ark's movement begins, and with the Levites finally carrying the ark, does the Chronicler call it the 'ark of the covenant of Yahweh' in harmony with Deut 10:8. . . . For the Chronicler the ark is the symbol of the covenant relationship between Yahweh and Israel and also the symbol of Yahweh's presence in Jerusalem" (*1 Chronicles*, p. 356).

The next verse (1 Chron. 15:26) indicates that certain sacrifices were made along the way. According to the source text in 2 Samuel 6:13, David sacrificed "a bull and a fattened calf" every six steps. The Chronicler provides a motivation for this: **because God had helped the Levites who were carrying the ark of the covenant of the Lord;** but he also makes the Levites the ones bringing the sacrifices and changes the offerings into **seven bulls and seven rams.** These changes were made to indicate that it was not human effort that ensured the successful carrying of the ark to Jerusalem, but rather that God was helping them. The sacrifices therefore also had to be brought by consecrated cult officials, the Levites, making it a more formal and official transaction than does 2 Samuel 6, and the procession follows proper protocol, too.

Although 1 Chronicles 15:27 makes use of the source text in 2 Samuel 6:14, the writer made extensive changes to it. First Chronicles 15:27 starts with an extended addition that indicates that **David was clothed in a robe of fine linen.** The same applied to **all the Levites . . . , the singers, and Kenaniah, who was in charge of the singing of the choirs.** Mention is then made that **David also wore a linen ephod,** a piece of information taken over from the source text. Although 15:29 presupposes David's dancing before the ark (see 2 Sam. 6:14), this information is not present in 1 Chronicles 15:27. The Chronicler is careful to emphasize right conduct and reverence before Yahweh.

In 15:28 the Chronicler again employs his pet term **all Israel,** indicating those who **brought up the ark of the covenant of the LORD,** compared to the source text (2 Sam. 6:15), which mentions that "the entire house of Israel brought up the ark of the LORD." The Chronicler furthermore adds to the list of musical instruments used on this occasion, probably to exaggerate the joy and celebration at the entry of the ark into Jerusalem.

First Chronicles 15:29 takes over the source in 2 Samuel 6:16 almost unchanged. It is strange that the Chronicler retained this information here. This verse indicates that **Michal daughter of Saul watched from a window** when the procession entered the **City of David,** and **she saw King David dancing and celebrating** before the ark. Both Chronicles and the source text indicate that **she despised him in her heart.** In 2 Samuel this incident is followed up with more information in 6:20–23. The conversation between Michal and David recounted there indicates that there were some sexual overtones to the dancing and celebration. It is not surprising, then, that the Chronicler, wanting to present an unblemished portrayal of David, omitted that part of the source text. However, one would therefore have expected the Chronicler also to eliminate the information in 1 Chronicles 15:29. That this was taken over from the source text is not in line with the trend seen elsewhere in the Chronicler's work.

First Chronicles 16:1–3 (using 2 Sam. 6:17–19a) now concludes the procession of the ark to Jerusalem. The ark was brought and **set inside the tent that David had pitched for it.** The ark would remain there until it was taken to the temple during Solomon's reign (2 Chron. 5). Sacrifices were again brought at this point, David **blessed the people in the name of the LORD,** and he gave them food to eat in celebration of the coming of the ark to the City of David. The remark in 2 Samuel 6:19b about the people going "to their homes" is not included at this point in the Chronicler's narrative. It is rather kept until the very end of the Chronicler's ark narrative in 1 Chronicles 16:43.

16:4–7 / These verses are without parallel in other biblical texts and may therefore be the Chronicler's own creation. This section narrates David's appointment of **some of the Levites** for special service before the ark. The Levites chosen for these duties were **Asaph and his associates.** Their task is described as **to make petition, to give thanks, and to praise the Lord, the God of Israel.** The Hebrew verb rendered in NIV as "to make petition" (*lehazkir*) can also be translated "to commemorate, cause to remember." Some think that the commemoration referred to here may be associated with the role some priests played during the morning and evening prayers when they had to blow a trumpet to bring the people to remember God's deeds. The three functions mentioned here, namely, "to make petition, to give thanks, and to praise," are echoed in the terminology used in the psalmic composition that follows (16:8, 9, 12).

First Chronicles 16:7 forms the bridge to the next section, which is presented in poetry. It starts with the temporal indication, **that day,** which gives the recitation of the psalm in the next section an imminent dimension. It is as if time is stopped for a moment now that the ark is in Jerusalem and officials have been appointed to serve before it in order to bring praise and **thanks to the Lord.** The verse says: **David first committed** (literally "gave") **to Asaph and his associates this psalm.** The suggestion is that David supplied "this psalm" to the Asaphites for thanksgiving and praise singing. The source materials from which this psalm is composed (Ps. 105, 96, 106) are not associated (by means of superscriptions) with either David or Asaph. This shows that the Chronicler assigned these source materials a unique context within the ark narrative.

16:8–36 / These verses are the longest of only a few poetic sections in Chronicles. (Interestingly enough, another quotation from a psalm, in this case Ps. 132, can be found in the narrative in 2 Chron. 6:40–42, where Solomon's transfer of the ark to the temple is described. The excerpt from Ps. 132 is used as part of Solomon's prayer.) First Chronicles 16:8–22 is paralleled in Psalm 105:1–15; 1 Chronicles 16:23–33 in Psalm 96:1–13; and 1 Chronicles 16:34–36 in Psalm 106:1, 47–48. Whereas earlier commentaries did not devote due attention to the unique way in which the Chronicler reworked and utilized this psalmic material (and even referred readers to Psalm commentaries for expositions of these texts!), more recent studies emphasize that the quotation of these psalm selections develops its own dynamic in the Chronicler's hand.

This view focuses our attention on the function of this new composite psalm in the Chronicler's construction. Although some earlier studies thought that the psalm was inserted by later editors and was not originally from the Chronicler's hand, the thematic and terminological links with the surrounding narrative now convince scholars that the psalm material represents a careful selection by the Chronicler himself. We have already seen that 1 Chronicles 16:4b (where it is indicated that the Levites were appointed to promote remembrance, to give thanks, and to praise the Lord) echoes in the composite song. Similar terminology occurs in the introductory part of the song (16:8–14), and some commentators even see three sections in the song associated with the three concepts: 16:15–22 as a "remember section," 16:23–33 as a "praise section," and 16:34–36 as a "giving-thanks section." Another theme that binds the psalm to the Chronicler's narrative construction is the "covenant." This concept plays a prominent role in the ark narrative. It is likewise prominent in particularly the first part of the composite psalm. A last theme is seeking Yahweh. For the Chronicler this concept expresses the ideal attitude toward Yahweh, and it leads to rest and peace. This theme is also prominent in the composite psalm (see, e.g., 16:10–11). My suggestion is that the singing of this psalm in the presence of the ark would be an expression of the seeking of Yahweh.

In order to determine the function of the composite psalm in the Chronicler's construction, one has to look carefully at the changes and selections made by the writer. Doan and Giles summarize the most important changes concisely, and I take their summary as a point of departure here (Doan and Giles, "Song of Asaph," pp. 29–43).

In 16:13 the Chronicler changed "Abraham" of Psalm 105:6 into **Israel.** With this change the Chronicler made the first half of the verse parallel to the second (with "Israel" another name for Jacob, and the name preferred instead of Jacob elsewhere in Chronicles), in contrast to the canonical psalm's reference to two ancestral generations. Doan and Giles explain the effect of this change as follows: "The substitution of 'Israel' for 'Abraham,' especially when quoting a psalm most likely familiar to the readers, could only have a surprise effect. . . . The Chronicler's use of 'Israel' drew the audience into the performance of the song as they . . . suddenly found the song to be about them!" ("Song of Asaph," p. 36).

In 16:15 the Chronicler changed the finite verb in Psalm 105:8, "he remembers" (with Yahweh as subject), into a plural imperative. Although the NIV translates it **he remembers,** to stay in line with Psalm 105:8, the literal translation of the Hebrew would rather be "[you all must] remember." With this small change the Chronicler created a structural link with 1 Chronicles 16:12, where the same verb is used, also as plural imperative. The change of the statement in Psalm 105:8 ("Yahweh remembers his covenant") into a command to the audience to remember **the covenant** draws them into the song again. Like 1 Chronicles 16:12, this verse addresses the covenant community (that is, the community gathered at the installation of the ark of the covenant in the City of David) but also implies the audience of the Chronicler's work.

Another change that draws in the audience of the Chronicler's psalm occurs in 16:19. Whereas Psalm 105:12 has "when they were but few in number" (referring to the patriarchs), the Chronicler changed the verb to read "when you were but few in number" (although the NIV again opted to translate the phrase in line with the source text: **when they were but few in number**). Although the following verb in 1 Chronicles 16:20, **they wandered,** does not show the same change, some manuscripts attest also in this case a change to "you" (plural). This slight change would again involve the audience, as the worshipers of David's day are called to identify themselves with the patriarchs. By making this change, the Chronicler succeeded in involving his own audience, which also casts 16:22 in another light. Whereas the source text in Psalm 105:15 has a reference to the patriarchs (who are called "anointed ones" and "prophets" there), the change in 1 Chronicles 16:19 makes the audience in the Chronicler's time the referent in 16:22. The call **do not touch my anointed ones; do my prophets no harm** in the Chronicler's construction is now applied to the audience. If one were to assume that the Chronicler addressed his work primarily to the cultic and provincial political community in Jerusalem during the Persian period, this warning would be a call (to the Persian leadership) to recognize the legitimacy of the cultic and political community in Jerusalem.

Two changes in 16:27 and 16:29 show how the Chronicler dealt with anachronistic references in his source text. The verses quoted from Psalm 96:6 and 96:8 contain references to the completed temple, which was still not a reality in David's time. In order to apply these texts to the historical context of David, he changed the second phrase in Psalm 96:6, "strength and glory are in his sanctuary," into **strength and joy in his dwelling place** (1 Chron. 16:27). The word "sanctuary" (*miqdash*) in Psalm 96:6, which is associated with formal sacrifices in a temple, was changed into the word that is used in Chronicles to indicate the future location of the temple, namely, "place" (*maqom*). The reason for the change from "glory" to "joy" remains a mystery.

In 16:29 a similar change was made when "bring an offering and come into his courts" (Ps. 96:8) was changed into **bring an offering and come before him.** The reference to "courts" in Psalm 96:8 again presupposes the completed temple, while the changed version in Chronicles is merely referring to the presence of Yahweh. Doan and Giles remark about these changes: "The alteration of references to the sanctuary and those courts was a necessary condition if the Chronicler's audience was to feel part of the song and to have the ability to 'enter' the song as participants" ("Song of Asaph," 37).

The Chronicler made two changes in 16:30–31. First, the phrase **let them say among the nations, "The LORD reigns!"** was taken over from the source text in Psalm 96:10, but it was moved to another position. Whereas this phrase stands at the beginning of Psalm 96:10, it was moved in 1 Chronicles 16:31 to a position following the phrase **let the heavens rejoice, let the earth be glad.** In doing this the Chronicler made the "heavens" and the "earth" the ones that must declare "among the nations" that "the LORD reigns!" In Psalm 96:7 the "families of nations" are the ones who have to declare that "the LORD reigns." The other change made here might provide us with a clue as to why the "heavens" and the "earth" were involved instead of the "nations." The Chronicler chose to omit the phrase "he will judge the people with equity" in Psalm 96:10b. A similar phrase in Psalm 96:13b, "he will judge the world in righteousness and the peoples in his truth," was also omitted. Political considerations are probably at the root of this omission.

A final change that will be highlighted here occurs in the very last verse of the song, namely, 16:36. Whereas the source text in Psalm 106:48b closes with the command "Let all the people say, 'Amen!'" followed by the phrase that closes book 4 of the Psalter, "Praise the LORD," the Chronicler made these into a piece of narrative (the verb "say" was changed into a *wayyiqtol* form) reporting how **the people said "Amen" and "Praise the LORD"** (with the last phrase joined with a copulative "and" to the former part). These changed words from Psalm 106 are therefore employed by the Chronicler to report that the congregation that gathered at the installation of the ark in the City of David confirmed the words of the psalm that he "gave" them (1 Chron. 16:7).

All the above changes and small omissions emphasize that the Chronicler made use of psalmic source materials, but that he transformed them into a song that fitted the context of David and also invited the addressees of his own context to be part of the performance of the psalm. This example shows how much contemporary interpreters of Holy Scriptures can learn from the Chronicler about hermeneutics! The Chronicler showed great sensitivity for his contemporary audience in his interpretation of the transmitted traditions.

Whereas the discussion in the previous paragraphs concentrated on the small but significant changes and omissions the Chronicler made, it also emphasizes that the Chronicler used his source materials very selectively in order to fit the bigger picture of his presentation. A telling example is his quotation from Psalm 105. The first fifteen verses of this psalm are used in the Chronicler's construction, but the rest of the psalm is simply omitted. With this omission the themes of Israel in Egypt, the exodus event, and the desert wanderings (which form the content of the remainder of Ps. 105) are excluded. This fits in, however, with the macrostructure of Chronicles. The Chronicler starts his historical construction with Adam (in 1:1), but then uses the patriarchal line of Jacob to structure the further genealogies, without mentioning the time in Egypt, the exodus, or the desert wanderings either. Immediately after the genealogies follows Saul's history (thereby also skipping over the conquest of the land and the period of the judges) and then David's. The macrostructure and the selective quotation from Psalm 105 show that the Chronicler did not see those omitted periods to be constitutive of All-Israel's identity in the Persian period. The focus is rather strongly on the kingship of David as well as on the cult in Jerusalem. In this, God is shown to be the promise keeper, and the focus is not so much on God the rescuer (like in Exodus and Judges).

In conclusion, 1 Chronicles 16:8–36 is composed of two enclosing elements: an introductory call to praise in 16:8–13 and a closing call to praise in 16:34. In between we find three sections giving content to the praise: 16:14–22 contains thanksgiving for Yahweh's judgments in the past; 16:23–29 is a declaration of Yahweh's present sovereignty; and 16:30–33 anticipates Yahweh's future rule. With the addition of the command **cry out** at the beginning of 16:35 the Chronicler turned 16:35–36 into a concluding liturgy. First Chronicles 16:35b contains a petition to God to **save** and **deliver,** whereas 16:36a expresses a benediction to Yahweh. First Chronicles 16:36b closes the whole section by reporting that **all the people** responded with "**Amen**" and "**Praise the** L**ORD.**"

16:37–42 / This section, again without parallel in other biblical literature, continues from 16:4–7 to narrate further appointments made by **David.** Apart from appointing **Asaph and his associates** (see 16:4–7) **before the ark of the covenant of the** L**ORD,** he also appointed **Obed-Edom** and **associates to minister with them** as **gatekeepers.**

Another cultic site comes into focus from 16:39, however. The Chronicler mentions that David appointed **Zadok the priest and his fellow priests before the tabernacle of the** L**ORD at the high place in Gibeon.** This part suggests that there were two cultic centers during David's reign: the ark in the City of David and the tabernacle in Gibeon. Some dispute the historical reliability of this information. Nevertheless, it seems that the Chronicler is not giving this information for historical purposes but is rather using it to prepare the way for the construction of the temple under Solomon (narrated in 2 Chron. 2–4). During Solomon's reign both the ark and the tabernacle were taken to the temple in Jerusalem. Second Chronicles 1:3 still mentions that Solomon went to "the high place in Gibeon," but when the ark and the tabernacle came to the temple in Jerusalem, the cult was united in one center.

The mention of the ark and the tabernacle in two locations in 1 Chronicles 16 might also be related to the tribal composition of postexilic Yehud. The City of David was clearly associated with the tribe of Judah, while Gibeon was one of the Benjaminite places. Bringing the two main cultic symbols to the temple from a Judahite and Benjaminite location, respectively, might have been the Chronicler's attempt to unite these tribal interests in the centralized Jerusalem cult.

16:43 / This last verse of the ark narrative is a reconstruction of the source material. It indicates that **all the people left, each for his home** (taken from 2 Sam. 6:19b) and that **David returned home to bless his family** (taken from 2 Sam. 6:20a). We have already seen that the Chronicler chose to omit the continuation of this narrative from 2 Samuel 6:20b (the Michal incident). The suggestion is clear: the blessing that the ark brought to the house of Obed-Edom was transferred to the City of David but is now also bestowed on David's family (literally "his house"). The house of David is, of course, the royal line that runs from Judah's first king, David, through all the other Judahite kings (whose histories will be narrated in 2 Chron. 10–36). The same Hebrew verb used in 1 Chronicles 10:14 (*sbb*), to say that "the LORD . . . turned the kingdom over to David son of Jesse," is now used here in 16:43. This blessing is now "turned over" to the house of David, extending its effect from the City of David to David's family line.

The ark narrative in 1 Chronicles 13–16 is full of theological significance. It starts with a first attempt to bring the ark to Jerusalem, but this attempt is aborted because of the Uzzah incident. This incident highlights that bringing the ark to Jerusalem is a serious matter that may not be approached in a simply human way. The failure indicated in 1 Chronicles 13 contrasts with the successful attempt narrated in 1 Chronicles 15–16. Whereas the first attempt is portrayed as an impulsive move based on human effort, the second attempt forms part of a well-organized cultic event. First Chronicles 14 serves as interlude to prepare the way for 1 Chronicles 15–16. It forms the bridge along which the blessings on the house of Obed-Edom can be transferred to the kingship of David and the cultic community. In this respect the hymn in the center of 1 Chronicles 16 plays an important role. By using poetic source materials for the construction of his hymn, the Chronicler creates a pause in the progress of the narrative to let the theological significance of the transfer of blessings sink in. Additionally, the hymn also draws the Chronicler's audience into participation in the ancient events and, in so doing, reenacts the original scene as a way of affirming something about their community.

The ark narrative concludes in 16:43 with all the people going to their homes, while David goes to his home to bless his family ("house"). With this remark the reader is led to conclude that not only has the cult in Jerusalem now been firmly established, but also the dynasty of David. With the ark's presence in Jerusalem, divine blessings on the Davidic dynasty are guaranteed.

Additional Notes §2.3

13:1–16:43 / Some scholars suggest the existence of a precanonical ark narrative in all or parts of 1 Sam. 4–6 and 2 Sam. 6. The Chronicler would then also have made use of this precanonical source for his construction of 1 Chron. 13–16. It is uncertain whether this hypothesis holds true. However, one may assume that the Chronicler made use of the Samuel version of this narrative, selecting such material as supported his cause. The information in 1 Sam. 4–6 was omitted by the Chronicler, and he has concentrated his version on 2 Sam. 6. In terms of the Chronicler's version 1 Chron. 14 poses a problem for biblical scholarship, since it is seemingly unrelated to the previous (1 Chron. 13) and following (1 Chron. 15–16) chapters. It furthermore quotes from 2 Sam. 5, although 2 Sam. 6 has been quoted already in 1 Chron. 13. John Wright concludes that the existence of an ark narrative, running from 1 Chron. 13 to 1 Chron. 16, is negated by "the intrusive role of 1 Chronicles 14" (J. W. Wright, "The Founding Father: The Structure of the Chronicler's David Narrative," *JBL* 117 [1998], pp. 45–59, at p. 47). Wright sees 1 Chron. 14:2 as the nexus between two greater narratives, 10:1–14:2 ("the rise of the founding father") and 14:3–22:1 ("the reign of the founding father"). Tamara Eskenazi holds another view. On the basis of a literary analysis she divides the narrative as follows: 13:1–4 ("objective defined: to bring the ark to Jerusalem"); 13:5–15:29 ("process of actualization: the transfer of the ark"); and 16:1–43 ("objective reached: celebration of the ark's arrival in Jerusalem") (T. C. Eskenazi, "A Literary Approach to Chronicles' Ark Narrative in 1 Chronicles 13–16," in *Fortunate the Eyes That See: Essays in Honor of David Noel Freedman in Celebration of His Seventieth Birthday* [ed. A. B. Beck et al.; Grand Rapids: Eerdmans, 1995], pp. 258–74). Although there is merit in Wright's arguments about 1 Chron. 14 and although Eskenazi's literary arguments for unity are sometimes unconvincing, it remains unlikely that the Chronicler envisioned 1 Chron. 13 and 1 Chron. 15–16, respectively, as separate units. That 2 Sam. 6 was quoted in both these sections points in the direction of some sort of a compositional unity at least. In my opinion, the peculiar position of 1 Chron. 14 should be explained in another way. It might be that 1 Chron. 14 (quoting from 2 Sam. 5:11–25) was detached from its original position after 1 Chron. 11:9 (quoting from 2 Sam. 5:1–3, 6–10). There the content of 1 Chron. 14 would have made good sense. If 1 Chron. 13 was directly followed by 1 Chron. 15–16, this would equally have created a direct connection with the unsuccessful attempt to bring the ark to Jerusalem (in 1 Chron. 13), followed by the further preparations and final bringing of the ark (in 1 Chron. 15). However, since there is no additional support for such a textual order in any of the other versions, this proposal remains hypothetical. What remains plausible, however, is the explanation of the present position of 1 Chron. 14 as a deliberate attempt by the Chronicler to present the bringing of the ark to Jerusalem and the capturing of the city as David's first acts as king after his coronation.

13:1–4 / The symbolism of the **ark** of the covenant should not be overlooked. It was considered in Israel to be the symbol of Yahweh's presence among them. The bringing of the ark would therefore have very clear theological overtones for the people during David's time. But why did the Chronicler consider the ark to be so important although the ark no longer existed in his time? Hicks responds to this issue as follows: "David's attitude toward the ark is the kind of attitude the postexilic community must have for the temple. Just as David sought God through the ark, so postexilic Israel must seek God through the temple" (*1 and 2 Chronicles*, p. 143).

13:5 / Rather than allude to the Davidic-Solomonic empire, the geography may simply reflect an idealistic portrait of broad support for David or summarize the wide spectrum of places represented among the participants in David's national assembly. According to Knoppers, having participants from all over the land paying appropriate honor to David's leadership implies wide public support for his transfer of the ark and models for the Chronicler's own time an inclusive Judaism in line with its present international character (*1 Chronicles 10–29*, pp. 585–86).

13:5–7 / We have seen different expressions being used to refer to the **ark**. Van den Eynde shows that the Chronicler links the ark and the theme of kingship and closely connects ark, temple, and kingship. The ark stories shape the structure of the overall story line and form the setting in which the Chronicler develops his view on kingship. She suggests that the divine covenant promises to David are the background behind the use of "covenant" (*berith*) in some of the ark's names (Van den Eynde, "Chronicler's Use," pp. 422–30).

13:13–14 / **Obed-Edom** was a **Gittite** according to both the source text and the Chronicler's version, which means he came from the (Philistine) city of

Gath. Klein therefore hypothesizes that "Obed-Edom was apparently a Philistine expatriate who was loyal to David" (*1 Chronicles*, p. 335). It seems strange that the ark is again finding a resting place among Philistines (see 1 Sam. 4–6). That the Chronicler did not omit the Philistine connection of Obed-Edom probably shows that the central problem that drives the narrative here was not simply that the ark was in Philistine hands but that the ark was not in Jerusalem.

14:12 / The attentive reader would notice that, whereas 2 Sam. 5:21 mentions that "David and his men carried . . . off" the Philistine idols after the battle, the Chronicler's text indicates that **David gave orders to burn them**. Klein (*1 Chronicles*, pp. 338, 342) cautions that one should not attempt too bold an interpretation of the Chronicler's motive here, since it can be seen from some other versions of 2 Sam. 5:21 that there might have been a variant of this text available other than the Masoretic Text of Samuel, on which the Chronicler probably based his text. However, the variant text would have fitted the Chronicler's cause quite well, since it does not give an indication (as in the Masoretic Text of 2 Sam. 5:21) that the idols were carried off. That would have been a blemish on David's reputation. The burning of the idols rather gives expression to what was commanded in Deut. 7:5, 25–26; 12:3. The Chronicler changed the imperative of the source text (the command "burn") into a *wayyiqtol* form of the verb, indicating that they have indeed burned the idols.

15:1–16:43 / Since numerous repetitions and conflicting pieces of information occur in 1 Chron. 15–16, the compositional history of these chapters has been the topic of scholarly debate. The debate revolves around whether the information on the different priestly groups, musicians, and gatekeepers was part of the Chronicler's material or whether these parts were added after the substantial completion of the book. On the one side of the debate are those who would attribute a minimal portion of the texts to the Chronicler, and on the other are those who would attribute everything—with few exceptions—to the Chronicler's hand. Knoppers indicates that the complexity of the text "may reflect shifting circumstances relating to the status of the singers over the course of this long era," but also reflects "disputes among different groups and individual authors over what the precise status and classification of the singers would be" (*1 Chronicles 10–29*, pp. 658–59). In this way 1 Chron. 15–16 bears witness to processes of identity formation among the clergy groups in the Second Temple period, in which the singers, musicians, and gatekeepers are presented as full-fledged Levites.

15:26 / The change of the number of sacrificial animals ("a bull and a fattened calf" in 2 Sam. 6:13, compared to **seven bulls and seven rams** in 1 Chron. 15:26) goes back to a Hebrew text of Samuel (4QSam^a), which differed slightly from the one in the Masoretic Text. One should therefore not interpret this change as representing part of the Chronicler's ideology.

16:8–36 / Different structures have been identified in the psalm through the history of scholarship. The simplest division is naturally according to the psalm source materials used. This would produce three subsections, namely, 16:8–22; 16:23–33; and 16:34–36. However, with the emphasis on the Chronicler constructing his own unique psalm from the source materials, scholars have lodged further investigations into the texts and on the basis of these analyses have come up with other suggestions. The most convincing is by M. Throntveit ("Songs in a New Key," pp. 153–70), who suggests the following structure (used in my commentary):

1. thanksgiving hymn (16:8–34)
   - a introductory calls to thanksgiving (16:8–13)
     - b for past "judgments" (16:14–22)
       - c for present sovereignty (16:23–29)
     - b′ for future "rule" (16:30–33)
   - a′ concluding call to thanksgiving (16:34)
2. concluding liturgy (16:35–36)
   - a liturgical summons (16:35a)
     - b petition (16:35b)
     - b′ benediction (16:36a)
   - a′ congregational response (16:36b)

Throntveit indicates that each subsection in part 1 "displays its own structural integrity in terms of both form and content" ("Songs in a New Key," p. 167). He also agrees with those scholars who indicate that 16:35–36 forms a concluding liturgy that stands outside the well-structured thanksgiving hymn. Throntveit furthermore reminds the reader that many scholars see a concentric structure in the whole of 1 Chron. 16, which puts the Chronicler's hymn in a central position:

- a David blesses the people (16:1–3)
  - b David appoints Levites for worship in Jerusalem (16:4–7)
    - c The Chronicler's hymn (16:8–36)
  - b′ David appoints Levites and priests for worship at Gibeon (16:37–42)
- a′ David blesses his house (16:43)

§2.4 A House for Yahweh and for David (1 Chron. 17:1–27)

The Chronicler's narrative now moves to the all-important oracle of Nathan in which divine promises to David are made and in which the issue of temple building is addressed. The Chronicler took his material from 2 Samuel 7, where this oracle is also presented (see Additional Note on 17:1–2).

This section opens with a back reference to the interlude in 1 Chronicles 14, where it was indicated that David built "a palace" (literally "a house") for himself with the assistance of "Hiram king of Tyre." First Chronicles 17:1 also connects with the last verse of the previous chapter, where it was indicated that "David returned home to bless his family" (literally "his house"). The double reference to "house" in the previous chapters forms the background to 17:1, where, in David's direct speech to Nathan, a contrast is made between David's house and the "tent" in which the ark had to reside at that stage.

This chapter can be divided into two major sections, namely, 17:1–15, in which Nathan's oracle is given, and 17:16–27, where David responds to the oracle with a prayer. The first section can be subdivided into 17:1–2 (the conversation between David and Nathan) and 17:3–15 (Nathan receives and reports the oracle to David).

17:1–2 / First Chronicles 17:1 corresponds to 2 Samuel 7:1–2 but shows some important differences. Here (as well as in 17:2) the personal name **David** is used instead of "the king" of the source text. The renominalization is probably the Chronicler's strategy to show that this section about the establishment of David's dynasty and temple building is now a next step in his narrative construction.

The Chronicler omits the rest of 2 Samuel 7:1, which says "the LORD had given him rest from all his enemies around him." At first sight this omission is strange, since the theme of rest and peace plays such an important role in the Chronicler's narrative. However, when the reader gets to the Nathan oracle, it becomes clear that the Chronicler wanted to contrast David and his son Solomon. Solomon was the one who would be given "rest" and would therefore be the builder of the temple. David is indicated (1 Chron. 22:8; 28:3) to have too much blood on his hands, which disqualified him from building the temple. The phrase in 2 Samuel 7:1b, therefore, did not fit into the Chronicler's larger narrative construction and was thus omitted.

In the direct speech of 1 Chronicles 17:1 a contrast is established between David (indicated with the first person pronoun **I** in the initial position of the sentence), who was **living in a palace of cedar,** and **the ark of the covenant of the** Lord (called "the ark of God" in 2 Sam. 7:2), which was at that stage **under a tent.** Although **Nathan the prophet** initially confirmed (in 1 Chron. 17:2 ∥ 2 Sam. 7:3) that David should do **whatever** he had **in mind,** because **God** was with him, the next oracle sheds a different light on David's plans. The oracle lets the reader realize that David's announcement of his intention to build a permanent abode for "the ark of the covenant of the Lord" has the same inappropriate quality as the impulsive gesture by Uzzah when the ark was carried from Kiriath Jearim. It was not the bringing of the ark to Jerusalem that was denounced when Uzzah was killed by Yahweh, but the improper, exclusively human effort exerted in doing so (see commentary on 1 Chron. 13). The same applies here: It is not David's idea of building a permanent abode for the ark that is denounced, but rather his doing this with blood on his hands. Just as the transfer of the ark to Jerusalem was an action stemming from divine command, so the building of the temple should also be done in response to Yahweh's command.

17:3–15 / After Nathan's initial positive response, he receives **the word of God** during **that night.** The expression used here is typical of divinely inspired prophetic oracles. Nathan is ordered by Yahweh to go and tell David: **You are not the one to build me a house to dwell in.** Although the sentence construction is somewhat different here than in the source text (where it is formulated as a rhetorical question, "Are you the one?"), the implication is the same. It is not the building of "a house to dwell in" that is criticized, but rather that "David" will do so.

The manner in which Yahweh's response is formulated (17:5–6) helps the reader to realize that a permanent location for the ark (17:1) is closely related to building "a house to dwell in" for Yahweh. The ark as a symbol of Yahweh's presence is thus affirmed. Although Yahweh's words to David in 17:5–6 leave the impression that he has never before required **a house of cedar** and that a temple will be unnecessary, the issue of building the temple still remains part of the promise to David's son Solomon. McKenzie also does not see a total repudiation in these words.

He rather concludes (in the light of the rest of the oracle that follows from 17:7) that "David is simply not the right man at the right time for the job of building the temple" (*1–2 Chronicles*, p. 156).

In 17:7 we find a renewed opening of the divine word (as in 17:4). Yahweh reminds David that it was he, Yahweh, who **took** David **from the pasture and from following the flock, to be ruler over** God's **people Israel**. The divine initiative is therefore emphasized. In light of Yahweh's previous protection of David, Yahweh promises David to make his name **like the names of the greatest men of the earth**. This promise, which was taken from the source text in 2 Samuel 7, is a reminder of the promise made to Abraham in Genesis 12. Yahweh will also **provide a place for** God's **people Israel** where they will be able to live in peace. Furthermore, Yahweh **will . . . subdue all** David's **enemies**. The latter phrase was slightly altered from the source text, which mentions rest again. Here again it seems that the Chronicler is rather reserving the issue of rest for the Solomon narrative. In 17:10 there follows a solemn declaration that Yahweh **will build a house for** David. This declaration gives an ironic twist to the initial opening of the narrative, where David declares that he wants to build a house for Yahweh. The irony is created by means of the wordplay on "house," which can refer to a physical palace (such as David's; 17:1), to a family (such as David's; 16:43), to a temple (such as the one David wanted to build; 17:4), and to a dynasty (such as David's; 17:10). First Chronicles 17:11 clarifies that one of David's **own sons** will be raised up by Yahweh, and Yahweh **will establish his kingdom**. This son will be **the one who will build a house** for Yahweh, and Yahweh **will establish his throne forever**.

The Chronicler made a small change in 17:10 that the reader should note. This change not only is important for the Chronicler's portrayal of David but also is a significant building block in the construction of his narrative. Whereas 2 Samuel 7:11 says, "I will also give you rest from all your enemies," the Chronicler's version in 1 Chronicles 17:10 has **I will also subdue all your enemies**. The Chronicler changed the Hebrew verb from "give rest" to "subdue" in order to avoid again (as in 17:1) any indication that David experienced rest. This again contrasts David and Solomon. And it also anticipates the war narratives that will follow in 1 Chronicles 19–20 and indicates that David's victories will not be because of his own strength but will be a result of Yahweh's initiative.

First Chronicles 17:13 (like the source text in 2 Sam. 7:14) clarifies that Yahweh sees a very close relationship between him and David's son: **I will be his father, and he will be my son**. The father-son metaphor was often used in ancient Near Eastern environments to express the relationship between the deity and the king (e.g., Ps. 2:7, where this expression is used with reference to the king). But the Chronicler made a significant change in this verse. Whereas the source text (2 Sam. 7:14) adds "when he does wrong, I will punish him with the rod of men, with floggings inflicted by men," the Chronicler omits any possibility of Solomon doing something wrong. This forms part of the Chronicler's strategy to present a blameless Solomon in 2 Chronicles 1–9. The point of comparison here is again Saul, from whom Yahweh took away the kingship (1 Chron. 10).

The oracle ends with a remark in 17:15 (taken from the source text) that **Nathan reported to David all the words of the entire revelation.**

17:16–27 / The narrative continues with David's response to the oracle. First Chronicles 17:16, which for the first time calls David **king,** says that he **went in and sat before the** LORD. The location is not specified, although one may assume that he went to the place where the ark was kept. Some commentators speculate whether "sitting" was an appropriate position for kings at prayer, since we know that standing, kneeling, or lying prostrate was more customary. However, the Hebrew word for "sitting" is the same word used in 17:1 to refer to David's "living" in his own house. The Chronicler, following his source text, probably suggested that David was now responsive to Yahweh's presence, instead of acting in response to his own personal sphere.

In the next verses (17:16–19) a series of rhetorical questions (**Who am I, O** LORD **God?** and **What more can David say to you?**) express David's surprise at Yahweh's gracious promise to his house. David shows his humility by calling himself Yahweh's **servant** (once in 17:17, twice in 17:18, and once in 17:19). He confesses that his past and Israel's past were in the hands of Yahweh and that he therefore also believes that the future of his house will be in Yahweh's hands.

In 17:20–22 (taken from the source text in 2 Sam. 7:22–24) David confesses, first, **There is no one like you, O** LORD, **and there is no God but you,** and second, **You made your people Israel your own forever** by becoming their God. Especially the second confession is filled with covenantal overtones.

The logical marker **and now** in 17:23 leads to David's petition to God: **Let the promise . . . be established forever.** If this will be the case, **then men will say, "The** LORD **Almighty, the God over Israel, is Israel's God!"** The Chronicler (following his source text again) knows that the realization of the divine promise to David's house will be a confirmation that Yahweh is really their God.

Whereas 2 Samuel 7:29 continues with the petition of the previous verses by utilizing two further imperatives ("be pleased" and "bless"), the Chronicler changed those imperatives into past tense: **you have been pleased to bless** (1 Chron. 17:27). The Chronicler suggests that God has already blessed David's house by making the eternal promise.

Different possibilities have been explored in the interpretation history of this section in the Chronicler's work. Some see in the divine promise of eternal kingship the royalist expectation of the Chronicler that God will resurrect the Davidic kingship after the exile, despite the Persian imperial context. Others see in the preservation of the Nathan oracle and David's prayer an indication that the Chronicler had eschatological expectations. Particularly the emphasis on the word "forever" in this section (it is repeated eight times) leads some interpreters to see the Chronicler as somebody who wanted to evoke hope for a future salvation that Yahweh would bring to Israel. Still others, particularly in the Christian tradition, see messianic allusions in the oracle. The "house of David," so the New Testament proclaims, produced the line from which Jesus of Nazareth was born. Therefore some Christian interpreters would see in Nathan's oracle an Old Testament prediction of the true king who would be born in Bethlehem.

None of these lines of interpretation do full justice to the Chronicler's narrative. Other sections in Chronicles do not leave the impression that the Chronicler was a political activist who wanted a resurrection of the Davidic kingdom. On the contrary, it often seems that the Chronicler wanted to convince the people of Yehud to accept Persian rule as a fulfillment of a prophecy (see 2 Chron. 36:22–23). An eschatological interpretation neglects the numerous indications in Chronicles that the writer did not expect future salvation but rather intended to convince his audience that God's salvation of his people could also be realized in their own time under Persian rule. A messianic interpretation also overlooks that the Chronicler wrote primarily for the cultic community in Jerusalem during the Persian period to assist them to understand who they were now that the exile was over. He wanted to open their eyes to their being Yahweh's covenant people and their very existence being the result of Yahweh's loyalty to the covenant. Although Christian interpreters may in hindsight, and through the lens of the New Testament, relate Nathan's promise to Jesus Christ, it is unlikely that it had this connotation in the Chronicler's time.

One should therefore be careful not to overinterpret the Chronicler's preservation of the Nathan oracle and David's prayer. These are not new elements created by the Chronicler; they were taken over from the earlier Deuteronomistic tradition. However, the Chronicler allowed himself some small changes so that this part of his source material would fit his overall theological construction well. The developing plot of the Chronicler's narrative takes on a few more building blocks, which will be amplified further in (particularly) the narrative dealing with Solomon. This chapter's building block of "divine promise of eternal kingship" feeds into a greater narrative that includes Solomon.

Additional Notes §2.4

17:1–2 / Second Sam. 7 served as source text for the Chronicler's construction in this chapter. When the two versions are compared, one notes only a few minor changes, the most important being the omission of 2 Sam. 7:1b and 7:14b. However, on the basis of technical text-critical arguments, scholars (such as Knoppers and Klein) argue that the Chronicler's source text was probably an older version than both the one we find in the Masoretic Text of 2 Sam. 7 and the version found in the Septuagint. Scholars also agree that the text in 2 Sam. 7 probably went through an extensive process of expansion. Many Chronicles commentators rightly assume, however, that the Chronicler knew only the final form of 2 Sam. 7. Psalm 89 seems to be a poetic version of "the divine promise to David and his house," which (according to the scholarly consensus) is probably "an interpretation, extension, and reapplication of the Davidic promises" of 2 Sam. 7 (Knoppers, *1 Chronicles 10–29*, pp. 673–74).

17:5–6 / Generally, Chronicles omits references to the exodus, desert wanderings, conquest of the land, and the period of the judges. But here the Chronicler retained some slight allusions to these themes from the source text of 2 Sam. 7. First Chron. 17:5–6 still includes **the day I brought Israel out of Egypt,** Yahweh's moving **from one tent site to another,** and **their leaders.** (The NIV keeps the direct reference to "out of Egypt" although it is absent from the Hebrew text of Chronicles.) According to Avioz, the retention of these expressions here (and in a few other texts) indicates that the Chronicler did not ignore or diminish the exodus and other earlier events (as Sara Japhet argues). The Chronicler is instead underplaying those events in order to give greater priority to the Davidic-Solomonic kingship in his construction of All-Israel's history (Avioz, "Nathan's Prophecy," pp. 546–47).

17:10 / The verb **build** is used in Chronicles, compared to "established" in the source text of 2 Sam. 7:11. The combination **build a house** is mostly used in connection with a dynasty. The Chronicler's change in this case was probably meant to show that Yahweh is now referring to David's dynasty. Willi, however, argues that the expression should not be understood as "dynasty" but rather as "temple." He is of the opinion that the Chronicler is referring to the divine kingdom here, which includes not only Israel but also the whole world of nations. The earthly anchor for the divine kingdom is the temple and not an earthly dynasty (Willi, "Gibt es in der Chronik eine 'Dynastie Davids'? Ein Beitrag zur Semantik von *byt*," pp. 393–404).

§2.5 David's Wars (1 Chron. 18:1–20:8)

In 17:10 the Chronicler made a small change to the verb of his source text. The result was a promise of Yahweh that he would subdue David's enemies. The narratives that follow in the next three chapters provide proof that Yahweh did indeed fulfill this promise. These chapters emphasize that it is not David's valor or his political aspirations that drove these military victories. It is rather Yahweh's initiative in preparing the way for the dispensation of peace and rest that will prevail under King Solomon's reign.

The Chronicler again followed his source texts in 2 Samuel closely but selected only certain war narratives, leaving aside many other family narratives contained in 2 Samuel. The material was mainly taken from 2 Samuel 8, 10, 12, 21, and 24. Some examples of omitted narratives are the following: David's showing kindness to Mephibosheth (2 Sam. 9), David's adultery with Bathsheba (2 Sam. 11), Amnon's rape of Tamar (2 Sam. 13), Absalom's revolt (2 Sam. 14), and rebellion in David's family (2 Sam. 15–20). Many scholars show that several of these omitted narratives shed a negative light on David and would thus not have suited the Chronicler's portrayal of David. Yet the Chronicler does not hesitate to show David's dark side. In fact, the Chronicler rather downplays David a bit in order to elevate Solomon.

This section can be divided into three subsections. It is structured by the repetition of the temporal indication "in the course of time," which occurs in 18:1; 19:1; and 20:4. First Chronicles 18 (∥ 2 Sam. 8) contains narratives of battles against a whole variety of neighboring nations, as well as indications of booty taken from them. First Chronicles 19:1–20:3 (∥ 2 Sam. 10; 11:1; 12:29–31) focuses on the Ammonite war, while 1 Chronicles 20:4–8 (∥ 2 Sam. 21:18–22) narrates some battles against the Philistines. Since the first subsection starts with victories over the Philistines (18:1) and the last subsection (20:4–8) also deals with the Philistines, the war narratives are enclosed by these accounts. This observation is strengthened by the same verb, "to subdue," being used in both 18:1 (taken from the source text) and 20:4 (introduced by the

Chronicler). The only other place where this verb occurs is in 17:10 (also introduced by the Chronicler).

18:1–17 / This chapter provides an overview of battles fought in all directions: against the **Philistines** (18:1; to the west), **Moabites** (18:2; to the east), **Hadadezer** and the **Arameans** (18:3–8; to the north and northeast), and **Edomites** (18:12–13; to the southeast). This military itinerary reminds one of the presentation of all the tribes of Israel in 1 Chronicles 1–9 but also of the indication in 1 Chronicles 13:5 that "David assembled all the Israelites, from the Shihor River in Egypt to Lebo Hamath," for the transfer of the ark to Jerusalem. The Chronicler's attempt to present an inclusive definition of All-Israel probably determined this geographical description. In 1 Chronicles 21 (David's census) we will come to yet another interesting example in this regard.

The selection of nations presented in the battle accounts of 1 Chronicles 18 may also have been determined by the imperial provincial geography during the Chronicler's time. During the Persian era, Philistia to the west, Moab to the east, Damascus to the far north, and Idumea to the south were influential provincial areas. Apart from this narrative intending to show how Yahweh's promise has been fulfilled, it might also have been an attempt to differentiate Yehud from its neighbors.

First Chronicles 18:2 shows an interesting example of the Chronicler's omission. Whereas the source text in 2 Samuel 8:2 tells of David's very ruthless killing of some "Moabites," the Chronicler mentions only that **they became subject to him and brought tribute.** The reason for the omission remains a mystery, but one may assume that once again this information did not fit the Chronicler's purpose. His aim was to present a quick overview of victories and not to go into detail.

First Chronicles 18:3–6 narrates the campaigns in the far north and northeast; 18:7–8 gives an account of the booty taken from Hadadezer and his men; 18:9–11 recounts the friendly approach by **Tou king of Hamath,** who brought David **all kinds of articles of gold and silver and bronze;** and 18:12–13 reports on the victories over the Edomites.

First Chronicles 18:14–17 stands somewhat outside the line of the battle narratives, although these verses were taken over from the source text in 2 Samuel 8:15–18. The subsection provides a very brief overview of the main officials of David's administration. Six offices are mentioned, namely, military commander (**Joab**), recorder (**Jehoshaphat**), priests (**Zadok and Ahimelech**), secretary (**Shavsha**), commander of David's elite troops **the Kerethites and Pelethites (Benaiah),** and **chief officials at the king's side (David's sons).**

19:1–20:3 / A new subsection is opened with the temporal indication **in the course of time** (19:1). The topic of the next verses is the battle against, and the defeat of, the **Ammonites**, who fought in coalition with the **Arameans.** The war is sparked off by a misunderstanding by **the Ammonite nobles** of the **delegation** David sent to the new Ammonite king, **Hanun,** after the latter's father died. David wanted **to express** his **sympathy** in order to return in this way the **kindness** the deceased king had shown to him. The "nobles" interpret the visit of the delegation as an attempt to **spy out the country and overthrow it.** The delegation is therefore **greatly humiliated** by Hanun's shaving them and cutting **off their garments in the middle at the buttocks.** The Chronicler's version differs slightly from the source text in 2 Samuel 10:1–5 insofar as it mentions "shaving" in general instead of the source text's version of "shav[ing] off half of each man's beard." The change was probably meant to exaggerate the humiliation, since shaving of the beard was not permitted to Israelites (as reflected in the priestly legal tradition in Lev. 19:27).

First Chronicles 19:6–9 reports that the Ammonites approached the Arameans to hire **chariots and charioteers** from them for the battle against David. The Chronicler's text (19:6–7) shows some additions to the text in 2 Samuel 10:6, indicating that a large sum of **a thousand talents of silver** was offered for the Arameans' military assistance. Some other additional information is also provided. Although some of these differences may be attributed to a different Hebrew source text than the one we have in the Masoretic Text, the more elaborate description of the enemy's frantic preparations gives prominence to David's military stature.

First Chronicles 19:10–15 narrates the preparations that were made on Israel's side. **Joab,** who was indicated in 18:15 as the military commander, prepares two military units, the one under his own command that was supposed to fight against the Arameans and the other under the command of **Abishai** to fight the Ammonites. The two units would provide cover for one another. Joab encourages the troops with the following words (which were taken over from the source text): **Be strong and let us fight bravely. . . . The L**ORD **will do what is good in his sight.** This fits in well with the Chronicler's emphasis on Yahweh fighting the wars for David in order to prepare the dispensation of rest under Solomon. In 19:14–15 it is reported that both the Arameans and the Ammonites fled even before the troops engaged in any fight. After that **Joab went back to Jerusalem.**

In 19:16–19 we hear that the Arameans regrouped in order to attack David's army again. First Chronicles 19:17 states that **when David was told of this, he gathered all Israel** and took the initiative to form **battle**

lines opposite the Arameans. The Masoretic Text of 2 Samuel 10:17 puts it slightly differently and gives the initiative to the Arameans. (This difference between the two versions is probably due to the Chronicler making use of another Hebrew text here.) David and his army won the battle decisively, so much so that the Arameans **made peace with David and became subject to him.** They even withdrew their support for the Ammonites.

With the Arameans already subjugated and with the Ammonites now without their coalition partner, it would not take long for David to also achieve military success against the latter. The Chronicler follows his source text's narrative line in 2 Samuel 11:1 when he continues his version in 1 Chronicles 20:1, but then skips over the greatest part of 2 Samuel 11–12, only to link up with the text again in 2 Samuel 12:29. First Chronicles 20:1 is therefore a merged version of 2 Samuel 11:1 and 12:29. This creates a logical contradiction in the text, however, because David is indicated to have remained in Jerusalem (according to 1 Chron. 20:1) but is then involved in the battle in the next verse. These verses report the final battle against the Ammonites, in which David not only won political control over them (with David putting the king's **crown** on his own head) but also **took a great quantity of plunder from the city.** Afterward, **David and his entire army returned to Jerusalem,** the center that gained still further control over the nations by means of this war.

20:4–8 / With the third use of the structuring element **in the course of time** the Chronicler returns to the battles against the Philistines. He takes his material from 2 Samuel 21:18–22 and, with minor differences in detail, presents his source text's version of some further individual combats that took place against the Philistines. Like in the narrative of David and Goliath in 1 Samuel 17 (which is not included in the Chronicler's narrative), this subsection (1 Chron. 20:6–7) again associates the Philistines with a gigantic figure.

This section (18:1–20:8) features the many wars and battles conducted by David. The materials that were taken over (with minor changes) from the source texts in 2 Samuel each time report on the successful outcome of all these wars for David. This section fits well not only into the Chronicler's construction of showing how Yahweh prepared the way for the full establishment of David's kingdom under Solomon, but also into his theological concept of Yahweh taking the initiative in these battles. The reader gets the impression from these battle accounts that they are probably programmatic in the sense that they reflect something of Israel's self-understanding in the Chronicler's time, rather than being historical accounts of real events. The point the Chronicler wants to drive home here is that All-Israel can count on Yahweh's guidance and protection and that their Davidic royal tradition of the past derived from Yahweh's providence. The reference to the past traditions created hope for the future.

Additional Notes §2.5

18:4 / Although the NIV does not reflect the difference, the indication in Chronicles of David capturing **a thousand of his chariots, seven thousand charioteers and twenty thousand foot soldiers** is somewhat different in the source text in 2 Sam. 8:4. There it says that David captured 1,700 charioteers, without any mention of the number of chariots he captured. Since we know from textual finds at Qumran, as well as from the Septuagint text of 2 Sam. 8, that another Hebrew text than the Masoretic Text must have been in existence at the time, we may assume that the numbers were not altered by the Chronicler but that he probably had another Hebrew text available (see Dirksen, *1 Chronicles*, p. 243). The NIV therefore followed the alternative reading in its translation of 2 Sam. 8:4.

18:8 / In this verse the Chronicler made use of 2 Sam. 8:8. However, the following words are added in the Chronicler's version: **which Solomon used to make the bronze Sea, the pillars and various bronze articles.** This information reflects a later era when the temple had already been built and furnished with all kinds of cultic-symbolic objects. Since these words do not occur in the Hebrew source text, some scholars conclude that they must be from the Chronicler's hand. However, the Septuagint, the Old Latin version, and Josephus all contain this indication. This therefore confirms that the Chronicler must have had another source text available in addition to the Masoretic Text and that these words are not his original statements (see Klein, *1 Chronicles*, p. 394).

18:12 / It remains unclear who led the battle against the **Edomites.** Whereas 2 Sam. 8:13 credits David, the Chronicler gives the glory to **Abishai son of Zeruiah.** The reason for the difference remains a mystery. We do know, however, that Zeruiah was David's sister and that Abishai was therefore his nephew.

18:17 / The Hebrew source text in 2 Sam. 8:18 calls David's sons "priests," while the Chronicler terms them **chief officials.** Some scholars argue that the Chronicler made the change since it would have been inappropriate for the king's sons to act as priests.

19:18 / The Masoretic Text of 2 Sam. 10:18 has "seven hundred" charioteers killed by David, but 1 Chron. 19:18 mentions **seven thousand.** The difference might be the result of a scribal error. The high numbers here and elsewhere (18:4–5) were probably used as a literary device to emphasize the comprehensiveness of David's military successes.

20:3 / The Masoretic Text of 2 Sam. 12:31 indicates that David's men consigned the Ammonites "to labor with saws and with iron picks and axes," but the MT of 1 Chron. 20:3 has the Ammonites "hacked to pieces" with those same tools (unlike NIV, which does not follow the Masoretic Text of 1 Chron. 20:3 but rather that of 2 Sam. 12:31). The difference between these two readings is just one letter of the verb! The Chronicler's version is either the original one or a scribal error.

§2.6 A Place for the Temple (1 Chron. 21:1–22:1)

We have seen thus far that the ark of the covenant was brought to Jerusalem (1 Chron. 13–16); that Yahweh denied David's request to build a "house" for him but made him an eternal promise that he, Yahweh, would build a "house" for David (1 Chron. 17); and that Yahweh subjugated the neighboring nations to David's rule through a series of wars (1 Chron. 18–20). Through all these narratives two important theological themes emerge: (1) the initiative to establish All-Israel as well as its cult center in Jerusalem could come only from Yahweh and not human effort; and (2) the eternal promise to David's house, the promise of "rest," would materialize only under Solomon's reign. In 1 Chronicles 21 the Chronicler made extensive use of 2 Samuel 24, but he altered some words and sentences, omitted some information, and added other information. There are also numerous instances where it is clear that the Chronicler worked from another Hebrew text than the one preserved in the Masoretic Text of 2 Samuel 24.

21:1–7 / First Chronicles 21:1 shows an interesting departure from the source text in 2 Samuel 24:1. The latter says that "the anger of the LORD burned against Israel, and he [i.e., the LORD] incited David against them" to take a census. The Chronicler makes **Satan** the instigator of the census, probably because of the theological difficulty in the source text. If Yahweh instigated the census, it remains theologically problematic that Yahweh would then punish this transgression. The Chronicler solved the problem by making Satan the instigator, while Yahweh is still the one exercising the punishment.

Also, the Chronicler omitted 2 Samuel 24:5–8a, which indicates the route that Joab and the military leaders took when conducting the census. They first crossed the Jordan into the Transjordan and from there proceeded along a counterclockwise route, returning to Jerusalem once they had finished. The Chronicler abbreviates this description in 1 Chronicles 21:4 by stating that **Joab left and went throughout Israel and then came back to Jerusalem.** The text in 2 Samuel additionally indicates how long the census took, information that is also omitted in

Chronicles. It should be noted that the whole of the area described in 2 Samuel 24 is indicated by the Chronicler to be *kol-yisra'el* (**all Israel**). This term, which occurs so frequently in the Chronicler's own textual material, is a prominent reflection of the self-definition that the Chronicler wanted to attribute to the returned community in Yehud after the exile. The use of this term should therefore not be seen merely as an abbreviation of the Deuteronomistic version; it in itself has significance within the broader scope of Chronicles. Although the detailed itinerary is omitted by the Chronicler, it is still indicated in 21:2 that the census was taken from the south (**Beersheba**) to the north (**Dan**). Interestingly enough, the direction is the reverse of 2 Samuel 24:2, which has "from Dan to Beersheba," probably reflecting the Chronicler's southern perspective.

Unlike the previous verses, in 1 Chronicles 21:6–7 the Chronicler added some information not present in 2 Samuel 24, the much-discussed addition that **Joab did not include Levi and Benjamin in the numbering, because the king's command was repulsive to him. This command was also evil in the sight of God; so he punished Israel.** The omission of Levi may be due to the priestly regulation in Numbers 1:47–49 and 2:33 that the Levites were not to be counted together with the other Israelites. One can only speculate on the reason for Benjamin's omission. It may somehow relate to Gibeon—and probably Jerusalem—being in Benjaminite tribal territory.

21:8–14 / This subsection was taken over with minor changes from 2 Samuel 24:10–15. In some cases the information of the source text was summarized in a shorter version. First Chronicles 21:8 contains David's remarkable confession of guilt: **I have sinned greatly by doing this.... I have done a very foolish thing.** Within the context of the previous chapters (1 Chron. 13–20) this sinful act of David's census should be interpreted as another example of human hubris. After the military successes in which Yahweh delivered victory to David and his men, David wanted to give an account again of his own sphere of influence. Neither the omission of Levi and Benjamin from the census nor the census in itself is sinful. The census is rather an expression again (analogous to Uzzah's touching the ark en route to Jerusalem) of David's own attempt to establish his "house." But David realizes his sinful act and confesses his guilt before Yahweh. In a divine oracle through the **seer Gad** the Lord gives David three options for his punishment. David chooses to **fall into the hands of the Lord, for his mercy is very great,** rather than **into the hands of men.** Therefore, **the Lord sent a plague on Israel, and seventy**

thousand men of Israel ("from Dan to Beersheba" in 2 Sam. 24:15) fell dead. David's attempt to establish his own power has a direct impact on Israel.

21:15–27 / The scene now zooms in on Jerusalem because God sent an angel to destroy the city. David's observation that Yahweh is a God of mercy is then confirmed when Yahweh withholds the destruction at the last moment. In 21:15 the Chronicler's addition (but as the angel was doing so, the LORD saw it) emphasizes the compassion of God for the city. Yahweh stopped the angel from destroying the city precisely when the angel of the LORD was . . . standing at the threshing floor of Araunah the Jebusite. This remark introduces the specific location of the threshing floor that will play an important role later. The whole of 21:16 (which is an addition to the source text in 2 Sam. 24) makes the impending destruction even more dramatic: David looked up and saw the angel of the LORD standing between heaven and earth, with a drawn sword in his hand extended over Jerusalem. Then David and the elders, clothed in sackcloth, fell facedown. David's renewed petition to God (in 1 Chron. 21:17, which is a heavily adapted form of the source text in 2 Sam. 24:17) shows that David takes responsibility for the wrongdoing of the census. He therefore asks, O LORD my God, let your hand fall upon me and my family ("my house"), but do not let this plague remain on your people. He realizes that this incident has implications for Yahweh's eternal promise to "his house."

Without any direct response from Yahweh, 21:18 relieves the tension by indicating that the impending destruction has been withdrawn. Instead of destroying the city with his sword, the angel of the LORD ordered Gad to tell David to go up and build an altar. Differently from the source text in 2 Samuel 24:18, the Chronicler here again involves "the angel of the LORD." By now the reader knows that "the angel" is the representative of Yahweh himself. The significance of the threshing floor of Araunah the Jebusite now becomes apparent. "The angel" ordered David to go up and build an altar to the LORD on the threshing floor of Araunah the Jebusite. David immediately obeyed the word that Gad had spoken in the name of the LORD.

In 1 Chronicles 21:20 the Chronicler provides a short interlude, which is not present in the source text of 2 Samuel 24: While Araunah was threshing wheat, he turned and saw the angel; his four sons who were with him hid themselves. If this verse indeed is part of the Chronicler's own material (see Additional Note on 21:20), one may assume that he wanted to provide an explanation for Araunah's very gracious act later in the narrative, when he offers his threshing floor to David for free. Because Araunah then knew that David's request to have the threshing floor was related to divine activity, he was more magnanimous in the financial transaction.

The actual transaction is then narrated in 21:21–25 (‖ 2 Sam. 24:20–24). However, the attentive reader will notice some subtle differences between the Chronicler's version and the source text. Since, according to the Chronicler's presentation, Araunah already knew about the divine intervention, Araunah's question in 2 Samuel 24:21, "Why has my lord the king come to his servant?" is omitted. David instead makes his intentions clear immediately: **Let me have the site of your threshing floor so I can build an altar to the Lord.** He also mentions that he wants to buy it **at the full price.** The latter expression is again the Chronicler's addition to the text. In the further deliberations Araunah first offers the site to David for free, but David insists on paying "the full price." In the end **David paid Araunah six hundred shekels of gold for the site** (compared to "David bought the threshing floor and the oxen and paid fifty shekels of silver for them" in 2 Sam. 24:24). The huge difference in price indicates that the Chronicler wanted to ensure that David's conduct would come across as being without any blemish. After the Uzzah incident (1 Chron. 13), as well as after the census and the consequential punishment, David knows well that right conduct and reverence are necessary when Yahweh's presence is at stake. The transaction entailed in acquiring the threshing floor that would become a cultic site had to reflect David's piety and reverence. In this way the Chronicler's contemporary audience received confirmation of the legitimacy of their own cultic site, which was the same site that David bought.

First Chronicles 21:26–27 again contains extensive reworking of the source material (in 2 Sam. 24:25) to reflect the Chronicler's theological intentions. First Chronicles 21:26 reports that **David built an altar to the Lord there.** After he **called on the Lord** (which is not mentioned in the source text), **the Lord answered him with fire from heaven on the altar of burnt offering.** With the addition of "fire from heaven" to his source material, the Chronicler turns this event into a theophany (i.e., an appearance of God). We know from many other Old Testament passages (e.g., Moses at the burning bush, the revelation of the Torah at Sinai) that the appearance of Yahweh was often accompanied by fire in some form. By recounting the event in this way the Chronicler emphasizes the cultic importance of what was happening here. Whereas the source text mentions that "the Lord answered prayer on behalf of the land, and the plague on Israel was stopped" (2 Sam. 24:25), the Chronicler's version is again more dramatic and visual, with **the LORD speaking to the angel, and the angel putting his sword back in its sheath.** That the punishment for David's census was countermanded forms the climax of the source text's version. However, the Chronicler's version continues in order to drive another important point home.

21:28–22:1 / These verses are without parallel in the source text of 2 Samuel 24. The Chronicler (see Additional Note) indicates that after the dramatic event at Araunah's threshing floor (which is indicated with the temporal expression in 21:28, **at that time**), David continued to offer **sacrifices there.** With another temporal indication in 21:29, **at that time,** the Chronicler achieves a contrast between the sanctuary that was at Gibeon and the newly established altar on the Jebusite threshing floor. The Chronicler provides the background to his statement in this verse when he indicates that **the tabernacle of the LORD, which Moses had made in the desert, and the altar of burnt offering were at that time on the high place at Gibeon.** The Chronicler expresses no negative sentiment toward the sanctuary in Gibeon but rather indicates that, **because he was afraid of the sword of the angel of the LORD,** David was prevented from going to Gibeon to worship there. This then leads to David's programmatic statement: **The house of the LORD God is to be here, and also the altar of burnt offering for Israel.**

In the Chronicler's modification of the census and cultic site narratives, it seems that he tried to achieve three purposes. First, the writer modifies the story to become an All-Israel narrative. He ties the census to the genealogical construction in 1 Chronicles 1–9, which is clearly a perspective from the context of the Persian period. The Persian-period definition of All-Israel in this way includes the time of David's kingship, even if it is through a negative episode of the census.

Second, the Chronicler's exclusion of Levi and Benjamin from the census serves the purpose of protecting Jerusalem—as common denominator between these tribes—to ensure that it retains the moral high ground as cultic center. In this strategy Benjamin is thus closely connected to Jerusalem.

Third, and closely related to the second point, the Chronicler wanted to claim a special position for Jerusalem in contrast to the Benjaminite sphere of influence, emphasizing that this is the right place for bringing sacrifices to God, in contradistinction to Gibeon, where the tabernacle was kept at that stage. By claiming that this exact site is the place where the sanctuary should be built, the Chronicler establishes neutral terrain for the temple site. Jebus now becomes the Chronicler's trump card against any Benjaminite claim of authority.

The reader may be surprised to hear again that these all-too-human ideologies determined the Chronicler's reconstruction of the past. Yet it is worth being reminded that one of the prominent theological features in Chronicles is that Yahweh's presence among and guidance of his people is acted out in the realm of human history.

Additional Notes §2.6

21:1–22:1 / At this stage the reader should be reminded of the earlier discussion of Benjamin in 1 Chron. 10. During the exile the Benjaminite territory was less affected by the destruction, and Mizpah (as administrative center) and Gibeon (as cultic center) gained significant influence. After the exile, when Jerusalem was reestablished as political and cultic center, some rivalry arose between Jerusalem and these Benjaminite towns. The Chronicler's version of the census narrative and the narrative about the acquisition of the Jebusite threshing floor might indicate the Chronicler's active participation in the discourse about Judah and Benjamin.

21:1 / The occurrence of **Satan** in this verse might be an indication that the personification of evil had already started during the time of the Chronicler, a trend that is also visible in late literature such as Job 1. Whereas supernatural dualism was not customary in earlier forms of Israel's belief systems (with good and bad being attributed to Yahweh), this tendency started developing in the late postexilic period, probably under the influence of Persian Zoroastrian dualism. We know from the Christian writings in the New Testament that the personification of evil was adopted in Christianity and was already well established during the time when the New Testament writings developed. For further discussion on the development of the understanding of Satan, see C. Breytenbach and P. L. Day, "Satan," in *Dictionary of Deities and Demons in the Bible* (ed. K. van der Toorn et al.; 2nd ed.; Leiden: Brill, 1999), pp. 726–32.

21:6–7 / Japhet sees the connection with Jerusalem as the common denominator between Levi and Benjamin in the Chronicler's omission of both from the census. She argues that the guilt upon Israel caused by the census justified God's punishment, but the omission of Levi (with its cultic relationship to Jerusalem) and Benjamin (with its geographical relationship) also warranted the exclusion of Jerusalem from this guilt (*I and II Chronicles* [London: SCM, 1993], p. 378).

21:15 / Although the NIV refers to **Araunah the Jebusite**, the Hebrew text has "Ornan the Jebusite." The name Araunah, which is spelled similarly to

Ornan in Hebrew (which originally had only consonants and no vowels), is used in the source text in 2 Sam. 24. The NIV translators therefore chose to keep that form in order to avoid any confusion.

21:20 / The introduction of **the angel** here complicates the flow of the narrative compared to the source text in 2 Sam. 24. There the events follow logically from David receiving the command to "go up and build an altar" on Araunah's threshing floor to Araunah seeing "the king and his men" coming and his bowing before David. The Hebrew words for "king" and "angel" differ by only one letter, so the introduction of the angel may go back to a scribal error in the textual transmission process.

21:28–22:1 / These verses are the last addition in this chapter. The main point of contention here is whether the whole section should be seen as an addition by the Chronicler or whether part of it should be attributed to later interpolators. Japhet provides a lengthy discussion of the issue in her commentary. According to her, "there is therefore no doubt that vv. 28–30 constitute a self-contained passage which can be interpreted in one of two ways: as a parenthetical element in the Chronistic composition itself . . . , or as a later interpolation" (*I and II Chronicles*, pp. 388–89). She sees 22:1 as the narrative sequel to 21:26–27 and therefore treats 21:28–30 as a separate unit. Both Dirksen (*1 Chronicles*, p. 263) and Klein (*1 Chronicles*, p. 429) opt for the first probability, but Knoppers (*1 Chronicles 10–29*, p. 760) attributes 21:28–30 to a later scribe who wanted to explain why David did not bring sacrifices to Gibeon, where the tabernacle altar was. All these commentators are, however, in agreement that 22:1 belongs to the Chronicler's own material.

§2.7 David Orders Solomon to Build the Temple (1 Chron. 22:2–19)

The previous text (1 Chron. 21:1–22:1) dealt with an important nexus in the Chronicler's construction of his narrative. Before the identification of the Jebusite threshing floor as site for the future temple, the most prominent aspect of the narrative was the history of David. We saw how Yahweh transferred the kingship from Saul to David (1 Chron. 10). We journeyed with David through the first, unsuccessful attempt to bring the ark of the covenant to Jerusalem (1 Chron. 13), and we witnessed how the Levites carried the ark from Kiriath Jearim to the City of David (1 Chron. 15–16). We heard the eternal promise spoken by Yahweh to David's "house" through the oracle of Nathan (1 Chron. 17), and we noted how David and his men subjugated the surrounding nations to Jerusalem (1 Chron. 18–20). And then (at the end of the previous pericope) the Chronicler let us stand in awe as "fire from heaven" indicated the site where the temple for Yahweh would be built.

The time was ripe for the central sanctuary in Jerusalem to be built. But the Chronicler's construction made it clear to the reader that David would not build the temple. Yahweh appointed David's son Solomon to perform this task. With the identification of the future temple site, the reader thus comes to the nexus between David's reign and that of Solomon. From this point on the transition to Solomon's reign is described.

From the beginning of 22:2 until the end of 1 Chronicles, the Chronicler no longer depended on canonical source materials. The description of the transfer of power from David to Solomon is therefore the Chronicler's own creation, probably following another biblical example to compose this part of his history. The transition of the leadership from Moses to Joshua described in Deuteronomy 31 and Joshua 1 probably served as the model for the Chronicler. Ironically enough, the Chronicler did not make use of the materials in 2 Samuel 23:1–7 and 1 Kings 2:1–9, which also deal with the transition from David to Solomon, probably because these materials did not fit the Chronicler's agenda.

The present text immediately starts with David preparing the labor force and the materials for the construction of the temple (22:2–4). This is followed by a speech in which he addresses his son Solomon (22:5–16) and the leaders of the people (22:17–19) in connection with building the temple.

22:2–4 / This section starts with David giving **orders to assemble the aliens living in Israel** in order to employ them in the temple-building activities, specifically **stonecutters to prepare dressed stone.** The Hebrew term used for "aliens" (*gerim*) occurs frequently in the legal material of the Old Testament and normally denotes people of non-Israelite origin who have settled among the people of Israel and have adopted their religion. This category of people remained without legal rights in society, however. Many legal stipulations in the Pentateuch therefore give them protection together with widows and orphans. Klein is of the opinion that the Chronicler's involvement of "aliens" in the temple-building process is an attempt to show "that only non-Israelites served as forced laborers" (*1 Chronicles*, p. 432), information that could have been significant for the Chronicler's contemporaries who served the Persian Empire. These "aliens" had the task of constructing **the house of God.**

The splendor of the future temple is preempted by description of the exuberant quantities of building materials in 22:3–4. Mention of **the Sidonians and Tyrians** in 22:4 reminds one of the earlier episode (1 Chron. 14) when "Hiram the king of Tyre" also provided cedar logs for building David's "house." These Phoenician craftsmen were well known for their expertise in transporting and cutting timber, and the Lebanon mountains were the prime area for growing cedar trees.

22:5–16 / First Chronicles 22:5 contains David's introduction to the personal communication with his son Solomon, which will follow in direct speech from 22:7. Because **the house . . . should be of great magnificence and fame and splendor in the sight of all the nations,** David announces that he **will make preparations for it.** The Chronicler's psalm in 1 Chronicles 16 stressed that All-Israel should proclaim the greatness of Yahweh "among the nations," and 22:5, too, says that the temple should be a place that will be recognized and revered by "the nations." This statement might well be the Chronicler's subtle way of promoting the cultic center in Jerusalem in his own time within the Persian imperial context. "The nations" might be a reference here not only to the neighboring nations but also to the entire Persian Empire.

David then **called for his son Solomon and charged him to build a house for the LORD, the God of Israel.** He addresses his son in a speech reported in 22:7–16. David's speech starts with the background to this momentous occasion. He tells his son that it had been his intention **to build a house for the Name of the** Lord **his God.** But Yahweh prevented it. Interestingly enough, the Lord's words to David are then also included in the first person as direct speech (22:8–10). Although these words are not directly quoted from the Nathan oracle (see 1 Chron. 17), the Chronicler certainly intended them as a report of Yahweh's response. The reference to **he will be my son, and I will be his father,** in which Yahweh (also in first-person direct speech) adopts the king, confirms this impression.

In Yahweh's direct speech reported in 22:8–10 we come to one of the central themes in the Chronicler's theology, namely, **peace and rest.** We have already seen how this theme functioned in the account of David's reign. Here, the transition to Solomon's reign is made explicit. Solomon is called **a man of peace and rest,** and Yahweh promises that he **will give him rest from all his enemies on every side.** Earlier discussions (see commentary on 17:1–2) showed that the Chronicler avoided this expression in describing David's reign. The "rest from all his enemies on every side" was reserved for David's son Solomon, the "man of peace and rest."

It is clear that the Chronicler intended a pun on the name of David's son (*Shelomoh*) and peace (*shalom*). This is unique in the Hebrew Bible, since the association of a name with "peace" occurs nowhere else in the Old Testament. The Chronicler's unique statement is that Solomon will be a king of peace who will have rest and quietness throughout his reign, since the Lord will grant him respite from his enemies. The peace, rest, and quietness (which all refer to a state of harmony, not only with the enemies, but also with Yahweh) stand in stark contrast to the "shedding of blood" and "waging of wars" of which David is again accused in 22:8. Although David prepares the way for the building of the temple, he is disqualified from executing the actual task, and it falls to Solomon, the "man of peace," to accomplish this.

The theme of rest, peace, and quietness is continued in David's speech to the leaders of Israel reported in 28:2–12. There the temple is called "a house of rest"—a deliberate attempt by the Chronicler to associate the "house of rest" with the "man of rest." Solomon's reign is presented to the audience of Chronicles as the kingpin around which the history of Israel revolved. Moreover, the temple as cultic institution is intricately interwoven into this portrayal of Solomon's kingship. Temple building under Solomon appears to be a central theme of the Chronicler's construction of history.

David's speech continues in 22:11–16 with the good wishes for his son Solomon. These wishes are now given in the light of what was said in 22:7–10. This is signified by the logical marker at the beginning of 22:11, now, my son, as well as the confirmation **the** L**ORD** **be with you.** David wishes for his son that **the** L**ORD** **give him discretion and understanding when he puts** him **in command over Israel.** This theme will be taken up again in 2 Chronicles 1–9, which recounts the excellence of Solomon. The "discretion and understanding" should lead Solomon to **keep the law of the** L**ORD** **his God.** If he will **observe the decrees and laws that the** L**ORD** **gave Moses for Israel, he will have success.** The theme of seeking Yahweh through obedience to his law, which was already present in the earlier parts of the David narrative, now becomes prominent. This will also serve as a leading theme in the narration about the Judahite kings in 2 Chronicles 10–36. David's speech to his son concludes in 1 Chronicles 22:14–16 with a confirmation of all the preparations that David has already done. Again, the exaggeration of quantities and types of materials increases the reader's expectations of the future temple's grandeur.

22:17–19 / In this subsection David addresses **all the leaders of Israel** to request their help for **his son Solomon.** Again, the speech is pregnant with theological terminology. David starts with two rhetorical questions: **Is not the** L**ORD** **your God with you? And has he not granted you rest on every side?** In the Bible such questions are in reality affirmations. Clearly, the Chronicler wanted to portray the "leaders of Israel" as grasping the theological significance of what was happening here. This speech follows the same structure as the previous speech to Solomon. It starts with a confirmation of God's presence and control, and continues (**now . . .**) to encourage these leaders for the work ahead. They should, however, **devote** their **heart and soul to seeking the** L**ORD** **their God.** Also those who will work on the temple construction should adhere to the requirements of "seeking the L**ORD**."

Additional Notes §2.7

22:2 / The Hebrew phrase **the house of God** (*beyt ha'elohim*) occurs almost exclusively in postexilic biblical texts. It occurs once in Judges, once in Ecclesiastes, and once in Daniel, but eighteen times in Ezra-Nehemiah and thirty-four times in Chronicles. The occurrence here in 22:2 is the first use of the phrase in the narrative part of Chronicles (excluding the genealogies in 1 Chron. 1–9, where it also occurs five times in connection with Levitical service). This signals the start of the era of the temple, here called "the house of God." Remarkably, the last occurrence of the phrase is in 2 Chron. 36:19, which reports that the

Babylonians burned "the house of God" and broke down the wall of Jerusalem. From then on Israel would enter a templeless age, until they returned from exile and could restore the temple in Jerusalem. The Chronicler is, of course, writing in the time of this Second Temple.

22:5 / Most commentaries include 22:5 in the previous subsection (22:2–4), but I see this verse, rather, as the introduction to David's direct speech in the following verses. The last phrase in 22:5, **so David made extensive preparations before his death,** does not mark the closure of the preceding section but is rather a proleptic summary of what follows.

22:9 / Various studies show that the theme of rest, peace, and quietness is not only characteristic of the Chronicler's version of Solomon's history but also forms a golden thread running throughout the books of Chronicles. Terminological patterns in Chronicles confirm (1) that Solomon's reign is seen as a paradigm of the rest, peace, and quietness that Yahweh gives to Israel; and (2) that this rest, peace, and quietness was not something achievable by military means but was only the result of the Judahite king seeking Yahweh and relying on him. The distribution of key terms shows that 1 Chron. 22:2–19 is a key pericope that is paradigmatic in the Chronicler's overall theological construction. The theme of peace, rest, and quietness that starts here forms the golden thread throughout the Chronicler's narratives about the "good" kings.

§2.8 David Organizes the Cultic and Secular Officials (1 Chron. 23:1–27:34)

According to 1 Chronicles 10–22, David prepared everything for the building of the temple, including full instructions to his son Solomon. First Chronicles 23–27 now describes the division of the Levites for various kinds of service and gives an elaborate and intricate overview of how the cultic service was organized in Jerusalem.

The short, opening comment that David made Solomon king serves as the bridge between David's and Solomon's reigns. From 23:2 onward we find the extensive description of the organization of cultic officials, starting with the indication that David gathered (Hebrew *'asaf*) all the officials for the occasion. Since 28:1 contains a similar comment on David gathering the leaders, but with another Hebrew word (*qahal*), one may assume that a new section starts there.

It may help the reader of this intricate part of the text to know that the term "Levites" is used here (as in some other sections) in two different senses. In some contexts the term refers to those people who belonged to the Levite tribe; I will call this the generic use. The term refers in other instances to a special group of (generic) Levites who served alongside the Aaronites in the temple service; I will call them the cultic Levites. The table on the following page provides an overview.

Since this section utilizes the list genre extensively, there is not much of a narrative line here. *Wayyiqtol* forms of the verb (customary in Hebrew narratives) are sparsely distributed throughout these chapters. David, being the subject of some of the key verbs, is indicated as being the main figure in the narrative line. He makes Solomon, his son, king over Israel (23:1); he assembles the commanders, priests, and Levites (23:2); and he organizes them into divisions according to the sons of Levi (23:6). David is also the one organizing them in their appointed duties (24:3); he sets apart the sons of Asaph, Heman, and Jeduthun for special service (25:1); and he appoints officials (26:32). In concluding these lists (27:23) the Chronicler makes the point that David did not count those below twenty years of age, for "the LORD had promised to make Israel as numerous as the stars in the sky."

Generic Levites
•general introduction (23:3–5)—38,000 total
•in continuity with ancestral past
•introduction according to families (23:6–24, 27)
•Davidic kingship forms basis for division

Aaronites (associated with cultic Levites)	Rest of Generic Levites
•division on authority of David (plus Zadok and Ahimelech)	•division on authority of David (plus Zadok and Ahimelech)
•functions of Aaronites (24:1–19)	•overview (24:2–31)
•functions of (cultic) Levites (23:25–26, 28–32)—24,000 total (see 23:2–5)	•musicians (25:1–31)—4,000 (see 23:2–5)
•duties assigned by Yahweh	•gatekeepers (26:1–19)—4,000 (see 23:3–5)
	•other officials—6,000 (see 23:3–5)
	treasurers (26:20–32)
	commanders (27:1–15)
	officers (27:16–22)
	interlude (27:23–24)
	storehouse keepers (27:25)
	farm workers (27:26–31)
	counselors (27:32–34a)
	commander (27:34b)

23:1 / The opening clause **when David was old and full of years** indicates that the end of David's reign is near. David now makes **his son Solomon king over Israel.** Although the information in this verse is not a direct quotation, the Chronicler probably meant to summarize the information in 1 Kings 1, which also starts with an indication that the king had become "old and advanced in years" (1 Kgs. 1:1) and—after an elaborate narrative containing Adonijah's attempted coup—that David made Solomon king. The present abbreviation of that story prepares the way for the occasion narrated in 1 Chronicles 29:22, where the assembly of Israel confirms Solomon's kingship without any indication of opposition.

23:2 / David then **gathered together all the leaders of Israel, as well as the priests and Levites.** This comment serves as a general introduction to the sections on the assignment of functions to these leaders and clergy (23:3–27:34).

23:3–5 / It might seem strange that **the Levites thirty years old or more were counted,** since they (together with the Benjaminites) are explicitly excluded in the census of 1 Chronicles 21. The difference, however, is that there the census was undertaken for military purposes, while the counting described here was done in order to implement the division of assignments for the cultic service. The number indicated in 23:3, **thirty-eight thousand,** is the sum of all the different divisions indicated in the following verse. Commentators are in agreement that the number is probably exaggerated, indicating the great significance of the Levites instead of their actual number.

A summary of four groups is given in 23:4–5, namely, those who had **to supervise the work of the temple of the** LORD (24,000 total), **officials and judges** (6,000 total), **gatekeepers** (4,000 total), and those who were **to praise the** LORD **with the musical instruments** (4,000 total).

23:6–24 and 23:27 / The present subsection gives another description of the Levites, namely, from the perspective of the family divisions. First Chronicles 23:6 indicates that **David divided the Levites into groups corresponding to the sons of Levi: Gershon, Kohath and Merari.** This tripartite division of the Levites is already known from the genealogy in 1 Chronicles 6. The family line of Gershon is listed in 23:7–11, that of Kohath in 23:12–20, and the line of Merari in 23:21–23. First Chronicles 23:24 and 23:27 form a conclusion to the description in 23:7–23 of the Levites along family lines (see Additional Note on 23:27).

It is not clear how the family division relates to the division of functions mentioned in the immediately preceding verses. It seems that the Chronicler wanted the section on the family divisions to serve as confirmation that David's divisions were in strict continuity with tradition. Although it is quite obvious, one should not overlook that the description of these families in 23:6–24, 27 is not an indication of the divisions that David made—those divisions were inherited by tradition—but rather an indication of the genealogical norm that David used when organizing the Levites into divisions. By presenting the process in this way, the Chronicler portrayed David as acting in accordance with tradition. Moreover, the Levites are presented as being organized in accordance with tradition. This claim probably gave legitimacy to the clergy in the Chronicler's own days. The organized cult in the postexilic age is thereby portrayed as a continuation of the past and not as something new that developed during the Persian period.

23:25–26 and 23:28–32 / Up to this point references to the Levites were in the generic sense. In 23:25–32 (excluding 23:27; see Additional Note) it becomes clear, however, that a special group of Levites is now meant, namely, those who had a special position in the cultic service. Their functions are explicated in the only direct speech section in these chapters, the subsection under discussion here. David is the speaker.

First Chronicles 23:25–26 indicates that David announced a new dispensation for the cultic Levites: **The Levites no longer need to carry the tabernacle or any of the articles used in its service.** In the light of other references in Chronicles, the indication that the Levites had carried "the tabernacle" seems strange. We know from other sections in Chronicles that they used to carry the ark of the covenant, but not "the tabernacle." This confusion is probably witness to the composite character of the literature here, but it also reminds one of the information in Numbers 3:21–37 and 10:17, which note that Levite families had special duties regarding the tabernacle. The new dispensation for the Levites is motivated with reference to the **rest** that **the** Lord, **the God of Israel, has granted** to his people and to his having **come to dwell in Jerusalem forever.** The background to David's new dispensation is the planned temple building as well as the promise that Yahweh will grant rest to All-Israel through Solomon.

The new **duty of the Levites** is indicated as being **to help Aaron's descendants** (literally "at the hand of the Aaronites") **in the service of the temple of the** Lord. The expression explaining the relationship between the Levites and Aaronites is interpreted differently by various commentators (see Additional Note on 23:25–26 and 23:28–32). However, it seems that the Chronicler wanted to relate the Levites to the Aaronites. The distinction is one of function and not so much of status.

24:1–19 / It already became clear in the previous subsections that the two sons of Amram, namely Aaron and Moses, were considered very important. The following description of Aaron was given there (23:13): "Aaron was set apart, he and his descendants forever, to consecrate the most holy things, to offer sacrifices before the Lord, to minister before him and to pronounce blessings in his name forever." No other member of the Levite families is given such an elaborate description. This description made it clear that the Aaronites would form the cultic clergy.

The line of **Aaron** now becomes the focus of the present subsection (24:1–19). The division of the Aaronites for service is described in the following way: **David separated them into divisions for their appointed order of ministering.** David was assisted in this task by **Zadok a descendant of Eleazar** (one of Aaron's sons) **and Ahimelech a descendant of Ithamar** (another of Aaron's sons). As in the high priestly genealogies in 6:3–9 and 6:50–53, Zadok is connected to Eleazar. However, the connection between Ahimelech and the Aaronide line is problematic. According to 15:11, as well as 2 Samuel 15:35 and 17:15, the two priests serving under David were "Zadok and Abiathar" (not Ahimelech). It is only here that Ahimelech is connected to the Aaronide priesthood. Abiathar's association with Adonijah (according to 1 Kgs. 1) might have disqualified him in the Chronicler's eyes from being associated with the Aaronite priesthood, and he was then replaced with Ahimelech.

First Chronicles 24:5 furthermore indicates that they undertook the division **by drawing lots.** The suggestion here is that, although the king and priests performed the division, they were guided by Yahweh's will (reflected in the "lots").

The remark in 24:6 that **the scribe Shemaiah son of Nethanel, a Levite, recorded their names** indicates that some Levites performed scribal tasks; that a Levite recorded the names also underwrites the authenticity of the list presented here. We do not have any other information about Shemaiah.

The last verse of this subsection provides another legitimization for the twenty-four priestly duty groups described in the previous verses: all this happened **according to the regulations prescribed for them by their forefather Aaron, as the LORD, the God of Israel, had commanded them.** This remark indicates not only that the division of priestly courses is in line with that of their ancestor Aaron but also that it has divine sanction. This is probably a claim made from a later era when the priesthood was operative rather than a reflection of a system that might have been in operation during the monarchy.

24:20–31 / In 24:20 we now come to **the rest of the descendants of Levi.** This subsection is taken by some commentators to be a later insertion into the Chronicler's material. It is problematic in the sense that the descendants of **Kohath** and **Merari** are mentioned, but not of Gershom. In terms of the structure, I see this section as a general overview that introduces the second group of Levites (in the generic sense). The first group, the Aaronites and associated cultic Levites, was dealt with in the previous subsections. I treat the present subsection as the equivalent of the description of the Aaronites *cum* Levites (cultic) on the basis of the formulation in 24:31. The Hebrew phrase translated in the NIV as **they also,** as well as the indication **just as their brothers the descendants of Aaron did,** draws a syntactical parallel between the casting of the **lots** for the division of "the rest of the Levites" and the casting of lots for the Aaronites. The same procedure is followed here, that is, the lots were cast **in the presence of King David and of Zadok, Ahimelech, and the heads of families of the priests and of the Levites.** This group therefore enjoys the same legitimacy, although there is no indication here that the division was done with divine sanction (as described in 24:19 with reference to the Aaronites). In this way a contrast is created between the two groups.

25:1–31 / This subsection deals with the division of the musicians. It takes its structure from the three main figures associated with the musical ministry in the temple, namely, **Asaph, Heman,** and **Jeduthun** (see Additional Note). These three figures were already mentioned in the genealogy of 6:33–47, where they are traced back to the three sons of Levi: Gershon, Kohath, and Merari. It is strange that **the commanders of the army** assisted **David** in dividing the musicians. However, the term used in Hebrew may also be understood as "the officials of the liturgical host" (Klein, *1 Chronicles*, p. 479). The task of the musicians would be **the ministry of prophesying, accompanied by harps, lyres and cymbals.** It is not exactly clear what the relationship between the musical role and the prophetic role of these Levites was. Some argue that the uttering of prophecies was accompanied by music, while others hold that the music in itself had a prophetic function. Furthermore, the relationship between these cultic officials and the classical prophets (of whom we have numerous books included in the Old Testament) also remains a mystery. Did the cultic officials take over the role of the prophets in the time of the Chronicler? Or were they "cultic prophets" in contrast to "noncultic prophets"? These questions have attracted much scholarly debate, but a definitive answer will probably not be possible.

This subsection first offers name lists of the three singer families: the four sons of Asaph in 25:2, the six sons of Jeduthun in 25:3, and the fourteen sons of Heman in 25:4–6. Then, in 25:7–31, a description follows of the lot-casting ceremony by means of which the singers were divided into twenty-four teams. This part follows a fairly strict format. However, the order of the names mentioned here differs from that of the names mentioned in the first part (25:2–6). Some commentators attribute this to the random outcome of casting lots. Klein offers a more interesting and plausible logical explanation: "The redactor's strategy is apparently to select a son of Asaph and a son of Jeduthun until the sons of Asaph run out, and then select a son of Jeduthun and a son of Heman until the sons of Jeduthun run out. The final ten names are all sons of Heman" (*1 Chronicles*, p. 478).

26:1–19 / The **gatekeepers,** who are also part of "the rest of the Levites," are now presented. The same bipartite presentation as in the previous subsection is used: first, the genealogical list of the "gatekeepers" (26:1–11), and second, the different positions that were assigned to them (26:12–19). The position of **Obed-Edom** is uncertain, since it seems that 26:4–8 and probably also 26:12–18 were later insertions. Obed-Edom had been mentioned in earlier lists as a Levitical singer (15:21; 16:5) and as a gatekeeper (15:18, 24; 16:38). The insertions probably wanted to clarify the matter of Obed-Edom's association with the gatekeepers.

26:20–32 / This subsection deals with the **Levites who were in charge of the treasuries of the house of God and the treasuries for the dedicated things.** Whether these two types of "treasuries" reflect a historical reality during the reign of David, or any other historical period, is uncertain. First Chronicles 26:26–28 gives the reader an impression of the goods that were kept in the "treasuries." Many of these are indicated as **dedicated** gifts. The Hebrew word used here is similar to "holy" and refers to the practice of keeping certain objects (gifts or plunder from war) apart as dedication to Yahweh. First Chronicles 26:27 indicates that **some of the plunder** was used to **repair . . . the temple.** This remark probably reflects that this description is retrospective, since in the chronology of the narrative the temple had not been built yet. First Chronicles 26:28 mentions that some of the "dedicated" gifts kept in the "treasuries" came from **Samuel the seer, Saul son of Kish, Abner son of Ner and Joab son of Zeruiah.** This is the very last reference to Saul in Chronicles.

27:1–15 / First Chronicles 27:1 seems to introduce the lists in 27:2–15 as well as 27:16–22, although the reference to **month by month** duty applies only to the first list. First Chronicles 27:2–15 presents the **commanders** of the twelve monthly **army divisions** who **served the king.**

27:16–22 / First Chronicles 27:16–22 lists **the officers over the tribes of Israel.** Since the order of the tribes reflected in this list is not attested in any other biblical text, it remains uncertain whether it should be seen as historical. It creates the impression of a literary construction.

27:23–24 / These two verses are presented as a conclusion to the preceding lists. However, their contents make it clear that they were probably added at a later stage to provide a commentary on the counting of the Levites reflected in these chapters. The information contained in these verses reminds one of the census narrative presented in 1 Chronicles 21. First Chronicles 27:23–24 indicates that when **wrath came on Israel on account of this numbering, . . . the number was not entered in the book of the annals of King David.** In the Deuteronomistic tradition the first mention of the annals of a king appears in 1 Kings 11:41, which refers to "the book of the annals of Solomon." The present text, however, is the only place in the Old Testament that indicates that there was a "book of the annals of King David." This might therefore be a retrojection.

27:25 / This verse mentions officials who were in charge of the royal storehouses as well as the storehouses in the outlying districts.

27:26–31 / These verses deal with officials who were in charge of different kinds of farming activities. Reference is made to those **who farmed the land** and those who were **in charge of the produce of the vineyards and the olive and sycamore-fig trees in the western foothills.** Animal farming also features prominently, with officials in charge of **the herds, the camels, the donkeys,** and **the flocks.** These descriptions are not only an indication of the officials who were employed for these purposes; they also leave the impression of an affluent kingdom with abundant food stocks.

27:32–34a / The titles given to a few other officials in these verses (**counselor, a man of insight and a scribe; took care of the king's sons; king's counselor; king's friend**) remind one of the wisdom schools often associated with royal courts in the ancient Near East. That these officials are included here in a list dealing with the Levites may suggest that the priestly duties and the duties of wisdom teachers were intertwined during the Chronicler's time.

27:34b / The long list of Levite officials (in the generic sense) closes with an indication that **Joab was the commander of the royal army.**

We have come to the end of the discussion of the subsections in which the Levite (generic) functions are described. Since these chapters deal so explicitly with the divisions within the cultic community, we should pause for a moment to reflect on the factors that could have motivated the construction of such a prototype and could have contributed to such a process of intragroup self-categorization. The establishment of a separate province of Yehud during the Persian period and the shifting of the administrative center back to Jerusalem from Mizpah brought a new sociopolitical dynamic that could have sparked off renewed processes of identity negotiation. Against this background, one could theorize about the following possibilities.

First, one may assume that the common fate of all the subgroupings of the Jerusalemite society could have contributed to such a self-understanding. During the time of the restoration, when the community in Jerusalem and Yehud was still struggling to come to grips with their changed political, social, and cultic realities, their political subjection and vulnerability could have been a motivation for finding continuity in the ancestral and royal past. In such circumstances the common fate of all subgroupings could have drawn them together in anticipation of a new present, and especially new future, under Persian dominion.

Second, the way in which the Aaronites and Levites (cultic) are presented in these chapters could be an indication that there was a need to build self-esteem within the cultic sphere. By emphasizing their special position and function, and by indicating that their status within the cult was legitimated by Yahweh, these specific subgroupings would have bolstered their position over against other contenders, such as priests in Samaria with southern aspirations.

Third, in the very unstable conditions of the restoration period of Persian-period Yehud, the need for self-verification or reduction of uncertainty could have been a real motive. Adherence to the group norms as spelled out in these chapters would have assisted individuals to validate themselves against the background of a bigger structure in order to find their rightful place in the changed society.

And last, the process of self-categorization that we witness in the texts under discussion could have been motivated by the need for optimal distinctiveness. This process of self-categorization, which builds on continuity with other groups in society but also clarifies the discontinuities, would help the group described in this section in Chronicles reach a better understanding of their own distinct role and status and would certainly assist in imposing that understanding on society.

Additional Notes §2.8

23:1–27:34 / Until fairly recently the majority of studies on 1 Chron. 23–27 focused on the history of the origin of these chapters. Questions such as What sources underlie these chapters? and What redaction processes can be detected in this literature? formed the focus of main interest of many Chronicles scholars. Following Klein's summary (*1 Chronicles*, pp. 445–47), we may distinguish three basic positions in the debate on the origin of these texts. First, some scholars consider all of the lists in 1 Chron. 23–27 to be secondary. This group of scholars argues, on the basis of the repetition of 23:2 in 28:1, that the five chapters in between them form an interruption of the narrative about David. The inconsistency of the materials in these five chapters is furthermore seen as an indication that these interrupting lists were not added at the same time and by the same hands. Second, some scholars argue that certain lists are original but others belong to a secondary level. These scholars do not regard 28:1 as a duplicate of 23:2 but rather see it as a repetitive resumption of the narrative after some lists that were inserted by the Chronicler himself. A third position adopted by some scholars is the originality of all or almost all the lists. The main argument here is again that the repetition in 23:2 and 28:1 should not necessarily be interpreted as an indication of composite sources. More recently, particularly through the work of Wright and Knoppers, scholars have started moving away from a preoccupation with sources and redactions and have shifted their attention to the social, political, and religious concerns reflected in the final composition. I accept that there might have been a process of growth of the literature in 1 Chron. 23–27. However, I agree with Knoppers and Wright that the interpreter of Chronicles should determine how this (probably) composite literature was used in the Chronicler's overall narrative construction and what its pragmatic-rhetorical function was. By focusing on the composition of this piece of literature, one should not neglect to ask how the final form functioned in the broader literary construction. My relating this section with the Chronicler's identity negotiation processes is an attempt to reflect on the pragmatic-rhetorical function of the final form.

23:27 / Commentators agree that 23:27 should not be positioned between 23:26 and 23:28. It interrupts the flow of thought there. A later hand probably made a comment on 23:24, and this remark then became included in the text. The later addition probably wanted to legitimize the information here by indicating that it was **according to the last instructions of David.**

23:25–26 and 23:28–32 / Both Knoppers and Klein point out that the expression in 23:28 (literally "at the hand of the Aaronites") emphasizes a coordinate relationship and not subordination. According to G. N. Knoppers ("Hierodules, Priests, or Janitors? The Levites in Chronicles and the History of the Israelite Priesthood," *JBL* 118 [1999], p. 59) and Klein (*1 Chronicles*, p. 455), subordination would have been indicated with the Hebrew expression *'al yad* (instead of *leyad*, used here), a term that is used in quite a few instances in Chronicles. Dirksen does not agree with this view. He is of the opinion that the expression indeed denotes subordination. But he adds: "Of course this does not mean less respect. The writer holds that priests and Levites both have their indispensable function within the order of the cult, while emphasizing only the prerogatives of the priests" (*1 Chronicles*, p. 286). Knoppers studied the functions assigned to the Levites here in comparison with the indications in the Priestly Writing (P) and in Ezekiel. There are four cases where the terminology in this direct speech section is not paralleled in P or Ezekiel. The most significant of these is the indication in 23:30 that the Levites had **to thank and praise the** Lord. This appointment of Levitical singers and musicians "is a case in which the Chronicler goes beyond Deuteronomic and Priestly precedent" ("Hierodules, Priests, or Janitors?," p. 67). This evidence, together with the other terminology considered by Knoppers, leads him to conclude that the Chronicler was heir to and interpreter of both the pro-Priestly and pro-Levitical traditions. He furthermore rightly indicates that "the Chronicler's work is inevitably affected by his own time and social circumstances, but his presentation is also affected by his tradition, outlook, commitments, and imagination. . . . Indeed, one could argue that in writing about the past, the Chronicler attempts to shape the present" ("Hierodules, Priests, or Janitors?," p. 71).

24:3 / **Zadok** is a problematic figure in the cultic history of Israel. See Additional Note on 6:8.

25:1–31 / An influential study that attempted to provide a history of the development of the Levitical singers is the essay by Hartmut Gese ("Zur Geschichte der Kultsänger am zweiten Tempel," in *Vom Sinai zum Zion: Alttestamentliche Beiträge zur biblischen Theologie* [Munich: Kaiser, 1974], pp. 147–58). Gese distinguished four stages in the development of the cultic singers: (1) after the return from exile the cultic singers are simply called "sons of Asaph" and are not yet regarded as Levites (Ezra 2:41 = Neh. 7:44); (2) by the time of Nehemiah (latter half of the fifth century B.C.) the singers are regarded as Levites and divided into two groups, the sons of Asaph and the sons of Jeduthun (Neh. 11:3–19; 1 Chron. 9:1–18); (3a) by the time of the Chronicler the Levitical singers are described in three family groups: Asaph, Heman, and Jeduthun (1 Chron. 16:4–7, 38–42; 2 Chron. 5:12; 29:13–14; 35:15); (3b) three groups remain, but Jeduthun has been replaced by Ethan, and Heman has become more prominent than Asaph (1 Chron. 6:31–48; 15:16–21). Since the publication of Gese's work more detailed studies of Chronicles have been undertaken, some of which have made adaptations to his theory (see Klein, *1 Chronicles*, pp. 348–49).

§2.9 Final Arrangements for Building the Temple and Transfer of the Kingdom to Solomon (1 Chron. 28:1–29:25)

After the major insertion into the Chronicler's narrative dealing with David's preparations for handing over power to his son and for building the temple, the writer now returns to the narrative line interrupted at the end of 1 Chronicles 22. There we read David's speeches to Solomon and some officials. A theme that was already subtly present in the previous David narratives, namely, the issue of being granted "rest and peace," was explicated in 1 Chronicles 22. Solomon is explicitly referred to there (22:9) as "a man of peace and rest," his name being etymologically related to the Hebrew word for "peace."

Whereas the previous reported speech of David to his son Solomon in 1 Chronicles 22 seemed to be a private affair, the introduction to the present section (28:1) indicates that David now makes the transfer to his son a public occasion. In this way the dubious circumstances of the transfer as reflected in 1 Kings 1 are avoided. His speech follows in 1 Chronicles 28:2–10 (with 28:2–8 addressed to the assembly and 28:9–10 to Solomon again), with a narrative section in 28:11–19 reporting David's planning for the new temple building. Then David addresses Solomon once more, assuring him of the temple craftsmen's loyalty and readiness to help (28:20–21).

First Chronicles 29 opens with David addressing the whole assembly again (29:1–5), telling them about all the materials he had already collected for the temple construction and asking who of them would be willing to pledge their support. The Chronicler then describes the very positive response from the people (29:6–9) and recites David's prayer to Yahweh (29:10–19) as well as his last command to the congregation to bless Yahweh (29:20). The last verses of this subsection (29:21–25) report the climax of the whole David narrative, namely, the enthronement of Solomon his son. The death notice for David (29:26–30) will be dealt with in a separate subsection.

28:1 / This verse sets the scene for David's last speeches. He **summoned all the officials of Israel to assemble at Jerusalem.** This remark is similar to the one in 23:2, when David also gathered all the leaders for the division into different service groups. The verb "to assemble" used here is different from that in 23:2, however. The verb used in 28:1 (*qahal*) is normally used in contexts of religious-cultic gatherings. It emphasizes that this last occasion of David's reign is of special significance. Different groups are assembled, namely, **the officers over the tribes, the commanders of the divisions in the service of the king, the commanders of thousands and commanders of hundreds, and the officials in charge of all the property and livestock belonging to the king and his sons, together with the palace officials, the mighty men and all the brave warriors.** This impressive list reminds one of all the divisions of cultic and secular officials in 1 Chronicles so far, particularly those in 1 Chronicles 23–27.

28:2–10 / The speech reported in these verses is very similar to David's speech to Solomon reported in 22:7–16. Here **David** addresses the assembly as **my brothers and my people.** He indicates that it was his intention **to build a house as a place of rest for the ark of the covenant of the LORD, for the footstool of our God.** The connection of "temple" and "ark of the covenant" is made explicit here once again, and the ark is now also called "the footstool of our God." This is not a strange metaphor, since it also occurs elsewhere with reference to the temple as a whole, to Jerusalem or Mount Zion, and even to the earth (e.g., Isa. 66:1; Ps. 99:5; 110:1; 132:7; Lam. 2:1).

The designation of the temple as (literally) "a house of rest" links back to the speech in 1 Chronicles 22, where Solomon is called "a man of rest." This wordplay (with the same word in Hebrew) is certainly not a coincidence (see Additional Note on 28:2).

The reason for David's disqualification from building the temple is repeated here (as in 22:8): **because you are a warrior and have shed blood.** The Chronicler emphasizes this not so much as a blemish on David's character but to prepare the way for Solomon's reign, which will be a period of rest and peace.

Differently from the speech reported in 1 Chronicles 22, the Chronicler now emphasizes David's lineage and divine election (28:4–5). The divine election narrows down from **he chose Judah as leader,** through David's **family** and through himself, to **he has chosen my son Solomon to sit on the throne of the kingdom of the LORD of Israel.** Not only is the Judahite connection of the chosen house important to take note of, but also the kingdom being designated "the kingdom of the Lord of Israel."

This reflects the Chronicler's view that the actual king of Israel is Yahweh. The house of David, with Solomon as its finest member, is earthly custodian of Yahweh's reign. This aspect reminds one of the selection of psalm material that the Chronicler presented in 1 Chronicles 16. The central exclamation in that cultic song is that "Yahweh reigns!" And exactly that will become known "among the nations." The Chronicler's view might be the product of the sociopolitical times in which he wrote. In the Persian era Israel had no Davidic king any longer. But they could still confess to the nations that the kingdom belongs to Yahweh, who is their actual king.

The rest of David's speech to all the leaders and officials follows more or less the same line as the speech reported in 1 Chronicles 22. The report of the oracle turns into an exhortation to the people (**so now** in 28:8) in which they are encouraged, **Be careful to follow all the commands of the LORD your God.** The two Hebrew verbs here (*shamar*, "keep," and *darash*, "seek") are programmatic. This **charge** comes **in the sight of all Israel and of the assembly of the LORD, and in the hearing of our God.** The "commands" should be sought **that** the people **may possess this good land and pass it on as an inheritance to your descendants forever.** The connection between the people's obedience to Yahweh's law and the possession of the "good land" is something typical of Deuteronomistic writings. The occurrence of this phrase here shows that the Chronicler made use of ideas he found in known written traditions of his time, although he did not quote directly.

From 28:9 David addresses his **son Solomon** again (introduced with **and you**). The charge to **seek** Yahweh also applies to Solomon individually. This verse is full of theological language: what is required of Solomon is **wholehearted devotion** and **a willing mind.** Yahweh is portrayed as **the LORD who searches every heart and understands every motive behind the thoughts.** Therefore: **if you seek** (Hebrew *darash*) **him, he will be found by you; but if you forsake** (Hebrew *'azab*) **him, he will reject you forever.** With this strong theological statement, the pattern is set for the Chronicler's evaluation of further Judahite kings (2 Chron. 10–36). The speech to Solomon concludes with the exhortation in 1 Chronicles 28:10: **Be strong and do the work!**

28:11–19 / In 28:11–12 the Chronicler reports that David gave Solomon the detailed **plans** of the building that had to be constructed. The specifications reflect ancient Near Eastern temple architecture, where storerooms and other amenities were included alongside cultic spaces. As in 28:19 (**from the hand of the LORD upon me**), the indication here is that the plans had a divine origin: **all that the Spirit had put in his mind** (see Additional Notes on 28:12 and 28:19).

After giving Solomon the plans, David gives him **instructions for the divisions of the priests and Levites** and related matters (28:13). This short summary might be a back reference to the extensive description in 1 Chronicles 23–27.

The narrative then (28:14–18) reports on all the precious metal cultic objects that were to be made for the temple and notes that David gave his son all the calculations for them. The exuberant wealth reflected in these indications contributes to the glamorous cultic status of the Solomonic temple.

28:20–21 / Another direct speech of **David** to his son **Solomon** follows. It is linked to the final remark in the previous direct speech (see 28:10) and serves as further encouragement to Solomon to start building the temple. David assures Solomon, **The Lord God, my God, is with you.** Solomon may depend on this God, since **he will not fail** him **or forsake** him. David also assures his son that all the clergy and craftsmen **are ready for all the work on the temple of God.**

It is remarkable that Solomon has not yet spoken a word in the Chronicler's narrative. Although it has already become clear that the narrative is building to a climax with Solomon's reign, David is still the main speaking figure.

29:1–5 / These verses follow after David's encouragement of his son in the previous subsection. It is also direct speech, again directed at **the whole assembly.** It reminds one again of the speech presented in 22:5. In the speech David indicates that he has already provided for many of the materials needed for the construction but that he, **in his devotion to the temple of** his **God,** also wants to contribute from his **personal treasures.** He is setting the example by giving offerings of his own free will. David therefore challenges his audience with the question: **Now, who is willing to consecrate himself today to the Lord?** It is clear that the Chronicler depended on the tabernacle narrative in Exodus 35:4–29, where Moses also requested some freewill offerings from the people to construct the desert sanctuary.

29:6–9 / The response of the **people** and all the **leaders** is overwhelmingly positive. The Chronicler indicates that they all contributed willingly and abundantly. The subsection concludes with rejoicing: **The people rejoiced at the willing response of their leaders, and David the**

king also rejoiced greatly. Joy forms an important point of reference during Solomon's reign.

29:10–19 / First Chronicles 29:10–19 contains the remarkable prayer of David, which sets the theological scene for his son Solomon's reign. The introduction to the prayer in 29:10 states that **David praised the LORD.** The Hebrew word used here can also be translated "to bless" or "to speak words invoking divine favor." David's prayer is spoken **in the presence of the whole assembly,** and it therefore has a liturgical character.

God is addressed in the prayer with the expressions **O LORD, God of our father Israel, from everlasting to everlasting** (29:10) and **O LORD, God of our fathers Abraham, Isaac and Israel** (29:18). It is clear that David acknowledges that the God who is building "a house" for himself and for David is the covenant God of Israel's ancestors. These divine titles establish continuity with the religious traditions of the past.

David's words in 29:14 resemble those used in the prayer reported in 17:16. David confesses that everything he and his people have donated willingly for the construction of the temple comes from the Lord, who is the provider of **everything.** David confesses that **all this abundance . . . comes from your hand, and all of it belongs to you,** and he expresses his joy about the freewill offerings of the people.

With the second invocation of God's name in 29:18 David presents a petition. He asks that the people will **keep this desire in** their **hearts** and **will keep their hearts loyal** to God. He furthermore asks for **wholehearted devotion** for his **son Solomon . . . to keep** the Lord's **commands, requirements and decrees.** He also asks that his son will have the "devotion" **to build the palatial structure.**

29:20 / In 29:20 David urges **the whole assembly** also to **praise the LORD** their **God** and to do so with the typical gesture of reverence and respect for the deity: **they bowed low and fell prostrate before the LORD and the king.** It is strange that "the king" is also included here. The suggestion is probably, just as earlier in the Chronicler's narrative, that the king is the custodian of Yahweh's kingship and prostration before the king implies reverence for the Lord.

29:21–25 / The temporal indications in 29:21–22, **the next day** and **that day,** move the narrative forward to the next main event, namely, the enthronement of Solomon. The day starts off with **sacrifices in abundance for all Israel** as well as eating and drinking **with great joy in the**

presence of the LORD. The element of joy is again prominent. This was followed by the actual enthronement of Solomon, when the people **acknowledged Solomon son of David as king a second time.** The reference to "a second time" here probably refers to 23:1, where it was already stated that David "made his son Solomon king over Israel." Now, the "second time," Solomon is made king by the people. The people anointed both **Solomon and Zadok before the** LORD, Solomon as **ruler,** and Zadok as **priest.** Since Zadok already served as priest under King David, it is surprising to see that he is anointed again here. We know from the Deuteronomistic succession narrative in 1 Kings 1–2 that Zadok was made the main priest in the place of Abiathar, who had backed Adonijah in the race for the kingship. The Chronicler's reference to Zadok's anointment might be a reflection of that background.

Solomon is described as sitting **on the throne of the** LORD **as king.** The Chronicler, differently from the writer of Kings, is clear that the actual king is Yahweh and that the earthly king is a custodian of Yahweh's kingship. The new king received support from various leaders, and **all Israel obeyed him.** The section closes with the declaration that **the** LORD **highly exalted Solomon in the sight of all Israel** and that the **royal splendor** he received was **such as no king of Israel ever had before.**

Additional Notes §2.9

28:2 / The strong emphasis on "rest" and "peace" might be the Chronicler's subtle engagement with the international sociopolitical situation. We know from Greek and Persian sources (both written and archeological) that there was a prominent peace discourse, particularly between Greece and Persia, from the beginning of the fourth century B.C. The Persian imperial government had representatives in Jerusalem, so perhaps the Chronicler also wanted to provide a theological evaluation of this international discourse, emphasizing that real peace does not come from treaties and imperial power but from "seeking" Yahweh and acknowledging the theological significance of the cult center in Jerusalem. For a detailed discussion of this aspect, see L. C. Jonker, "Chronicler's Portrayal of Solomon," pp. 653–69.

28:11 / **The place of atonement** (literally "the house of the mercy seat") is probably the innermost sanctuary of the temple, elsewhere called the Most Holy Place. Although the use of the term "mercy seat" (*kapporeth*) in connection with Solomon's temple is unique, it is well known from the Priestly tradition (e.g., Exod. 25–40 and Lev. 16). The Chronicler did not shy away from juxtaposing materials from the Deuteronomistic and Priestly traditions.

28:12 / In the NIV the temple plans are called **the plans of all that the Spirit had put in his mind.** In the light of 28:19 one may certainly deduce that divine inspiration is meant here. The Chronicler indicates that the strength to build the temple does not derive from human effort but from Yahweh. By translating the Hebrew word *ruach* with a capital ("Spirit"), the NIV suggests to Christian readers that the third person of the Trinity is meant here. According to pre-Christian Jewish understanding, the word would rather refer to Yahweh's active involvement (i.e., "spirit" with lowercase).

28:19 / This verse is difficult to translate. The NIV renders it as another direct speech by David. In the Hebrew text one of the words (translated in NIV as **upon me**) carries a first-person suffix. A text-critical note (with the Septuagint as support), however, indicates that one Hebrew letter, which would have made the suffix third-person singular, probably fell away in the transmission process of the text. If so, the verse would still continue the third-person report of the previous verses.

29:1 and 29:19 / The NIV translates the noun for the temple building as **palatial structure.** The Hebrew word (*habbirah*) often describes a fortified structure on top of a hill. That Araunah's threshing floor, the building site for the temple, was on a high-lying area might have determined the choice of vocabulary.

29:7 / The mention of **darics** in this verse is anachronistic. The narrative context, that is, the time of David and Solomon, predates the minting of "darics" under the Persian King Darius in 515 B.C. by centuries. The use of the word reflects the time of origin of Chronicles (i.e., at least after 515 B.C.).

§2.10 Conclusion to David's reign (1 Chron. 29:26–30)

With this last section we come to the conclusion of David's reign and life. In the previous section his successor as king was enthroned and anointed, and it was therefore time to conclude the David narrative.

29:26–30 / The narrative about David's reign started in 1 Chronicles 10:14 with the death of Saul. There David was called "son of Jesse." The Chronicler uses that title here again to complete the circle at the end of David's reign. The basic information about his reign (length, capital cities) is provided in 29:27, after which we come to David's final moment: **he died at a good old age, having enjoyed long life, wealth and honor.** This comment paints a considerably different picture from the one in 1 Kings 1–2. There David is portrayed as frail and feeble, not completely in command of his faculties. In Chronicles, however, David remains the active king until the very end.

The section concludes with a reference to three other accounts of David's reign, namely, **the records of Samuel the seer, the records of Nathan the prophet and the records of Gad the seer.** It is highly unlikely that these refer to noncanonical writings. The references to three prophetic figures are probably an indication that the Chronicler had in mind the so-called Former Prophets, that is, the canonical books Samuel and Kings.

Additional Note §2.10

29:26–30 / The Chronicler probably made use of 1 Kgs. 2:11–12 in his writing of this last notice on David. However, he has expanded it considerably so that it can hardly be seen as a direct quotation.

Summary of §2

The Chronicler's David narrative (1 Chron. 10–29) derives mostly from source materials found in the Deuteronomistic History (mainly in Samuel), but with significant changes and additions to them. The Chronicler also worked highly selectively with his canonical source. From the extensive narratives about David in the Deuteronomistic History, the Chronicler primarily selected material of theological rather than political significance.

The David narrative presents David, not Saul, as the first real king of Israel (1 Chron. 10). Saul's death marks the beginning of David's reign, and the Chronicler's theological addition to Saul's death notice (10:13–14) makes it clear that David's kingship stems from Yahweh's initiative.

The two main events of David's history in the Chronicler's construction are the transfer of the ark of the covenant of Yahweh to the City of David and the preparation for the building of the temple in the reign of his son Solomon. The narrative line develops around these two thematic complexes and emphasizes again that David's significance lies in his contribution to the establishment of the sanctuary in Jerusalem.

Although the Chronicler's David narrative is much more extensive than his Solomon narrative in 2 Chronicles 1–9, Solomon's reign, not David's, is the climactic point toward which the Chronicler is heading. Solomon will be "the man of rest" who will establish "the house of rest." A clear story line from David to Solomon starts with David's desire to bring the ark to Jerusalem and continues through his ill-fated census that ultimately leads to the identification of the site for the future temple. When Yahweh confirms the eternal promise to David's house, David realizes that Yahweh wants his son to build the temple. The story of David therefore ends on a high note of expectation. Everything is now ready for the temple to be built under Solomon.

The psalms, speeches, and prayers of David contribute significantly toward the formulation of the Chronicler's theology. The Chronicler understood All-Israel to be the covenant people of the covenant God. Continuity with the traditions of the ancestors is therefore emphasized. It is also important to observe the kind of piety depicted in these parts of Chronicles. David humbles himself before God by constantly asking, "Who am I / are we?" David's words come to express that Yahweh is the provider of everything, that he keeps his promises to his people, and that he will guide them into the age of the temple. However, Yahweh is also portrayed as one who punishes transgressions, who is holy, and who should be revered. David, his son Solomon, and All-Israel should seek Yahweh in obedience. Only then will they find rest and peace.

The David narrative has a strong theological focus, but prominent indications of the processes of identity negotiation also lie in the background. The tribal rivalry between Judah and Benjamin may underlie the identification of Araunah's threshing floor as the site of the future temple. On the one hand, the Chronicler features Benjamin as an inclusive All-Israel prototype, while, on the other hand, he establishes Jerusalem as the preferred cultic site over against some Benjaminite centers. This process of intragroup categorization probably reflects the Chronicler's sociohistorical context during the Persian era. The Chronicler's clear preference for the Levites as a religious prototype over other cultic officials (e.g., 1 Chron. 23–27) similarly reflects the discourses during the Chronicler's time on the status of different cultic groups.

Further, the Chronicler's psalm (1 Chron. 16) indicates that identity negotiation during the Chronicler's time also involved engagement with the imperial context. The Chronicler's selection of psalm materials probably reflects rivalries with the cults of neighboring provinces and subtle polemics directed at the Persian Empire. Finally, the portrayal of Solomon as "the man of rest" and the temple in Jerusalem as "the house of rest" may indicate the Chronicler's participation in the international peace discourses of the late Persian era. The clear message is that real peace is attainable not by international treaties and campaigns but by those who seek Yahweh and acknowledge the significance of the sanctuary in Jerusalem.

§3 Solomon, the Man of Peace and Rest (2 Chron. 1:1–9:31)

The reign of Solomon is the focus of 2 Chronicles 1–9. The Chronicler has already prepared the reader to expect that the next chapters contain the climax of the royal history that culminates in the accession of Solomon and his building of the temple in Jerusalem. Solomon is explicitly called "a man of peace and rest" in 1 Chronicles 22:8–10, and Yahweh promises to give David's son "rest from all his enemies on every side." It therefore comes as no surprise that 2 Chronicles 1–9 reports neither battles nor strife during the transition of leadership from David to Solomon (contrast 1 Kgs. 1–2). The Chronicler's description of Solomon's reign projects a tone of peace and rest. Even the pinnacle of Solomon's achievements, the temple, is to be "a house . . . of rest" (1 Chron. 28:2). All the preparations that David made for the temple attain their goal under his son Solomon. The Chronicler selectively uses the Deuteronomistic literary materials (167 verses of the latter's 434 plus 34 of his own) to achieve this clear goal.

Many commentators believe that the Chronicler's narrative of the transition from David to Solomon has been modeled on the transition from Moses to Joshua (Deut. 31; Josh. 1). Two other models may lie behind this portrait: Solomon as a second David, and Solomon and Huram-Abi as a new Bezalel and Oholiab. The second-David motif is quite obvious and may even be inherent in the Deuteronomistic version. The parallel between Solomon/Huram-Abi and Bezalel/Oholiab is less obvious but makes literary sense. Bezalel built the tabernacle, the temple's architectural ancestor (Exod. 31:1–11; 35:20–36:2; 38:22–23), and 2 Chronicles 1:5 credits him with making the bronze altar that stood before the tabernacle in Gibeon. Huram-Abi, the skilled craftsman made available to Solomon by King Hiram of Tyre, in turn parallels Oholiab of the Exodus texts. As Oholiab assisted Bezalel with the tabernacle building, so Huram-Abi assisted Solomon with the temple building. In fact, the Chronicler indicates that Huram-Abi's mother came from the tribe of Dan (2 Chron. 2:14), the same tribal ancestry as Oholiab's (Exod. 31:6; 35:34; 38:23). In short, whatever the role each model played in the Chronicler's construction of the Solomon narrative, it is clearly the Chronicler's deliberate literary aim to embed Solomon's reign in some other significant contexts.

Some scholars see a ring structure in this narrative. According to this suggestion, Solomon's request for wisdom (2 Chron. 1) parallels the elaborations on his wealth and wisdom (2 Chron. 9); the recognition by the gentiles and the dealings with Hiram (2:1–16) parallel later international connections (8:17–9:12); the temple construction with gentile labor (2:17–5:1) has subsequent echoes (8:1–16); and the dedication of the temple (5:2–7:10) parallels the later divine response (7:11–22). The latter two sections therefore form the core of the chiastic structure. One problem with this suggestion, however, is that textual units of unequal length and weight are forced into their positions in the supposed chiastic structure. This may explain why this structure plays no significant role in some commentaries' discussion of the Solomon narrative.

This commentary will follow a structure adapted from McKenzie (*1–2 Chronicles*, p. 227). First Chronicles 1, God's appearance to Solomon at Gibeon, introduces the narrative. The next three episodes all deal with temple building. First Chronicles 2 describes how Solomon made preparations for building the temple, while 3:1–5:1 gives an account of the actual construction. The next episode (5:2–7:22) elaborates on the dedication of the temple. The following two episodes focus on Solomon's other projects (2 Chron. 8) and his international fame (9:1–28). The narrative concludes with the death notice of Solomon, the man of peace and rest (9:29–31).

Additional Note §3

1:1–9:31 / Zipora Talshir ("Reign of Solomon," pp. 233–49) investigates whether the Septuagint form of the Deuteronomistic version of Solomon's reign could be traced back to the same source as the Chronicler's version. She concludes that the interrelationship between the versions is too complex and varied to suggest that an original, short version of 3 Kingdoms underlies them.

§3.1 God Appears to Solomon at Gibeon (2 Chron. 1:1–17)

Second Chronicles 1:1 opens with the remark that "Solomon son of David established himself firmly over his kingdom" and that "the LORD his God was with him and made him exceedingly great." These words complete the transition from David to Solomon and set the scene for Solomon's history.

As a first incident, the Chronicler tells how Solomon convened "all Israel" in Gibeon to bring sacrifices at the local sanctuary (1:2–6). The location is significant, since reference has already been made to Gibeon in 1 Chronicles 16:39 and 21:29. Gibeon was associated with Benjaminite tribal territory. With the ark in Jerusalem (which was part of Judah's tribal area) and the tabernacle under the supervision of Zadok in Gibeon, the cult was still split between these two territories under the reign of David. Solomon's reign is therefore presented as the time during which the cult was unified in one location, namely, in the temple in Jerusalem.

After Solomon and "all Israel" made sacrifices on the altar in front of the tabernacle in Gibeon, "God appeared to Solomon" on the same night (1:7–13). In the conversation between God and Solomon, the king is established as somebody who receives the gift of wisdom from God. This characteristic is not only necessary in preparation for the temple building, but it also forms the motivation for the account of the splendor and international fame of King Solomon. The episode therefore ends in 1:14–17 with further elaboration on his wealth.

The Chronicler clearly made use of the Deuteronomistic version of the Gibeon incident in 1 Kings 3:4–15. However, the Chronicler used this text creatively and selectively. The opening words, in which it is said that Solomon strengthened his reign, were probably taken from 1 Kings 2:12b and 2:46b, where a similar expression occurs. From the start the Chronicler makes clear that Solomon's reign is closely related to God's presence (see the expression "God was with him," which is not in 1 Kgs. 2). From 2 Chronicles 1:2 onward the relationship to 1 Kings 3 is clear, although the Chronicler added some information about whom the king commanded to go with him to Gibeon. This stands in contrast to the version in 1 Kings 3, which indicates that the king went to Gibeon alone. The last few verses, in which the wealth of Solomon is indicated (2 Chron. 1:14–17), were taken over from 1 Kings 10:26–29, where more or less the same information is provided.

1:1 / Unlike the Deuteronomistic version in 1 Kings 1–2, the Chronicler portrays the transition from David's to Solomon's reign as smooth and without resistance. As was already announced in David's blessings in 1 Chronicles 22:1 and 28:20, **the Lord his God was with him.** As in 29:25, it is confirmed again that **the Lord his God . . . made him exceedingly great.** Exactly the same expression was also used in 22:5 as an indication of the temple that Solomon had to build for Yahweh in Jerusalem. The Chronicler omits the killings in 1 Kings 1–2 in order to sustain the difference between the warrior David and the "peace" of Solomon.

The Chronicler uses the verb "to make himself strong" (*chazaq*) (translated **established himself firmly** by NIV) as an indication of Solomon's settling into the kingship. This differs in two ways from the probable source texts in 1 Kings 2:12b and 2:46b. There another verb, "be established" (*kun*), was used. It is strange that the Chronicler did not take over this verb, since it plays a significant role elsewhere in the book. A second difference is that the Deuteronomistic version suggests that God established Solomon's kingship, while the Chronicler indicates that Solomon strengthened **himself . . . over his kingdom.** Although this deviates from the Chronicler's normal pattern, it seems that he wanted to emphasize the human contribution of Solomon as excellent king, as if he did not want this aspect to be hidden behind the emphasis on Yahweh being with Solomon.

1:2–5 / The Chronicler once again takes pains to show that **Solomon** had the full support of **all Israel** in his going up to **Gibeon.** This designation is a prominent theme in Chronicles. In a certain sense the whole literary construction of the Chronicler is intended to define who "all Israel" was after the exile. Here it is claimed that "all Israel" was the community (consisting of different leadership groups) that supported Solomon in his cultic endeavors. In 1:3 this community is called **the whole assembly,** a term that often refers to the organized cultic community. The location indicated here, **the high place at Gibeon,** links this text to 1 Chronicles 21:29, where it was already indicated that "the tabernacle of the Lord, which Moses has made in the desert, and the altar of burnt offering were at that time on the high place at Gibeon." This information is repeated here in 2 Chronicles 1:3 and 1:5, with additional information about **the bronze altar.** Here it is specified (probably with reference to Exod. 38:1–8) that **Bezalel son of Uri, the son of Hur,** had made the altar. This reference could point to the Bezalel-Oholiab account as a possible model that the Chronicler followed in his description of this event. Second Chronicles 1:4–5 can be considered parenthetical, since it provides background information on why "Solomon and the whole assembly" had to go to Gibeon to offer sacrifices to the Lord. The last phrase of 1:5 states, **So Solomon and the assembly inquired of him there.** The verb used here, "to seek" (*darash*), refers to a very prominent concept in Chronicles. It expresses the basic cultic and religious inclination that the Chronicler wanted to foster among the postexilic community.

1:6 / In this verse the Chronicler again resorts to the Deuteronomistic version in 1 Kings 3:4. He specifies, however, that **the bronze altar** stood **before the** Lord **in the Tent of Meeting.** The Chronicler considers it important to emphasize that the tabernacle was in Gibeon at that time, a reference that alludes to its Benjaminite background again (see commentary on 1 Chron. 21:28–22:1).

1:7–12 / The next part of the narrative deals with the appearance of **God** to **Solomon.** The following conversation, starting with God's introductory **ask for whatever you want me to give you,** leads to Solomon asking in 1:9–10 that the Lord's **promise to** his **father David be confirmed,** as well as for **wisdom and knowledge.** This is done on account of the **great kindness** that God showed to David (as expressed by Solomon in 1:8). The Hebrew word for **great kindness** (*hesed*) used here (as well as in the source text) is a clear indication of the covenant relationship envisioned between God and David/Solomon. God's reaction to Solomon's requests is given in 1:11–12. Solomon is granted "wisdom and knowledge" **to govern** God's **people over whom** he has **made** Solomon **king,** as well as incomparable **wealth, riches and honor,** although Solomon did not request this. This indication prepares the way not only for the last verses in this episode (1:14–17) but also for the elaboration on Solomon's international fame in 2 Chronicles 9.

1:13 / This verse concludes the Gibeon episode and changes the setting to **Jerusalem,** from where Solomon **reigned over Israel.**

1:14–17 / The episode ends with a report on all Solomon's wealth and splendor. This section was taken over from 1 Kings 10:26–29, where the same information is provided in the context of the end of

Solomon's reign. Here it is put at the beginning of his reign, and it serves the immediate function in the Chronicler's text of a confirmation of the promises made by God (expressed in 2 Chron. 1:11–12) that manifested in Solomon's wisdom.

Additional Notes §3.1

1:2–5 / This section is paralleled by only half a verse in the Deuteronomistic version, namely, 1 Kgs. 3:4a. There it is merely indicated that Gibeon "was the most important high place," without any elaboration about the tabernacle and altar that were kept there.

1:7–12 / The Chronicler abbreviates the information in his source text, 1 Kgs. 3:4–15, significantly. However, commentators are careful not to read too much into the abbreviations. The selective use of source materials might have been motivated by the need for brevity here rather than for some ideological reason.

1:13 / This verse is a parallel to 1 Kgs. 3:15. However, two significant aspects of the source text are left out by the Chronicler. First, the Deuteronomistic version mentions that God appeared in a dream. Since the Chronicler does not mention this information, some commentators theorize (with reference to Num. 12:6–8) that this might have been an indication of an antidream sentiment that prevailed in the Chronicler's time. The other aspect omitted by the Chronicler is the sacrifices brought by Solomon before the ark of the covenant and the feast he organized after his return to Jerusalem. Thompson theorizes about this omission: "Perhaps he [the Chronicler] wanted to avoid any confusion in the picture of legitimate worship that he had taken such trouble to develop" (J. A. Thompson, *1, 2 Chronicles*, The New American Commentary [Nashville: Broadman & Holman, 1994], p. 205). This information is rather replaced by another confirmation of Solomon's "reign over Israel."

1:14–17 / This section was taken over from 1 Kgs. 10:26–29. However, a significant part of it can also be found in 2 Chron. 9:25–28, a section describing the end of Solomon's reign. This correlates better with the original position of the source text in the Solomon narrative. Some commentators are therefore of the opinion that one of these occurrences is secondary. McKenzie rightly indicates, however, that "the repetition may also be viewed as a structuring device—a bracket or framework for the account of Solomon, whose wealth and international prestige—both gifts from God—allowed him to build the temple" (*1–2 Chronicles*, p. 231).

§3.2 Solomon Prepares to Build the Temple (2 Chron. 2:1–18)

In 1 Chronicles 22 and 28–29 the Chronicler indicated that King David had paved the way for the building of the temple in Jerusalem and had already made extensive preparations. It is therefore somewhat strange that, according to the Chronicler's narrative, Solomon had to appoint craftsmen again and had to gather building material from Lebanon. However, the narrative reaches its climax here, when the actual building of the temple is credited to Solomon. Second Chronicles 2 therefore introduces the history of the building process, which stretches to the end of 2 Chronicles 7.

This episode starts with an introductory remark in 2:1 in which the building of the temple and the palace is announced; 2:2 and 2:17–18 frame the episode with information on the craftsmen whom Solomon conscripted; 2:3–16 contains the report on the correspondence between Solomon and Hiram of Tyre, in which Solomon requests some building material and assistance for his project.

2:1 / **Solomon** orders the building of **a temple for the Name of the LORD** and **a royal palace for himself**. The so-called name theology is prominent in Deuteronomistic literature. It probably expressed the understanding that Yahweh, the God of Israel, dwelled among his people without being physically present or being confined to the sanctuary. McKenzie (*1–2 Chronicles*, p. 233) mentions that this theological understanding is probably related to the practice in the ancient Near East whereby a king would lay claim to a site by placing his name there. The Chronicler adopted this name theology here in order to reflect his understanding of the status of the sanctuary, namely, as the place chosen by Yahweh. Although the palace of King Solomon is also mentioned in this context (and is therefore closely related to the temple), the focus is rather on the building of the temple itself.

2:2 and 2:17–18 / These verses form an enclosure around the negotiations in direct speech between Solomon and Hiram of Tyre in

2:3–16. The verb "to count" opens both 2:2 and 2:17 with the reminder in the latter verse of the census undertaken by David (1 Chron. 21). These verses consist of an abbreviation of the source text (1 Kgs. 5:13–18). The numbers mentioned in the two versions are not significantly different. Chronicles differs only in terms of the number of foremen (3,600 according to both 2 Chron. 2:2 and 2:18, instead of 3,300 in 1 Kings 5:16). One significant difference, however, is that the Chronicler omitted the phrase "Solomon conscripted laborers," which is used in 1 Kings 5:13. The word used in this verse refers to "forced labor," as it is translated in 5:14. It is indicated that Solomon took "forced laborers" "from all Israel." The Chronicler, who did not want to blemish Solomon's reputation in any way, rather replaced this point with the mention of a census, indicating that those being counted were the **aliens** (2 Chron. 2:17), that is, those non-Israelites who settled down among the Israelites and who had only limited rights. In doing so the Chronicler also avoided any suggestion that this census could be considered sinful, such as the census ordered by David (see 1 Chron. 21) that was conducted among the Israelites.

2:3–16 / The section in which the negotiations between **Solomon** and **Hiram of Tyre** are mentioned is in significant aspects an extended version of the source text found in 1 Kings 5:1–12. Whereas the Deuteronomistic version starts with Hiram sending a messenger to Solomon after he heard that David's son had become king, the Chronicler suggests the initiative came from Solomon by omitting 1 Kings 5:1. Solomon is the one taking the initiative in contacting his northern neighbor to support his temple-building project. In this way the focus remains on Solomon as the temple builder.

At the beginning of Solomon's address to Hiram, 1 Kings 5:3–5 includes an explanation of why David could not build the temple, and states that he, Solomon, was granted "rest on every side" and therefore intended to build the temple in fulfillment of the promise Yahweh made to his father. This section is significantly changed and expanded in 2 Chronicles 2:3–6 to refer to the future temple being a place where Yahweh's **lasting ordinance for Israel** (2:4) will be given expression. It will be a place where the cultic rituals and celebrations will be performed. The future temple will therefore stand in continuity with those cultic rituals and appointed festivals of the past. The Chronicler's theological understanding of the temple as a cultic site is furthermore incorporated into this direct speech. Chronicles reflects the understanding that the temple should be **great, because our God is greater than all the other gods.** However, the temple will not be a place that will contain Yahweh. The Chronicler adds the theologically loaded exclamation uttered by Solomon: **But who is able to build a temple for him, since the heavens, even the highest heavens, cannot contain him?** (2:6). This addition to the source text relates well to the Chronicler's persistent use of the name theology (which was taken over from Kings), in which care is taken not to portray Yahweh as a deity who can be contained in any earthly structure. The name theology manages to keep in creative tension what is often called the immanence and transcendence of Yahweh.

In the source text (1 Kgs. 5:6) the actual request to Hiram follows only after the explanation of why Solomon is going to build the temple. The basic request is for "cedars of Lebanon" as well as craftsmen who will work with Solomon's men. In the Chronicler's version the basic request already appears at the beginning of Solomon's message. Then follows the elaboration on the reason for building the temple as well as a theological appraisal of the future structure. Only after that, in 2 Chronicles 2:7–9, the request for well-skilled craftsmen and more wood is made (2:7). The payment offered to these craftsmen is specified in 2:10.

Hiram's reaction in a **letter** now follows in three stages. First is an introductory acknowledgment (2:11) by this foreign king that **because the Lord loves his people, he has made** Solomon **their king;** second is elaborate praise (2:12) of **the Lord, the God of Israel, who made heaven and earth!** Again, the foreign king exclaims that God has given the kingship to Solomon and that he has made him **a wise son** to David, **endowed with intelligence and discernment.** It is this king **who will build a temple for the Lord.**

Only after these two remarks by the foreign king does the third stage of his reaction follow, in which he replies to Solomon's request for a craftsman (2:13–14) and wood (2:16). **Huram-Abi** is named as the skilled craftsman who will be sent to work with Solomon's men. He not only complies with the requirements set out by Solomon but also has a familial link with the tribe of **Dan.** The description of Huram-Abi might be a deliberate attempt by the Chronicler to draw a parallel between this Sidonian craftsman and Oholiab, who was credited in Exodus 31:6 as the artisan who constructed the tabernacle. In this way the Chronicler emphasizes with his own additions to the text that the future temple will stand in continuity with the tradition of the tabernacle.

Additional Notes §3.2

2:2 and 2:17–18 / The Hebrew word *mas*, which can be translated "forced labor" (used in the Deuteronomistic source text), has been replaced here in Chronicles. The concept does, however, occur in the book in 2 Chron. 8:8 and 10:18. In both cases it has been taken over from the source texts in 1 Kings. There it is clear, however, that the forced labor was taken from other, Canaanite nations, who had remained in the land. The omission of the word "forced labor" in 1 Chron. 2 can best be explained in terms of the Chronicler's attempt to present a very positive image of King Solomon.

2:3 / The name of the king of Tyre is spelled "Huram" in the Hebrew text. It is, however, well known that this is an alternative spelling for **Hiram**, which is usually used in the Deuteronomistic version to refer to this king. The name **Huram-Abi,** which is given to the Sidonian craftsman who was made available to Solomon, might be related to the king's name (with the suffix -*abi* meaning "my father"). Some commentators think that the ending -*abi* is a deliberate construction to relate it to the name of Oholiab, who is mentioned as the builder of the tabernacle in Exod. 31:6 and 35:30–33. McKenzie (*1–2 Chronicles*, p. 234) remarks on the presentation of Hiram by the Chronicler: "Huram is quite familiar with Israelite theology; indeed, his confession in verse 12 of Yahweh as maker of heaven and earth makes him appear as something of a convert to Israelite religion." Hicks disagrees: "These words are surprising on the lips of Hiram, but they may be nothing more than diplomatic politeness" (*1 and 2 Chronicles*, pp. 269–70).

2:7 and 2:14 / McKenzie points out that the word for **purple** is Aramaic, while the word for **crimson** is Persian: "The vocabulary in the letter . . . indicates the relative lateness of this passage and makes it clear that the letter was composed by the Chronicler, not by Solomon" (*1–2 Chronicles*, p. 234).

2:10 / **Cor** and **bath** were ancient measurement units. Cor (approximately 220 volume liters) was used as a dry measure, while bath (approximately 22 fluid liters) served as a liquid measure.

2:11 / Ehud Ben Zvi ("When the Foreign Monarch Speaks," in *The Chronicler as Author: Studies in Text and Texture*, ed. M. P. Graham and S. L. McKenzie [JSOTSup 263; Sheffield: Sheffield Academic Press, 1999], pp. 209–28) provides an analysis of all the speeches by foreign monarchs in Chronicles. One aspect Ben Zvi points to is Yahweh's love for his people being mentioned only twice in Chronicles, once in the mouth of Hiram of Tyre (2:11) and the other in the mouth of the queen of Sheba (9:8). As a matter of fact, both of these are foreign monarchs. It seems that the Chronicler wanted to insinuate that even the foreign monarchs are well aware that Yahweh loves his people.

§3.3 Solomon Builds the Temple
(2 Chron. 3:1–5:1)

We now enter the section in which the long-awaited process of building the temple is described. The reader's expectations have already been focused on the actual building of the temple in Jerusalem from the narration of David's history in 1 Chronicles 21–22 and 28–29.

The Chronicler used 1 Kings 6–7 as his main source for the description of the building of the temple under Solomon. But as has become familiar to the reader, the Chronicler not only abbreviated the source account significantly but also took the liberty of making some changes and adding some minor details.

It is clear that 2 Chronicles 3:1–2 serves as introduction to this episode in the Solomon narrative, with 5:1 concluding the account. The structure of the description between the introduction and the conclusion, however, is difficult to unravel. The description starts with a basic overview of the ground plan of the temple (3:3), then moves to a description of the portico in front of the temple (3:4–7), and then provides a detailed account of the Most Holy Place, its contents, and separating curtain (3:8–14). After this (3:15–4:22) there are descriptions of a variety of cultic objects, decorations, structural elements, and so on. As in the source texts in 1 Kings 6–7, the repetition of the verb "and he made" punctuates references to the different objects that were made. Unlike in the source texts (where the vocabulary is very technical), however, the descriptions are not as detailed here. Hicks is probably correct that "the Chronicler's emphasis is liturgical rather than architectural. . . . His interest is sufficient to verify the magnificence of the temple, but he does not detract from . . . divine presence and human seeking" (*1 and 2 Chronicles*, p. 272). Because the focus is different in Chronicles, the technical vocabulary of Kings was simplified.

3:1 / The phrase used here at the beginning of the temple-building narrative, **Solomon began to build the temple of the LORD,** and the later phrase **when all the work . . . was finished** of 5:1, frame the narrative. The location is specified with information that is not provided in the source text. According to the Chronicler, the temple was built in Jerusalem on Mount Moriah, where the Lord had appeared to his father David. It was on the threshing floor of Araunah the Jebusite, the place provided by David. The reference to Araunah's threshing floor comes from 1 Chronicles 21, where the reader was told that David bought this piece of land from the Jebusite. The choice of the neutral ground between Judah and Benjamin was probably deliberate. Here, in 2 Chronicles 3:1, however, the location is further specified as "on Mount Moriah." This mountain is mentioned only twice in the Old Testament, namely, here and in Genesis 22 as the location of Abraham's offering of Isaac. This is a very clear attempt by the Chronicler to embed the building of the temple in the ancestral history of Israel. The Chronicler's insinuation is clearly that the Lord's presence will be experienced in the temple in Jerusalem as their ancestor Abraham experienced it on Mount Moriah. In this way it is shown that the Lord's presence in this place is already well established in their long-standing ancestral traditions, which gives further legitimacy for the temple construction on the same site.

3:2 / The temporal indication of this verse correlates approximately to that in 1 Kings 6:1. The Chronicler, however, omits the reference to the exodus in the source text, which indicates that the building of the temple was started "in the four hundred and eightieth year after the Israelites had come out of Egypt." Many commentators note that the Chronicler does not give prominence to the exodus event. Together with the previous verse, this verse creates the impression that the cultic community of Israel should seek its foundations in ancestral times and not in the exodus event (which was still constitutive for the Deuteronomistic version). This might be an indication that the Chronicler foresaw a future that was rooted in the ancestral promise rather than in the obedience associated with the exodus and desert wanderings.

The concurrence of the start of the temple building and the commencement of Solomon's reign is the same in the two versions, namely, **the second month of the fourth year of his reign.** The Chronicler adds that it was **on the second day** of that month.

3:3 / The measurements of the basic ground plan, consisting of the Holy Place and the Most Holy Place, but excluding the portico, were taken from the source text in 1 Kings 6:2. A parenthetical remark in 2 Chronicles 3:3 specifies that **the cubit of the old standard** was used for these measurement. According to Ezekiel 43:13, another variation of "the old standard," namely, the "long cubit" (which was a handbreadth longer than the old cubit standard), came into use at a certain stage. It is not completely certain when this change was made, but some accept that it might have been sometime in the tenth or ninth century B.C. The parenthetical information in 2 Chronicles 3:3 is therefore another indication that this text originated at a time when the new standard was already in use. It remains interesting, however, that the Deuteronomistic version in 1 Kings 6:2 did not feel the need to specify this information.

The NIV specifies in a footnote that, according to the accepted measurement of about 18 inches (or 0.45 meters) for one old-standard cubit, the ground plan was "about 90 feet (about 27 meters) long and 30 feet (about 9 meters) wide."

3:4–7 / This section contains a description of the **portico at the front of the temple.** It seems that the measurements of this part were not included in the measurements provided in the previous verse. Although the Chronicler took his information about the measurements of the "portico" from 1 Kings 6:3, he deviates from his source text. That text indicates that the length was twenty cubits and the breadth ten cubits. The Chronicler agrees about the length, but he omits the measurement of the breadth and adds an indication of the height. Commentators are in agreement with H. G. M. Williamson (*1 and 2 Chronicles* [New Century Bible Commentary; Grand Rapids: Eerdmans, 1982], p. 206) that 120 cubits for the height of the portico is probably the result of a textual error. The differences in measurements might also be the result of a difference in overall dimensions between the first and second temples (the latter of which the Chronicler would have been familiar with).

It is difficult to know whether the further description of the decorations refers to the portico or to the temple as a whole. It is also difficult to know which sections in 1 Kings 6 served as source text for this part, since the information was altered and abbreviated somewhat randomly. What is clear, however, is that **gold** played a very important role in the temple decorations.

3:8–14 / These verses, which can be associated with a source text in 1 Kings 6:16–28, deal with the construction and decoration of the **Most Holy Place.** We know from ancient Near Eastern architecture that the innermost part of the sanctuary was considered to be the dwelling place of the deity or, as Israel understood this, of the name of Yahweh. Special cultic regulations applied for this part of the sanctuary. As in the source text, **gold** once again plays an important role in the decorations.

This precious metal signifies the high cultic and theological status of this part of the temple.

Contained in the Most Holy Place were the **cherubim** (the plural of "cherub"). Their splendor is again emphasized, and their measurements are an indication that they filled the space of the inner sanctuary. According to McKenzie, cherubim were "composite creatures, similar to the great Sphinx in Egypt, which were typically represented in ancient Near Eastern iconography as the guardians of entrances to temples and palaces" (*1–2 Chronicles*, p. 239).

The Most Holy Place with the cherubim was separated from the rest of the temple by means of a **curtain**. This detail in 3:14 is not present in the source text and is therefore the Chronicler's own addition. The material from which the curtain was made, namely, **blue, purple and crimson yarn and fine linen,** was certainly extremely valuable. Although the suggestion is that Solomon himself made the curtain (Solomon is the subject of all the verbs "and he made" in this construction narrative; see commentary on 4:11–18), it was precisely for this purpose that he requested an artisan from King Hiram of Tyre.

3:15–17 / These verses are an abbreviated version of the source in 1 Kings 7:15–22, with a minor difference in the height measurement of the **pillars** (eighteen cubits in the Deuteronomistic version, and **thirty-five** here in Chronicles). It is not clear what the function of the pillars was, but McKenzie is of the opinion that "the fact that they are named suggests that they may have had a liturgical or theological purpose that has been lost to us" (*1–2 Chronicles*, pp. 239–40).

4:1–10 / The next ten verses, which are loosely paralleled in 1 Kings 7:23–39, provide a description of the following objects, all of which had distinct cultic functions: **bronze altar** (4:1), where sacrifices of atonement could be brought; **Sea of cast metal** (4:2–5), where ritual cleansing could take place; **ten basins** (4:6), which were used for washing the offerings; and **ten gold lampstands** (4:7), **ten tables,** and **a hundred gold sprinkling bowls** (4:8), which all probably had some liturgical function in the sacrificial cult.

Second Chronicles 4:9 (without a parallel in the source text) now elaborates further on the spatial division of the temple area. **The court-yard of the priests** and **the large court** are distinguished from the rest of the design and probably reflect the understanding of temple design of the Chronicler's own day (i.e., the spatial division in the so-called Second Temple, which had an inner court for the priests and a bigger, outer court for laypeople).

Second Chronicles 4:10 returns to the position of the "Sea" with an accurate quotation from the source text in 1 Kings 7:39b.

4:11–18 / This part of the temple-building episode introduces **Huram** for the first time as an artisan who furnished many of the detailed decorations in the temple. The verb "and he made" occurs frequently in the temple-building episode, but it is never specified who "he" is. From the context it seems as if the Chronicler intended Solomon to be regarded as the real builder of the temple in all its glory. In the previous episode, however, Huram-Abi was explicitly offered to Solomon by King Hiram of Tyre to perform these duties. In 4:11 the name Huram occurs twice (in both variations: Huram and Hiram). It is thus clear that he was the designer of all the artful decorations mentioned in the next verses. In 4:18 **Solomon** becomes the explicit subject of the verb again in accordance with the source text in 1 Kings 7:47. At this point it becomes clear that, although the Sidonian artisan Huram was responsible for the creation of many of the objects in the temple, Solomon is credited with building the temple.

4:19–22 / These verses contain a summary of all the objects that were made for the temple. The Chronicler follows the source text in 1 Kings 7:48–50 with some minor alterations.

5:1 / This clearly forms the conclusion to the actual temple-building process, including the point that **all the work Solomon had done for the temple of the LORD was finished.** This comment, as well as the indication that Solomon brought into the treasury of the temple building **the things his father David had dedicated,** was taken over from the source text in 1 Kings 7:51. The temple is now ready to be dedicated to Yahweh.

Additional Notes §3.3

3:1 / It is not only the mention of **Mount Moriah** that creates the impression that the temple building is embedded in the ancestral history of Israel. The use of the phrase **had appeared to . . . David** also echoes the appearance of Yahweh to Abraham on Mount Moriah, so much so that Gen. 22:14 mentions that the mountain was called "the LORD will see" (which is the alternative translation provided in a footnote in NRSV, which better expresses the verb used here). The verb "to see" (*r'h*) figures prominently in Gen. 22. The name Moriah might even be an echo of the same verb "be seen" used in these phrases. This observation does not, however, exclude the possibility that the reference to seeing/appearing also had further overtones. In the prophetic tradition, for example, this term and theme occurs frequently, with the technical term "seer" often used for some prophetic figures.

3:2 / It is extremely difficult to ascertain an absolute date for Solomon's reign (because the biblical information provided on the length of his reign probably consists of symbolic numbers, and also because of scanty archeological evidence from the tenth century B.C.). For thorough discussions of the tenth century B.C. in ancient Israel, see Israel Finkelstein's and Amihai Mazar's contributions in part 4 of *The Quest for the Historical Israel: Debating Archaeology and the History of Early Israel* (ed. Brian B. Schmidt; Leiden: Brill, 2007). A very rough indication of the beginning of Solomon's reign would be between 970 B.C. and 960 B.C. E. R. Thiele's establishing the date of Solomon's death as 931 B.C. has been accepted in scholarship (Thiele, *A Chronology of the Hebrew Kings* [Grand Rapids: Zondervan, 1977]). If the forty-year reign of the biblical narrative can be regarded as factually correct, then his reign would have started in 970 B.C., with the beginning of the temple building in 967 B.C. But the forty-year indication may simply be a symbolic reference to one generation.

3:6 / The reference to **gold of Parvaim** cannot be explained. H. G. M. Williamson suggests that it must have been a place name no longer known in later times. He refers to studies that associate Parvaim with Ophir, which was also known for its gold. He theorizes: "It is . . . possible that even by the Chronicler's time this literal meaning had been overshadowed, or even forgotten, so that the place-name was used more in the sense of a superlative for 'finest gold'" (*1 and 2 Chronicles* [New Century Bible Commentary; Grand Rapids: Eerdmans, 1982], pp. 207–8).

3:14 / The term used in the Hebrew for **curtain** is the same as the term used in Exod. 26:31 and 36:35 for the curtain that formed part of the tabernacle. This is yet another indication that the Chronicler wanted to portray the temple as a continuation of the tabernacle cultic tradition.

3:17 / Some commentators speculate about the meaning of the names **Jakin and Boaz**. The first may mean "he sets/holds up" (from the Hebrew verb *kun*, which plays a significant role in the Chronicler's construction), and the second "in strength/with might." It is clear from the Septuagint version that the Greek translators understood these words in exactly this way, translating them with the equivalent Greek terms (and not with transcriptions of the Hebrew words). If the **pillars** had no structural function in the temple, the combination of these terms could have been a reminder at the entrance of the temple that he (probably a reference to Yahweh, the deity of the sanctuary) establishes Israel (or the temple) with strength.

4:9 / Japhet points out that three courts are distinguished in Kings, namely, "the inner court" (1 Kgs. 6:36; 7:12), "the great court" (7:12), and "the other court" (7:8), but that not one of these references was taken over by the Chronicler from the source text. First Chron. 4:9 is the only verse in the temple-building narrative that mentions the courts. Japhet suggests: "It would seem that the architectural picture is the same, with the two courts having somewhat different designations" (*I and II Chronicles* [London: SCM, 1993], p. 567).

§3.4 Solomon Dedicates the Temple
(2 Chron. 5:2–7:22) ·

At the end of the previous episode (5:1) the scene is set for the dedication of the temple. The following episode now deals with this great event, which stands at the center of the Chronicler's reconstruction of the monarchical past. The dedication of the temple has different elements and is accompanied by speeches, prayers, sacrifices, music, and a theophany. The whole description from 5:2 to 7:22 bears a liturgical character, as if the Chronicler wanted the reader of his history to experience the glory of the temple again and to reenact the worship performed there. This would, of course, have a clear message to the Second Temple cultic community of the Chronicler's own day.

In this section the Chronicler adhered to the source text in 1 Kings 8:1–9:1 very closely, with only minor insertions. It is clear from one small section of the episode (1 Chron. 6:41–42) that the Chronicler also had access to another biblical text, namely, Psalm 132:8–10.

It is important to point out at this stage how artful the Chronicler's narrative composition is. An important part of the David narrative was the bringing of the ark of the covenant to Jerusalem. We then heard the promise of Yahweh to David of an eternal kingship, and we read about all David's preparations for his son's kingship and the building of the temple. The previous episode describes the completion of the temple, and the narrative can resume by giving an account of the unfulfilled task of bringing the ark of the covenant into the sanctuary. The expectations associated with the ark that were created in the reader but frustrated by the slow development of the narrative from 1 Chronicles 17 can now be fulfilled. By regulating the tension level in this narrative, the narrator of Chronicles succeeds in conveying to the reader that Solomon's reign is actually the climax of the development of the monarchy. In Solomon's achievements—with the completion of the temple and the bringing of the ark to the sanctuary—All-Israel has achieved its divine purpose.

The episode therefore starts with a subunit on the bringing of the ark to the temple (2 Chron. 5:2–14). This is followed by the narration of Solomon convening the whole assembly before the temple and making a speech to them (6:1–11), the prayer of Solomon (6:12–42), and a description of the sacrifices and festivities performed by Solomon and the people (7:1–11). This episode closes with Yahweh's response in a divine revelation (7:12–22).

5:2–14 / This section corresponds closely to the source text in 1 Kings 8:1–11, although some alterations were made to the last part (namely, 1 Chron. 5:11b–13a being an addition to 1 Kgs. 8:10–11). These alterations are typical of the Chronicler's sentiments. The addition deals first with the consecration of the priests: **all the priests who were there had consecrated themselves, regardless of their divisions.** This is a motif already encountered in 1 Chronicles 13, which describes the first, unsuccessful attempt to bring the ark to Jerusalem. The Uzzah incident has already underlined what may happen if humans trespass into divine territory. This theme is continued in 1 Chronicles 15, where David ordered "the heads of the Levitical families" to consecrate themselves before bringing the ark to the City of David. When the continuation of the ark's journey once again becomes the theme of the narrative in the present episode, the Chronicler deems it very important to mention again that those who will be responsible for carrying the ark will have "consecrated themselves."

Second, the addition emphasizes the role of the **Levites** in providing the musical accompaniment during the ceremony (5:12–13a). The prominence of the Levites—already well known from the elaborate section in 1 Chronicles 23–27, where the organization of the Levites is explained—had already been emphasized by another small change to the source text in 2 Chronicles 5:4. There it is said that **the Levites took up the ark,** although the source text in 1 Kings 8:3 refers to "the priests" taking up the ark. The active role of the Levites is therefore emphasized in the Chronicler's version. It is interesting to note, however, that the Chronicler kept the Deuteronomistic version in 2 Chronicles 5:7, which states that **the priests then brought the ark of the LORD's covenant to its place in the inner sanctuary of the temple, the Most Holy Place.** The Chronicler therefore does not exclude the priests from this important task. Second Chronicles 5:5, which forms the transition from the Levites taking up the ark (5:4) to the priests bringing the ark (5:7), mentions that **the priests, who were Levites,** did the carrying. This translation represents another minute change that the Chronicler made to his source text, which reads "priests and Levites." By identifying the priests who helped with the carrying as being of Levitical lineage, the Chronicler achieved his goal of highlighting the role of the Levites without omitting the priests from the occasion altogether. The addition in 5:11 of "regardless of their divisions" therefore also indicates that both priests and Levites had consecrated themselves, because both groups had to participate in the bringing of the ark to the temple. The priestly divisions, elaborately described in 1 Chronicles 23–27, are in the background here again.

The position of the ark in the temple, namely, **in the inner sanctuary of the temple, the Most Holy Place,** . . . **beneath the wings of the cherubim** (taken over from the source text), is highly symbolic. The Most Holy Place was seen as the place of Yahweh's presence, the earthly dwelling of the name. This was already symbolized by the ark of the covenant, which was closely associated with Israel's wandering in the desert. By bringing the ark into the Most Holy Place, this symbolic meaning is now being transferred to the temple.

One should, however, take note that—although the focus is very strongly on the ark of the covenant in this section—5:5 adds (in accordance with the source text in 1 Kgs. 8:4), **And they brought up the ark and the Tent of Meeting and all the sacred furnishings in it.** "The Tent of Meeting" refers to the tabernacle, kept at Gibeon—as the reader was informed in 2 Chronicles 1. Although the rest of the narrative in the present section does not give further prominence to the tabernacle, it becomes clear that this ceremony also brings the tradition associated with Gibeon to a close. With both ark and tabernacle now brought to the temple, their respective functions and symbolical meaning are transferred to one united sanctuary in Jerusalem.

Both the Deuteronomistic version (1 Kgs. 8:8) and Chronicles (2 Chron. 5:9) mention, **And they are still there today.** This remark not only indicates that the texts were written long after the event being narrated, but it also serves as an indication of the continuing significance and effect of these holy objects in the religious life of Israel. As the Chronicler was writing in the Second Temple period, one may assume that this remark was quite influential in affirming the ongoing significance of the Second Temple in Jerusalem during the late Persian period.

The section about the bringing of the ark and the tabernacle to the temple in Jerusalem concludes with the singers exclaiming, **He is good; his love endures forever** (5:13), and **a cloud** filling the whole temple so that **the priests could not perform their service because of the cloud** (5:14). Following the Deuteronomistic source text again at the end of this section, the Chronicler interprets the appearance of the cloud as indicating that **the glory of the LORD filled the temple of God.** The appearance of a cloud is a well-known motif in the Old Testament associated with a theophany. It symbolizes the presence of God himself. This appearance of the cloud concludes the transferring of the symbolic meaning of the ark and the tabernacle onto the temple.

6:1–11 / **Solomon** now responds to the glorious events described in the previous pericope. This section again closely follows the Deuteronomistic version in 1 Kings 8:12–21, with one small addition in 2 Chronicles 6:5b–6a (see Additional Note). Solomon first of all quotes the Lord in saying, **The LORD has said that he would dwell in a dark cloud** (6:1). The word used for "dark cloud," which occurs only fifteen times in the Old Testament, is prominently associated with the theophany at Sinai (Exod. 20:21). Second Chronicles 6:2 seems to be addressed to Yahweh. Although "the LORD" is mentioned in the third person in the previous verse, Solomon's words continue with direct speech to a second person (**for you**), which can be understood in this context only as Yahweh.

After **the king turned around and blessed them,** Solomon addressed **the whole assembly of Israel.** His speech opens with praise to Yahweh (6:4), **who with his hands has fulfilled what he promised with his mouth to my father David.** The greater part of the speech contains reminders of the divine promises about the election of Jerusalem and David (6:5–6) and about the construction of the temple (6:7–9). Then (6:10–11) follows the confirmation that **the Lord has kept the promise he made.**

6:12–42 / This section contains the well-known prayer of Solomon, one of the most elaborate nonpsalmic or prose prayers in the Old Testament (see Additional Note). The Chronicler adhered closely to his source text in 1 Kings 8:22–53, with one prominent addition in 2 Chronicles 6:13 and some changes to the end of the prayer.

Second Chronicles 6:12–13 provides the narrative framework for the prayer. Second Chronicles 6:12 still follows the source text (1 Kgs. 8:22), and the last part of this verse is repeated in 2 Chronicles 6:13b: **and** Solomon **spread out his hands toward heaven.** The information about the **bronze platform, five cubits long, five cubits wide and three cubits high, . . . placed . . . in the center of the outer court,** is new, however. The verse not only mentions the "bronze platform" that Solomon made as an elevation from which he could address the people, but also changes the place from **before the altar of the LORD** (6:12) to "the center of the outer court" (6:13). Japhet is probably correct in assuming that "Solomon prayed 'before the altar of the Lord,' namely, in the inner court. It was inconceivable to a later generation that a public address of any type could have been made in that area, and therefore the reference 'before the altar' is replaced by the more general *ʿªzārāh*, probably (although not explicitly) the outer court" (*I and II Chronicles* [London: SCM, 1993], p. 590).

The prose prayer itself consists of the following parts (based on O'Kennedy's analysis in "Twee Weergawes van die Gebed van Salomo [1 Kon. 8 en 2 Kron. 6]," pp. 155–77): prayer for the Davidic dynasty (6:14b–17), transition to the seven petitions (6:18–21), seven petitions under different circumstances (6:22–39), and conclusion (6:40–42). The seven petitions form the core of the prayer, with a similar structure followed in each of them (namely, particular circumstances are first mentioned, followed by the petition with the words **then hear from heaven and act/forgive**/etc.). The last petition, in 6:36–39, which deals with the circumstances of exile, is the longest of all the petitions and probably forms the climax of this section.

The conclusion to the prayer deviates from the source text. First, the information contained in 1 Kings 8:50–51 and 8:53 was omitted by the Chronicler; 1 Kings 8:52 is retained in an adapted form in 2 Chronicles 6:40. O'Kennedy (p. 159) agrees with other commentators that the omission of the other verses was probably determined by the reference to the exodus and Moses tradition. There is a tendency (although not absolute) in Chronicles to omit references to the exodus and the desert wanderings. Second, 2 Chronicles 6:41–42 is an addition that quotes from Psalm 132:8–10. This section and 1 Chronicles 16:8–36 are the only parts of Chronicles that include quotes from known psalmic material. O'Kennedy (pp. 163–68) provides a thorough discussion of theories on why the Chronicler included this specific quote here. For our purposes, however, only two of these possible reasons need to be emphasized. A prominent theme contained in the words is **now arise, O Lord God, and come to your resting place, you and the ark of your might**. Solomon is portrayed by the Chronicler as "the man of peace and rest" and the temple as "the house of rest." Here, at the dedication of the temple to Yahweh, the Chronicler's inclusion in Solomon's prayer of an invitation to the deity to come and occupy "your resting place" might be a deliberate way of linking the temple with the above-mentioned portrayal of Solomon. Another possible reason might be linked to a further prominent theme in this closing section of the prayer, namely, the reminder: **O Lord God, do not reject your anointed one. Remember the great love promised to David your servant.** This petition might be an allusion to the eternal promise made to David, which will be upheld for Solomon.

These two prominent themes show how earlier promises have been fulfilled in Solomon, and they contribute to this king becoming the

Chronicler's prototype of Israelite kingship. And the temple becomes the prototype of the rest and peace associated with Yahweh. The temple and the cultic worship taking place there reflect the harmonious interchange between Israel's God and his people. The temple symbolizes a reality that has to have effect in society as well.

7:1–11 / Solomon's prayer is followed by the report on **the glory of the LORD** taking possession of the temple. This section draws strongly on 1 Kings 8:62–9:1, but with significant deviations. First of all, the three verses (2 Chron. 7:1–3) describing how "the glory of the LORD" filled the temple are from the Chronicler's own hand. The phrase "the glory of the LORD" occurs three times in these verses, emphasizing that Yahweh's presence has now become visible in the new temple. The description of the theophany accompanied by fire resembles the description of how "the glory of the LORD" filled the tabernacle after its construction (see Exod. 40:34–38). The Chronicler emphasizes again that the temple stands in continuity with the tabernacle tradition. McKenzie, however, notices one small difference between the two portrayals: "In contrast to the tabernacle event where those who are present run away in fear, when the people in 2 Chron. 7:3 witness the divine activity, they are inspired to worship and give thanks" (*1–2 Chronicles*, p. 248). The people react with the well-known phrase **he is good; his love endures forever.**

The dramatic theophany is followed by **the king and all the people** offering **twenty-two thousand head of cattle and a hundred and twenty thousand sheep and goats.** The number of sacrificial animals mentioned in 7:5 is taken from the Deuteronomistic source text. The Chronicler continues, however, by providing additional information (in 7:6) about the cultic personnel who were involved: **the priests took their positions, as did the Levites with the LORD's musical instruments.** As in previous examples, it is not denied that the priests performed their appropriate duties, but the emphasis is on the Levites assisting them and providing the musical accompaniment for the occasion. And when the priests **blew the trumpets, . . . all the Israelites were standing,** an expression emphasizing the inclusive concept of Israel.

Second Chronicles 7:7–11 narrates how **Solomon consecrated the middle part of the courtyard in front of the temple of the LORD** (7:7) and **observed the festival at that time for seven days** (7:8). The section concludes with the words, **Solomon had finished the temple of the LORD and the royal palace, and had succeeded in carrying out all he had in mind to do in the temple of the LORD and in his own palace.** This concludes the whole episode of the temple's construction and its dedication.

7:12–22 / The conclusion of the temple construction and dedication is followed by Yahweh's response in a divine revelation. Whereas the source text in 1 Kings 9:2 refers back to the Lord's appearance to Solomon in Gibeon, the Chronicler merely mentions the LORD appeared to him at night, apparently the same night after the dedication of the temple. Second Chronicles 7:12b–15 is not represented in the source text in 1 Kings 9 but refers back to the content of Solomon's prayer, particularly to 2 Chronicles 6:26–31. Very important are the opening words of the divine response: I have heard your prayer and have chosen this place for myself as a temple for sacrifices. The rest of the report of the divine response (7:16–22) adheres closely to the Deuteronomistic version (1 Kgs. 9:3–9). The Lord's words confirm the acceptance of the temple: my Name may be there forever (2 Chron. 7:16). Yet this confirmation is conditional: but if you turn away and forsake the decrees and commands I have given you and go off to serve other gods and worship them, then I will . . . reject this temple I have consecrated for my Name (7:19–20). McKenzie is probably right in remarking: "It is difficult to avoid the impression that the Chronicler here warns those in the Second Temple period by recalling the destruction of the first temple brought on by apostasy" (*1–2 Chronicles,* p. 250). Because Solomon's temple was regarded as the earthly dwelling place of Yahweh in which his presence was tangible, the destruction of this temple before the exile sparked intense theological reflection. In the wake of this theological reflection about the relationship between Yahweh and his people through the temple, the Chronicler's words would have been a clear warning to the Second Temple community.

Additional Notes §3.4

5:2–7:10 / Hicks (*1 and 2 Chronicles,* p. 279) proposes a chiastic structure for this text. According to this suggestion, the narrative starts with a summons (5:2–3) and concludes with a dismissal (7:8–10). The sacrifices are described in two corresponding units, namely, 5:4–10 and 7:4–7. The corresponding sections 5:11–13a and 7:3 narrate the musical interludes, with the appearance of the glory cloud in 5:13b–7:2 forming the centerpiece of this chiastic construction. Again, one should be careful not to force literary units into a rigidly chiastic structure. It rather seems more sensible to take the narrative structure itself, with its temporal and spatial markers, as the point of departure for the analysis of subunits. The division suggested in the commentary (based on McKenzie, *1–2 Chronicles,* p. 243) works within the wider narrative context (connecting this episode with the previous narrative, about David bringing the ark to Jerusalem), but also suggests that the climax of the dedication ceremony is reached when Yahweh responds in a divine revelation (7:11–22).

5:2–14 / There are numerous similarities between this section and the account in 1 Chron. 15–16. The same verb was used in 1 Chron. 15:3—with David as subject—to refer to the convening of All-Israel to bring the ark to Jerusalem. In the present section **Solomon** performs this role. The role of the **Levites** is also very similar in these sections. Particularly the Chronicler's additional material in 2 Chron. 5:12–13a recalls the musical accompaniment described in 1 Chron. 15–16. The mention of the three Levitical families, **Asaph, Heman,** and **Jeduthun,** is in line with the Chronicler's tendency to give prominence to these families in the cultic celebrations. As discussed in the commentary, these references probably reflect the Chronicler's own cultic situation. The praise song to Yahweh of the Levitical singers, **he is good; his love endures forever**—a phrase also well known from the Psalter—was already featured in 1 Chron. 16:34 and 16:41 as part of the celebration after the bringing of the ark to Jerusalem.

6:1–2 / McKenzie (*1–2 Chronicles*, p. 243) sees these two verses as part of the previous pericope. The idea of the **cloud,** which was mentioned at the end of the previous part, continues here. However, since the verses report a first short speech by Solomon, they form a transition from the theophany of 5:2–14 to Solomon's speech (6:3–11) and prayer (6:12–42). These verses could therefore be considered part of either of the two sections.

6:5a and **6:11** / I have already referred to the Chronicler's apparent omission of the exodus tradition from his version of history (see commentary on 3:2). The present section, however, offers ambiguous evidence. In 6:5a the reference to the exodus was retained from the source text in 1 Kgs. 8:16, although it was omitted in 2 Chron. 6:11 (compared to 1 Kgs. 8:21). At least one could confirm on the basis of these examples that no general conclusion can be drawn about the Chronicler's usage of the exodus tradition. McKenzie's speculation about this particular instance seems plausible: "It may be that the Chronicler suppresses such references, as some scholars contend, but then it is unclear why he retained the one in 2 Chron. 6:5. Perhaps his change here was motivated by his concern to avoid the implication that the covenant was only with the exodus generation and to show that it involves all Israel, including his contemporaries" (*1–2 Chronicles*, p. 246).

6:5b–6a / The Hebrew equivalent for **nor have I chosen anyone to be the leader over my people Israel. But now I have chosen Jerusalem for my Name to be there** does not appear in 1 Kgs. 8. H. G. M. Williamson remarks that these words should, however, not be seen as the Chronicler's own addition, and he offers a text-critical explanation for the difference: "These two clauses . . . were only lost . . . by homoioteleuton [a scribal error which occurred when the eye of the scribe who copied the manuscript jumped from one phrase to a similar phrase later in the text, omitting what comes between the two phrases] after the time of the Chronicler. They are thus not to be regarded as his addition, indicative of his particular interests" (*1 and 2 Chronicles* [New Century Bible Commentary; Grand Rapids: Eerdmans, 1982], p. 216).

6:12–42 / Certainly the most extensive discussion of Solomon's prayer in 1 Kgs. 8 (which forms the basis for the Chronicler's version) is the published dissertation of Eep Talstra, *Solomon's Prayer: Synchrony and Diachrony in the Composition of 1 Kings 8,14–61* (Contributions to Biblical Exegesis and Theology 3; Kampen: Kok Pharos, 1993). As his subtitle suggests, Talstra first does a synchronic analysis that "takes the text as a unity, as a meaningful whole to which all textual elements contribute" (p. 82). This is followed by a diachronic analysis that "reconstructs the growth of the text and the corresponding situations in which existing texts were received and interpreted" (p. 82).

7:8–10 / The Chronicler made some significant changes to the chronology of the Feast of the Dedication of the temple in these verses. Drawing from his source text in 1 Kgs. 8:65–66, he changed the dismissal of the people from the eighth day to **the twenty-third day**, with **the eighth day** becoming the day on which **they held an assembly**. These changes create some tensions in the text. McKenzie indicates that the new "timetable causes some tension with the Chronicler's dating of the dedication ceremonies at 'the festival' [= Sukkot] in 5:3. Perhaps more problematic, the Chronicler apparently failed to recognize that his dates for the dedication encompass Yom Kippur, the day of atonement, to be observed on the tenth day of the seventh month according to Lev 23:26–32" (*1–2 Chronicles*, pp. 248–49).

§3.5 Solomon's Other Projects (2 Chron. 8:1–18)

Whereas the construction of the temple in Jerusalem carries the most emphasis in the Chronicler's narrative about Solomon, some of the other projects of the king are summarized in a brief section as well. The temporal remark in 8:1 indicates that the temple construction took twenty years and that at the end of this period some other projects were initiated. Second Chronicles 8:1–6 briefly summarizes some other building projects that were undertaken. Second Chronicles 8:7–10 reports on Solomon's conscription of laborers and his appointment of his officials, concluding in 8:11 with the mention of Solomon's Egyptian wife. A short description is given of the rituals performed in the temple (8:12–15) before 8:16 wraps up the whole narrative with the remark, "So the temple of the Lord was finished." Second Chronicles 8:17–18 provides some information on Solomon's maritime expeditions to Ophir in pursuit of gold. The Chronicler made use of 1 Kings 9:10–28 in developing his narrative in this section. There are, however, numerous differences in presentation, with omissions and additions abounding.

8:1–6 / This subunit differs considerably from the source text in 1 Kings 9:10–17. Not only does Chronicles provide different information than the Deuteronomistic source text, but there is at least one contradiction between the two versions. Whereas 1 Kings 9:11–13 mentions that "King Solomon gave twenty towns in Galilee to Hiram" and that the Sidonian king was not satisfied with the payment, 2 Chronicles 8:2 states that Hiram gave cities to Solomon (**the villages that Hiram had given him**). It is clear that the Chronicler wanted to provide a more positive depiction of the relationship between Hiram and Solomon, in which the latter is the superior party.

8:7–10 / These verses closely follow the source text in 1 Kings 9:20–23. The distinction between foreign Canaanites being conscripted as forced labor and Israelites who served as commanders and chiefs of his army was taken over from the Deuteronomistic version.

8:11 / Although both versions report about Solomon's Egyptian wife, who moved from the **City of David** to the new **palace** built by Solomon, the Chronicler adds an interesting motivation for this move: **For he said, "My wife must not live in the palace of David king of Israel, because the places the ark of the LORD has entered are holy."** The Chronicler therefore takes pains to indicate that this move was not just for her convenience, but took place in order not to defile a place where the ark had entered before. It is not clear, however, whether it was her status as an Egyptian foreigner or her status as a woman that determined this move. Although the first option seems most plausible within a context where the wife's ethnic background is explicitly mentioned, it remains doubtful, since the Chronicler is known to have a fairly inclusive attitude toward foreigners.

8:12–15 / Whereas 1 Kings 9:25 very concisely mentions the offerings brought by Solomon to the altar in the temple, the Chronicler adds elaborate material on the offerings sacrificed and the feasts celebrated in the temple. Although these verses are mainly from the Chronicler's account, it seems that he could have obtained the information contained in them from Pentateuchal texts such as Leviticus 23 and Numbers 28–29, where similar festivals are described. The section might also be related to 1 Chronicles 23–27, where the division of David's officials was detailed. Second Chronicles 8:14 therefore mentions that these appointments were made **in keeping with the ordinance of his father David** and **because this was what David the man of God had ordered.** The expression "man of God" in relation to David is quite strange. This phrase is normally used in the Old Testament to refer to prophets. McKenzie remarks that "its use here is likely connected to the description of the activity of the Levitical singers as prophecy" (*1–2 Chronicles*, p. 255).

8:16 / This verse—which has no equivalent in the source text—is another conclusion (like 7:11) to the temple-building episode. It is suggested that all these other projects stood within the framework of the construction of the temple. Therefore, the verse concludes: **So the temple of the LORD was finished.**

8:17–18 / The last two verses present yet another project of Solomon's, namely, his maritime expeditions from **Ezion Geber and Elath** in pursuit of precious metals. King **Hiram** of Tyre again (as in the temple-building exercise) came to Solomon's assistance by providing **men who knew the sea.** The huge amount of **gold** brought back from **Ophir**

provides the background to the next episode, in which Solomon's wealth is the center of attention.

Additional Notes §3.5

8:16 / The Hebrew verb *kun*, used in this verse (translated in the phrase **all Solomon's work was carried out**), is a term that structures the Chronicler's understanding of the monarchical history. The verb occurs five times in the Solomon narrative (1:4; 2:7, 9; 3:1; 8:16), with the present reference being the last one. The very last occurrence in Chronicles is in 35:20, where it is stated after the celebration of Josiah's Passover: "After all this, when Josiah had set the temple in order . . ." According to the Chronicler's view, Solomon's building of the temple was completed only after the proper celebration of the Passover under Josiah.

8:18 / The location of **Ophir** is unknown. Some scholars suggest that the place must have been somewhere on the African continent, where the commodities associated with it could readily be found. Some older studies even associated it with the wealth of the ancient Zimbabwean kingdom (the ruins of which were discovered in southern Africa in the nineteenth century). Manfred Görg ("Ofir und Punt," *BN* 82 [1996], pp. 5–8) associates Ophir with Punt and comes to the conclusion that these places must have been along the African coast (although no more precise indication is given). McKenzie remarks ironically: "Unfortunately for treasure seekers, the location of Ophir is unknown" (*1–2 Chronicles*, p. 255). The mention of **four hundred and fifty talents of gold** is probably an exaggeration in order to enhance Solomon's reputation. A "talent" is normally taken to weigh between thirty and thirty-five kilograms, which would bring the weight of gold mentioned here to approximately sixteen metric tons.

§3.6 Solomon's International Fame (2 Chron. 9:1–28)

Now that the Chronicler's narrative has reached its climax in the building and dedication of the temple in Jerusalem, the focus shifts to King Solomon himself. His outstanding achievement was, of course, the construction of the sanctuary. However, the Chronicler goes to great lengths to emphasize the glorious reputation of this king. He is somebody who acts with wisdom, which is a confirmation that Yahweh granted his wish (2 Chron. 1:10–12). But he also possesses abundant wealth, because the Lord his God is with him.

His wisdom and wealth lead to international fame. This is dramatically confirmed in the next episode, in which the visit of the foreign queen of Sheba is described (9:1–9, 12). She was just one example of international royalty confirming Solomon's reputation. Second Chronicles 9:22 states that "King Solomon was greater in riches and wisdom than all the other kings of the earth," and 9:23 mentions that "all the kings of the earth sought audience with Solomon to hear the wisdom God had put in his heart." It is quite significant that Solomon receives this recognition from foreign royalty.

Furthermore, numerous anecdotes about Solomon's wealth and other projects confirm this reputation in 9:10–11 and 9:13–28. They include Hiram's maritime assistance to get further precious metals and wood for enhancing the glory of the temple and palace; the making of shields, throne, goblets, and household articles from gold; and the organization and equipment of his cavalry.

The Chronicler follows his source text in 1 Kings 10 very closely, with only a few minor deviations occurring in the text, particularly toward the end of the episode.

9:1–9 and 9:12 / The account of the visit of **the queen of Sheba** to **Solomon** in **Jerusalem** serves a dual purpose. On the one hand, it emphasizes the wisdom of Solomon. Her intention in coming to Jerusalem was **to test him with hard questions** (9:1)—an expression associated with wisdom practice. Furthermore, **Solomon answered all her questions;**

nothing was too hard for him to explain to her (9:2). The queen's surprised reaction to Solomon's wisdom is stated very elaborately in 9:3–7. Such an overwhelming confirmation of Yahweh's granting Solomon wisdom cannot be missed by any reader!

The narrative serves another purpose, however—to emphasize Solomon's wealth. The queen of Sheba herself has a great reputation. She arrived **with a very great caravan—with camels carrying spices, large quantities of gold, and precious stones** (9:1). And the summary in 9:9 is telling: **there had never been such spices as those the queen of Sheba gave to King Solomon.** Although this queen appears only briefly on the scene of history in the Deuteronomist's and Chronicler's versions of the past and then disappears again, her reputation as somebody who can give extraordinary gifts to whom she wants serves as a powerful instrument in the characterization of Solomon.

Although this account follows the Deuteronomistic source text closely, an interesting deviation occurs in 9:8. Whereas 1 Kings 10:9 reads, "Praise be to the LORD your God, who has delighted in you and placed you on the throne of Israel," the Chronicler's version differs in the last part: **and placed you on his throne as king to rule for the LORD your God.** The change from "the throne of Israel" to Yahweh's throne is in line with the way in which Solomon's kingship is presented in the Chronicler's own material in 1 Chronicles 28:5: "he has chosen my son Solomon to sit on the throne of the kingdom of the LORD over Israel." This reflects the Chronicler's understanding that the actual king of Israel is Yahweh. Solomon might be the center of literary attention in this episode, but with this small change to the source text the Chronicler reminds his readers that Solomon was not occupying his own throne but was rather representing Yahweh. In the time of the Chronicler, when Israel had no earthly king of its own, this claim might have had special significance for the restoration community. The Chronicler's easy acceptance of Persian rule over them (see commentary on 2 Chron. 36:22–23) might even be related to this conviction that earthly kings are not the real kings. Yahweh is the real king.

9:10–11 and 9:13–28 / The insertion in 9:10–11 (see Additional Note) rejoins the narrative about Solomon's relationship with **Hiram** of Tyre. It seems that the maritime connection with this foreign king over a long period contributed to increasing Solomon's splendor (9:21).

However, it was not only the queen of Sheba and King Hiram who contributed in this way to Solomon's prestige: **also all the kings of Arabia and the governors of the land brought gold and silver to Solomon** (9:14).

The wisdom and wealth of Solomon are central in the queen of Sheba narrative. These themes are again confirmed in 9:24–25, which acts as a type of summary of the section on the further splendor of this king: **the whole world sought audience with Solomon to hear the wisdom God had put in his heart. Year after year, everyone who came brought a gift.** The section in 9:25–28 deviates significantly from the source text in 1 Kings 10:26–29. Second Chronicles 9:25, 27–28 abbreviates the information of the text in 1 Kings 10, but the information contained in 2 Chronicles 9:26, **he ruled over all the kings from the River to the land of the Philistines, as far as the border of Egypt,** does not occur in this position in the source text. It was taken from 1 Kings 4:21, where the same description is provided to indicate Solomon's territory.

Additional Notes §3.6

9:1 / **Sheba** is normally associated with Yemen on the southwestern shores of the Arabian peninsula. G. W. van Beek ("The Land of Sheba," in *Solomon and Sheba* [ed. J. B. Pritchard; London: Phaidon, 1974], p. 41) states that Sheba was located in the southwestern corner of the Arabian peninsula, with boundaries roughly corresponding to those of modern Yemen. It was more than 1,400 miles south of Palestine, with barren terrain in between. This region must have been extremely difficult to cross unless one was well provided with camels and experienced guides. Van Beek also remarks (p. 43) with reference to the date of the Sabean settlement that it still cannot be fixed precisely, although its outer limits must be between 1600 B.C. and 1200 B.C. Van Beek also contains interesting material about the presence of a "queen of Sheba" in other traditions, such as the Ethiopian and Christian traditions (e.g., Matt. 12:41 and Luke 11:31). If **the queen of Sheba** of 2 Chron. 9 can be associated with the Sabean area and settlement, it indicates that the use of this figure in relation to Solomon (who lived much later) is probably a legendary literary construction. The queen of Sheba was probably seen as the ultimate symbol of a very wealthy and wise ancient Near Eastern royal line, and when the biblical texts have her confirming Solomon's greatness, the effect is to enhance his reputation tremendously.

9:10–11 / These verses interrupt the account about the queen of Sheba. Japhet thinks that "their more appropriate place was probably after v. 21" (*I and II Chronicles* [London: SCM, 1993], p. 638). Another possibility would be that these verses belonged to the end of the previous chapter (i.e., after 8:18) but were dislocated during the history of transmission. One should note that this interruption is already present in the Deuteronomistic source text in 1 Kgs. 10:11–12 and should not be attributed to a change made by the Chronicler. The corruption in the source text was closely followed by the Chronicler.

9:15–16 / The unit used here is **beka.** It is known from the reference in Exod. 38:26, where it is specified as "half a shekel." The metric equivalent of a beka is about 5.5 grams.

9:16 and 9:20 / **The Palace of the Forest of Lebanon** is only mentioned in these verses without any further description. In contrast, the construction of this storehouse or arsenal by Solomon is described more fully in 1 Kgs. 7:2–5.

9:19 / One of the luxurious objects manufactured by Solomon from all the precious metals he had at his disposal was "a great throne inlaid with ivory and overlaid with pure gold" (9:17). One little detail of the description, however, was altered from the version in the Deuteronomistic source text. Whereas 1 Kings 10:19 mentions that "its back had a rounded top," scholars are in agreement that the Hebrew term in that verse is a scribal error for another word meaning "calf." The Septuagint, for example, preserved this reading, referring to "calf heads." H. G. M. Williamson suggests with reference to the expression "footstool of gold": "The Chronicler has substituted this for I Kg. 10:19, 'at the back of the throne was a calf's head,' probably because of the latter's unacceptable religious overtones" (*1 and 2 Chronicles* [New Century Bible Commentary; Grand Rapids: Eerdmans, 1982], p. 235). McKenzie disagrees, however: "It is doubtful that a calf's head on the rear of the throne would be perceived as idolatrous" (*1–2 Chronicles*, p. 257).

§3.7 Solomon's Death (2 Chron. 9:29–31)

This final episode presents—in the usual fashion—a summary of Solomon's reign as well as a note on his death, burial, and succession. For this description the Chronicler makes use of the Deuteronomistic version in 1 Kings 11:41–43.

9:29–31 / Whereas the source text in 1 Kings 11:41 refers the reader to "the book of the annals of Solomon" for more information on "the other events of Solomon's reign—all he did and the wisdom he displayed," the Chronicler's version differs considerably. The latter refers to **the other events of Solomon's reign, from beginning to end,** and the reader is referred to a list of prophetic writings. It seems as if 1 Chronicles 29:29 could rather have been the source text used here in 2 Chronicles 9:29. There a similar formulation is used with reference to the life of King David. This might be the Chronicler's way of giving expression to the close relationship between David's and Solomon's respective reigns.

Additional Note §3.7

9:29–31 / It is noteworthy that the Chronicler skips over the preceding narratives in the source text, 1 Kgs. 11:1–40. These recount Solomon's many wives and their idolatrous influence on him, Solomon's adversaries, and Jeroboam's rebelling against Solomon. These narratives blame Solomon for the division in the monarchy that followed his reign. Given the Chronicler's desire to idealize Solomon as a prototype of royalty, it is understandable that these Deuteronomistic narratives were not included in the Chronicler's construction.

Summary of §3

In retrospect, several key ideas clearly dominate the Chronicler's Solomon narrative.

Interestingly, the Chronicler sets it in the context of the transfer of cultic functions from Gibeon to Jerusalem. The Chronicler apparently wanted to reconfirm the religious-historical claim of Jerusalem as the chosen place to worship Yahweh. This claim stood over against that of Gibeon, closely associated with the Benjaminites (1 Chron. 21). The transfer of the tabernacle from Gibeon to Jerusalem's temple forever established the temple in Jerusalem as the place where Yahweh's name lives. The bringing of the ark of the covenant by consecrated Levites and priests to the Most Holy Place in the temple consummates a long history by which the Jerusalem cult achieves centrality.

The all-important theme of the temple building probably reflects the discourse in Persian-period Judah concerning the status of the rebuilt temple. Other biblical writings of the time (such as Haggai) voice the disappointment in some circles about the lack of splendor in the postexilic temple. The Chronicler's narrative emphasizes the value and significance of the Second Temple.

The depiction of foreign nations and rulers in the Solomon narrative is noteworthy. Apparently, Solomon conscripted Canaanite tribes living within Israel for slave labor, but this episode portrays two foreign rulers, King Hiram of Tyre and the queen of Sheba, very positively in their confirmation of Solomon's wealth and wisdom.

Clearly, the Chronicler wanted to draw a parallel between David and Solomon. However, there is also a clear development from David to Solomon. Yahweh's promise of eternal kingship to David finds fulfillment in Solomon. David prepared the way for the building of the temple, but Solomon is the king who accomplishes this formidable task. Davidic kingship comes to its fullest expression in the reign of Solomon.

Solomon is therefore presented as a prototype of Israelite kingship. Rest and peace characterize his reign, but he is also the one who receives the gift of wisdom from Yahweh. Even foreign kings confirm Solomon's splendor (2 Chron. 9:8). However, he sits on Yahweh's throne, and his reign is closely associated with Yahweh's covenant relationship with All-Israel.

Might the Solomonic prototype constructed by the Chronicler also have had a polemic function during the late Persian period? With the establishment of Yehud as a Persian province and the reestablishment of the temple in Jerusalem, one may assume that this text also contributed to a wider discourse on the status of the Yehudite leadership and cultic community within the Persian imperial context.

§4 The Kings of Judah (2 Chron. 10:1–36:23)

With the narratives of David and Solomon (1 Chron. 11–29 and 2 Chron. 1–9, respectively) the Chronicler has thus far succeeded in establishing a very clear prototype of Israelite kingship. This kingship rests in the eternal promise made to David by Yahweh, the deity of Israel. And it finds its highest expression in the kingship of Solomon, who sits on Yahweh's throne. Solomon established a cultic center by building the temple in Jerusalem, where both the tabernacle and ark of the covenant are resting, and he embodies Yahweh's rest and peace for both his own people and foreign nations. As Johnstone puts it: "The sovereignty of God is acknowledged by Israel paying all that is due to him and by all the world bringing their tribute. The magnificence and wealth of the temple, and the splendor of the court and throne of Solomon, maintained by these dues and tribute, are thus the outward sign of this universal recognition of the reign of God" (W. Johnstone, *1 and 2 Chronicles*, vol. 2 [JSOTSup 254; London: T&T Clark, 1976], p. 10).

This prototype forms the background to the discussion of Judah's kings in the rest of Chronicles. In 2 Chronicles 10–36 a total of nineteen Judahite kings (or twenty, if Athaliah is also considered a separate monarch) are discussed. The Chronicler's narrative includes all Judahite monarchs who are already known from the Deuteronomistic History in the book of Kings, and the Chronicler follows the same order as the Deuteronomist in his presentation. However, the Chronicler's royal narratives are cast in a new framework. Not only does the David-Solomon complex form a new entry into the further royal narratives, but the Chronicler's portrayal focuses exclusively on the Judahite monarchy, not the divided kingdoms. The Chronicler ignores the northern kingdom's history for the most part and mentions it only where Israel's past impinged on the Judahite history. This confirms that the Chronicler's version is not merely a reduction or abridged version of the Deuteronomistic text—it is surely another history that stands in continuity, but also in discontinuity, with the older historiographical tradition.

The concept of All-Israel figures prominently in the genealogical introduction to the book (1 Chron. 1–9) as well as in the David-Solomon narratives. Does the exclusion of the northern kingdom's history alter the understanding of All-Israel in the next section of Chronicles? No! In the next part it becomes remarkably clear that the Chronicler's understanding of All-Israel is not related to a united monarchy. Although the focus is on the Judahite kings, the Chronicler very clearly understands that the people of Yahweh as All-Israel do not exclude the northern tribes (as seen in 1 Chron. 1–9). But the next section of the book defines All-Israel as those who "seek" Yahweh. All-Israel is therefore primarily defined in religious-cultic terms, not in terms of ethnicity.

The Chronicler bases his description of the Judahite kings strongly on the Deuteronomistic version (1 Kgs. 2–2 Kgs. 25). However, he does so very freely. Much more than in the Solomon narrative, the Chronicler has the courage to omit great parts of the source texts, alter other parts, and even add his own materials (see the introduction). The significant number of differences in this section of Chronicles has sparked a debate on whether the Deuteronomistic History was really used by the Chronicler or whether both the Deuteronomists and the Chronicler rather made use of a common source, each in their own way. This theory has not found general acceptance, so one may still assume that the differences between Chronicles and 1–2 Kings derive mainly from the Chronicler's own ideological agenda.

How are the royal Judahite narratives (2 Chron. 10–36) structured? M. A. Throntveit (*When Kings Speak: Royal Speech and Royal Prayer in Chronicles* [Atlanta: Scholars Press, 1987], pp. 113–20) divides them into two parts: 2 Chronicles 10–28 and 2 Chronicles 29–36. His analysis of their royal speeches leads him to conclude that the period from Rehoboam to Ahaz marks an era when the unity featured in the time of David and Solomon has ended. The narratives call for a reunion of north and south by seeking Yahweh and obeying his prophets as Jehoshaphat did. In Throntveit's view, the period from Hezekiah until the exile (i.e., 2 Chron. 29–36) represents a period of a reunited monarchy.

In this commentary I will follow another structure, however. There are mainly two reasons for this: (1) I am not as convinced as Throntveit that the Chronicler had any intention of advocating a united kingdom in a political sense; and (2) the structural indications that delimit the different royal narratives suggest a structure in which the narrative of each king forms a unit, with the death and burial notice forming its end and the note about who succeeded the king indicating the transition to the following narrative. I treat the narratives of Athaliah and Joash together

(22:10–24:27), since it is not clear whether Athaliah is considered a separate monarch by the Chronicler. Furthermore, for practical reasons, I will treat the short narratives of Jehoahaz, Jehoiakim, Jehoiachin, and Zedekiah together in one unit. The whole book closes with a unit on the fall of Jerusalem (36:15–21) and another on the imminent liberation under the Persian Empire (36:22–23).

§4.1 Rehoboam (2 Chron. 10:1–12:16)

The first king of the kingdom of Judah was Rehoboam, the son of Solomon. Rehoboam was a transitional figure. At the beginning of his reign the united kingdom of his father came under severe pressure. Under the leadership of Jeroboam, the son of Nebat, the northern tribes rebelled against the southern leader. When they did not get a satisfactory reaction from Rehoboam of Judah, a schism between the southern and northern tribes was the inevitable consequence. The schism into two kingdoms, that of Judah in the south and Israel in the north, occurred in approximately 931/930 B.C.

The Deuteronomistic historian simply blamed the dissatisfaction with the southern leadership on Solomon. According to that version of Israel's history, Solomon conscripted slave laborers from the northern Israelites. The Chronicler takes pains to indicate that Solomon did not put his fellow Israelites under the yoke of slavery but rather conscripted laborers from the Canaanite tribes who had remained in the land. Since the Chronicler wants to present a blameless Solomon as the zenith of royal obedience to Yahweh, the following schism presented the Chronicler with a difficult task. He had to reconcile the historical reality and the older Deuteronomistic version with his own theological agenda in which an idealized Solomon occupies central position.

In doing so, the Chronicler cleverly made use of some of the older Deuteronomistic traditions about Rehoboam and the schism, but also made significant alterations and additions. The resultant literary structure of the Chronicler's narrative is as follows: 2 Chronicles 10:1–19 closely follows the source text in 1 Kings 12:1–20 in presenting the narrative about the schism (although the Chronicler eliminates the last verse of Kings). This narrative consists of an introduction in 2 Chronicles 10:1–2, followed by a report on all the conversations that took place (10:3–15) and a description of the resultant schism (10:16–19). In 11:1–4 (following 1 Kgs. 12:21–24 closely) it is indicated that a prophetic intervention kept Rehoboam and Judah from battling against their northern neighbors. Then follows a section of the Chronicler's own material in which Rehoboam's consolidation of the southern kingdom is narrated (2 Chron.

11:5–12), the defection of some priests and Levites from the north to the south is described (11:13–17), and Rehoboam's familial growth is featured (11:18–23). The narrative then goes over into a description of Shishak's campaign against Jerusalem (12:1–12). Although the first few verses of this account follow the source text in 1 Kings 14:25–28, the Chronicler also altered his source and added an elaborate portion of text about the prophet Shemaiah speaking to Rehoboam. The narrative concludes (2 Chron. 12:13–16) with a summary of Rehoboam's reign using the usual formulas (adapting some source material from 1 Kgs. 14:21–31).

The overall structure of the Chronicler's Rehoboam narrative, which differs from the Deuteronomistic version, may be understood in the light of the Chronicler's theological agenda. McKenzie is therefore right when he states: "The division of the kingdom at the beginning of Rehoboam's reign had to be at least partly his fault, since it could not be blamed on Solomon. Similarly, the invasion of Shishak had to be punishment in response to Rehoboam's sin" (*1–2 Chronicles*, p. 261).

10:1–2 / The Chronicler—like his source text—locates the enthronement as king of **Rehoboam**, Solomon's son, in **Shechem**, to the north of Jerusalem. This is probably an indication that there had already been some signs of discontent among the northern tribes and that Rehoboam wanted to consolidate support for his reign by this gesture. That **Jeroboam**—who, as it will become clear in the narrative, had close allegiance with the northern tribes—**was in Egypt, where he had fled from King Solomon** is an additional sign of unrest emerging in the north. Although both the Deuteronomistic and the Chronicler's versions indicate that **all the Israelites** (*kol-yisra'el*) went to Shechem for the occasion, the term here (and in 10:3) probably refers to the northern tribes only.

10:3–15 / The northern delegation, with Jeroboam among them, now convenes in Shechem. The request (in direct speech in 10:4) to **lighten the harsh labor and the heavy yoke** comes within the context of their carrying the "heavy yoke" that Solomon placed on them. The Chronicler took over this formulation from Kings and did not bother to omit this negative reflection on Solomon (which would have been expected in the light of his idealization of Solomon). After **Rehoboam** asks for **three days** to reflect on the matter, the new king sets out to gather some perspectives from different groups in the community. After consulting **the elders who had served his father Solomon** (10:6–7), he ignored their **advice** (10:8). He rather followed **the young men who had grown up with him and were serving him** (10:8–11), who responded that he should make his father's **heavy yoke . . . even heavier.** This conduct of Rehoboam stands in sharp contrast to the portrayal of Solomon, his father. At the occasion of the queen of Sheba's visit, "Solomon answered all her questions; nothing was too hard for him to explain to her" (9:2). And because of his wisdom and wealth, "all the kings of the earth sought audience with Solomon to hear the wisdom God had put in his heart" (9:23). Whereas Solomon could provide words of wisdom, Rehoboam had to go and seek wisdom.

10:16–19 / The narrative now reaches its deepest point. Having heard that Rehoboam does not want to make any concession to them, the Israelites exclaim: **What share do we have in David, what part in Jesse's son? To your tents, O Israel! Look after your own house, O David!** This spells rebellion and schism. That Rehoboam sent **Adoniram, who was in charge of forced labor,** to deal with the matter was certainly not the wisest thing to do. He was stoned to death by the Israelites, and Rehoboam escaped narrowly. What happened there at Shechem is seen as **rebellion against the house of David to this day.** The Hebrew word used here, translated "rebellion" in the NIV, refers to "break away from" or "to be disloyal." Rehoboam's support base was now reduced to **the Israelites who were living in the towns of Judah.**

Whereas the Chronicler followed his source text in 1 Kings 12:1–19 very accurately, one verse is omitted. First Kings 12:20 states: "When all the Israelites heard that Jeroboam had returned, they sent and called him to the assembly and made him king over all Israel. Only the tribe of Judah remained loyal to the house of David." It is clear that the Chronicler did not want to give any credibility to the kingship of Jeroboam and also did not want the reality of "only the tribe of Judah" remaining loyal to the house of David to be emphasized. This would run counter to his course of focusing on Judah.

11:1–4 / These verses, which were taken over with only a few minor changes from 1 Kings 12:21–24, conclude the schism of David's and Solomon's united kingdom. Although Judah and Benjamin started preparing for a battle against Israel **to regain the kingdom for Rehoboam,** a **word of the Lord** that **came** through **Shemaiah the man of God** (a customary expression for a prophet) intervened, and **they . . . turned back from marching against Jeroboam.** In the intervening "word" the Israelites are explicitly called **your brothers,** an expression that emphasizes the blood relationship between Judah-Benjamin and those tribes following a non-Davidide (Jeroboam) as king.

The prophetic word emphasizes another theological aspect, namely, that the schism should be accepted, **for this is my doing** (11:4). In this phrase, taken over from the source text, Yahweh's role in the division of the kingdom is acknowledged.

11:5–12 / This section does not occur in the source text in Kings or anywhere else in the Hebrew Bible. Some scholars suggest that the city list provided here should rather be associated with the time of Hezekiah. Although the content of this section would probably not fit into the historical-geographic context of Rehoboam, it is quite clear what the Chronicler's intention was with these verses. After the conclusion of the schism in the previous section, it was necessary to emphasize the consolidation of the kingdom of Judah again. It confirms **Jerusalem** as capital of the kingdom, as well as the inclusion of **Judah and Benjamin** under Rehoboam's dominion.

11:13–17 / The next subsection, which also belongs to the Chronicler's own material, continues the trend set in the previous verses, namely, to provide a consolidated image of Rehoboam's kingdom. It simultaneously polemicizes against the cult of the northern kingdom by narrating how some **priests and Levites from all their districts throughout Israel** defected from the north to the south. On the one hand, this is a confirmation that the royal cult in Jerusalem was still the only legitimate cult, but, on the other hand, it indicated that Jeroboam's worship was nothing more than idol veneration. **He appointed his own priests for the high places and for the goat and calf idols he had made** (11:15). The Levites—who we know play such an important role in the Chronicler's understanding of the cult—even came to Jerusalem **because Jeroboam and his sons had rejected them as priests of the LORD** (11:14). And these "priests and Levites" were not alone: they were joined by **those from every tribe of Israel who set their hearts on seeking the LORD, the God of Israel** (11:16). Here, the very important Chronistic concept of "seeking the LORD, the God of Israel" occurs (in this case with the Hebrew root *biqqesh*). In spite of the political trouble, Rehoboam's reign became a time of consolidation for those who sought the Lord in the cult in Jerusalem. As seen in 7:14, and as we will also see later, "seeking the LORD" is the basic constituent of being Yahweh's people. By showing this inclination, they were **walking in the ways of David and Solomon** (11:17). The continuation of the Davidic-Solomonic kingdom is not so much dependent on the political support of All-Israel as it is constituted when All-Israel is "seeking the LORD."

11:18–23 / These verses are also without parallel in the source text in Kings. This subsection still continues the theme of the previous two pericopes, in which the consolidation of the kingdom under Rehoboam is a central motif. Whereas 11:5–12 confirmed the Judahite king's sphere of influence in terms of city building and defense, 11:13–17 had the consolidation of the Jerusalem cult as its theme. In the present subsection the consolidation of Rehoboam's family becomes the focal point. It is clear that the Chronicler is already starting to prepare the way for the succession of **Rehoboam** by his son **Abijah** (see 11:22). This confirms that the kingdom of Judah is not ruled by usurpers or deserters but by the legitimate lineage of the eternal Davidic kingship. But it also confirms that Rehoboam continues his reign with the wisdom of his father. **He acted wisely** in establishing his sons' influence **throughout the districts of Judah and Benjamin** (11:23).

12:1–12 / The Chronicler now moves on to report on the campaign of **Shishak king of Egypt** against **Jerusalem**, which took place in approximately 926/925 B.C. This is not, however, a neutral report about a military event in Judah's history. The Chronicler's very creative usage of source material from 1 Kings 14:21–28 indicates that this subsection presents the turning point in Rehoboam's reign. As soon as his kingdom **was established** (Hebrew *kun*) and **he became strong, he and all Israel with him abandoned the law of the** LORD (12:1—a radical adaptation of the source text in 1 Kgs. 14:22–24). This abandoning (Hebrew *'azab*) of Yahweh and his Torah stands in sharp contrast to the "seeking" of Yahweh still prominent in the previous subsection. In the next verse this downward trend in his career is continued when it is indicated that, **because they had been unfaithful to the** LORD (the Chronicler's own addition to the source text in 1 Kgs. 14:25), Shishak (including some **Libyans, Sukkites and Cushites** in his army) comes to attack Jerusalem. Here the programmatic Hebrew word "be unfaithful" (*ma'al*) is used—a term last used in 1 Chronicles 10:13 in connection with King Saul.

The Chronicler continues his description of the Egyptian campaign until 2 Chronicles 12:12, but only 12:9–11 can be traced back to the source text in 1 Kings 14:26–28. The rest of the narrative is the Chronicler's own material. Battle accounts—including this battle during Rehoboam's reign—are programmatic in the Chronicler's narrative. The introduction of a "new" prophet, namely, **Shemaiah**, into the account of the battle has the function of interpreting the word of Yahweh for the king. The prophetic formula **this is what the** LORD **says** introduces a theological appraisal of the military event. The Chronicler's own material contains abundant use of programmatic terms: **you have abandoned me; therefore, I now abandon you to Shishak** (with the term *'azab* being used twice in 12:5). After **the leaders of Israel and the king** heard the prophet's message, they **humbled themselves** before the Lord. The term used here (*kana'*, "humble oneself") occurs four times in 12:6–7, 12 (which belong to the Chronicler's own additions). The effect of "humbling themselves" to the Lord is indicated in 12:12: **the LORD's anger turned from him, and he was not totally destroyed. Indeed, there was some good in Judah.** Although there was a downward spiral in Rehoboam's reign in terms of his and his people's dedication to the Lord, the intervention by Yahweh through his prophet Shemaiah during the Egyptian campaign turned things around again.

12:13–16 / In this subsection we now come to the summary of **Rehoboam's reign** as well as to a report of his death and burial. The text follows 1 Kings 14:21, 29–31, but adapts the information at will. Second Chronicles 12:14, which has no parallel in the source text, contains the programmatic summary: **he did evil because he had not set his heart on seeking the LORD.** The Hebrew terms *kun* ("to set/establish") and *darash* ("to seek" the Lord) occur here again. The citing of prophetic sources for further reference about the king's reign is also typical of the Chronicler's style. The Chronicler's evaluation of Rehoboam concurs with that of the Deuteronomistic version, but this is done in the Chronicler's own programmatic language.

Additional Notes §4.1

10:2–3 / NIV mentions in a footnote at 1 Kgs. 12:2 that another possible translation for **he returned from Egypt** would be "he remained in Egypt." This seemingly contradictory suggestion can be understood from the Hebrew verbal root *yashab*, when vocalized differently, being translated either "live/remain" or "return." The Hebrew text of 2 Chron. 10:2 reads "he returned from," while the Hebrew text of 1 Kgs. 12:2 reads "he remained in" (with the preposition also differing in Hebrew). Since the Septuagint and Vulgate translations of 1 Kgs. 12:2 also have the equivalent of "he returned from," this is probably the more original reading. However, the change in vocalization and preposition to read "he remained in" is understandable in light of the beginning of 2 Chron. 10:3, which states that **they sent for Jeroboam.** This may, however, also mean that, while he settled somewhere else after his return from Egypt, he was summoned to accompany the people to Shechem.

10:4 / The expression that the NIV translates **and we will serve you** could be better translated "so that we will serve you." The suggestion is that their support for Rehoboam is dependent on whether he is going to soften their yoke. The omission of the same sentence in 10:9 reiterates the point.

10:10 / The sentence **my little finger is thicker than my father's waist** is difficult to interpret, because the word for "finger" is absent from the Hebrew phrase (literally "my little thing"). If "finger" is correct as many think, the line would brag that what Solomon had to go to war to achieve (i.e., to "gird [his] loins"), Rehoboam could get done simply by moving his "little finger." Another possibility, however, is that "my little thing" is a euphemism for the penis. If so, the words "would add rash vulgarity to the charge of foolishness against the young men" (so McKenzie, *1–2 Chronicles*, p. 263). Whether brash, foolish, or crude, the **young men** come off looking very bad.

10:15 / This verse mentions **the word the LORD had spoken to Jeroboam son of Nebat through Ahijah the Shilonite.** In the Deuteronomistic version this is a back reference to 1 Kgs. 11, where the prophecy of Ahijah is mentioned. However, that text was not adopted by the Chronicler. This was probably just an oversight in the Chronicler's editing of the older material, but it emphasizes at least that the Chronicler had access to a fuller text and that his use of that tradition was deliberately selective. The Chronicler assumes his reader has the background to this remark.

11:3 / A small change to the source text in this verse should be noted: Whereas 1 Kings 12:23 states, "Say . . . to the whole house [*kol-bet*] of Judah and Benjamin, and to the rest of the people," the Chronicler changed the phrase to **Say . . . to all the Israelites** (*kol-yisra'el*) **in Judah and Benjamin.** The phrase *kol-yisra'el* had been used earlier in this narrative referring to the northern tribes who rebelled against Solomon's son. Here, however, it becomes an ideological concept that gives expression to the Chronicler's understanding of those who constitute postexilic Israel. H. G. M. Williamson therefore states: "The Chronicler's view in brief is that for the period of the divided monarchy both north and south may legitimately be called 'Israel,' so that the phrase **in Judah and Benjamin** is geographical only" (*1 and 2 Chronicles* [New Century Bible Commentary; Grand Rapids: Eerdmans, 1982], p. 239).

11:5–12 / Israel Finkelstein ("Rehoboam's Fortified Cities," pp. 96–107) shows that the city list provided in these verses does not correspond to any Iron Age reality but fits the period of Hasmonean rule, probably in the days of John Hyrcanus in the second half of the second century B.C. He remarks, however, that "my observations . . . do not call for dating the entire work of the Chronicler to the late 2nd century BCE. . . . It seems possible that II Chron 11,5–11 . . . is a later addition to the main text of Chronicles. If one removes the seven verses, the text reads fluently both thematically and structurally" (p. 106).

11:18–23 / McKenzie indicates that this subsection "is remarkable in several respects" (*1–2 Chronicles*, p. 266). Not only is the detail of the list unusual, but its historical reliability is also uncertain. McKenzie theorizes that the information was included here in the Chronicler's construction (and not in the regnal summary at the end) to imply "that Rehoboam received God's blessing during this period of his reign" (p. 267).

11:20–22 / A difficulty arising in these verses is the mentioning of **Maacah** as Rehoboam's wife and Abijah's mother. Elsewhere, Maacah is mentioned as Asa's mother, that is, Abijah's wife. Some scholars try to harmonize these indications by assuming that Abijah and Asa were brothers rather than father and son. They would have had the same mother, Maacah, then. This contradicts the information in 1 Kgs. 15:8 that Asa was Abijah's son. As long as biblical scholars do not have access to any more evidence, this enigma will remain.

12:2 / The Hebrew term "be unfaithful" (*ma'al*) occurs eleven times in Chronicles (1 Chron. 2:7; 5:25; 10:13; 2 Chron. 12:2; 26:16, 18; 28:19, 22; 29:6; 30:7; 36:14), of which all except one (1 Chron. 2:7, which could be related to Josh. 7:1) are part of the Chronicler's own material. These statistics show the great programmatic importance of this term.

§4.2 Abijah (2 Chron. 13:1–14:1a)

Whereas the history of King Abijah (who ruled approximately 912–911/910 B.C.) occupies only seven and a half verses in the Deuteronomistic source text (1 Kgs. 15:1–8a), the Chronicler's version is much more extensive (twenty-two and a half verses). The reason for this expansion is that the Chronicler completely altered the portrayal of this king. In Kings, Abijah is described as somebody who "committed all the sins his father had done before him; his heart was not fully devoted to the LORD his God, as the heart of David his forefather had been" (1 Kgs. 15:3). In Chronicles he becomes a pious leader who delivers a remarkable speech to Jeroboam when Judah goes into battle with the kingdom of Israel. And he leads his people to a great victory in this battle.

It seems that the Chronicler used the figure of Abijah to rectify the blemishes left by the schism of the kingdom under Rehoboam. Whereas the idealized image of the Davidic kingdom and Solomonic cult came under severe pressure under Rehoboam's reign, the Chronicler's version of Abijah returns the splendor and dedication of that prototypical image. Abijah becomes a model of proper kingship and pious dedication to Yahweh in the Chronicler's version.

The Chronicler's narrative starts with the usual regnal formula with some background information on the king (2 Chron. 13:1–2). In this introduction the Chronicler uses his source text (1 Kgs. 15:1–2, 7b). In the conclusion to this royal narrative (2 Chron. 13:22–14:1a) the Chronicler again draws on his source text (1 Kgs. 15:7a, 8). In between, that is, in 2 Chronicles 13:3–21, we find the Chronicler's own material, where the typical style and theology of this Persian-period writer abound. Second Chronicles 13:3 introduces the reader to a battle that Abijah initiated against Jeroboam of Israel. In 13:4–12 the Chronicler presents the remarkable speech by Abijah, which he delivered from Mount Zemaraim in the hill country of Ephraim. Second Chronicles 13:13–20 recounts the battle itself together with its outcome, while 13:21 is a concluding statement about Abijah's successes.

13:1–2 / The expression **in the eighteenth year of the reign of Jeroboam,** which synchronizes the Judahite king's reign with that of its northern neighbor, is untypical in Chronicles. Although such synchronization occurs frequently in Kings, this is the only instance in Chronicles. It was probably retained from the source text in 1 Kings 15:1 because of the content to follow, namely, a battle against the northern kingdom, Israel. This is one clear instance that shows that the Chronicler did not eliminate the northern kingdom from his presentation completely. Wherever the histories of the two kingdoms intersect (even when Judah comes off badly), the Chronicler retains information on Israel's monarchy.

Second Chronicles 13:2 continues with the statement **there was war between Abijah and Jeroboam.** The Chronicler used a remark occurring at the end of his source text (1 Kgs. 15:7) as a type of heading for the following narrative.

13:3 / It is clear that **Abijah** initiated the war against Jeroboam: **Abijah went into battle.** Although this stands directly in contradiction with the prophetic warning from Shemiah mentioned in the previous episode (11:4), the Chronicler does not judge Abijah's action negatively. The great numbers mentioned for Abijah's and Jeroboam's troops are exaggerated. The point is clear, however: Jeroboam had double the number of troops on the ground. This would make a victory for Judah over Israel remarkable.

13:4–12 / The geographical setting for Abijah's speech—**on Mount Zemaraim, in the hill country of Ephraim**—is the border region between Judah and Israel. The practical setting makes one realize that this speech, which comes completely from the Chronicler's hand, is a construction intended to highlight the Chronicler's theology. The literary function is not to present Abijah speaking to **Jeroboam and all Israel,** but it is rather to offer a way in which the Chronicler could convey his theological ideas to his Persian-period audience.

In the rhetoric of the speech Abijah takes his point of departure in the eternal kingship that Yahweh promised to David: **Don't you know that the LORD, the God of Israel, has given the kingship of Israel to David and his descendants forever?** (13:5). The accusation comes next: **Yet Jeroboam son of Nebat, an official of Solomon son of David, rebelled against his master** (13:6). What Jeroboam did stands in direct opposition to the eternal covenant made by Yahweh with the Davidides. It is interesting to note that Jeroboam is characterized here as "an official of Solomon son of David," and not as king over Israel, in order to emphasize the wrongness of what Jeroboam did. The matter is also blamed on those **worthless scoundrels** who supported Jeroboam. They took advantage of Rehoboam's inexperience. The wordplay in the Hebrew text is notable: whereas Rehoboam could not **resist** (*chazaq*, "to strengthen oneself") them (13:7), Jeroboam and his supporters plan **to resist the kingdom of the** LORD (13:8).

In 13:8–9 the Chronicler's narration of Abijah's speech turns to the apostasy of the northern kingdom. Not only are **the golden calves that Jeroboam made to be your gods** mentioned, but also the ill treatment that **the sons of Aaron, and the Levites** received from Jeroboam and the cheapening of the priesthood (**whoever comes to consecrate himself with a young bull and seven rams may become a priest of what are not gods**) become accusations against Israel on account of which a war against them is legitimized.

In sharp contrast to the apostasy of the northerners, the piety of the Judahites is emphasized in 13:10–11. Aaronide **priests,** assisted by **Levites,** have taken care of all the aspects of the temple cult. In doing so, they were **observing the requirements of the** LORD. The main difference between Judah and Israel is that the Judahites **have not forsaken** (*lo' 'azab*) Yahweh (13:10), while the Israelites **have forsaken him** (*'azab*) (13:11).

Therefore, the strong claim is made in 13:12: **God is with us; he is our leader.** Israel should know that they are engaging in a holy war now (see Num. 10:9) in which Yahweh is fighting the battle for Judah. Therefore, the northern neighbors are warned: **Men of Israel, do not fight against the** LORD, **the God of your fathers, for you will not succeed.**

13:13–20 / When it became clear to Abijah and his troops that Jeroboam had relied on good battle tactics in the meantime, **they cried out to the** LORD (13:14). Therefore, **God routed Jeroboam and all Israel before Abijah and Judah,** with God himself being the subject of the routing/striking (Hebrew *nagaph*, repeated in 13:20). The difference between Judah and Israel, as illustrated by this battle, is that **the men of Israel were subdued** (*kana'*) **on that occasion, and the men of Judah were victorious because they relied** (*sha'an*) **on the** LORD, **the God of their fathers** (13:18). Whereas Jeroboam never recovered from this battle (13:20), Abijah was able to extend his kingdom to include some of the border region towns (13:19).

13:21 / The successes of **Abijah** are confirmed by the phrase **grew in strength,** expressed with *chazaq* ("to make oneself strong") again. While Rehoboam could not make himself strong (*chazaq*) against

Jeroboam and while Jeroboam made himself strong (*chazaq*) against
Yahweh, Abijah could make himself strong (*chazaq*). Like his father
Rehoboam (11:21, 23), he had many **wives, sons,** and **daughters.**

13:22–14:1a / The regnal summary and death-and-burial notice
of Abijah were taken over from the source text in 1 Kings 15:7–8, although
some stylistic and content changes were made. The other information
about Abijah is described in 2 Chronicles 13:22 as **what he did and what
he said,** an expression that differs from the Deuteronomistic "all he did."
This change was probably made on account of the Chronicler's version
of Abijah's history consisting mainly of the speech the king made. Furthermore, the sources cited by the Chronicler are **the annotations of the
prophet Iddo.** We have seen before (with reference to Solomon's reign
in 9:29 and Rehoboam's reign in 12:15) that the Chronicler is fond of
citing a prophetic source (instead of the Deuteronomist's "the book of
the annals of the kings of Judah"). Here Iddo's work is referred to as
"annotations" (so the NIV for Hebrew *midrash*). The narrative ends with
the note that **Asa his son succeeded him as king.**

Additional Notes §4.2

13:1–2 / The Hebrew text of 1 Kgs. 15:1 calls the king Abijam, while
2 Chron. 13:1 has **Abijah.** These were probably alternative spellings of the same
name. There is also some uncertainty about his **mother's name.** Whereas the
Hebrew text of 2 Chron. 13:2 calls her **Micaiah, a daughter of Uriel of Gibeah,**
she is indicated in 1 Kings 15:2 as "Maacah daughter of Abishalom" (which
corresponds to the indication in 2 Chron. 11:20). The NIV translates the name in
2 Chron. 13:2 as **Maacah** in order to harmonize it with 1 Kgs. 15:2 and 2 Chron.
11:20.

13:2 / The remark **there was war between Abijah and Jeroboam** comes
from 1 Kgs. 15:7. In 1 Kgs. 15:6 we have a similar remark: "There was war between
Rehoboam and Jeroboam throughout Abijah's lifetime." This text is, however,
probably the result of some scribal error in the process of textual transmission.

13:3–21 / This section, which is normally taken to be the Chronicler's
own material, may have been compiled from some older sources. This acknowledgment, however, does not prevent us from showing the very distinct Chronistic
theological traits of the addition to the Deuteronomistic version (e.g., typical
expressions like "seeking Yahweh," "relying on Yahweh," and "not forsaking
Yahweh").

13:5 / The background of **a covenant of salt** is unknown. It has been suggested that it signifies an eternal covenant. Perhaps the preservative qualities of salt underlie this metaphor.

13:13–21 / The Abijah narrative illustrates a larger interpretive principle: Wherever the Chronicler introduced his own slant over against the Deuteronomistic version, this does not mean that he did so at will. The Chronicler was heir to a complex theological tradition that could be appropriated in different ways.

§4.3 Asa (2 Chron. 14:1b–16:14)

The Chronicler dedicates the next narrative episode to the reign of King Asa of Judah (ca. 911/910–900 B.C.). As in the Abijah narrative, the Chronicler introduces a significant portion of his own material, creatively restructuring the Asa narrative in the source text (1 Kgs. 15:9–24) within a coherent theological framework. The Deuteronomistic version communicates a positive image of Asa as a king who ensured religious-cultic purity (1 Kgs. 15:11–15), and it narrates an unrelated episode of successful military strategy and diplomacy (15:16–22). One could say that the Deuteronomistic narrative presents religious-cultic and political information about Asa's reign. The Chronicler's account, however, reformulated the two sections into two theological alternatives. It contrasts a clear change from "having rest/peace/not war" in the first section to "having wars from now on" in the second. Two specific temporal indications (2 Chron. 15:19 and 16:1) establish the break between the two: rest prevailed until the thirty-fifth year of Asa's reign, but the situation then suddenly turned around from the thirty-sixth year of his reign. The narrative as a whole now has a logical flow that also better integrates the introduction (14:1b) and conclusion (16:11–14). No longer merely notes about political history and royal succession, they now signify the turnaround from the land having rest (14:1b) to a king becoming ill and dying because he did not rely on Yahweh (16:11–14).

Rather than communicate mere historical information about a past king, the Chronicler urges his audience to make a choice between two basic modes of existence. Cleverly, the Chronicler interrelates thematic terms and their associated themes to build the narrative: those seeking Yahweh and relying on him experience rest, peace, and absence of war. Successful building projects, religious reforms, and victory in battle are associated with this style of existence. The opposite mode of existence is formulated by the negation of the same constellation of concepts: those who do not seek Yahweh and do not rely on him (or rely on worldly powers such as foreign kings or doctors!) will experience war and unrest, as well as disease and death.

The narrative communicates its theological slant by the organization of actors. Yahweh (who never acts in the Deuteronomistic version) is always the subject of *nuach* ("give rest") in the Chronicler's narrative. When Asa relies (*sha'an*) on Yahweh, Yahweh wins the battle on Asa's behalf; when Asa relies (*sha'an*) on Ben-Hadad of Aram for his battle, wars (plural) are the result. When Asa and the people seek (*darash*) Yahweh, they experience rest and security; when Asa does not seek (*darash*) Yahweh, the king becomes ill with a foot disease and dies. These two modes of existence are then highlighted by speeches by two prophets, Azariah and Hanani, as the mouthpieces of Yahweh who ensure the right interpretation of reality. The speeches turn the military strategies of Asa into theological paradigms.

14:1b / The first sentence in the **Asa** narrative is still part of the previous section in the Hebrew Bible, so Asa is introduced merely by a pronominal suffix in the phrase **in his days.** (Interestingly, the Septuagint substituted the pronominal suffix with Asa's name.) At that time **the country was at peace for ten years,** a phrase not found in the source text. The theme of peace and rest, which was already so prominent in the Solomonic history, returns here as a structuring element in the account of Asa's reign. Further, the first section of the narrative (14:2–15:19) expounds the full meaning of the introductory phrase of 14:1b, culminating in 15:19: **there was no more war until the thirty-fifth year of Asa's reign.** The latter temporal clause sounds an ominous note that this condition of having rest ended at some stage.

14:2 / The positive evaluation of King Asa in the Deuteronomistic version in 1 Kings 15:11 is repeated: **Asa did what was good and right in the eyes of the LORD his God,** although with one difference. First Kings 15:11 has only "what was right in the eyes of the LORD." The Chronicler added "his God," as if he wanted to increase the positive evaluation in Kings.

14:3–5 / The Chronicler significantly altered and expanded the source text (1 Kgs. 15:12), which already mentioned the king's cultic reform measures. The terminology used in Chronicles, namely, **foreign altars, high places, sacred stones, Asherah poles** (2 Chron. 14:3), and **high places** and **incense altars** (14:5), reminds one of the prescriptions given in the Deuteronomic legal material (e.g., Deut. 7:5; 12:3). These are mentioned, instead of the "male shrine prostitutes" and "idols his fathers had made" in the source text. The expansion of the Chronicler is also programmatic: **he commanded Judah to seek the** Lord. Again, the word *darash* features prominently. And equally programmatic is the Chronicler's own description of the time: **the kingdom was at peace under him** (2 Chron. 14:5, with *shaqath*).

14:6–7 / Prosperity in the land is expressed by means of building projects. Asa could build **fortified cities and towns** with **towers, gates and bars,** since **the land was at peace** and **the** Lord **gave him rest** (14:6, with both *shaqath* and *nuach*). **The land still belonged to them, because they have sought the** Lord **their God; they sought him and he has given them rest on every side** (14:7, with *darash* twice and *nuach*). These verses, which are not taken from a source text, abound with typical Chronistic theological terminology.

14:8–15 / The account of the war against **Zerah the Cushite** is a novel element in the Chronicler's narrative. The contrast in military power between Judah and Cush is made clear with reference to the numbers of armed men and chariots. Asa had at his disposal **three hundred thousand men from Judah, equipped with large shields and with spears, and two hundred and eighty thousand men from Benjamin, armed with small shields and with bows**—in total, therefore, 580,000 men. Zerah the Cushite, however, had **one million men** (literally "thousands of thousands," translated in NIV as **a vast army**) and **three hundred chariots** at his disposal. Like the previous account of Abijah, the narrative dynamics in the Asa narrative are clearly meant to emphasize the miraculous nature of Judah's victory over the Cushites, emphasizing the role of Yahweh as the one who actually **struck down** (*nagaph*) **the Cushites** on Asa's behalf. The success of Asa thus cannot be attributed to his military power—it was solely the result of his relying on Yahweh (14:11, with *sha'an*). This is confirmed again in the second half of the Asa account, when Hanani reminds Asa of the miraculous nature of this victory over the Cushites and Libyans ("a mighty army"). Asa "relied [*sha'an*] on the Lord," and he "delivered them into [Asa's] hand" (16:8).

15:1–15 / Prophetic figures are often introduced in the Chronicler's narratives to act as theological interpreters of events. The same strategy is followed in 15:1–7, where **Azariah son of Oded** is introduced as somebody on whom **the Spirit of God came** (a typical formula to indicate prophetic status). The Chronicler's typical terminology occurs here repeatedly. The prophet's basic message is: **if you seek** (*darash*) **him, he will be found by you, but if you forsake** (*'azab*) **him, he will forsake**

(*'azab*) you. And, although for a long time Israel was without the true God, they turned to the LORD, the God of Israel, and sought (*biqqesh*) him, and he was found by them. This was meant as an encouragement to the king on account of his cultic-restoration measures. Those acts were seen as "seeking" Yahweh, which would result in "being found" by Yahweh. However, this also provides encouragement for the future: be strong (*chazaq*) and do not give up, for your work will be rewarded. This is then indeed what Asa did when he heard these words and the prophecy of Azariah son of Oded the prophet, namely, he took courage (*chazaq* again). The cultic reforms therefore culminated in an assembly of all Judah and Benjamin and the people from Ephraim, Manasseh and Simeon who had settled among them for making sacrifices and entering into a covenant with God. The content of this covenant basically boils down to being faithful in seeking (*darash* twice in 15:12–13) Yahweh. This is indeed what all Judah did: they sought (*biqqesh*) God eagerly. And the outcome—which is by now not unexpected in the Chronicler's typical theology—is that the LORD gave them rest (*nuach*) on every side.

15:16–19 / This subsection uses some source material from Kings again (1 Kgs. 15:13–16). Asa's cultic reforms continued with more cultic objects being cut down, broken up, and burned. For the first time since the end of Solomon's history, we encounter a reference to the temple: he brought into the temple of God the silver and gold and the articles that he and his father had dedicated (15:18). This is a clear indication that cultic purity and seeking of and relying upon Yahweh are closely associated with temple worship in Jerusalem. And the effect of this can clearly be observed: there was no more war until the thirty-fifth year of Asa's reign (15:19). This remark confirms that rest, peace, and quiet will be experienced if Yahweh is sought, but it simultaneously points forward to a time when there will be war. This verse therefore forms a structural turning point in the Chronicler's Asa narrative.

16:1–6 / The second section (16:1–10) introduces a new period in Asa's history. In the very next year of Asa's reign (the thirty-sixth year) things drastically changed: Baasha king of Israel went up against Judah (16:1). In self-defense, Asa immediately sought alliance with Ben-Hadad king of Aram (16:2), sending to Ben-Hadad as inducements silver and gold out of . . . the LORD's temple and of his own palace. The turnaround for Asa is dramatic, at least initially. When Baasha learned of the alliance, he stopped building Ramah (16:5). Asa carried off timber and stones from there to build up nearby Geba and Mizpah (16:6).

16:7–10 / The Deuteronomistic account of this battle (1 Kgs. 15:17–22) ends quite positively for Asa. However, unlike that source text, the Chronicler introduces through his own material another prophetic voice, **Hanani the seer,** to reinterpret the alliance between Asa and Ben-Hadad. His direct speech abounds with familiar terminology but with a negative slant: **because you relied on** (*sha'an*) **the king of Aram** rather than **on the** Lord **your God, the army of the king of Aram has escaped from your hand.** Hanani also reminds Asa of the king's previous victory against the Cushites: they fell to him because he **relied on** (*sha'an*) **the** Lord. Reliance/nonreliance makes the difference, so henceforth Asa **will be at war.** This new construction clearly reads the alliance between Asa and Ben-Hadad as the beginning of the end for Asa.

16:11–14 / The notice about Asa's disease, death, and burial brings this period to an end. The temporal indication in 16:13 (**the forty-first year of his reign**) therefore creates another point of closure that relates the second narrative section (16:1–10) to the conclusion (16:11–14). The source text is again 1 Kings 15:23–24. However, significant alterations here relate the king's disease to the preceding event. He sought (*darash*) a cure **from the physicians** rather than **the** Lord (2 Chron. 16:12). The Chronicler's significantly different version of the king at the end of his life, representing him as turning from somebody who did "the right and the good" in the Lord's eyes into somebody who "did not seek" the Lord for help in his illness required alteration and expansion of the simple burial notice of 1 Kings 15:24. Like other kings, **Asa died and rested with his fathers,** but (unlike them) he **was buried . . . in the tomb that he had cut out for himself in the city of David.** His funeral was elaborate: he lay **on a bier covered with spices and various blended perfumes, and they made a huge fire in his honor** (2 Chron. 16:13–14). The ambiguity of the Chronicler's portrayal of Asa continues up until his death notice. Although honor was given to this king, he could not be buried with his ancestors in the City of David.

Additional Notes §4.3

14:1b / The Hebrew term that the NIV translates **was at peace** (*shaqath*) occurs three times in the Asa narrative (14:1b, 5, 6). It occurs six times in the book of Judges, and the close connection to Judges becomes particularly apparent in Azariah's speech (2 Chron. 15:1–7).

14:8–15   /   Why did the Chronicler choose the battle against the otherwise unknown **Zerah the Cushite** from Asa's past to make this particular point?
The scholarly proposals concerning his identity include a Nubian general of
Pharaoh Osorkon I (a Libyan), a Nubian mercenary of Pharaoh Shoshenq living
around Gerar, or a member of a small Bedouin-like ethnic group living in the
vicinity of Judah (the majority view; cf. "Cushan" in Hab. 3:7). Clues to why the
Cushites were introduced into this narrative should be sought in the Persian era,
when the Chronicler wrote. Jonker ("Cushites in the Chronicler's Version," pp.
863–81) indicates, with reference to various Greek texts, that the Cushites had a
reputation at the time of being invincible. Ethiopia (or Cush) was regarded by the
Persians (and Greeks) as the southern extreme of the known world. Furthermore,
excavations in Nubia indicate that the Persian invasions never managed to take
complete control of this remote part of the world. Although the evidence from
classical writers is scanty (and biased), people in the Persian province of Yehud
may have known this reputation of the Cushites, perhaps through the Elephantine Jewish community on the southern border of Egypt with Nubia. Could
one perhaps imagine that these classical Greek traditions about the relationship
between Persia and Nubia/Libya were in the back of the Chronicler's mind when
he adapted the narrative about Asa's reign? One could perhaps imagine that the
traditions about Cush being the most extreme part of the known world, as well
as about the military reputations of Cush and Libya—particularly in relation
to the Persians—were known among the elite in Jerusalem and Samaria through
classical Greek literature. Persians are depicted in this literature, not as conquerors,
but with the insinuation that they are weak. Whatever the case, the Chronicler
may have used the classical Greek traditions to emphasize that Yahweh's power
is even greater than that of the Cushites (and by implication greater than that
of the Persians). The Persian officials in Jerusalem and Samaria were probably
Judean/Samarian and would probably have understood that the Chronicler's
message in the Asa narrative was a subtle polemic directed at them.

15:16   /   **Maacah** is called the **grandmother** of **King Asa** (see Additional
Note on 13:1–2).

§4.4 Jehoshaphat (2 Chron. 17:1–21:1)

Judged by the length of text that he dedicates to King Jehoshaphat of Judah, the Chronicler certainly considered this king of great importance for his historiographical reconstruction. Not only is this one of the longest royal accounts in Chronicles (together with those of Hezekiah and Josiah), but it also contains the most substantial portion of the Chronicler's own material. Apart from 18:1–34 and 20:31–21:1, which make use of source materials in 1 Kings 22:1–35 and 22:41–50, respectively, the rest of the Jehoshaphat account consists of the Chronicler's own material. There is much ambiguity in the structure of the Chronicler's account. Second Chronicles 17:1–6 introduces Jehoshaphat with references to his righteousness in the eyes of the Lord and to the successful establishment of his kingdom; 17:7–11 tells of the king's campaign to teach Judah "the Book of the Law of the LORD"; and 17:12–19 deals with the king's growing military power. All the materials thus far are from the Chronicler's own hand.

Second Chronicles 18:1–19:3 is an extensive account of Jehoshaphat's joint military campaign with King Ahab of Israel to Ramoth-Gilead. This narrative (taken over from the source text in 1 Kgs. 22, with only a few changes) also contains the episode with the prophet Micaiah, son of Imla. Second Chronicles 19:4–11 deals with some judicial reforms that Jehoshaphat initiated. This material comes from the Chronicler's own hand again.

The major part of 2 Chronicles 20 recounts Jehoshaphat's defeat of the coalition of the Ammonites and Moabites (20:1–30). Prominent features are the prayer of Jehoshaphat (20:5–12) and a description of the role of Jehaziel the Levite (20:14–17). The Jehoshaphat account closes (20:31–21:1) with the normal summary of the king's reign and some other minor events. In this last section the Chronicler rejoins his source material in 1 Kings 22.

17:1–6 / The establishment of Jehoshaphat's kingship is— typically in the Chronicler's style—expressed with the verb *chazaq* ("to strengthen oneself"). In this case it is mentioned that he **strengthened**

himself against Israel (17:1). This means that he stationed troops in the border towns between Judah and Israel **that his father Asa had captured** (17:2). A very positive evaluation of the king already sounds here: **the LORD was with Jehoshaphat** (17:3). Again, in typical Chronistic style, the motive for this evaluation follows: **he did not consult** (Hebrew *darash*, "seek") **the Baals but sought** (*darash*) **the God of his father** (17:3–4). This is contrasted to following **the practices of Israel**. Therefore **the LORD established** (*kun*) **the kingdom under his control**. This resulted in the king's receiving wealth and honor from the Judahites and Jehoshaphat's performing some cultic purifications (removing **the high places and the Asherah poles from Judah**).

17:7–11 / This very positive portrayal of Jehoshaphat is continued in the next subsection, which describes the king's attempts to educate the Judahites in **the Book of the Law of the LORD** (probably some early form of the Pentateuch). The latter also plays an important role in another royal narrative, the account of King Josiah's reign (2 Chron. 34), which tells that the law book was found in the temple during its renovation.

The **priests** had the duty to instruct the people in the Torah (e.g., Lev. 10:11 and Deut. 31:9–13), so it is noteworthy that the Chronicler includes other **officials** and some **Levites** in the list of people sent out by Jehoshaphat. This may reflect the Chronicler's own time, when the difference in function between these groups started to become vague. It is important to note that the king himself promulgates the law, not as his own law but as God's.

Second Chronicles 17:10 details the effect of this process of educating the Judahites in "the Book of the Law of the LORD": **the fear of the LORD fell on all the kingdoms of the lands surrounding Judah**. Other royal narratives in Chronicles portray the **Philistines** and **Arabs** as enemies who have battled against Judah, but here they bring Jehoshaphat all kinds of **gifts** and **flocks** (17:11).

17:12–19 / This section elaborates further on Jehoshaphat's increasing influence: **Jehoshaphat became more and more powerful.** His military power is closely associated with his building **forts and store cities in Judah** and his enormous army. In total he had 1,160,000 soldiers available (**besides those he stationed in the fortified cities throughout Judah**), a number double the size of Asa's troops (2 Chron. 14). The number is obviously not to be taken literally but is rather a sign of the importance the Chronicler attributes to his king.

18:1–19:3 / Previous sections concentrated on the very positive aspects of Jehoshaphat's reign, but the "northern shadow" now started to fall over the Judahite kingship when the king **allied himself with Ahab by marriage.** The alliance between the southern kings and their northern counterparts shapes the next series of royal narratives until the reign of King Joash (see §4.7).

The present section deals mainly with Jehoshaphat's joint military expedition with King Ahab of Israel against **Ramoth Gilead** (a city in the tribal area of Gad, which became a point of contention between Israel and Syria-Damascus). This account is based on the source text in 1 Kings 22:1–38 (with some minor changes). The Chronicler supplies another introduction to the story (cf. 1 Kgs. 22:1), which reconfirms the **wealth and honor** of **Jehoshaphat** and reports the alliance with **Ahab.** After that, the narrative follows the source text in the sections on the treaty between Ahab and Jehoshaphat (2 Chron. 18:2–3 || 1 Kgs. 22:2–4), on the prophecies they consulted (2 Chron. 18:4–27 || 1 Kgs. 22:5–28), and on the campaign against Ramoth Gilead itself (2 Chron. 18:28–34 || 1 Kgs. 22:29–35). Rather than include the Deuteronomistic section on the very dramatic end to Ahab's life (1 Kgs. 22:36–38), the Chronicler added in 2 Chronicles 19:1–3 his own conclusion, which describes Jehoshaphat's safe return to Jerusalem as well as the prophecy of **Jehu the seer, the son of Hanani.** This prophetic voice rebukes the king for his support of Ahab's army (**should you . . . love those who hate the LORD?**) and announces that **the wrath of the LORD is upon** him. However, Jehu the seer also concedes that the king has done **some good:** he has **rid the land of the Asherah poles** and set (*kun*) his **heart on seeking** (*darash*) God. The very ambiguous evaluation of this king becomes apparent here.

19:4–11 / This section, which departs from the Deuteronomistic source text in Kings, describes the judicial reforms of King Jehoshaphat (see Additional Note on 17:7–9 and 19:4–11). The Chronicler sets the judicial reforms in a theological framework: **Jehoshaphat . . . turned them** (i.e., **the people from Beersheba to the hill country of Ephraim**) **back to the LORD, the God of their fathers.** Within this context, the appointment of **judges . . . in each of the fortified cities of Judah** (19:5) follows. Theologically, their judicial function is not to judge **for man but for the LORD.** Their style of justice conforms to this principle: **with the LORD our God there is no injustice or partiality or bribery** (19:7).

In Jerusalem a similar system is put in place. However, there **the Levites, priests and heads of Israelite families** have to officiate in it. They are equally encouraged to **serve faithfully and wholeheartedly in the**

fear of the LORD (19:9). Their task was **to warn** their countrymen **not to sin against the LORD; otherwise his wrath will come on** them **and their brothers** (19:10).

In the Chronicler's construction, Jehoshaphat's judicial reforms contribute enormously to the very positive portrayal of the king in this part of the narrative. It stands in contrast to the less positive perspective in the previous section (the alliance with Ahab).

20:1–30 / This battle account is typical of the Chronicler's novel approach, which includes a battle against foreign nations, a prayer to Yahweh, and a prophetic voice (this time in the form of Jehaziel the Levite).

The account starts with the report that **the Moabites and Ammonites with some of the Meunites** came to make war against Jehoshaphat (20:1). After his men came to tell him that a vast army had already advanced to the west bank of the Dead Sea, that is, at **En Gedi**, Jehoshaphat was **alarmed** and he immediately set out **to inquire** (*darash*) **of the** LORD. The whole of **Judah (from every town)** gathered with him **to seek** (*biqqesh*) **help from the** LORD. This "seeking" attitude of the king is a very positive sign. To the Chronicler, *darash* and *biqqesh* express the ideal religious inclination.

The seeking of Yahweh became material when **Jehoshaphat stood up** before **the assembly** gathered **at the temple of the** LORD (20:5) and started praying (20:6–12). The king introduces his call to God with the invocation **O** LORD, **God of our fathers, are you not the God who is in heaven?** The king's conviction is that the Lord has dominion over all nations. The king recalls the conquest of the land, when God drove out all the nations before them and gave the land **forever to the descendants of Abraham** his **friend** (20:7). This last expression clearly links the events of Jehoshaphat's reign with Israel's ancestral history. In 20:10 the king's prayer turns into an argument of sorts against Yahweh, who did not allow the people to drive out Judah's attackers (**men from Ammon, Moab and Mount Seir**). On this account the king calls upon God to **judge them**. Although this very king in an earlier episode of his reign had the biggest army, he now declares in prayer that **we have no power to face this vast army. . . . We do not know what to do,** he declares, **but our eyes are upon you** (20:12). This attitude differs greatly from that of an earlier section when Jehoshaphat used his own discretion to enter an alliance with Ahab to fight against Ramoth Gilead. The response to the king's prayer comes in a prophetic utterance by the Levite **Jehaziel.** First, **the Spirit of the** LORD (*ruach yahweh*) **came upon Jehaziel** (20:14). The employment of **a Levite** for a prophetic function might indicate that the Chronicler either favored an expanded role for the Levites or that at the time the distinctive roles of Levites and prophets (and priests) were becoming increasingly vague.

Jehaziel encourages Jehoshaphat to go into battle against the vast army, **for the battle is not** his, **but God's** (20:15), and he reassures the king of **the deliverance the** Lord **will give** him (20:17). The Chronicler conducts this battle with the liturgy of a holy war: the vanguard is **to sing to the** Lord **and to praise him for the splendor of his holiness.** Their battle cry is, **Give thanks to the** Lord, **for his love endures forever** (20:21). This description resembles that of the battle of Abijah against Jeroboam of Israel (2 Chron. 13). The praise song is also reminiscent of the bringing of the ark to Jerusalem. In the style of a holy war **the** Lord **set ambushes against the men of Ammon and Moab and Mount Seir** (20:22) and caused them to destroy themselves. Jehoshaphat and his men could therefore conquer them without actually taking part in the battle in any way. Their role was to collect the booty and to praise the Lord, who gave them victory at **the Valley of Beracah** (20:26) (which means "the valley of praise"). Jehoshaphat and his men could therefore return **joyfully** (20:27) to the temple in Jerusalem, where they could complete the liturgy of the holy war **with harps and lutes and trumpets** (20:28).

The fear of God was **upon all the kingdoms** who **heard** about the Lord's great victory (20:29). Meanwhile, **the kingdom of Jehoshaphat was at peace** (Hebrew *shaqath*) (20:30). The battle ushered in the ideal state (according to the Chronicler's vision): **God had given him rest** (*nuach*) **on every side.** The programmatic language with which the Chronicler ends this battle account reconfirms the very positive image of the king and simultaneously advances the Chronicler's ideology for his own time: rest and peace are the results of the king seeking Yahweh.

20:31–21:1 / This final episode contains another evaluation of Jehoshaphat, as well as a short account of the king's alliance with **Ahaziah king of Israel** in a failed maritime operation. Although the Chronicler used the source text in 1 Kings 22:41–50, he also made some significant changes to it and left out the material from 1 Kings 22:44, 46–47. For example, the source text mentions (1 Kings 22:43) that "the people continued to offer sacrifices and burn incense," but instead the Chronicler substituted the phrase **the people still had not set** (*kun*) **their hearts on the God of their fathers** (2 Chron. 20:33). The final judgment on this king is therefore expressed in the programmatic language of the Chronicler, using again the well-known term *kun* to reflect the writer's understanding of Yahweh's kingdom as well established and well ordered.

The failed maritime project comes as a very last confirmation that Jehoshaphat is not altogether an exemplary king. Another prophetic voice, **Eliezer son of Dodavahu of Mareshah,** interprets this event: **because you have made an alliance with Ahaziah, the** LORD **will destroy what you have made** (20:37). To rely on alliances means not to rely on Yahweh. The death-and-burial notices in 2 Chronicles 20:34 and 21:1 follow the Deuteronomistic versions in 1 Kings 22:45 and 22:50, with one exception. The latter refers the reader to "the book of the annals of the kings of Judah" (1 Kgs. 22:45) for further information about the king. The Chronicler instead cites **the annals of Jehu son of Hanani, which are recorded in the book of the kings of Israel** (2 Chron. 20:34). This change is in line with the Chronicler's tendency to substitute the source references of the canonical Book of Kings with references to figures who were active during the particular king's reign.

Additional Notes §4.4

17:1–21:1 / The Chronicler's narrative about King **Jehoshaphat** is even more ambiguous than the account about his father Asa. Both positive and negative elements appear alongside one another, with seemingly no relationship between them. In ambiguity, it compares to the portrayal of Rehoboam, but with one prominent difference: the ambiguity in the Rehoboam narrative is facilitated by Rehoboam humbling himself—an element absent from the Jehoshaphat account. The Chronicler's literary juxtaposition of comparable and contrasting episodes portrays Jehoshaphat as a complex, multifaceted character, viewed of course through the Chronicler's unique theological lens.

17:7–9 and 19:4–11 / Critical discussion in the past has probed the relationship between 17:7–9 and the account of Jehoshaphat's judicial reforms narrated in 19:4–11. The consensus view is that the latter account may reflect a pre-Deuteronomic phase in the development of the monarchical judiciary. But Knoppers argues instead that "the Chronicler draws on both past tradition and present reality" in order "to shape the present. . . . The Chronicler's depiction of Jehoshaphat's reforms ultimately reflects what he believes justice should be" (G. N. Knoppers, "Jehoshaphat's Judiciary and 'The Scroll of Yhwh's Torah,'" *JBL* 113/1 [1994], p. 80).

20:5–12 / Church historian Mary Jane Haemig shows that Jehoshaphat's prayer in Chronicles strongly influenced prayer practices and piety among sixteenth-century Lutheran reformers (see Haemig, "Jehoshaphat and His Prayer," pp. 522–35). Remarkably, the ambivalent figure of the king in the Chronicler's portrayal seems not to function in their interpretations.

§4.5 Jehoram (2 Chron. 21:2–20)

The previous three kings, Abijah, Asa, and Jehoshaphat, were (mainly) positive role models of the Davidic kingship in both Chronicles and Kings. (For darker episodes, see the turn of events in Asa's and Jehoshaphat's reigns in 16:1–14 and 20:35–37, respectively.) However, the Chronicler even enhanced their exemplary profiles with some of his own material. The same does not apply to Jehoram's history. His portrayal is very negative, with the ominous note already sounding early in the narrative: "he walked in the ways of the kings of Israel" (21:6).

The Chronicler's account starts with some of his own material (21:2–4), which describes Jehoram's early moves to establish his kingship. In the next verses (21:5–7) the Chronicler gives his evaluation of this king, following the source text of 2 Kings 8:17–19. After that (2 Chron. 21:8–10), again following the source text in 2 Kings 8:20–22, he gives an account of the Edomite rebellion and also mentions the high places that Jehoram built (2 Chron. 21:11). Then follow the so-called Elijah letter (21:12–15), a short account of the battle against the Philistines and the Arabs (21:16–17), and a report about the king's bowel illness already prophesied in Elijah's letter (21:18–19). The pericope ends with the Chronicler rejoining the source text in 2 Kings 8:24 with the usual death-and-burial notice (2 Chron. 21:20).

21:2–4 / These verses provide new information not in 2 Kings 8, but they also create confusion about whether the events happened in Israel or in Judah. Second Chronicles 21:2 suggests that the **brothers** of Jehoram were all **sons of Jehoshaphat king of Israel**, although Jehoshaphat was actually king of Judah. Second Chronicles 21:3, however, mentions that **fortified cities in Judah** were given to these brothers and that the kingship was given to **Jehoram**, who was **his firstborn son**. After establishing (*chazaq*) his power, Jehoram then **put all his brothers to the sword along with some of the princes of Israel** (21:4). This statement also confuses Judah and Israel.

In order to resolve this confusion in the text, some scholars emend "Israel" in 21:2 to read "Judah" (so also many ancient translations).

Another suggestion is that "Israel" in 21:2 refers not to the northern kingdom but rather to the southern and northern kingdoms as a whole (also suggested by a footnote in NIV). A third possibility sees the phrase "king of Israel" in 21:2 as an attempt by the Chronicler to link the Jehoram narrative to the Ahabite line of the northern kingdom (Athaliah, the daughter of Ahab of Israel, was married to Jehoram). Jehoram's horrendous deed of killing all his brothers would then be related to the nonlegitimate northern kingdom (in the Chronicler's view) and not to the Davidide Judah. Whatever the case may be, we should not ignore that the distinction between Judah and Israel is blurred here.

21:5–7 / Second Chronicles 21:6 provides (in line with the source text) a negative evaluation of King Jehoram: **he walked in the ways of the kings of Israel, as the house of Ahab had done.** It further explains that there was an official relationship with the Israelite monarchy: **he married a daughter of Ahab.**

Both versions indicate that the Lord did not destroy him, but they differ significantly in two details. First, they provide different motivations for that display of mercy. In 2 Kings 8:19 the reason is "for the sake of his servant David," whereas the Chronicler has **because of the covenant the Lord had made with David.** Second, the entity that "the Lord was not willing to destroy"—"Judah" in 2 Kings 8:19—becomes **the house of David** in 2 Chronicles 21:7. This change is significant in that it focuses attention on the continuation of the royal line of David instead of on the continuation of the kingdom of Judah. The reference to the "covenant" was probably intended to invoke the memory of the eternal promise made to David by Yahweh.

21:8–11 / An account of the Edomite (and Libnite) rebellion against Jehoram follows. Whether this reflects a historical reality is not certain. However, in the time of the Chronicler, the Edomites' later heirs, the Idumeans, played a significant role in Persian provincial politics. The mention of the Edomites might therefore have had a very contemporary ring to the Chronicler's audience. Libnah is mentioned in Joshua 10:29–30 as a so-called Levite city. Given the Chronicler's high esteem for the Levites in his own time, this might just have had a contemporary sound to it. The Chronicler follows his source text in 2 Kings 8:20–22 fairly closely but appends an elaborate theological motivation for the rebellion at the end of the Deuteronomist's version: **because Jehoram had forsaken the Lord, the God of his fathers.** The theologically loaded expression makes use of a verb typical of the Chronicler's theology, namely, *'azab,* "to forsake" the Lord. The theological motivation continues in 2 Chronicles 21:11 (which also belongs to the Chronicler's own material), indicting Jehoram for having **built high places on the hills of Judah,** having **caused the people of Jerusalem to prostitute themselves,** and having **led Judah astray.** This allusion probably intends to connect Jehoram's deeds with those of the house of Ahab of Israel. The Chronicler portrays the Edomite and Libnite rebellion as punishment for Jehoram's following of practices for which his northern in-laws were actually better known! The irony is, furthermore, that Jehoram is evaluated very negatively here (in line with the source text) in terms of his Ahabite connection, although Jehoshaphat, his father, who entered into an alliance with Ahab of Israel, is evaluated positively. The lines between Judah and Israel are blurred again.

21:12–15 / This section, which belongs to the Chronicler's own material, indicates that **Jehoram received a letter from Elijah the prophet.** The letter is introduced with the typical messenger formula **this is what the** LORD . . . **says** (with "the LORD" specified as **the God of your father David).** Again, as in the previous section, the accusation is made against Jehoram that he **walked in the ways of the kings of Israel** and he **led Judah and the people of Jerusalem to prostitute themselves, just as the house of Ahab.** This way of Jehoram contrasts with **the ways of your father Jehoshaphat or of Asa king of Judah.** That Jehoram **murdered** his **own brothers** also aggravates the matter. The letter therefore announces in typical prophetic fashion the punishment that the Lord is about to impose: he **is about to strike your people, your sons, your wives and everything that is yours, with a heavy blow.** The terminology used here (with a participle and noun related to the verb *nagaph,* "to strike") is typical of the Chronicler's style. It is often used in Chronicles to describe Yahweh's punishment for transgressions. The punishment in this case also has a personal dimension for Jehoram: it announces that he will become **very ill with a lingering disease of the bowels, until the disease causes** his **bowels to come out.** This indeed was shown to happen in the Chronicler's narrative (see 21:18–19). The introduction of prophetic voices in the Chronicler's own material is very typical. This is often done to provide a theological interpretation of the events during a monarch's reign. In the present narrative the prophetic voice of Elijah—this time in a letter (see Additional Note on 21:12)—serves this function. It is as if the Chronicler lets the prophetic utterance confirm his own assessment of Jehoram's reign.

21:16–17 / The themes of the letter are taken up in the continuation of the Chronicler's own material in 21:16–17 and 21:18–19. As a punishment against Judah and Jehoram in particular, Yahweh **aroused against Jehoram the hostility of the Philistines and of the Arabs.** The Hebrew word for "arouse" (Hifil of *'wr*) is also used in 36:22 (as in the present section, the Chronicler's own material), which states that the Lord "aroused" Cyrus to write his proclamation that would liberate Israel from exile. In the Chronicler's view the Lord can arouse nations or foreign kings to either exercise punishment on his people or facilitate their liberation. It is ironic that these foreign nations who were aroused against Jehoram will carry off all the king's sons, except **Ahaziah, the youngest.** This is reminiscent of the same Jehoram killing all his brothers.

21:18–19 / **After all this,** the prophecy of Elijah's letter was fulfilled when **the LORD afflicted** (*nagaph*) **Jehoram with an incurable disease of the bowels.** It is ironically mentioned that after Jehoram's death **in great pain** there was no honoring of this king: **his people made no fire in his honor, as they had for his fathers,** a sentiment echoed again in 21:20.

21:20 / The first part of this verse, the final summary of Jehoram's reign, repeats the information already provided in 21:5 (taken from 2 Kgs. 8:17). Then follows the Chronicler's own version of Jehoram's death and burial: **he passed away, to no one's regret, and was buried in the City of David, but not in the tombs of the kings** (cf. 2 Kgs. 8:24). In this final remark the Chronicler's great contempt for this king cannot be mistaken!

Additional Notes §4.5

21:2–20 / The historical question of Jehoram's genealogy is a prominent theme in previous studies that try to offer alternatives to the traditional interpretation that **Jehoram** was the son of Jehoshaphat, king of Judah, and the father of Ahaziah (with Athaliah, the daughter of Ahab of Israel and Jezebel, as mother). These studies also address the question of whether Jehoram of Judah and Jehoram of Israel were not the same king. For example, Boyd Barrick ("Another Shaking of Jehoshaphat's Family Tree: Jehoram and Ahaziah Once Again," *VT* 51 [2001], pp. 9–25) proposes the following alternatives: (1) that Ahaziah was son of Athaliah and Jehoram's unidentified older brother, Jehoshaphat's firstborn and heir apparent who died before both Jehoshaphat and Jehoram; (2) that Jehoram, a younger son not designated to become king of Judah, was married to an unnamed daughter of Ahab and Jezebel and became king of (north) Israel when his brother-in-law Ahaziah died; and (3) that Jehoram, as Jehoshaphat's oldest (or perhaps only) surviving son, also became king of Judah when his father died. It is impossible to confirm the historical reality from the biblical texts. However, whatever relationships might have been between the kings of Judah and Israel, the Chronicler used these relationships for his own theological purpose: to show that the borders between Judah and Israel were blurred and that the downfall of these Judahite kings was the result of their close relationships with the northern kings.

21:7 / It is uncertain what the expression **he had promised to maintain a lamp for him and his descendants forever** means. Ehud Ben Zvi ("Once the Lamp Has Been Kindled . . . A Reconstruction of the Meaning of the MT *Nir* in 1 Kgs 11.36; 15.4; 2 Kgs 8.19 and 2 Chr 21.7," *ABR* 39 [1991], pp. 19–30) suggests that the word for "lamp" should rather be translated "fiefdom" or "domain." See also Swanson's *Dictionary of Biblical Languages with Semantic Domains: Hebrew (Old Testament)* (electronic ed.; Oak Harbor: Logos Research Systems, 1997): "The reigning presence of an heir, with a special focus to keep or guard something, as a figurative extension of a lamp that gives light (as in the Temple)" (entry 5775).

21:12 / Elijah's **letter** is called a *miktab*. Christopher Begg ("Constructing a Monster: The Chronicler's *Sondergut* in 2 Chronicles 21," *ABR* 37 [1989], p. 49) indicates that this same word is used in 2 Chron. 36:22 in connection with Cyrus's proclamation. Begg argues that this is only one of the ways in which the Chronicler already opens a vision on the "exile and beyond" in the Jehoram narrative. He sees the relationship between these two verses as one of reversal: whereas the Elijah letter notes that Judah's destruction is preceded by a foreign coalition (the Philistines and Arabs), the Cyrus proclamation precedes the restoration of Judah.

21:20 / The NIV's **to no one's regret** is problematic. It literally means "not with precious/desirable things." This could mean that the dead king was not honored in the usual way by putting some precious objects in his tomb. The Septuagint translated it with a Greek phrase meaning "not to speak of the excellence of a person." Although it is difficult to find an appropriate translation for the phrase in the text, the connotation "dishonor" is clear.

§4.6 Ahaziah (2 Chron. 22:1–9)

The fatal relationship of the Judahite kingdom with the northern royal house continued during the reign of Ahaziah, who ruled approximately 841/840 b.c. The Chronicler's version of this king's reign is an abridged version of the Deuteronomistic source text in 2 Kings 8:24b–9:28. Significant changes have been made, creating some logical problems for the reader. First, Kings and Chronicles give different accounts of the sequence of events. In Kings Ahaziah is killed before the officials of Judah, but in Chronicles his death follows theirs. Second, according to Kings, Ahaziah died near Megiddo, while Chronicles says that he died in an unnamed place after he was found hiding in Samaria. Third, in Kings he was buried in Jerusalem, while Chronicles suggests that he was buried at the place of his death. I agree with McKenzie's assessment: "None of these differences is insurmountable, and it may be best to understand the Chronicles version as a theological elaboration of the story in Kings, with which the Chronicler assumed his audience was familiar" (*1–2 Chronicles*, p. 307).

The Chronicler's abbreviated account starts with a summary of Ahaziah's reign (22:1–2). After this follow accounts of the king's affiliation with the northern monarchy (22:3–6a) and how this close relationship eventually leads to his downfall and death (22:6b–9).

22:1–2 / Second Kings 8:24b announces the new king with the words: "And Ahaziah his son succeeded him as king." In 2 Chronicles 22:1, however, it is the inhabitants of **Jerusalem** who make **Jehoram's youngest son, Ahaziah,** king after him. The unusual incident of the youngest son becoming king is explained in 22:1b by referring to the killing of **all the older sons** in the battle against the **Arabs** (mentioned in 21:16–17).

22:3–6a / King **Ahaziah** is evaluated negatively (as in the source text) with the statements **he too walked in the ways of the house of Ahab** and **he did evil in the eyes of the LORD, as the house of Ahab had done.** The Chronicler adds three phrases, however, in which it becomes clear that Ahaziah's evil can be blamed on his following the advice of his northern affiliates: **for his mother encouraged him in doing wrong** (22:3), **for after his father's death they became his advisers, to his undoing** (22:4), **and he also followed their counsel** (22:5). In this way Ahaziah became involved in the events concerning the war that **Joram son of Ahab king of Israel** waged against **Hazael king of Aram.** The Israelite king was wounded in this battle.

22:6b–9 / Because **Ahaziah** was related to the northern royal court, he went to visit the wounded king of Israel. The Chronicler, however, sees in this visit the providence of God: **through Ahaziah's visit to Joram, God brought about Ahaziah's downfall.** According to the writer, it was no coincidence that it was exactly at the time of Jehu's revolt that Ahaziah arrived in the northern capital. The Chronicler's own material identifies Jehu as the one **whom the Lord had anointed to destroy the house of Ahab.** It implies that Ahaziah was also part of this "house of Ahab" and that his downfall was preordained by Yahweh. Ahaziah's death is therefore part of the divine eradication of the northern influence from Judah. Unlike the source text (in 2 Kgs. 9:28), the Chronicler again (as in the case of Jehoram) denies the king a burial in the kings' tombs in the City of David. This confirms the Chronicler's contempt for this king. This very short account of Ahaziah's reign ends with the ironic remark: **so there was no one in the house of Ahaziah powerful enough to retain the kingdom** (22:9). The eternal kingship of the house of David has been endangered by the fatal relationships of a series of Judahite kings with their northern neighbors. This had to be rectified by Yahweh himself.

Additional Notes §4.6

22:2 / The age of King **Ahaziah** at his accession is given by the Chronicler (in the Hebrew text) as **forty-two.** It is, however, generally accepted that this is a scribal error, and it is normally emended to read **twenty-two** (as in the NIV). The expression **Athaliah, a granddaughter of Omri** also requires comment. The Hebrew text has "daughter" instead of "granddaughter." The Septuagint therefore changed the name from Omri to Ahab. However, the Hebrew word "daughter" can also be understood more generally as "descendant," which would make any change to the name unnecessary. The NIV's "granddaughter" is also acceptable given this more general understanding.

22:7 / The Hebrew word used for the **downfall** (*tebusah*) of Ahaziah occurs only once in the Hebrew Bible and is translated in the Septuagint with the Greek word *katastrophē.* The word probably means "trampling on."

§4.7 Athaliah and Joash (2 Chron. 22:10–24:27)

We saw at the end of Ahaziah's reign that the house of David was seriously endangered. A power vacuum developed after the king's death. All the king's uncles (six of them) were killed by their brother, Jehoram, the previous king. And during Jehoram's reign all male heirs (except Ahaziah) were killed in a battle against the Philistines and Arabs. Ahaziah, the sole survivor, therefore became king. When he died and left a power vacuum, his mother, Athaliah, stepped in.

We know that Athaliah was a daughter of King Ahab of Israel and his wife Jezebel. The previous two Judahite kings' relationships with the northern kingdom, Israel, had proved to be fatal. This relationship now resulted in a situation where the house of David could potentially be replaced by a daughter of King Ahab of Israel. Athaliah moved swiftly after the death of Ahaziah to eliminate all contenders for the Judahite throne: "she proceeded to destroy the whole royal family of the house of Judah" (22:10), including her own grandchildren. One of them escaped, however. Through the intervention of a sister of the dead King Ahaziah (that is, a daughter of Jehoram, probably with a wife other than Athaliah) little Joash, Ahaziah's son, was saved and eventually became king of Judah. As the sole male survivor of the house of David, he was carrying the hope that Yahweh's eternal promise to David would remain valid.

Athaliah's queenship is narrated very briefly in both 2 Chronicles 22:10–12 and 2 Kings 11:1–3. The normal formulas announcing and concluding a king's reign are absent from both narratives. Although we know from ancient Near Eastern parallels that the queen mother played a prominent role in the royal court and could rule in the case of the unexpected death of the king, she was also seen as a substitute. The presentation in Kings and Chronicles uses Athaliah's substitution as a plot element to build suspense ("Will the house of David survive?") and to emphasize the miraculous salvation of David's house by the special circumstances surrounding Joash's becoming king. Differently from other commentaries, I therefore treat the Athaliah narrative as part of Joash's kingship.

The Chronicler made substantive use of the Deuteronomistic version of Athaliah and Joash in 2 Kings 11:1–12:21, albeit with some smaller changes here and there. The only major contribution by the Chronicler's own hand can be found in 2 Chronicles 24:15–22.

The narrative starts with a description of Athaliah's attempt to usurp the throne of Judah (22:10–12). This is followed by the narration of the planning by Jehoiada the priest of how to get Joash onto the throne (23:1–7). The execution of the plan follows (23:8–11), together with a description of Athaliah's reaction and death (23:12–15). Some cultic reforms followed after Joash became king (23:16–21), and a taxation system was put into place to restore the temple and its equipment (24:1–16). Up until this point in the narrative Joash has been an example of a good king by attending to the restoration of the cult and temple.

However, the end of the previous subsection (24:15–16, which has no parallel in the source text) describes the death of Jehoiada the priest. This signifies a turning point in Joash's career, because from then on the wickedness of this king surfaces. In a section also without parallel in the source text, the Chronicler describes the king's apostasy and the prophecy of Zechariah, the son of Jehoiada, against him (24:17–22). In this sad tale the king orders that the prophet be killed in the temple courtyard. The Joash narrative ends with a description of a battle against the Arameans in which the king dies, as well as with some final notes on his reign (24:23–27, which was taken over in an adapted form from the source text).

22:10–12 / After the death of Ahaziah, **Athaliah . . . proceeded to destroy the whole royal family of the house of Judah.** The Chronicler adds the words "of the house of Judah" to the source text in 1 Kings 11:1, probably to emphasize that the house of David is endangered here. For **six years** (2 Chron. 22:12) Athaliah took the place of the king by ruling the land.

Another woman, **Jehosheba** (Hebrew Jehoshabeath), appears on the scene (22:11). She is **the daughter of King Jehoram** (and therefore the aunt of Joash) **and wife of the priest Jehoiada.** McKenzie (*1–2 Chronicles*, p. 308) aptly describes her symbolic role in the narrative: "The tale of two women is also a tale of two houses. The house of David faces extinction at the hands of Athaliah, who, following Jehu's purge, is the last ruler of the house of Ahab. . . . She [Jehosheba] is also the wife of Jehoiada the priest. Thus, she has commitments to both dynasty and temple, and she uses the latter to protect the former, embodied in the baby Joash."

23:1–7 / **In the seventh year** of Athaliah's substitution the priest Jehoiada took the initiative to plan for Joash's enthronement. The expression Jehoiada **showed his strength** is formed in Hebrew with the familiar verb *chazaq*. Second Kings 11:4 mentions that Jehoiada sent for "the commanders of units of a hundred, the Carites and the guards" and that he gathered them at "the temple of the LORD." The Chronicler's version mentions only **the commanders of units of a hundred** but then specifies them by name. He furthermore adds to his source text that these commanders were sent **throughout Judah** and had to gather **the Levites and the heads of Israelite families from all the towns** (23:2).

The Chronicler inserts into his source text (in 23:3) mention of **a covenant with the king at the temple of God** that **the whole assembly made**. It is not exactly clear to whom "the king" refers here. The previous king had already been dead for at least six years. This can therefore be interpreted only as a reference to Joash, the **king's son**, who is announced by Jehoiada as the one who **shall reign, as the LORD promised concerning the descendants of David** (23:3). The eternal promise to the house of David is thus invoked by the Chronicler's insertion.

Although the Chronicler's description of the plan set out by Jehoiada follows the source text in 2 Kings 11:5–7, the details differ slightly. The main difference, however, is again in line with the Chronicler's strict adherence to cultic regulations concerning who may enter the temple. The Chronicler added the words **priests and Levites** in 2 Chronicles 23:4 to ensure that the narrative portrays those entering the temple as consecrated cultic personnel. This change is in line with the addition in 23:6, specifying that **no one is to enter the temple of the LORD except the priests and Levites on duty . . . because they are consecrated**, as well as with the specification in 23:7 that **the Levites** had to surround **the king**. Again (as in 23:3) "the king" refers here to the young Joash.

23:8–11 / The plan is now put into practice. **The Levites and all the men of Judah** (instead of "the commanders of units" of the source text) organized their men just as **Jehoiada** had **ordered** them to do. Jehoiada gave to the commanders King David's own **spears** and **shields . . . that were in the temple of God** (probably a back reference to 1 Chron. 18:7 and 2 Chron. 12:9–10). This weaponry probably served a ceremonial function and was not intended for defending the king with violence.

Second Chronicles 23:11 narrates the actual crowning and anointing of Joash as **king** of Judah: **Jehoiada and his sons brought out the king's son and put the crown on him; they presented him with a copy of the covenant and proclaimed him king. They anointed him and shouted,**

"Long live the king!" The expression "copy of the covenant" actually refers to two different concepts in Hebrew, the vow of consecration and the witness or testimony. The Hebrew word for witness ('edut) probably refers to the Ten Commandments, perhaps in a double sense: "The law that the king was to copy and read daily according to Deut 17:18–20" (McKenzie, 1–2 Chronicles, p. 311).

With the exclamation "Long live the king!" the reader realizes that the house of David has been saved from extinction. This is not only a new beginning of the reign of young King Joash but also an expression of relief that the house of David can be continued. It is interesting that neither biblical version of this remarkable turn of events involves royals or politicians, but they both rather focus on the role that an otherwise insignificant woman (Jehoshabeath in Hebrew) and her priest husband (Jehoiada) played. It seems that both versions wanted to emphasize that the Jerusalem cult was indispensable for the continuation of the house of David and that the continuation is not in the hands of the powerful but in Yahweh's.

23:12–15 / This section describes Athaliah's reaction and follows the source text very closely. When she heard sounds coming from the temple, she went there to see what was going on. The revelation of the new king follows equally dramatically: **she looked, and there was the king** (23:13). The Hebrew particle of surprise, *wehinneh* ("and there was . . ."), is again used here. Her exclamation **Treason! Treason!** indicates that she knows that there has been a conspiracy without her knowledge, but also that the end of the road has come for her. **Jehoiada** therefore sent out **commanders** and **troops** to follow her with the command to kill her, only **not . . . at the temple of the** LORD (mentioned in both Kings and Chronicles). After the soldiers reached her, **they put her to death** (23:15). Unceremoniously, the substitute rule of Athaliah comes to an end, without any burial notice or further reference.

23:16–21 / After **Jehoiada . . . made a covenant that he and the people and the king would be the** LORD**'s people,** they immediately started to purge **the temple of Baal.** This covenant signifies a new commitment to Yahweh. Athaliah, who was a daughter of Jezebel and Ahab of Israel, was probably closely associated with the Baal cult, which had a strong influence in the northern kingdom. These remnants of Athaliah's influence are therefore immediately eradicated.

Jehoiada also organized **the oversight of the temple of the** LORD by giving responsibilities to the **priests** and **Levites, to whom David had**

made assignments in the temple (23:18). The Chronicler expanded on his source text to specify in greater detail the oversight of the sanctuary and in this way indicates that—with a real Davidide, Joash, as their king now—the cult instituted by David (see 1 Chron. 23–27) has been restored. The actual enthronement of Joash takes place only after the Baal temple has been destroyed and the supervision of the temple organized. Second Chronicles 23:20–21 (closely following the source text in 2 Kgs. 11:19–20) describes the young king being brought to the palace and set on **the royal throne.**

24:1–16 / This section closely follows the source text in 2 Kings 11:1–12:16, except in the last two verses, which belong to the Chronicler's own additions. Second Chronicles 24:1–3 contains the information normally provided at the beginning of a king's reign (ca. 835–796 B.C. in Joash's case). The positive evaluation of the king (**Joash did what was right in the eyes of the LORD**) sounds an ominous note already by mentioning that this was the case **all the years of Jehoiada the priest.** Later we will see that things changed dramatically after Jehoiada died.

In his version the Chronicler omits 2 Kings 12:3, which states that "the high places . . . were not removed; the people continued to offer sacrifices and burn incense there." That statement would not have suited the very positive beginning of Joash's reign according to the Chronicler's conception. This information is instead replaced in 2 Chronicles 24:3 with an indication that **Jehoiada chose two wives for him, and he had sons and daughters.** As in earlier royal narratives, here also the Chronicler considers wives and children as signs of a king's prosperity.

The following verses (taken with some changes from 2 Kgs. 12:4–16) describe the restoration of **the temple of the LORD** at Joash's command (2 Chron. 24:4, which differs from the source text). The initial attempt did not produce the desired response, and a long time lapsed (until the twenty-third year of the king's reign, according to 2 Kgs. 12:6) before an alternative taxation system of voluntary gifts was put in place by Joash. The Chronicler mentions that, just before the new system was implemented, Athaliah's sons **had broken into the temple of God and had used even its sacred objects for the Baals** (2 Chron. 24:7). This interjection, absent from Kings, prepares the way for another addition to the source text (24:14), which indicates that there was still some money left after the restoration of the temple, so they could replace the temple objects. In the end the restoration was successful, and **they rebuilt the temple of God according to its original design and reinforced it** (24:13).

In the following two verses (24:15–16) the Chronicler supplements the source text by adding a comment on the death and burial of Jehoiada. The high esteem the Chronicler bestows on this priest finds expression in his royal burial (with the kings in the City of David), something denied Kings Jehoram and Ahaziah. The death of Jehoiada foreshadows a dramatic turnaround of events in Joash's reign.

24:17–22 / Jehoiada was no longer available to give advice, so Joash turned to the officials of Judah. On their advice the king abandoned the temple of the Lord and turned to Asherah poles and idols again. He and his people did not even listen to those prophets who were sent by the Lord to call them back from their wicked ways. This is particularly illustrated in the Chronicler's own material inserted here. He narrates the event where Zechariah son of Jehoiada the priest was inspired by the Lord's spirit to prophesy against the king. His message bears key concepts of the Chronicler's theology: because you have forsaken ('azab) the Lord, he has forsaken ('azab) you (24:20; cf. 24:18, 24, 25). This dark hour in Joash's reign reached its deepest point when by order of the king they stoned him to death in the courtyard of the Lord's temple. Whereas Jehoiada earlier ordered that Athaliah—"that wicked woman" (24:7)—should not be killed in the temple (23:14), Joash orders that Jehoiada's son, a prophet of the Lord, be killed in the temple. In his last words, Zechariah says: May the Lord see this and call you to account; this expression uses the Hebrew term darash again ("call to account"). Zechariah's words call for Yahweh to seek Joash, because the king did not seek the Lord. The irony is dramatic!

24:23–27 / Because of the turnaround in Joash's conduct, a battle against the Arameans becomes appropriate retribution for his apostasy. This account, which very broadly follows the source text in 2 Kings 12:17–21, confirms that though the Aramean army had . . . only a few men, the Lord delivered into their hands a much larger army. The Chronicler makes clear that military power does not count when the Lord wants to use an enemy as punishment for his apostate king. Judgment was executed on Joash, because he led Judah to forsake ('azab) the Lord (2 Chron. 24:24).

After being wounded by the Arameans, Joash was killed in his bed by his own officials for murdering the son of Jehoiada the priest (24:25). Although he was buried in the City of David, he did not get a resting place in the tombs of the kings. This latter piece of information comes from the Chronicler's own hand again and expresses his contempt for Joash, the good king who had gone astray.

An after note (24:26–27) specifies the names of the officials who killed Joash and gives some further references: **the record of the restoration of the temple of God** can be read in **the annotations on the book of the kings** (see Additional Note on 24:27). **A new era dawned when Amaziah his son succeeded him as king.**

Additional Notes §4.7

22:10 / Although the NIV translates **to destroy** here, the verb used in Chronicles (*dabar*) rather means "to turn (one's) back on." The Chronicler has replaced the verb from the source text in 2 Kgs. 11:1 (*'abad*, "to destroy").

23:3 / The NIV unfortunately did not translate the Hebrew word *hinneh* ("see/observe/look"), which introduces the reference to **the king's son**. *Hinneh* here highlights the moment when Jehoiada revealed to the commanders, the Levites, and the family heads that the young boy was actually the king's son, who was hidden from Athaliah for almost six years. An alternative translation is: "Here is the king's son!" (as in the NRSV).

24:1–16 / On January 13, 2003, a newly discovered inscription was made known to the world. The inscription on sandstone contained information on the temple restoration under King Joash, and claims were made that this could be the oldest evidence available not only about the historicity of the biblical accounts of King Joash but also about the temple in Jerusalem. However, after close examination by experts and intensive discussions by scholars, it was concluded that the inscription must be a fake. A person who was active on the antiquities market in Israel was arrested and convicted after investigations. A number of scholarly articles discussed the inscription in the aftermath of this "discovery." Although the majority (e.g., Gross and Knauff) were very certain that this was a fake, some (e.g., Achenbach and Norin) asked that it should not be abandoned totally, since there might be something historical behind the inscription after all. At least, as one writer concludes, if this is a fake, the person producing it was a master at his work! The *Jerusalem Post* reported on March 14, 2012, about the conclusion of the case: "In his verdict, the judge said the prosecution was unable to prove that the findings were fabrications beyond a reasonable doubt. However, the court also ruled that it was unable to conclude that the finds were authentic, and at least one of Golan's [the antiquities dealer acquitted of forging the inscription] associates confessed to aiding the antiquities dealer in a fabrication conspiracy." For good scholarly discussions on the inscription, see Achenbach, "Einige Beobachtungen zu der sogenannten 'Jeho'asch-Inschrift,'" pp. 5–14; Gross, "Vorsicht: Archäologische Objekte zweifelhafter Herkunft," pp. 177–78; Knauf, "Jehoash's Improbable

Inscription," pp. 22–26; Norin, "Die sogenannte Joaschinschrift—Echt oder Falsch?," pp. 61–74.

24:20–22 / Two New Testament Gospels (Matt. 23:35; Luke 11:50–51) present words of Jesus that are normally taken as references to the killings of Abel (Gen. 4) and Zechariah the prophet (2 Chron. 24:20–22). These references raise some difficulties (e.g., the Matthew text calls Zechariah "son of Berekiah" instead of **of Jehoiada,** and both New Testament texts indicate that the killing happened "between the altar and the sanctuary" instead of **in the courtyard of the temple**). Nevertheless, in the history of interpretation Abel (who is mentioned in the first book of the Hebrew Bible, Genesis) and Zechariah (who is mentioned in the last book of the Hebrew Bible, Chronicles) may have become the epitome of innocent people who have died at the hand of an apostate. See the discussion of Kalimi: "Story about the Murder," pp. 246–61.

24:27 / The expression **the annotations** (*midrash*) **on the book of the kings** occurs only here and in 13:22. Whether the term denotes simply "annotations," "commentary," or even something akin to later rabbinic exegesis remains a matter of speculation.

§4.8 Amaziah (2 Chron. 25:1–28)

After the house of David was saved from extinction in the previous royal narrative, Amaziah continues the Davidic line as king after the death of his father, Joash. His reign (ca. 796–767 B.C.) lasted for twenty-nine years. The ambiguity in the Chronicler's presentation of many of Judah's kings—for example Asa, Jehoshaphat, and Joash—continues in the next episode.

The Chronicler's version features two prominent insertions into the source material, 2 Kings 14:1–20. Second Chronicles 25:5–10 (from the Chronicler's own hand) describes Amaziah's mustering of his troops and hiring of additional mercenaries from his northern neighbor, Israel. An anonymous "man of God" warns him in this section that it would be fatal if he were to ally with northern military resources, and he therefore dismisses these soldiers. The second insertion (25:13–16) describes in great detail the battle against the Edomites and its aftermath. The Chronicler expands the single verse (2 Kgs. 14:7) in the Deuteronomistic source text recounting the battle. Both substantial additions in Chronicles elaborate on that brief comment.

For the rest of the Amaziah narrative the Chronicler follows his source text, making some changes necessitated by his major insertions. There are also some small omissions (e.g., the coordinating dating in 2 Kgs. 14:1).

The text starts with the usual information about the king, an evaluation of his reign, and some anecdotes about him establishing his kingship after the death of his father (25:1–4). This is followed by the extensive description of the preparation, execution, and aftermath of the battle against the Edomites (25:5–16). The outcome of this battle was positive in military terms but fatal in terms of Amaziah's religious convictions. After the victory over the Edomites, he imported some Edomite idols into the Judahite cult. The narrative therefore takes a turn toward the negative. Second Chronicles 25:17–24 gives an account (following the source text closely) of Amaziah's battle against Israel, an incident that leads to his downfall. Second Chronicles 25:25–28 gives final remarks about his reign, death, and burial.

25:1–4 / The Chronicler does not alter the positive evaluation of **Amaziah** given in the Deuteronomistic version, but certainly paints a more complex picture of this king by adding some material that emphasizes the king's apostasy and stubbornness. The Chronicler also changes the evaluation formula slightly: whereas 2 Kings 14:3 compares the king to David and Amaziah's father, Joash, the Chronicler changes this to **he did what was right in the eyes of the** LORD, **but not wholeheartedly.** It is clear that the Chronicler did not want to compare this king in any way with David and Joash. The Chronicler also omits the remark in 2 Kings 14:4 about the people still bringing sacrifices on the high places. This does not fit into the Chronicler's promotion of total dedication to Yahweh, and he therefore prefers the more neutral expression "but not wholeheartedly."

The new king moved swiftly to establish his reign, and **after the kingdom was firmly in his control** (Hebrew *chazaq* is used again), he killed **the officials who had murdered his father** but did not kill **their sons.** This qualification was made to adhere to **what is written in the Law, in the Book of Moses.** Second Chronicles 25:4 quotes Deuteronomy 24:16, showing that the expression "the Law, in the Book of Moses" already referred to Deuteronomy (at least in some early form) during the writing of the Deuteronomistic History (where the same quotation occurs). The Chronicler is apparently well acquainted with the Deuteronomic tradition.

25:5–6 / Amaziah then starts preparing an army. At this stage of the narrative the purpose of this action is uncertain, but it will later (25:11) become clear that a battle against the Edomites was planned. Amaziah **called the people of Judah together and assigned them according to their families to commanders of thousands and commanders of hundreds.** This was done **for all Judah and Benjamin** (25:5). The expression "Judah and Benjamin" occurs ten times in 2 Chronicles in the contexts of the narratives about Rehoboam (11:1, 3, 12, 23), Asa (15:2, 8, 9), Amaziah (25:5), Hezekiah (31:1), and Josiah (34:9). In seven of these ten cases (including in 25:5), the expression is introduced by the same element used in the term "All-Israel," namely, *kol*—thus "All Judah and Benjamin."

Amaziah could muster **three hundred thousand men ready for military service,** a significantly smaller number than the armies that Rehoboam and Jehoshaphat could muster. However, in the next account of a battle (against the Edomites) it will become clear again (as so often in the Chronicler's royal narratives) that victory is not dependent on military strength. What counts is the amount of dedication to Yahweh and his cause. The small number was probably the reason why the king considered hiring mercenaries from Israel to strengthen his army in the coming battle. Although this seems to be good military strategy, it turns out to be a fatal move in the end (see commentary on 25:13).

25:7–10 / The hiring of Israelite mercenaries brings an anonymous **man of God** (normally a prophet) onto the scene. A section containing the Chronicler's own material gives the conversation between the prophet and the king. When the prophet warns the king that he should not make use of Israelite soldiers, **for the LORD is not with Israel** (25:7), and because such a move would lead to his defeat, the king expresses his concern about the **hundred talents of silver** he has already paid. The prophet responds that the economic argument does not fit the situation, because **the LORD can give you much more than that** (25:9). The king obeys the prophet's words and sends those troops back home. The reaction of those troops in 25:10 (**they were furious . . . and left . . . in a great rage**) will have repercussions later in the narrative (25:13).

25:11–12 / A description of the battle against the **men of Seir** is now provided. Seir, Edom, and Esau are always closely related in the Hebrew Bible, and they are often taken as synonyms. The geographical area is to the southeast of the Dead Sea (referred to here as **the Valley of Salt**), where the Edomites (later replaced by the Nabateans) had their stronghold. Although 25:11 refers to 2 Kings 14:7 (the only mention in the Deuteronomistic version of the battle against Edom), the Chronicler alters this text to fit his own portrayal of this battle. He starts his version with the typical expression **Amaziah then marshaled his strength** (Hebrew *chazaq*) and adds to the source text's version another **ten thousand** Edomites who were **captured alive** and thrown off a **cliff** to dash them **to pieces** (25:12). This further elaboration ensured that the reader would be impressed by the dramatic victory that a relatively small Judahite army could achieve.

25:13 / This verse, which is part of the Chronicler's own material, forms an interlude in the description of the Edomite excursion. It presents the reader with some background information about what happened to those **troops that Amaziah had sent back and had not allowed to take part in the war.** They were in the meantime causing havoc by raiding **Judean towns from Samaria to Beth Horon,** killing **three thousand people** and carrying off **great quantities of plunder.** This interlude picks up the narrative thread from 25:10 (also part of the Chronicler's own material) and prepares the way for the battle against Israel described from 25:17 onward. Although the Deuteronomistic version also describes that battle (2 Kgs. 14:8–14, 17–20), the Chronicler creatively provided it another prelude. The Chronicler focuses on the ironic twist that plagued the reign of Amaziah. Because he had obeyed the prophet and sent back the Israelite troops, they caused the trouble that necessitated the later battle (which the king tragically lost)!

25:14–16 / This section, which consists of the Chronicler's own material, contains the core of his critique against King **Amaziah.** Although the king achieved a military victory against the Edomites with a relatively small army, he did not attribute this achievement to wholehearted dedication to Yahweh. Instead, he **brought back the gods of the people of Seir. He set them up as his own gods, bowed down to them and burned sacrifices to them** (25:14). Because of this syncretistic move, **the anger of the** LORD **burned against Amaziah,** and the Lord sent another **prophet** to the king with the pertinent question: **Why do you consult** (*darash*) **this people's gods?** This time the king did not listen, however, and treated the prophet with contempt: **Have we appointed you an adviser to the king? Stop! Why be struck down?** (25:16). The prophet's last words before he disappears from the scene, **I know that God has determined to destroy you,** forebode no good fortune. It is therefore incomprehensible to the reader why Amaziah continues with his plans to take revenge on Israel.

25:17–24 / In 25:17 the Chronicler rejoins the source text at 2 Kings 14:8. To sharpen the contrast with the previous pericope, where the king chased away the prophet of the Lord, the Chronicler adds as an introduction to the account of the battle with Israel: **after Amaziah king of Judah consulted his advisers.** This phrase reminds us of Rehoboam, Solomon's son, who listened to the wrong advisors (1 Kgs. 12). The reader is therefore prepared for a turnaround in events. The introduction of the Edomite gods into Judah started a second phase in Amaziah's reign, which cannot be reconciled with the evaluation at the beginning: "He did what was right in the eyes of the LORD" (2 Chron. 25:2).

The Chronicler follows the source text in 1 Kings 14:8–14 closely but nevertheless makes a significant change in 2 Chronicles 25:20. He added the words **for God so worked that he might hand them over to Jehoash, because they sought the gods of Edom** to the earlier version. It is clear that the Chronicler wanted to provide a theological explanation for what happened in the battle against Israel. On the surface it seems as if Amaziah just wanted to strike back at those Israelite soldiers who had plundered his area after being dismissed from the king's army. However, the Chronicler provides a deeper insight into these military-political endeavors. Behind the scenes God was working, because Amaziah was not wholeheartedly dedicated to Yahweh.

25:25–28 / The Chronicler follows the source text in 2 Kings 14:17–20 closely but makes three small changes. First, whereas the Deuteronomistic version refers the reader to "the book of the annals of the kings of Israel" for more information about the king, the Chronicler mentions **the book of the kings of Judah and Israel** (2 Chron. 25:26). This reference to an additional source is probably another of the Chronicler's attempts to give expression to the unity of Judah and Israel in the postexilic context. Second, the Chronicler specifically dates the conspiracy against King Amaziah to **the time that Amaziah turned away from following the LORD** (25:27). This is clearly an indication that the Chronicler saw the bringing of the Edomite deities to Jerusalem as the beginning of the end for this king. Eventually, the history of Amaziah is determined not by his military losses or victories but by his fatal turning away from Yahweh. Third, whereas the source text indicates that he was buried "in the City of David," 25:28 mentions that it was **in the City of Judah.** This is an unusual phrase and is probably the result of some scribal error. The history of Amaziah therefore ends (as in the case of so many of his predecessors) on a low note.

Additional Notes §4.8

25:12 / "Sela" in the Deuteronomistic version becomes in the Chronicler's elaboration the **cliff** off which the Edomites were pushed (Sela means "rock" or "cliff"). Sela or the rock cliff could be associated with Petra (it also means "rock" or "cliff"), the city carved out of rock by the Nabateans who later occupied the Edomite homeland to the southeast of the Dead Sea. The Chronicler's concern with the Edomites, and his vague reference to Sela, could betray some concern of his own time. During the late Persian era, when the Chronicler probably wrote his history, the province of Idumea (related to Edom) was established alongside Yehud (related to Judah) in the Persian Empire. That there was some rivalry may be assumed with a great amount of certainty.

25:13 / The mention of **Samaria** seems strange here, because that city formed part of the northern kingdom of Israel. Some commentators offer explanations for this confusion—none of which are satisfactory.

25:14 / This verse contains the only information available in the Hebrew Bible on the religion of the **Edomites.** It implies that they served more than one deity and that these deities were represented in visible form. The reason that the Chronicler felt the need to introduce this aspect of the Edomite deities into the narrative should probably be sought in the sociohistorical circumstances of the time of the Chronicler's writing, when the Persian province of Idumea existed alongside Yehud. The Chronicler therefore interacts not so much with Edom of the past but with the Persian province Idumea of his present.

25:24 / The reference to **Obed-Edom** is an addition to the source text of 2 Kgs. 14:14. Since Obed-Edom means "servant of Edom," the mention of this name may subtly allude to Amaziah's apostate worship of the gods of Edom. Since Obed-Edom was custodian of the temple treasures, the name may also highlight the connection between Amaziah's loss of that treasure to Israel because he had served the gods of Edom.

§4.9 Uzziah (2 Chron. 26:1–23)

Uzziah, who reigned approximately 792/791–740/739 B.C., is yet another example of a king who started off well but ended in shame. In this case the Chronicler was solely responsible for presenting this picture of the king. The major part of this narrative (26:5–20) belongs to the Chronicler's own material, which expanded on a very concise account in the Deuteronomistic version, found in 2 Kgs. 14:21–22; 15:1–7. The former text is part of the Deuteronomist's conclusion to Amaziah's reign, while the latter gives the actual account on Uzziah, complete with the usual date of accession correlated with that of the northern king (2 Kgs. 15:1). The Chronicler omitted this comment, together with the remark that the people still brought sacrifices to the high places (2 Kgs. 15:4), something typical of the Chronicler's style. The narrative continues in the Deuteronomistic version in 2 Kings 15:5 with a remark, "The LORD afflicted the king with leprosy until the day he died." This follows logically after 2 Chronicles 26:4, indicating that the high places were still in operation. But since this information was omitted by the Chronicler, he had to provide other reasons for the king's skin disease. So he reconstructed the whole narrative, adding an expanded section on Uzziah's successes (26:5–15), probably to explain this king's very long reign of fifty-two years. He also added a section on Uzziah's pride (26:16–20), which explains the king's skin disease, his troublesome last years, and his death.

26:1–4 / These introductory verses to King Uzziah's reign conflate two texts from the Deuteronomistic source (2 Kgs. 14:21–22 and 15:1–2). The Chronicler's account follows these verses exactly, except that he calls this king **Uzziah** and not "Azariah" as in 2 Kings 14:21. Although the name Azariah is used in the Chronicler's genealogy in 1 Chronicles 3:12, he probably used the other name of the king to avoid causing any confusion with the prophet Azariah (mentioned in the Asa narrative), but particularly with the priest Azariah, who accompanied Uzziah into the temple (see 26:17, 20).

Following the source text (2 Kgs. 15:3), the Chronicler indicates the king **did what was right in the eyes of the LORD, just as his father Amaziah**

had done (2 Chron. 26:4). The reader of Chronicles knows, however, that
the unique account of Amaziah provided in the previous chapter leaves
a very ambiguous impression of that king. The description that follows
will confirm that ambiguity with reference to Uzziah.

26:5–15 / The section on the successes of Uzziah (all from the
Chronicler's hand) starts with the telling remark: **He sought** (*darash*)
God during the days of Zechariah. . . . As long as he sought (*darash*)
the LORD, God gave him success. It is very clear that the Chronicler relates these successes to the king's dedication to Yahweh's cause. These
successes were clearly visible in three areas. First (26:6–8), he conducted
successful campaigns against a whole series of foreign and neighboring
nations (**Philistines, Arabs, Meunites,** and **Ammonites**) in order to expand
his territory and initiate various building projects. This caused **his fame
to spread as far as the border of Egypt, because he had become very
powerful.** Second (26:9–10), he succeeded in fortifying **Jerusalem** and
in providing **cisterns** for his **livestock** and **fertile lands** for his **fields and
vineyards.** In a remarkable side note the Chronicler indicates: **For he loved
the soil.** Third, Uzziah was also successful in building up a remarkable
army and military machinery (26:11–15), so that **his fame spread far and
wide, for he was greatly helped until he became powerful** (26:15). The
Hebrew word for "help" (*he'azer*) is a sound play on the name Azariah
(*'azaryahu*), which means "the LORD helped." This is the name given to
Uzziah in Kings. The insinuation is clear that, although the Lord is not
explicitly mentioned as subject here, Uzziah's fame was given to him by
the Lord. The phrase "until he became powerful" uses the well-known
word *chazaq* again, which could be a double entendre here, leading to
the dark period in the king's history. This verb resonates with the king's
name in Chronicles, Uzziah (which means "Yahweh is strong"). The
name change from Azariah to Uzziah might be the Chronicler's way of
indicating the two phases in this king's career: the period of fame (when
he was helped, presumably by Yahweh) and the period of shame (when
he did not rely on Yahweh's strength, but on his own).

26:16–21 / The word *chazaq* opens the new section, which
shows the result of the king becoming "strong": **but after Uzziah became powerful, his pride led to his downfall.** The king's "pride" is
further explained with the phrase **he was unfaithful to the LORD his
God,** which uses the significant term *ma'al* ("be unfaithful") again.
In the Rehoboam history (see Additional Note on 12:2) this is one
of the Chronicler's programmatic terms that signifies the opposite of

darash and *biqqesh* ("to seek" the Lord). This is indeed a turnaround in Uzziah's history.

The king's pride and unfaithfulness were particularly exemplified on one specific occasion when he **entered the temple of the LORD to burn incense on the altar of incense** (26:16). The reader of Chronicles would know that proper cultic behavior is of the utmost importance for this writer. This was already made very clear in the Uzzah narrative in 1 Chronicles 13. Uzzah (whose name remarkably resembles that of King Uzziah) touched the ark of the covenant while it was en route to Jerusalem, and the Lord struck him dead for this transgression. Improper behavior in the cult, such as a king performing the duty of a priest, is the extreme example of unfaithfulness.

Azariah the priest with eighty other courageous priests of the LORD (2 Chron. 26:17) confronted the king while he was preparing "to burn incense on the altar of incense." Their accusation is crystal clear: **you have been unfaithful** (*ma'al* again) (26:18).

While the king was still **raging at the priests, leprosy broke out on his forehead** (26:19). The word translated **leprosy** by the NIV can also be translated more generically "skin disease." By mentioning the skin disease in 26:19–20, the Chronicler prepares the way to rejoin his source text in 2 Kings 15:5. There, without citing any background circumstances, the Deuteronomist writes that "the LORD afflicted the king with leprosy until the day he died." The Chronicler adds that the priests **hurried him out** of the temple and that the king **himself was eager to leave, because the LORD had afflicted him.** As in the source text, 2 Chronicles 26:21 states that the king **lived in a separate house,** but the Chronicler adds that he was **leprous, and excluded from the temple of the LORD.** Whereas 26:15 ended with the fame of the king spreading over all the neighboring areas, 26:21 ends with the king being expelled from the temple because of his pride. How the mighty have fallen!

26:22–23 / The narrative ends with the usual summary notes taken from the source text in 2 Kings 15:6–7. Two small changes are noteworthy, however. First, whereas the Deuteronomist's version refers to "the book of the annals of the kings of Judah" again, the Chronicler claims he tells events **recorded by the prophet Isaiah son of Amoz.** This is normally taken as reference to the eighth-century B.C. prophet Isaiah, who was a contemporary of King Uzziah of Judah (Isa. 1:1; 6:1). The change was probably made by the Chronicler in line with his inclination to involve prophetic voices in his history. Second, another well-known change was made to the note about the king's burial place. Whereas

2 Kings 15:7 mentions that "he was buried . . . in the City of David," Chronicles says, **Uzziah . . . was buried near his fathers in a field for burial that belonged to the kings.** His burial was on royal property nearby but not in the official burial plot reserved for kings. The reason: **for people said, "He had leprosy."** This note is a final confirmation of the Chronicler's contempt for this king.

Additional Note §4.9

26:6–8 / Steven Ortiz ("Urban City Planning," pp. 361–81) argues that many of the building projects uncovered by archeologists at Tel Gezer and in the Shephelah, which are normally attributed to King Hezekiah, were actually part of the successful expansions of King Uzziah.

§4.10 Jotham (2 Chron. 27:1–9)

This very short passage describes the reign of King Jotham (ca. 748–733 B.C.), the first king since Abijah to be judged wholly positively. The Chronicler closely followed the even shorter version in the Deuteronomistic History (2 Kgs. 15:32–38) but added some information on the successes of the king. On the other hand, given the pattern evident in the previous royal narratives in Chronicles, it is strange that the Chronicler did not snatch the opportunity to extol the religious virtues of this righteous king even more. This may simply be because the Chronicler did not have access to more information about the king.

Second Chronicles 26:21 notes that "Jotham his son had charge of the palace and governed the people of the land." The reference is to the period after Uzziah's skin disease led to his being expelled from society. Given this comment, some scholars theorize that Jotham was coregent with his father for a number of years. Two pieces of evidence cast doubt on this suggestion. First, 26:21b credits Jotham only with management of the palace and perhaps with limited governing (literally "judging"). Second, according to 26:22, Jotham comes to reign only after Uzziah's death. This section starts with the normal introduction to and evaluation of the new king (27:1–2), followed by a description of his building projects (27:3–4) and his military campaign against the Ammonites (27:5); 27:6 provides a summary of his reign, before 27:7–9 concludes the narrative with the usual summary information.

27:1–2 / As usual, the Chronicler omits the coordinated dating of the kings of Judah and Israel (as in 2 Kgs. 15:32) but copies the biographical details about King **Jotham** from 2 Kings 15:33. The positive evaluation of the king is also taken from the source text in 2 Kings 15:34. The phrase **just as his father Uzziah had done,** which occurs in both versions, refers to the positive evaluation of King Uzziah in the previous passage. However, the Chronicler qualifies this in the light of his own version of Uzziah's reign by adding **but unlike him he did not enter the temple of the LORD,** which serves as negative judgment on Uzziah. Typically, the Chronicler leaves out the Deuteronomistic comment that the people still continued bringing sacrifices at the high places (2 Kgs. 15:35a). In this narrative he indeed includes that aspect but with a change: **the people, however, continued their corrupt practices.** It is, however, absolutely clear that these "corrupt practices" of "the people" did not blemish King Jotham's righteous reputation in any way. Theologically, the Chronicler works with an understanding of individual responsibility, a view that already emerges in some prophetic material (e.g., Ezek. 18).

27:3–4 / These verses focus on the successful building projects of Jotham. The Chronicler adds to the source text (2 Kgs. 15:35b) a reference to the king's work **on the wall at the hill of Ophel,** the hill that extends southward from the temple mount and where the City of David was situated. The Chronicler also adds information about the king building **towns in the Judean hills and forts and towers in the wooded areas.** We know by now that successful building projects are one sign of the divine blessings a righteous king would experience.

27:5 / The same applies to military successes, which are seen as closely associated with a righteous rule. Jotham's successful conquering of **the Ammonites** (with the verb *chazaq* again) and their paying regular tribute to the king in huge amounts of **silver, wheat,** and **barley** (reported in the Chronicler's own material) are in line with the writer's theological vision of the relationship between the deity and the monarch. Righteous kings reap the rewards of prosperity.

27:6 / Second Chronicles 27:6 draws a theological conclusion from the previous information about the building projects and military successes: **Jotham grew powerful** (*chazaq*) **because he walked steadfastly** (*kun*) **before the LORD his God.** This verse, which belongs to the Chronicler's own material, uses two of the typically Chronistic terms.

27:7–9 / The Chronicler rejoins his source text in 2 Kings 15:36 with the normal reference to other sources about the king. As usual, the Chronicler replaces "Judah" in the source text with **Israel and Judah** in order to emphasize the All-Israel concept again. Second Chronicles 27:8 repeats the introductory information in 27:1 and could be either the result of some error in textual transmission or a literary feature intended to enclose the Jotham narrative. The final remark about the burial of the king (27:9) follows the source text (2 Kgs. 15:38) but omits the words "with his fathers." The reader would note that this is the first king since Jehoshaphat to be granted burial **in the City of David.** The Chronicler typically uses the burial note to give a final assessment of the king's reign, so he confirms Jotham's righteousness by locating his burial in the royal burial site in the City of David.

Additional Note §4.10

27:3 / Could the reference to **the wall at the hill of Ophel** be a reference to the Millo, or stepped stone structure, uncovered by archeologists in this area? We know from 32:5 that King Hezekiah strengthened the Millo, and the present text may also refer to this structure, which probably supported a bigger structure on the Ophel hill.

§4.11 Ahaz (2 Chron. 28:1–27)

If the previous narrative about Jotham had created some hope for the reader of Chronicles that the kingship of Judah would survive, the present narrative about Ahaz (ca. 743/742–727/726 B.C.) would destroy that hope again! It marks one of the most negative portrayals of a king in Chronicles. Whereas many of the previous royal narratives (e.g., Asa, Jehoshaphat, Joash, Amaziah, and Uzziah) reflected some ambiguity about the virtues and vices of the kings, the present narrative provides a wholly negative account. The Chronicler even adapted some of the information in the source text (2 Kgs. 16) to create an even more negative portrait of King Ahaz. To some commentators, Ahaz is the Chronicler's substitute for the Deuteronomist's portrayal of Manasseh as the epitome of evil who was to blame for the exile of Judah. Although it is certainly true that Manasseh receives better treatment from the Chronicler, and Ahaz worse treatment, the Chronicler does not link Ahaz's reign in any way to the Judahite exile. Instead, Ahaz serves as a prominent warning against unrestrained apostasy.

There are two significant changes in the Chronicler's use of the Deuteronomist's version. First, the Chronicler added a substantial section (28:6–15) that describes an encounter with the northern kingdom, Israel. Second, the Chronicler omits the episode of Ahaz's installation of a copy of the Damascus altar in Jerusalem (in 2 Kgs. 16:10–16), replacing it with an abbreviated version of the encounter with Syria.

The order of events in the Chronicler's text seems illogical. Whether this is the result of textual transmission or the Chronicler's deliberate literary artistry to portray the chaotic state of King Ahaz's reign cannot be determined for sure. My discussion regroups the information contained in the text in order to provide a more logical commentary. Structurally, this narrative opens with an introduction that both contains the usual regnal information and elaborates substantially on the apostasy of the king (28:1–4). It then provides information about Ahaz's interaction with Damascus in Syria (28:5a and 28:23). Second Chronicles 28:5b–15 discusses Ahaz's defeat by Israel as well as the resultant events concerning the captives of Judah. His failed attempt to get help from Assyria is narrated in 28:16 and 28:20–22, while the account of his losses to the Edomites and Philistines follows (28:17–19). Second Chronicles 28:24–25 returns to the king's apostasy, which 28:1–4 described, before the normal concluding remarks about the king's reign close the narrative (28:26–27).

28:1–4 / Both the Chronicler and the Deuteronomist make their negative judgment on this king in comparison with David: **unlike David his father, he did not do what was right in the eyes of the Lord.** Both also qualify their negative evaluation, remarking that Ahaz **walked in the ways of the kings of Israel.** The latter comment probably necessitated the reference to David, the epitome of the righteous king. You have to go a long way back to find a king who was able to avoid this pitfall!

In elaborating on the apostasy of King Ahaz, the Deuteronomist mentions that the king "even sacrificed his son in the fire, following the detestable ways of the nations the Lord had driven out before the Israelites" (2 Kgs. 16:3). Child sacrifice, which is often related to the influence of the Canaanite Molech cult, is explicitly forbidden in various texts in the Old Testament (e.g., Deut. 18:10). These sacrifices were apparently associated with **the Valley of Ben Hinnom** (a valley running to the west and south of the old city of Jerusalem, joining the Kidron Valley to the southwest), which also served as a rubbish heap for Jerusalem through many centuries. The Chronicler adds another apostate action to the Deuteronomist's version, however: **he burned sacrifices in the Valley of Ben Hinnom** (28:3). Literally, this refers to smoke (or incense) offerings. In the next verse the Chronicler copies the information from his source text: **he offered sacrifices and burned incense at the high places, on the hilltops and under every spreading tree** (28:4). This remark comes as a surprise for two reasons. Almost all previous royal narratives in the Deuteronomistic version mention that "the people" still sacrificed on the high places. Now it is the king committing this sin! The second reason for our surprise is the inclusion of this remark by the Chronicler, whereas he had omitted all previous references to the remaining high places. This shows the Chronicler's deep disdain for King Ahaz.

28:5a and 28:23 / The Chronicler ignores the alliance of Aram-Damascus and Israel and the so-called Syro-Ephraimite war against Judah (2 Kgs. 16:5). Instead, he splits the information, presenting, first, Ahaz's defeat by the Arameans (**the Lord his God handed him over to the king of Aram. The Arameans . . . took many of his people as prisoners . . . to Damascus; 28:5a**). Then follows a description of a similar defeat by

Israel (he was also given into the hands of the king of Israel, who inflicted heavy casualties on him; 28:5b). Two grammatical touches, the Hebrew particle *gam* ("in addition") and the fronting of the prepositional phrase "into the hands of the king of Israel," picture two defeats in a row. Following the Chronicler's narrative portrayal, I therefore opt to treat these encounters as two different events.

The Chronicler abbreviates in 28:23 the elaborate information provided in the source text (2 Kgs. 16:10–16). There Ahaz orders Uriah the priest to build a copy of the Damascus altar in Jerusalem, on which regular sacrifices are then made. The Chronicler's shorter account reports that Ahaz sacrifices to Aramean gods so the latter **will help** him just as they have the victorious **kings of Aram.** Unfortunately, Ahaz's apostasy led to **his downfall and the downfall of all Israel** (2 Chron. 28:23). The Chronicler thus again (28:5a) provides a theological explanation for Ahaz's act and shows how it contributed to the downfall of both the king and All-Israel (i.e., the totality of the Chronicler's envisioned people).

28:5b–15 / The encounter with **Israel,** the northern neighbor, which makes up the greatest part of the Ahaz narrative, belongs fully to the Chronicler's own material. The Chronicler surely wanted to portray **Ahaz** within the context of his relationship with his northern neighbor. The motivation for the account of the heavy losses against Israel is again theological: **because Judah had forsaken** (*'azab*) **the Lord, the God of their fathers** (28:6).

This section introduces a number of ironic twists. Israel (and particularly the house of Ahab), normally portrayed as apostate and syncretistic, now becomes the instrument through which the Lord punishes the apostasy of Ahaz and Judah! Furthermore, **a prophet of the Lord named Oded** (28:9) addresses the Israelite (not Judahite) **army** on its way back to **Samaria** with thousands of captured **kinsmen** and **plunder** from Judah (28:8). The "prophet of the Lord," who normally addresses the Judahite king, now warns these Israelite soldiers not to bring the Judahites to Samaria, lest the Lord's **fierce anger** (28:13) come upon Israel! Although Israel defeated Judah **because the Lord, the God of** their **fathers, . . . gave them into** their **hand,** they do not have the right to slaughter **them in a rage that reaches to heaven** (28:9). They themselves are **also guilty of sins against the Lord** (28:10), a clear reference to the apostasy of the north that even the **leaders in Ephraim** realize (**our guilt is already great, and his fierce anger rests on Israel;** 28:13). The word for "guilt," which the verse repeats three times, resonates with the word of the prophet (in 28:10), and this deed is then called a **sin.**

This depiction, as well as the description of the encounter with the Arameans in the previous subsection, contrasts with the Deuteronomist's remark that the Syro-Ephraimite coalition "could not overpower him" (2 Kgs. 16:5). According to the Chronicler, they indeed overpowered Ahaz and Judah, although the sending back of the captives by Israel might be the Chronicler's way of relating to the Deuteronomist's portrayal.

28:16 and 28:20–22 / These verses describe the encounter with the Assyrians, while the short section on the Edomite and Philistine raids (28:17–19) interrupts the flow of the source text narrative (2 Kgs. 16:7–9). The next verses show the remarkable literary artistry of the Chronicler. With only a few minor changes and the swapping of verse order, he presents a totally different outcome of the encounter with the Assyrians than 2 Kings 16 does. In the latter, Ahaz requests help from Assyria against the Syro-Ephraimite coalition and presents silver and gold from the temple and palace as a gift to the Assyrian king. Tiglath-Pileser then responds by attacking Damascus and killing the Syrian king. According to Chronicles, however, Ahaz's request for help without the gift (2 Chron. 28:16) yields the opposite response: **Tiglath-Pileser king of Assyria came to him** (i.e., against Ahaz!)—but with **trouble instead of help** (28:20). To end the attack, Ahaz presented the Assyrian king with **things from the temple of the LORD and from the royal palace and from the princes . . . ,** but that did not help him (28:21). In Hebrew the latter verse starts with the particle *ki* (untranslated in the NIV), which introduces a reason for the preceding incident. Clearly, the Chronicler saw the giving of "things from the temple of the LORD" to Tiglath-Pileser as the reason that Ahaz was defeated by the Assyrians. The Chronicler adds another phrase to confirm his theological estimation of what happened between Ahaz and Assyria: **in his time of trouble King Ahaz became even more unfaithful** (*ma'al*) **to the LORD** (28:22).

28:17–19 / These verses (the Chronicler's own material) mention a defeat by the **Edomites** (28:17) as well as raids by the **Philistines** (28:18) in which they captured a number of villages from Judah. With these insertions into the account of Ahaz's reign, the Chronicler managed to incorporate into the narrative an imperial force (Assyria), Judah's kinsfolk to the north (Israel), and some neighboring nations (Edomites, Philistines). These insertions probably had a metaphorical function, evoking the political reality of the Chronicler's own time, when an imperial force (Persia), a related province (Samaria), and some other neighboring provinces (Idumea and Philistia) dominated the sociopolitical scene.

This section of the Chronicler's narrative also concludes with a theological assessment containing some familiar terminology: the LORD had humbled (*kana'*) Judah because of Ahaz king of Israel, for he had promoted wickedness in Judah and had been most unfaithful (*ma'al* [emphatic in Hebrew]) to the LORD (28:19).

28:24–25 / These verses, which are just vaguely related to the source text in 2 Kings 16:17–18, recap some of the prominent themes in the Ahaz account, but with 28:3–4 they also frame the narrative. In his reformulation of the source text the Chronicler intensifies the king's apostasy by indicating that he shut the doors of the LORD's temple and set up altars at every street corner in Jerusalem, a remark that is absent from Kings. Imagine: a Davidic king barring entrance to the very temple that David desired and Solomon built! The great irony of the king himself now also providing high places to bring sacrifices to other deities in every town in Judah bears repeating. It comes as no surprise that Ahaz's policy provoked the LORD, the God of his fathers, to anger.

28:26–27 / The death-and-burial notice is copied from the source text in 2 Kings 16:19–20, although the customary small changes are made. The most prominent of these is again (as in the case of so many previous kings) that the Chronicler changes reference to the burial place from "with his fathers . . . in the City of David" to in the city of Jerusalem, but he was not placed in the tombs of the kings of Israel. The mentioning of "kings of Israel" (and not Judah) is probably an indication of the Chronicler's All-Israel ideology again. As with so many of Ahaz's predecessors, his reign ends outside the realm of what the Chronicler would consider to be faithful kingship.

Additional Notes §4.11

28:8–15 / Although it is clear that Ahaz is made into the worst Judahite king by the Chronicler, the writer apparently does not attribute the same blame to him as the Deuteronomist does to Manasseh (who is held responsible for the exile). Some scholars suggest that there are similarities between the Ahaz narrative and the parable of the good Samaritan in Luke 10:25–37. Granted, the basic structure of the Ahaz narrative could have contributed to further interpretation in new contexts, but the connections usually made between the narrative and the parable rest on very limited analogies. The wider literary contexts are too different to be associated with one another.

28:16 and 28:20–22 / The campaigns of **Tiglath-Pileser,** the Assyrian king, against the Levantine states are discussed in many historical studies. However, it bears repeating that the Chronicler's depiction of the interaction between Judah and Assyria aimed not merely to convey historical information but rather to provide a theological perspective on these international political circumstances.

28:20 / The Chronicler constantly calls the Assyrian king **Tilgath-Pilneser,** instead of the more accepted form "Tiglath-Pileser." This might be a spelling mistake by the Chronicler, although it would then be strange that the mistake is repeated in all three cases where the name is mentioned (1 Chron. 5:6, 26; 2 Chron. 28:20). The Septuagint and Peshitta corrected the name in these cases to the more usual form.

§4.12 Hezekiah (2 Chron. 29:1–32:33)

Hezekiah (ca. 727/726–698/697 B.C.) is certainly one of the Chronicler's favorite kings. Excluding the Chronicler's accounts of David and Solomon, this is the most extensive of all the royal narratives, stretching over four chapters (2 Chron. 29–32). Here the Chronicler composed an almost completely new narrative with very specific ideas on how to portray this king.

A major event that is described in full by the Deuteronomist (in 2 Kgs. 17) but omitted totally by the Chronicler is the fall of Samaria and the northern kingdom, Israel, to the Assyrians in 722 B.C. (i.e., during Hezekiah's reign over Judah). This introduced a new phase in Judah's history in which they were the only surviving Israelite kingdom. M. A. Throntveit (*When Kings Speak: Royal Speech and Royal Prayer in Chronicles* [Atlanta: Scholars Press, 1987], pp. 40, 120–25) argues that new aspirations for a "reunited monarchy" emerged in these days. He therefore sees a new section starting in 2 Chronicles 29, which focuses on the reunited monarchy. I am not so convinced that these aspirations were political in nature. However, the new phase certainly gave new impetus to the understanding of All-Israel. The Chronicler promoted not a revived and reunified David-Solomon empire but a theological unity, a national reunion around the temple worship of Yahweh. The Chronicler, however, related Hezekiah and Josiah to one another in a way that is analogous to the relationship between David and Solomon.

The Chronicler made very eclectic and limited use of the text in Kings. He uses the introduction to the king's reign in 2 Chronicles 29:1–2 (adapted from 2 Kgs. 18:1–3) and inserts into his account huge portions of narrative about the cleansing and rededication of the temple (2 Chron. 29:3–36) as well as about the celebration of the Passover (30:1–27), before rejoining very briefly the source account in his description of Hezekiah's reform measures in 31:1–21 (an adaptation and expansion of 2 Kgs. 18:4–7). The most extensive use of source materials is 2 Chronicles 32:1–33, where the Chronicler (albeit again very selectively) uses 2 Kings 18:13, 17–37; 19:35–37; 20:1–21. Interestingly enough, large parts of the Deuteronomist's account are also attested in Isaiah 36–39, a narrative section that probably stems from the eighth-century B.C. prophet, who was a contemporary of King Hezekiah.

How did the Chronicler recast and restructure this narrative in order to shift its focus? The temporal organization of the Chronicler's narrative, as well as the constellations of acting subjects and indirect objects, shifts the narrative focus from the Deuteronomist's emphasis on political events to the Chronicler's emphasis on cultic events. The temporal focus in Chronicles is on year one of Hezekiah's reign, established by an elaborate and almost slow-motion description of the temple cleansing, Passover celebrations, and organization of the Levites and priests (29:3–31:21). This description (apart from one verse in 2 Kgs. 18:4) is not in the Deuteronomistic version. What can be categorized as "post–year one" in the Chronicler's account (2 Chron. 32:1–33) carries the main focus in the Deuteronomistic account (which even structures those events with precise temporal indications). The construction of this narrative by the Chronicler therefore reshapes (or retells) the account of the past in order to move it from the realm of political history to the realm of cultic history.

29:1–2 / As usual, the Chronicler omits the synchronism with the Israelite king (Kings no longer mentions northern kings after the house of Israel came to an end in 722 B.C.). The positive qualification of **Hezekiah** is made in the statement **he did what was right in the eyes of the Lord, just as his father David had done.** The comparison of Hezekiah with David (the only king thus far to get this qualification) is already present in the source text.

29:3–11 / Second Chronicles 29:3 opens quite a long section (the Chronicler's own material) with the very elaborate temporal indication **in the first month of the first year of his reign.** The Chronicler wanted to portray this king as immediately starting to reform the cult after the devastating events of his father Ahaz's reign. This "first year of his reign" is also the Chronicler's primary interest.

Whereas Ahaz closed the doors of the temple and started sacrificing "at every street corner in Jerusalem" (28:24), the new king **opened the doors of the temple of the Lord and repaired them** (29:3). The Hebrew word translated "repair" in the NIV (and most other translations) is prominent in Chronicles, *chazaq* ("to strengthen"). Here, the word is certainly used as a pun on the name of King Hezekiah (*chizqiyyahu*, "the Lord strengthens"), since the verb occurs another four times in this account.

In the next sections the Chronicler indicates that Hezekiah prepared the way for extensive temple renovations. He gives a prominent
role to the **priests and the Levites** in this whole endeavor. The king addresses them in the extensive direct speech in 29:5–11, opening with the
words **listen to me, Levites** (the latter term used in the generic sense here;
see introduction to §2.8). The king calls on them to perform two tasks:
**consecrate yourselves now and consecrate the temple of the LORD, the
God of your fathers** (29:5). The verb translated "consecrate" in the NIV
(a reflexive of the verb *qadash*) is used frequently in the king's speech
but also seems to have some programmatic overtones. Apart from two
instances (26:18 in connection with Uzziah, and 36:14 in connection
with the exile), all other occurrences of this verb are in the narratives on
David, Solomon, Hezekiah, and Josiah. The Chronicler develops a special
relationship between these four kings (see commentary on 34:1–36:1).
This is achieved by means of, among other things, the use of certain
programmatic terminology such as "consecrate." The consecration of the
temple is further described in the phrase **remove all defilement from the
sanctuary** ("sanctuary" is *haqqodesh*, a word related to "consecrate").
The choice of the word "defilement" (*niddah*) shows the Chronicler's
great contempt for the state of the temple before Hezekiah's restoration
started. The Hebrew word is related to the menstrual bleeding of women,
which was considered utterly impure in the cultic worldview of the time.

In 29:6–9 the Chronicler provides the historical reasons for Judah's
present disastrous state. It is clear that the description particularly refers
to the evils of Hezekiah's own father, Ahaz. These evils of the fathers
are strongly expressed in 29:6: **our fathers were unfaithful** (*ma'al*); **they
did evil in the eyes of the LORD our God and forsook** (*'azab*) **him**, again
with two strong programmatic words in the Chronicler's version of this
statement.

The intention of the king (29:10) is expressed clearly (**to make a
covenant with the LORD, the God of Israel**), and to do so, he calls upon
the "priests and Levites," whom **the LORD has chosen . . . to stand before
him and serve him** (29:11). We may assume that this strong call was also
intended for the priests and Levites in the Chronicler's own time, the
context to which this communication was primarily addressed.

29:12–14 / The response of the **Levites** is immediate, as they
set to work. In a short genealogical section the names of those Levites
who started working are provided. Three families who are already well
known from the genealogies in 1 Chronicles 1–9, as well as from the section on David's officials in 1 Chronicles 23–27, participate: **Kohathites,**

Merarites, and Gershonites. Of the next four groups mentioned in the list, three names are also well known as those of temple singers (Asaph, Heman, and Jeduthun) (see commentary on 1 Chron. 23–27).

29:15–19 / The actual cleaning is now described in 29:15–19. This was done as the king had ordered, following the word of the LORD (29:15). In the description of the restoration of the temple, as well as in the report to the king that follows, the word consecrate (qadash) is used four times—which underlines the programmatic nature of the Chronicler's description. The temporal indications in 29:17 (on the first day of the first month . . . by the eighth day of the month . . . for eight more days . . . finishing on the sixteenth day of the first month) again confirm that the restoration of the temple forms the very basis of Hezekiah's reign. With the report that they have prepared (kun) and consecrated (qadash) everything, the priests and the Levites turn the clock back to a pre-Ahaz age, when the dedicated temple service was still intact. The scene is set for a renewed dedication of the temple and the resumption of its cultic function.

29:20–36 / Different kinds of sacrifices are now performed on the altar by the priests, the descendants of Aaron (29:21). The description of these sacrifices in 29:20–24 is very detailed and graphic in order to give expression to the cultic context. It is important to note that the Chronicler indicates that the atonement sacrifices were brought for all Israel. The legitimacy of the restored and rededicated temple in Jerusalem is not limited to within Jerusalem or Judah but extends its cultic function to include All-Israel, that is, the complete postexilic people of Yahweh as envisioned by the Chronicler. Since we know that Samaria and its sanctuary were destroyed concurrent with the reign of Hezekiah, the Chronicler's claim is that Jerusalem is now, and always was, the sanctuary for All-Israel.

Second Chronicles 29:25–30 specifically involves the Levites in the celebrations. They are reinstated in the way prescribed by David and Gad the king's seer and Nathan the prophet; this was commanded by the LORD through his prophets (29:25). Their function is particularly to praise the LORD with the words of David and of Asaph the seer (29:30). This section is particularly reminiscent of the Chronicler's description of David's cultic organization. According to 1 Chronicles 23–27, the Levites are quite prominent in accompanying with their music and instruments the sacrificial worship (which is to be performed by the priests).

According to the Chronicler's depiction, this tradition is taken up again during the reign of Hezekiah. After Hezekiah had given the word, the assembly could join in the sacrificial celebrations. Enormous numbers of animals were slaughtered for the sacrifices, so much so that the priests could not handle the slaughtering alone, so **their kinsmen the Levites helped** (literally "strengthened," *chazaq*) **them** (29:34). This remark is particularly interesting. It may seem that the Chronicler wants to portray the Levites and priests in a good working relationship with one another. However, the motivational clause included in 29:34 also creates another impression: **for the Levites had been more conscientious in consecrating** (*qadash*) **themselves than the priests had been.** The entire book of Chronicles provides fairly equal portrayals of the Levites and the priests, but the present text sounds another evaluative note. One may assume that the Chronicler, without being overly biased, wanted to advance the Levites' cause by indicating that they had already consecrated themselves (the same sentiment is expressed in 30:3).

Another significant phrase occurs in 29:35: **so the service of the temple of the Lord was reestablished** (*kun*). This is a very important indication in the macrostructure of Chronicles. Here it indicates that the temple service was put in place again and could resume after being neglected for many years during Ahaz' reign. However, a similar phrase (also with *kun*) in the Josiah narrative closes the macrostructure in 35:20. Hezekiah's rededication of the temple service already prepares for the glorious era that will come with King Josiah's Passover celebrations. The idea expressed with *kun* is echoed in the last verse of this subsection (29:36), when the Chronicler says: **Hezekiah and all the people rejoiced at what God had brought about** (*kun*) **for his people, because it was done so quickly.**

30:1–27 / This subsection (which is the Chronicler's own material in full) is dedicated to the preparations for and celebration of the Passover. Passover occupies a very prominent place, not only in the Hezekiah narrative, but also in the Josiah account. However, it is here in the account of Hezekiah's reign that the Passover is mentioned for the first time in Chronicles.

It is introduced in 30:1 with the remark that **Hezekiah sent word to all Israel and Judah and also wrote letters to Ephraim and Manasseh,** an all-inclusive designation that leaves no misunderstanding that the northern tribes are seen as part of the cultic community of Jerusalem. They are invited by the king **to come to the temple of the Lord in Jerusalem and celebrate the Passover to the Lord, the God of Israel.** Whereas the traditional Passover celebration, according to Exodus 12, had to take place in the family sphere, the Chronicler's narrative makes clear that the Passover was celebrated as a national event during the time of Hezekiah. The king explicitly instructed and sent letters to the people **from Beersheba to Dan** (30:5) to come to Jerusalem for the celebration. In the end it seems that the ideal of an all-inclusive celebration was striven for, but this did not really materialize: people in **Ephraim and Manasseh, as far as Zebulun, . . . scorned and ridiculed** the royal **couriers.** The lone exception: **some men of Asher, Manasseh and Zebulun humbled themselves** (*kana'*) **and went to Jerusalem** (30:10–11).

The words of the king's letter are given in 30:6b–9. The people are called to **return to the** LORD, **the God of Abraham, Isaac and Israel** (30:6). This designation for Yahweh occurs only here in Chronicles, and the Chronicler hereby not only relates Hezekiah's Passover to the ancestral era before the existence of the monarchy but also thereby includes both southern and northern traditions. The king calls on the people to **not be like your fathers and brothers, who were unfaithful** (*ma'al*) **to the** LORD (30:7)—again a clear indication of the Chronicler's theological vision that promoted faithfulness to Yahweh. Although the king's letter is suffused with the Chronicler's style and language, it is also clear that the Chronicler took a leaf from the Deuteronomist's book in composing it (without the letter being represented in the Deuteronomistic version). A prominent Deuteronomic term, "to return" (*shub*), encompasses the letter's content. The call in 30:6 is: **people of Israel, return** (*shub*) **to the** LORD. And the promise in 30:9 is: **if you return** (*shub*) **to the** LORD, **then your brothers and your children . . . will come back** (*shub*) **to this land, for the** LORD **your God is gracious and compassionate.** Apparently, the Chronicler is playing on the exilic condition of the northern kingdom here. The Passover in Jerusalem should be the way in which Judah's brethren from the north can "turn back to" Yahweh so that they may be released from their captivity. This is typical of the Deuteronomic theology, which also exercised enormous influence on the Deuteronomistic History.

The portrayal of the **priests** over against the **Levites** also comes into focus again in the account of the Passover. We have seen in 29:34 that a distinction is made between these two groups in terms of their conscientiousness with regard to their consecration. The description of the preparation for the Passover in the present chapter states in no uncertain terms that the priests were coresponsible with the people for Passover being postponed to the second month: **not enough priests had consecrated themselves and the people had not assembled in Jerusalem** (30:3). They therefore had to celebrate it **on the fourteenth day of the**

second month (30:15) instead of the fourteenth of the first month. (The idea is further developed in 30:17, which says that the Levites had to take over some responsibilities because priests and people **had not consecrated themselves, . . . were not ceremonially clean and could not consecrate their lambs to the LORD.**) The Pentateuch prescribed (Exod. 12:6) that the Passover had to be celebrated on the fourteenth of the first month. Here the Chronicler probably draws on the Priestly narrative in Numbers 9:6–14, the only other place in the Hebrew Bible that mentions a concession Passover celebration in the second month. Whether the Chronicler's narrative reflects a historical reality in Hezekiah's time is doubtful. It rather seems that the description of the Passover forms part of the macrostructural development of the Chronicler's narrative (see commentary on 35:1–19).

The narrative moves forward in 30:13, reporting that a **very large crowd of people assembled in Jerusalem**, not for Passover, but **to celebrate the Feast of Unleavened Bread in the second month.** Passover and the Feast of Unleavened Bread had separate origins in prebiblical times but were later on celebrated together or even merged into one festival. Apparently, the Hezekiah narrative uses the different terminology interchangeably. It starts with reference to "Passover" (30:1, 2, 5), then refers to the same feast as "the Feast of Unleavened Bread" (30:13), continues with "Passover" terminology (30:15, 17, 18), and ends with reference to "the Feast of Unleavened Bread" again (30:21) (see Additional Note on 30:13).

The Chronicler's depiction of Hezekiah's Passover constantly reminds the reader that this was not really properly done. Although 30:16 states that the Levites took up their **positions as prescribed in the Law of Moses the man of God**, 30:18–20 makes clear that many people **from Ephraim, Manasseh, Issachar and Zebulun** ate the Passover lamb without consecrating themselves beforehand. **Hezekiah** then **prayed** to the Lord to pardon **everyone who sets** (*kun*) **his heart on seeking** (*darash*) God—even if they were not ritually clean according to the rules of the sanctuary. It is then stated that the **LORD heard Hezekiah and healed the people** (30:20).

The feast initially lasted **seven days** (30:21), but it was then decided to continue for **seven more days** (30:23). This is in line with the later development in Judaism to celebrate the joint Passover and Unleavened Bread festival for a total of fourteen days. What characterized these celebrations was **joy**. The Chronicler uses every opportunity to indicate that the people celebrated joyfully (30:21, 23, 25, 26).

The evaluation of the Passover provided in 30:26 is problematic: **since the days of Solomon son of David king of Israel there had been nothing like this in Jerusalem.** The mentioning of King Solomon as a historical point of comparison is strange, because there is no explicit indication in Chronicles that the Passover was celebrated in Solomon's time. Second Chronicles 8:13, however, states that the Feast of Unleavened Bread was celebrated, or rather reestablished together with other feasts, after the completion of the temple in Jerusalem. The evaluative reference in the Hezekiah account probably refers to this celebration.

Hezekiah's Passover celebrations end with a blessing on the people by **the priests and the Levites,** words that **God heard . . . , for their prayer reached heaven, his holy dwelling place** (30:17).

31:1 / **When all this** (i.e., the Passover) **had ended,** the land was cleansed of all idol worship. This verse relies on the source text in 2 Kings 18:4, but one notable difference is that Chronicles specifies the places from which these idols were removed: **the towns of Judah** and **throughout Judah and Benjamin and in Ephraim and Manasseh.** The Chronicler probably did not want his readers to think that these objects were also found in Jerusalem, because that would put blame on the cultic center. That assumption may also account for the addition: **after they had destroyed all of them, the Israelites returned to their own towns and to their own property.** Another notable difference is the Chronicler specifying the idol objects as **sacred stones, Asherah poles, high places,** and **altars.** The source text (2 Kgs. 18:4) mentions only the first two but adds "the bronze snake Moses had made . . . called Nehushtan" (see Additional Note on 31:1–21).

31:2–10 / This section, which deals with the freewill offerings given by the **king** (31:3), the inhabitants of **Jerusalem** (31:4), the **Israelites** (31:5), and **the men of Israel and Judah** (31:6), is absent from the source text and is another unique part in Chronicles. The **priests and Levites** (31:2, 4, 9) play a prominent role in the gathering and proper administering of these offerings. The attitude that the givers should have in bringing these offerings should be to **devote** (*chazaq*) **themselves to the Law of the** LORD. (Again, the verb, well known from other passages in Chronicles, is probably a wordplay on the name of King Hezekiah.) The abundance of the freewill offerings so that the "priests and Levites" **had enough to eat and plenty to spare** (31:10) is a clear illustration of this devout attitude.

31:11–19 / On account of the abundance of the freewill offerings that were brought to the temple, the king **gave orders to prepare** (*kun*) **storerooms in the temple of the** LORD, **and this was done** (*kun*). The **contributions, tithes and dedicated gifts** could be stored there (31:12a).

A long section (31:12b–19) describes how the **Levites and priests, the descendants of Aaron,** undertook the administration and redistribution of the freewill gifts **to all who were recorded in the genealogies of the Levites** (31:18–19). The Chronicler does not let the opportunity slip to indicate that the redistribution to the Levitical families was done because **they were faithful in consecrating themselves** (*qadash*) (31:18b).

31:20–21 / The final two verses of this chapter (which correspond approximately to the source text in 2 Kgs. 18:5–7a) provide a preliminary evaluation of King Hezekiah: he was **doing what was good and right and faithful before the LORD his God** (31:20). (Compare this to 14:2, where Asa was described as somebody who did "good and right in the eyes of the LORD." With Hezekiah we have reached even a higher level of righteousness.) What characterized all of Hezekiah's actions was that **he sought** (*darash*) **his God and worked wholeheartedly,** with the result that **he prospered** (31:21). The seeking of God is characteristic of a good king in the Chronicler's view, and this inclination leads to blessing from Yahweh.

32:1–23 / The next episode in Hezekiah's reign is opened here with the phrase **after all that Hezekiah had so faithfully done,** referring to his reestablishment of the temple and the cult. Although this subsection depends heavily on the source text in 2 Kings 18–19 (|| Isa. 36–37), the Chronicler omitted substantial parts of the texts and altered and appended them in order to fit his own ideological construction.

Second Chronicles 32:1 is based on 2 Kings 18:13, which introduces the Assyrian campaign under **Sennacherib** into the narrative. In 2 Chronicles 32:2–8, however, the Chronicler adds his own material to describe the many measures Hezekiah took to make **Jerusalem** more defensible against the Assyrian siege. He secured the **water** flow to the city and blocked off the **water from the springs outside the city** so that the enemy could not have access to them (32:3–4). He repaired the city **wall** and **towers** and **reinforced the supporting terraces** (or Millo; see Additional Note on 27:3) **of the City of David** (32:5). The Chronicler's formulation again utilizes his typical language. The repairing and reinforcing of the walls, towers, and Millo are described with the verb *chazaq* ("to strengthen"), which is particularly appropriate in the Hezekiah narrative. The same verb is also found in the king's encouraging words to his **military officers** to **be strong** (*chazaq*) **and courageous** (32:7). In his encouragement, the king indicates that **there is a greater power with us than with** the Assyrian king, which is obviously a reference to Yahweh.

This is then made explicit in the words **with us is the LORD our God to help us and to fight our battles** (32:8). The description of human preparations and the affirmation of divine help seem in tension. Theologically, the Chronicler may assume that the former is necessary because the latter depends upon God's choice rather than a divine guarantee. In this way the Chronicler transforms the encounter with the Assyrians into a holy war in which Yahweh fights the battle on Judah's account.

In 32:9–19 (which abbreviates the source text 2 Kgs. 18:17–37 ‖ Isa. 36:2–22 in 2 Chron. 32:9–16 and also adds 32:17–19) we find the Assyrian king, Sennacherib, speaking to **Hezekiah king of Judah** and **all the people of Judah** through his officers (quoted in 32:9–15) and in a **letter** (quoted in 32:17b). It is noteworthy that this is the only speech by a foreign monarch in Chronicles that has a negative tone. Hiram of Tyre (to Solomon), the queen of Sheba (to Solomon), Neco of Egypt (to Josiah), and Cyrus of Persia (at the end of the book) all speak very positively, even articulating Yahweh's voice. Sennacherib's role, however, is the opposite. He mocks the people and their God through his messengers and states in his letter that **the god of Hezekiah will not rescue his people from my hand** any more than **the gods of the peoples of the other lands** did (32:17). (This negative tone is already present in the source texts.) The Chronicler confirms the real point of this interaction: **they spoke about the God of Jerusalem** as if Yahweh, like **the gods of the other peoples, were the work of men's hands** (32:19). The Assyrian king, his army, and his messengers are not only a military force against which Hezekiah and his men should defend themselves; they are also foreigners who mock Yahweh, the God of Israel.

Hezekiah's reaction to these mocking tones of the Assyrians is described in 32:20: **King Hezekiah and the prophet Isaiah son of Amoz cried out in prayer to heaven about this.** And without further ado, **the LORD sent an angel, who annihilated all the fighting men and the leaders and officers in the camp of the Assyrian king** (32:21). The reference to the prophet Isaiah appears out of the blue here. We know from the source text (2 Kgs. 19), however, that Isaiah plays a major role in the Deuteronomistic account. The Chronicler omitted all the interaction between Isaiah and Hezekiah in order to make Yahweh's victory over the Assyrian army all the more dramatic. In the Chronicler's version salvation follows directly after the king and prophet prayed to the Lord. Kings just mentions that Sennacherib withdrew from Jerusalem, while the Chronicler indicates that it was "an angel" sent by the Lord who "annihilated" the Assyrians. This wondrous salvation is summarized and confirmed in 32:22: **So the LORD saved Hezekiah and the people of Jerusalem.** . . . . **He took care of**

them on every side. The result was that **many** started bringing **offerings for the LORD** and **gifts for Hezekiah** to Jerusalem. The outcome of this narrative is reminiscent of what we already heard about Solomon, but is said with reference to Hezekiah: **from then on he was highly regarded by all the nations** (32:23).

32:24–31 / These verses contain the account of Hezekiah's illness, which was substantially abbreviated from the source text in 2 Kings 20:1–11 (|| Isa. 38:1–21). In the Chronicler's adaptation of his source material, he allows the **pride** of Hezekiah (which is sketched in greater detail in the source text) to appear very briefly. But he immediately adds in his own words: **Then Hezekiah repented** (*kana'*, "to humble oneself") **of the pride of his heart, as did the people of Jerusalem** (32:26a); thus the Chronicler makes use of one of his programmatic words again. The outcome of his repentance is that **the LORD's wrath did not come upon them during the days of Hezekiah** (32:26b). Even in the king's illness and pride, the Chronicler manages to show that the right attitude before the Lord brings healing and salvation.

As a continuation of the previous verses, in which Hezekiah's repentance is mentioned, as well as the Lord's wrath not coming upon him again, the king's **very great riches and honor** are described. All these riches, together with the successful building projects he achieved (including the channeling of the **Gihon spring** into **the City of David**), once again remind the reader of Solomon. Hezekiah's righteous kingship and dedication to the Lord resulted in his succeeding **in everything he undertook** (32:30).

Second Chronicles 32:31 adds another ingredient to the narrative that we have come to know from some previous accounts: foreign kings (in this case, **the rulers of Babylon**) come to inquire about the success of this king. This verse is a very cryptic summary of a more extended narrative in the source text (2 Kgs. 20:12–19), and the final **God left him to test him and to know everything that was in his heart** creates difficulties in interpretation. This marks the only text in Chronicles in which testing mediates divine intervention. Its language (and perhaps meaning) echoes Deuteronomy 8:2, but how this verse fits within the broader theological framework of the Chronicler's writing remains an unsolved interpretive problem. The testing might have had the aim of seeing whether the king sought Yahweh and was relying on him.

32:32–33 / The final summary of Hezekiah's reign is taken from the source text in 2 Kings 20:20–21, but some of the Chronicler's customary changes are made. He omits the reference to the water channel, the engineering achievement on which the Deuteronomist's version focuses. The Chronicler also refers the reader to the usual sources and completes the expression **the book of the kings of Judah and Israel** (instead of "Judah" in the source text), but also adds what should be consulted in this source, namely, **the vision of the prophet Isaiah son of Amoz.** This is in line with the Chronicler's practice of adding prophetic source references, particularly a prophet who has been active in the royal narrative. Finally, as usual, the Chronicler changes the burial notice. Whereas 2 Kings 20:21 only mentions that "Hezekiah rested with his fathers," the Chronicler adds: **and was buried on the hill where the tombs of David's descendants are. All Judah and the people of Jerusalem honored him when he died.** The burial notice again serves as the Chronicler's final confirmation of the righteousness of King Hezekiah.

The Chronicler's Hezekiah account is one of the pivotal passages in his macrostructure of Israelite history. There are many parallels between the Chronicler's portrayal of Hezekiah and that of King David and King Solomon. I will come back to these parallels after discussion of the Josiah narrative, but at this stage one aspect should be emphasized: Whereas David started the planning and preparations for the building of the temple in Jerusalem, it was only his son, Solomon, who could complete it. The Chronicler's description of Hezekiah's Passover leaves a similar impression of incompleteness. With the celebration of the Passover on the concession date, and with so much trouble in getting all the priests and people consecrated for the celebration, this narrative creates the expectation that a proper Passover will be celebrated in the course of time. This expectation is fulfilled in the days of Josiah. Whereas temple building started under David and was completed under Solomon, so the Passover celebration was started under Hezekiah but completed only during Josiah's reign.

Additional Notes §4.12

29:3–36 / The historicity and extent of Hezekiah's cultic reforms are disputed among modern scholars. Whatever the case, I strongly assert that the Chronicler's (and, for that matter, the Deuteronomist's) writing was not primarily meant to reflect the historical circumstances of the monarchy about which he writes, but rather his own historical circumstances in the Second Temple period.

30:2 / Simeon Chavel ("The Second Passover," pp. 1–24) doubts whether the concession **Passover** of 2 Chron. 30 has anything to do with the narrative in Num. 9. The date of Hezekiah's Passover, however, should not be treated in isolation but rather be interpreted together with the Passover account in the Josiah narrative.

30:13 / Discussion of the Jewish festivals of **Passover** and the **Feast of Unleavened Bread** normally concerns two main problems. First, the Feast of Unleavened Bread and Passover apparently did not belong together from the start. Questions therefore arise about their respective origins and when, and for what purpose, these festivals were amalgamated. Second, it is also clear that the Priestly and Deuteronomic/Deuteronomistic descriptions of these festivals reflect different portrayals. Questions therefore probe whether, for example, the festivals were meant as family rites or as festivals to be celebrated at sanctuaries, and how the celebrations should be organized. Whatever the historical reliability of the biblical witnesses to these feasts, and in spite of the many theories about the feasts, the following (at least) can be said about them: (1) the Feast of Unleavened Bread (with its probable origin in Canaanite agricultural circles) was the first of the Israelite festivals to be celebrated at the sanctuary; (2) the Passover (with its probable origin in Canaanite pastoral circles) was initially practiced as a family rite; (3) the Passover was later removed from the family sphere to that of the sanctuary, and later became a centralized festival celebrated in the temple together with the other festivals; (4) the Passover and Feast of Unleavened Bread, both celebrated at the temple, were later amalgamated into one festival. Clearly, the late postexilic Yehudite community (i.e., in the days of the Chronicler) celebrated the amalgamated festival, starting on the fourteenth day of the first month and continuing for seven days, in a centralized sanctuary, the Second Temple. The possibility cannot be excluded, however, that this feast was also celebrated elsewhere among the Diaspora communities (as the Elephantine Passover letter shows).

31:1–21 / The elaborate description of the voluntary offerings and priestly duties in 31:2–19 is actually a substitution for the Deuteronomist's reference to the Nehushtan mentioned in 2 Kgs. 18:4. The phrase in the Deuteronomistic version that probably prompted the substitution is the motivational clause "for up to that time the Israelites had been burning incense [or: making smoke offerings] to it" (2 Kgs. 18:4b). The elaborate expansion in 2 Chron. 31:2–19 creates a few strategic contrasts to the Nehushtan remark. (1) The Chronicler certainly shies away from using the verb "making smoke offerings" here. He does so because of its explicit association with pagan worship in this specific context and also in the Deuteronomistic History. Instead, the Chronicler used a positive alternative as a substitute. As a contrast to, and correction of, the misbehavior inherent in Nehushtan worship, the Chronicler replaces "smoke offerings" to Nehushtan with **burnt offerings and fellowship offerings** (31:2–3) with the intention **to minister, to give thanks and to sing praises at the gates of the LORD's dwelling** (31:2) and to **devote themselves to the Law of the LORD** (31:4), all done **as written in the Law of the LORD** (31:3). (2) The Chronicler constructs a related contrast when he makes the priests and Levites, not the "children of Israel" (as in 2 Kgs. 18:4), the officials who should perform the "burnt offerings and fellowship offerings." Two remarks further bolster the status of the **priests and Levites:** 2 Chron. 31:10 and 31:19 associate these officials with **Zadok** and **Aaron.** Correct worship, according to the Chronicler, takes place not when everybody just burns offerings to whatever god they want to but when the priests and Levites, supported by the firstfruits and tithes of the king and people, perform their duties according to the Torah of Yahweh. (3) A third contrast is the one between the Nehushtan and the law of Yahweh. "The bronze snake that Moses had made" should not be the focus of Israel's worship now, but rather the Torah of Yahweh given to the people "by the hand of Moses." The Chronicler, therefore, does not merely omit the Nehushtan—he rather replaces it with the Torah of Yahweh. Obedience to the Torah should characterize true worship, and obedience results in abundance of produce (as indicated in Deut. 7:13).

32:20 / Traditional synopses of the accounts in Kings and Chronicles show that the active participation (also with speech) of the prophet **Isaiah** disappears in Chronicles. Through formal computer analyses, Wido van Peursen and Eep Talstra ("Computer-Assisted Analysis," pp. 45–72) show that "Hezekiah's words in Chronicles are clearly reminiscent of Isaiah's words to Hezekiah in Kings," a parallel often overlooked because "Isaiah's address to Hezekiah has been omitted from Chronicles" (p. 70).

32:21 / Different sources present the outcome of the Assyrian siege of Jerusalem differently. All three biblical accounts (2 Kgs. 19:35; Isa. 37:36; 2 Chron. 32:21) indicate that "an angel of the LORD" came and overpowered the Assyrian soldiers. The Assyrian version (in Sennacherib's Prism, an Akkadian text discovered in Nineveh, in present-day Iraq) states that the Assyrian king trapped King Hezekiah of Judah "like a bird in a cage." Rather than describe either the destruction of Jerusalem or the overpowering of the Assyrian army, it states that the Assyrian king simply decided to go back to Nineveh and that the king of Judah paid him tribute afterward. The Greek historian Herodotus, who lived and wrote in the fifth century B.C. (i.e., was approximately a contemporary of the Chronicler), mentions that the Assyrian army, in their campaign against the Egyptians (which was probably connected to the siege of Jerusalem in 701 B.C.), had to retreat because a plague of mice interfered with their military activities. For a discussion of the ideological positions represented by the different sources on Sennacherib's campaign, see Janse van Rensburg, "Attack on Judah," pp. 560–79.

32:23 / Other points of similarity between David, Solomon, and Hezekiah include the expression "the whole assembly" and its related theme of joy.

§4.13 Manasseh (2 Chron. 33:1–20)

Although King Manasseh is the Judahite king with the longest tenure (fifty-five years, ca. 698/697–643/642 B.C.), he is presented as the prime embodiment of evil in the Deuteronomistic History (2 Kgs. 21:1–18). He is particularly blamed for leading the people astray with the result that they had to be punished with exile. The portrayal of this king in Chronicles, however, is very different. We have seen examples of good kings (according to the Deuteronomistic version) turned into blemished kings by the Chronicler (of which Asa is perhaps the best example). Here, with Manasseh, we see the opposite happening: a bad king is turned into a repentant king by the Chronicler.

For example, the Chronicler's narrative omits the king's shedding of innocent blood (2 Kgs. 21:10–16) and instead describes the king's exile, repentance, pardon by Yahweh, and cultic reforms (2 Chron. 33:11–17).

As for the Chronicler's structure, after the usual introduction of the king (33:1), an extended negative evaluation of the king follows that describes many of his apostasies (33:2–8). The next two verses (33:9–10) summarize the evil of the king and people. The result of their apostasy is that Manasseh is taken captive to Babylon, where he repents (33:11–13). After his return he conducted a series of cultic reforms (33:14–17). The last verses (33:18–20) contain the normal summary information, death, and burial notice.

33:1 / The introduction to **Manasseh** follows 2 Kings 21:1 but omits the king's mother's name.

33:2–8 / Clearly, both the Deuteronomist and the Chronicler wanted to portray the king as having turned back to the era before Hezekiah, the time of the apostate King Ahaz (see the reference to child sacrifice, which occurs only here and in the Ahaz narrative). Although the Chronicler provides a more favorable picture of Manasseh later in the narrative, he agrees at this point with the Deuteronomist's very negative evaluation of the king.

33:9–10 / In providing a summary of the apostasy of King Manasseh, the Chronicler made use of 2 Kings 21:9: **they did more evil than the nations the LORD had destroyed before the Israelites.** Although the Chronicler took the introduction to the next discourse in 2 Kings 21:10, he changes the flow of the narrative from this point by not reporting what "the LORD said through his servants the prophets" (as in Kings), but rather substituting this with the short phrase **the LORD spoke to Manasseh and his people, but they paid no attention.** This phrase then leads to Manasseh's exile.

33:11–13 / These verses, which belong to the Chronicler's own material, describe how **the LORD brought against them the army commanders of the king of Assyria, who took Manasseh prisoner** (33:11) and humiliated him by putting **a hook in his nose, bound him with bronze shackles and took him to Babylon.** Second Chronicles 33:12 is pivotal in the Chronicler's portrayal of King Manasseh: **in his distress he sought the favor of the LORD his God.** He did what was, according to the Chronicler's theological understanding, the basic thing to do: he **humbled himself** (*kana'*) **greatly before the God of his fathers.** As a result, **the LORD was moved by his entreaty and listened to his plea.** Manasseh was therefore returned to **Jerusalem.** He then **knew that the LORD is God.** This image of a repentant king and God's giving heed to him are unexpected elements in the Chronicler's construction, which emphasizes the writer's courage in reinterpreting the older traditions (see Additional Note on 33:11–13 and 33:18–19).

33:14–17 / This section (absent from the Deuteronomistic source text) is a typical addition by the Chronicler that shows the achievements and successes of King Manasseh after his return to Jerusalem. Apart from new building projects in **the City of David,** he also instituted some cultic reforms in which **he got rid of** the idol objects and **restored the altar of the LORD** and **sacrificed fellowship offerings and thank offerings on it** (33:16). The Chronicler concedes that **the people, however, continued to sacrifice at the high places, but only to the LORD their God** (33:17). This indication of sacrificing at high places, which often occurs in the Deuteronomistic accounts, is normally omitted in the Chronicler's version (except in the case of Ahaz). Here we have the opposite situation, where it does not appear in the Deuteronomist's version, but the Chronicler adds it to his version. It seems that the Chronicler gives the formula a positive spin: the "high places" under Manasseh were sites for the worship, not of other gods, but of Yahweh alone. This might be to prepare the way for the proper cultic reforms that would come under King Josiah.

33:18–20 / The concluding notice draws from the source text in 2 Kings 21:17–18 but inserts an elaborate remark that picks up on the Chronicler's own material, whose center is Manasseh's **prayer to his God** and **how God was moved by his entreaty.** In this way the Chronicler manages to merge his own material successfully with the source material. The burial notices in the two versions are the same, except that the Chronicler omits that the king was **buried in his palace** garden (which is mentioned in Kings).

Additional Note §4.13

33:11–13 and 33:18–19 / A number of other texts relate to the Chronicler's portrayal of **Manasseh.** Jer. 15:4 offers a negative judgment of the king similar to the Kings version. In Judg. 18:30, later copyists changed the name of Moses to read Manasseh, blaming this king for the heterodox cultic activities at Dan. Two Assyrian royal records (Prism B and Prism C) mention Manasseh as a loyal vassal, and he receives comment in some Second Temple (second century B.C. to second century A.D.) Jewish Pseudepigrapha (*2 Baruch* 64–65; *Lives of the Prophets* 1; *Martyrdom and Ascension of Isaiah*; Prayer of Manasseh) and in some rabbinic sources (Mishnah, tractate *Sanhedrin* 10.2; and Babylonian Talmud, tractate *Sanhedrin* 102b). The prayer of Manasseh is included in the noncanonical psalms from Qumran (4Q381 33.8). Many studies of the Chronicler's account devalue his report of Manasseh's prayer and repentance as a theological explanation of this evil king (according to the Deuteronomist's portrayal) having the longest reign (fifty-five years) among Judah's rulers. However, recent studies rightly emphasize that both the Deuteronomistic and Chronicles versions had specific ideological intentions and therefore presented the data differently. The authors of 2 Kgs. 21 did not mention Manasseh's prayer for forgiveness and repentance, since their version sought to explain the severity of the exile. In that writing Manasseh was presented as the epitome of evil and apostasy and was blamed for the destruction of the kingdom of Judah and the resultant Babylonian exile. The Chronicler reappropriated these textual materials to suit his own purposes. His inclusion of the prayer of Manasseh (2 Chron. 33:12–13, 18–19) serves to symbolize another side of Manasseh—he becomes a repentant king who dedicates the latter part of his life to the restoration of the Yahwistic cult in Jerusalem.

§4.14 Amon (2 Chron. 33:21–25)

This is the shortest royal narrative in Chronicles. It is based on the (not much longer) account in 2 Kings 21:19–26. Amon ruled over Judah in approximately 643/642–641/640 B.C.

33:21 / The Chronicler omits the king's mother's name, which is given in Kings. This follows the pattern of the Chronicler's version of the Manasseh narrative.

33:22–23 / King **Amon** is evaluated negatively in these verses, which are taken—with some slight changes—from Kings. The Chronicler has more specific references to **Manasseh**, Amon's father, and he adjusts the present narrative to fit the additional information that was provided in the Manasseh account: **but unlike his father Manasseh** (who humbled himself, *kana'*), **he did not humble himself** (*kana'*) **before the LORD**. We have seen that the humbling of Manasseh was an element the Chronicler inserted into that narrative. Here, the same terminology is used, but in a contrasting way.

33:24–25 / Amon's death is described in the same way in Kings and Chronicles. He is the first king to be killed **in his palace. The people of the land killed** Amon's murderers and made **Josiah**, Amon's son, king. It is strange that the Chronicler has no burial notice (which is present in 2 Kgs. 21:25–26). Its omission in Chronicles either intends to show the writer's disdain for Amon or (more likely) results from an accidental scribal transmission error.

Additional Notes §4.14

33:21 / Dominic Rudman ("Note on the Personal Name Amon," pp. 403–5) proposes an Egyptian origin for the name **Amon**. He argues that Manasseh, who participated in Ashurbanipal's first campaign in Egypt (667 B.C.), named his son to commemorate the Assyrian's capture of the rebel capital Thebes (Hebrew Na-Amon) during his second campaign (663 B.C.). Although the name certainly has an Egyptian ring to it (cf. Tut-Ank-Amun), it seems strange that a king of any nation would name his son after a captured city. Given our meager information about these kings, any attempt to explain this name remains speculation.

33:25 / The sociopolitical identity of **the people of the land** is uncertain. The term may designate a wealthy social class (e.g., free landowners), (collectively) free people or citizens, people from provincial towns (versus residents of Jerusalem), lower-class ordinary people, or a kind of national council of elders.

The narrative about this new child king (reminiscent of another child king, Joash, who saved the Davidic dynasty from being destroyed by northern influence) has constantly fascinated Bible scholars. It is a common view that King Josiah, who reigned over Judah in approximately 641/640–610/609 B.C., is idealized as the zenith of Davidic kingship in the Deuteronomistic description in 2 Kings 22–23. There he represents the antithesis of Manasseh, who is seen as the nadir of Judahite history in the Deuteronomistic construction. The Chronicler altered the portrayal of Manasseh significantly. The question remains whether the Chronicler did the same for Josiah.

Four temporal markers determine the progress and focus of the narrative. It starts in the eighth year when King Josiah began to seek the Lord (2 Chron. 34:3a), progresses to the twelfth year when the king began to rid Judah and Jerusalem of all idols (34:3b), and ends in the momentous eighteenth year, the year of the temple's restoration, the discovery of the Book of the Law, and the celebration of Passover (34:8, 19). It should be noted here that this temporal organization differs from the Deuteronomistic version in 2 Kings 22–23, where everything is located in the eighteenth year.

The Chronicler also makes some significant changes to the macrostructure of this narrative. The story of Josiah in 2 Chronicles is once again framed with information that was taken, with small adjustments, from 2 Kings (2 Chron. 34:1 and 35:20–36:1). The report in the last section about the death of the king, however, is told in a significantly different way. The opening section is once again followed by a positive assessment of the king that is taken precisely from the older tradition (34:2). But the second assessment that appears in Kings is omitted from Chronicles.

Structurally, the Chronicles narrative has two units. The first (34:3–7) gives an indication of King Josiah's reform measures. This version is not only considerably shorter than the older version in Kings, but is also placed in a different position in the course of the narrative. While the text of Kings suggests that the reform measures were one of the consequences of the discovery of the Book of the Law in the temple, the

Chronicler shows that these measures flow from the king's piety. Since he was somebody who was seeking Yahweh, he could make decisions on purging the land of all idols.

The second large section of the Chronicles narratives (34:8–35:19) follows only after that. This large section has three smaller units. In 34:8–18 the point is made that the restoration of the temple is a consequence of Josiah's reform measures (34:8–13) and that "the Book of the Law of the LORD" was found during this process (34:14–18). In the second subsection, 34:19–33, the reactions of the king and the Huldah oracle (34:19–28) and the renewal of the bond by the king and the people (34:29–33) are adopted more or less unchanged from the older tradition. The third subsection, 35:1–19, is devoted entirely to the first celebration of Passover "since the days of the prophet Samuel." This version of the Passover celebration is not only considerably more elaborate than the version in Kings (which devoted slightly more than three verses to it), but it also provides completely different content.

Does this difference in narrative structure and content between the two accounts indicate different perspectives on King Josiah? The following remarks may help us in deciding on this question:

1. The differences between the two accounts of the cultic reforms and the Passover celebration cannot be used conclusively to decide which version is more historical than the other. One should realize that both versions were written with certain theological and ideological motives and were not meant primarily to convey historical facts.

2. The different narrative structures suggest different intentions. Whereas the structure of the Deuteronomistic account (2 Kgs. 22–23) contributes to the idealization of King Josiah and his deeds (his cultic reform measures, in particular) and to the portrayal of him as representing the zenith of the Deuteronomistic History, the structure of the Chronicler's account emphasizes the Passover celebration (and not so much the king).

3. Like the Deuteronomist, the Chronicler provides a positive picture of King Josiah. The evaluative remark in 2 Chronicles 34:2 serves, as is the case in all other Chronicles narratives about righteous Judahite kings, to categorize Josiah among the "good" kings. However, other aspects of the Chronicler's account, in comparison with the Deuteronomist's, suggest that King Josiah is not being idealized here. The telling second evaluative remark in the Deuteronomistic History (2 Kgs. 23:25–27) is, for example, absent from the

Chronistic account. Additionally, the elaborate description by the Chronicler of Josiah's campaign against Pharaoh Neco of Egypt and the circumstances of the king's death (2 Chron. 35:20–24) provides a false note at the end of King Josiah's reign (reminiscent of similar changes in other royal narratives in Chronicles). This even suggests that the foreign king knew the will of God better than did Josiah. Josiah ignored the pharaoh's warning, and this resulted in his own death. This ending does not cancel the positive evaluation of the king by the Chronicler, but it certainly negates any attempt to idealize King Josiah.

4. It therefore seems as if the main focus of the Chronicler's account is on the Passover rather than the king. In this account the king's deeds are referred to in order to emphasize the celebration of the Passover. King Josiah is therefore *instrumentalized* to focus on the Passover, rather than *idealized* as the best example of Davidic kingship. With this move the Chronicler takes Josiah out of the political frame emphasized in the Deuteronomistic account and depicts his actions within a mainly cultic setting.

34:1 / The Chronicler uses the introductory information given in 2 Kings 22:1, except that the information about the king's mother is omitted by the Chronicler.

34:2 / The evaluative note was also taken from the Deuteronomistic account (2 Kgs. 22:2), but one minor change was made. The Chronicler indicates that the king **walked in the ways of his father David,** whereas the Kings account mentions "in all the ways of his father David." This might be an attempt by the Chronicler to distance Josiah from some of David's deeds. We know that the Chronicler presents David as having too much blood on his hands and therefore being unable to construct the temple. This kind of association would have been problematic for the Chronicler, particularly because he instrumentalizes Josiah's reign to focus on the Passover, when "clean hands" were certainly indispensable.

34:3–7 / We have seen that 34:3 contains two temporal indications absent from the Deuteronomistic source text. The Chronicler first states that **in the eighth year of** King Josiah's **reign, while he was still young, he began to seek** (*darash*) **the God of his father David.** This remark emphasizes the piety of this young king, even at a stage in his career when the Book of the Law had not been discovered yet. This piety finds expression in the cultic reform measure, **to purge Judah and Jerusalem,** which the young king initiated **in his twelfth year.** In 34:3b–5 the concentration is on **Judah and Jerusalem.** The following cultic objects were removed: **high places, Asherah poles, carved idols and cast images** (34:3, which serves as a general introduction to the purging), **the altars of the Baals, the incense altars, the Asherah poles, the idols and the images** (34:4, which narrates the actual removal and destruction of the objects). Furthermore, Josiah **burned the bones of the priests on their altars, and so he purged Judah and Jerusalem** (34:5).

Second Chronicles 34:6–7 indicates that the reform measures were also extended to include the northern territories: **the towns of Manasseh, Ephraim and Simeon, as far as Naphtali, and in the ruins around them.** Since the northern kingdom had ceased to exist years before, the king of Judah could show his cultic influence by tearing down **the altars and the Asherah poles** and crushing **the idols to powder** and cutting **to pieces all the incense altars throughout Israel.**

34:8–13 / Second Chronicles 34:8 introduces **the eighteenth year** of King **Josiah's reign.** The greater part of this narrative takes place in this year. This subsection describes the administration of the temple restoration in Jerusalem. Although the Chronicler made use of the source text in 2 Kings 22:3–7, he made significant changes and additions to that material.

The words **to purify the land and the temple** (2 Chron. 34:8) were added by the Chronicler in order to link the temple restoration to the other cultic reform measures that were moved forward in his narrative. Whereas only Shaphan is sent by the king, according to the Deuteronomist's version, the Chronicler reports that three people were sent: **Shaphan son of Azaliah and Maaseiah the ruler of the city, with Joah son of Joahaz, the recorder** (34:8). Their task was to repair (*chazaq*) **the temple of the** LORD **his God.** The Chronicler inserts the term *chazaq* here. As we know by now, in Chronicles the term (which means "to strengthen") not only refers to the strengthening of the physical structure but also denotes the assumption of the right attitude toward Yahweh and the cult.

Whereas the Deuteronomist's version in Kings indicates that the king ordered Shaphan in direct speech in 2 Kings 22:4–7, the Chronicler changes this into a report in which it is indicated that Shaphan, Azaliah, and Maaseiah **went to Hilkiah the high priest and gave him the money.** By making small changes and adding some information, the Chronicler highlights the role of the Levites in the preparation for the temple restoration. "The doorkeepers" mentioned in 2 Kings 22:4 become **the Levites**

who were the doorkeepers, and whereas the money was collected from "the people" in Kings, the Chronicler turns this into the money that had been collected **from the people of Manasseh, Ephraim and the entire remnant of Israel and from all the people of Judah and Benjamin and the inhabitants of Jerusalem** (2 Chron. 34:9). It is clear that the Chronicler turns the temple restoration into a joint effort by All-Israel, but in the process emphasizes the northern tribes Manasseh and Ephraim and the southern tribes Judah and Benjamin. These represent the former northern and southern kingdoms.

The Chronicler leaves out the comment in 2 Kings 22:7 that no accounting was necessary for the collection money, but adds another elaboration on the Levites' roles (**skilled in playing musical instruments . . . supervised all the workers . . . secretaries, scribes and doorkeepers;** 2 Chron. 34:12–13). And of these workmen it is stated that **the men did the work faithfully.** We have become accustomed in the Chronicler's work to hearing the three Levite families together, but only two are mentioned here (the Merarites and Kohathites), with the Gershonites for some reason absent here.

34:14–18 / This subsection continues the narrative line of the previous one by focusing on the finding of **the Book of the Law** in the temple during the restoration. The version in Kings just mentions that "Hilkiah the priest" reported to "Shaphan" that he had "found the Book of the Law in the temple." The Chronicler first describes this event: **while they were bringing out the money that had been taken into the temple of the LORD, Hilkiah the priest found the Book of the Law of the LORD that had been given through Moses** (34:14). The consensus view among scholars is that the book was probably an early form of the book of Deuteronomy and that this find played an influential role in the development of the Deuteronomistic movement that continued over a period, with some ups and downs, into the exile. The Chronicler's elaborate reference to this book, however, suggests that he most likely understood it to comprise the whole Pentateuch. In the rest of the subsection the Chronicler adhered fairly strictly to his source text, ending with the dramatic reading of the book to the king: **and Shaphan read from it in the presence of the king** (34:18).

34:19–28 / The reaction of the king is described in this subsection, which was taken over from Kings very precisely, with only minor changes here and there. The king's order to a group of officials is: **go and inquire** (*darash*) **of the LORD for me and for the remnant in Israel and**

Judah about what is written in this book that has been found (34:21). The term *darash* ("to seek/inquire"), which we know by now plays an important role in the programmatic language of the Chronicler, is already present in the source text in 2 Kings 22:13. The same applies for the Huldah oracle, which is presented fairly unchanged. In that oracle we find a dense cluster of terms typical of the Chronicler's language: because they have forsaken (*'azab*) me (34:25); to inquire (*darash*) of the LORD (34:26); you humbled yourself (*kana'*) (twice in 34:27). The majority of occurrences of these terms in the Chronicler's work are in sections that belong to his own additions. The occurrence of these terms in the present section and in the Huldah oracle in particular could help us toward a more nuanced understanding of these terms. What is unique about the Chronicler is not so much his usage of these terms but rather his compulsion to insert them at every important theological junction in his narrative construction. As in the Deuteronomistic version, the Josiah account forms a climax in the Chronicler's construction, albeit with a different intention. Could it be that the Huldah oracle therefore formed a point of theological orientation for the Chronicler when he recomposed the history of Israel? The Chronicler, so it seems, used the language of this oracle (taken over from the Deuteronomistic source) but spread it over his own writing to such an extent that it becomes a stylistic trait of the new work. The Chronicler picked up a Deuteronomistic theme, but then fully developed its implications in his own construction of the royal past.

The last part of the Huldah oracle can corroborate this impression. Sharing the wording with the Deuteronomistic source again, the Chronicler indicates that Huldah prophesied to Josiah that the Lord says: I will gather you to your fathers, and you will be buried in peace (34:28). We saw in previous discussions that changes to the burial notices of royal narratives are typical in the Chronicler's narratives. Might it be that the relationship between "humbling oneself" and having a peaceful burial as expressed in the Huldah oracle influenced the Chronicler to present the burial information in his unique way?

34:29–33 / The Huldah oracle now leads to the king convening a meeting in the temple to read to all the people from the least to the greatest . . . all the words of the Book of the Covenant. Although another term is used here to refer to the book, the phrase which had been found in the temple of the LORD (34:30) shows that the same document was intended. The different name for the book is probably influenced by this reading leading to the king renewing the covenant in the presence of the LORD (34:31).

The Chronicler took over the source text in 2 Kings 23:1–3 in his construction of the present subsection. However, the one prominent change he made in 2 Chronicles 34:30, as well as the addition in 34:32–33, again illustrates the writer's inclusive attitude. In 34:30 the Chronicler includes **the priests and the Levites** in the group who had to convene in the temple. In Kings the reference is rather to "the priests and the prophets." This alteration is in line with the Chronicler's tendency to highlight the role of the Levites in all religious matters. It might also be an attempt to suggest that the Levites had assumed prophetic functions. In the last two verses the Chronicler expanded on the single phrase in Kings that states, "Then all the people pledged themselves to the covenant" (2 Kgs. 23:3), by changing it to: **then he had everyone in Jerusalem and Benjamin pledge themselves to it; the people of Jerusalem did this in accordance with the covenant of God, the God of their fathers** (2 Chron. 34:32). It is also significant that the king's role in the people's pledging themselves to the "covenant" is emphasized.

Second Chronicles 34:33 might be an indication that the Chronicler certainly had access to a source text that had the cultic reform measures in this position in the narrative. The Chronicler shifted the report on these measures to the beginning of his narrative in contrast to Kings, which has it after the covenant ceremony. The words **Josiah removed all the detestable idols from all the territory belonging to the Israelites, and he had all who were present in Israel serve the Lord their God** (34:33a) are probably a remainder from the older version. The subsection ends with words added by the Chronicler: **as long as he lived, they did not fail to follow the Lord, the God of their fathers** (34:33b).

35:1–19 / This section presents the most remarkable expansion of source material in this chapter (if not in the whole book). The Deuteronomistic version reports in 2 Kings 23:21–23 (only three verses!) that, following Josiah's cultic reform measures (2 Kgs. 23:4–20, 24a), the king commanded the people to celebrate the Passover. The Chronicler expanded this description, however, into an elaborate narrative of nineteen verses, which follow after the account of the covenant ceremony. The king's concluding a covenant before the Lord on behalf of the people leads to the glorious celebration of the Passover.

The Chronicler included the Deuteronomist's description in 2 Chronicles 35:1 and 35:18–19, but he did make some changes. Whereas 2 Kings 23:21 provided the order King Josiah gave directly to all the people, "Celebrate the Passover to the Lord your God, as it is written in this Book of the Covenant," the Chronicler turned it into a report again:

Josiah celebrated the Passover to the Lord in Jerusalem, and the Passover lamb was slaughtered. The temporal indication given at the beginning of the Passover account, **on the fourteenth day of the first month,** is quite significant. It not only focuses the reader's attention on this specific day in the eighteenth year of King Josiah, but also indicates that the Passover was celebrated in accordance with the prescription of the Torah. In the narrative of the Hezekiah Passover (2 Chron. 30) the date of that celebration, namely, the fourteenth of the second month, already created the expectation of a proper Passover celebration that would take place on the right date. Here, in the Josiah account, that expectation is now fulfilled. The insertion of the date (not present in the Deuteronomist's version) signifies the Chronicler's view that Josiah's Passover is the climax of the cultic development under the Judahite monarchy (see Additional Note on 35:1–19).

The information contained in 35:2–17 belongs completely to the Chronicler's own material. Second Chronicles 35:2–9 describes the preparations for the Passover, with the organizing of the officials being the focus in 35:2–6, and the provision of sacrificial animals in 35:7–9. Josiah **appointed the priests to their duties and encouraged** (*chazaq*) **them in the service of the Lord's temple** (35:2). However, the focus is notably on the **Levites** again (who are described as those **who instructed all Israel** [a function not typically ascribed to the Levites] **and who had been consecrated** [*qadash*] **to the Lord**). They are addressed in direct speech in 35:3–6, and the following commands are given to them. The first command is: **put the sacred ark in the temple that Solomon son of David king of Israel built** (35:3). This is an unusual command in the light of, according to the Chronicler's narrative (see 2 Chron. 5), the ark having already been put in the Most Holy Place of the temple during Solomon's days. The Chronicler may have intended this puzzling act to reenact the days of Solomon. As in the days of Solomon when the temple was finished in order to house the ark of the covenant, so the celebration of the Passover serves the same function of establishing the position of the ark. A remark in 35:20 corroborates this interpretation. The second command is to **serve the Lord your God and his people Israel** (35:3), while the third is to **prepare yourselves** (*kun*) **by families in your divisions** (35:4). The word *kun* occurs eight times in the Josiah Passover account. Here it refers to the preparation of the Levitical families for their service in the Passover celebration. The fourth command, **stand in the holy place with a group of Levites for each subdivision of the families** (35:5), still relates to the preparation of the Levitical families for the celebration. The next three commands, **slaughter the Passover** lambs, consecrate yourselves (*qadash*) and prepare (*kun*) the lambs for your fellow countrymen (35:6), emphasize the Levites' supporting role in the bringing of the Passover sacrifices.

The abundance of sacrificial animals provided for the Passover is described in 35:7–9. Not only did the king provide a vast number of animals, but his officials also contributed voluntarily. Again, the leaders of the Levites are quite prominent.

In 35:10–16 the actual celebration of the Passover is the point of focus (35:10–13), as well as the provisions for the priests and Levites (35:14–16). The description starts with a programmatic word again: the service was arranged (*kun*). This remark, and 35:16, so at that time the entire service of the LORD was carried out (*kun*), frame a section in which the term *kun* is used five times (four of which are in 35:14–16). There is no doubt that this term plays a very prominent role here. Its use is strongly related to the right celebration of the Passover as is written in the Book of Moses (35:12) and as the king Josiah had ordered (35:10). The verb is mainly used in Old Testament contexts where the formation or foundation of, for example, the earth or Mount Zion is described. In Psalms, it occurs mainly in hymns about creation. By using this verb so prominently in the Josiah Passover account, the Chronicler probably hinted at the universal significance of the temple and its rituals. The verb is used for the last time in 35:20 (not only in Chronicles but also in the whole Hebrew Bible) in connection with the temple.

Again, the Levites act prominently in the celebrations. They stood together with the priests . . . in their places . . . in their divisions as the king had ordered (35:10). While the priests did the slaughtering of the sacrificial lambs and the sprinkling of the blood, the Levites skinned the animals (35:11), and they took responsibility for distributing the burnt offerings . . . to the subdivisions of the families of the people (35:12). They (apparently a reference to the Levites) roasted the Passover animals over the fire as prescribed, and boiled the holy offerings in pots, caldrons and pans and served them quickly to all the people (see Additional Note on 35:13). After the celebration the Levites made preparations (*kun*) for themselves and for the priests (35:14), apparently because they were occupied with the service on behalf of the people during the celebrations and therefore had to perform the celebration for themselves only afterward. That this statement is repeated in 35:14 (so the Levites made preparations [*kun*] for themselves and for the Aaronic priests) and 35:15 (because their fellow Levites made the preparations [*kun*] for them) indicates that it was very important for the Chronicler to emphasize the Levites' prominent position alongside the other priests.

Second Chronicles 35:16 concludes the actual celebration account: **the entire service of the LORD was carried out (kun) . . . as King Josiah had ordered.** Second Chronicles 35:17–19 contains the evaluation and conclusion of the Passover celebration. Second Chronicles 35:17 mentions that **the Israelites . . . present celebrated the Passover at that time and observed the Feast of Unleavened Bread for seven days.** "The Israelites" probably refers to those people from the northern tribal areas who joined the celebrations in Jerusalem. The Feast of Unleavened Bread, which played a prominent role in Hezekiah's Passover, is mentioned only briefly here. The evaluation of the Passover is given in 35:18: **the Passover had not been observed like this in Israel since the days of the prophet Samuel; and none of the kings of Israel had ever celebrated such a Passover as did Josiah.** This remark is problematic on two levels. First, it seems as if the celebration of the Passover in Hezekiah's days (described only a few chapters earlier in Chronicles) is not taken into account here. Some interpreters try to explain the Chronicler's remark by indicating that the point of comparison is not whether the Passover had been celebrated in the past, but rather whether it had been celebrated in this particular way (i.e., with the king, the priests, Levites, and all Judah and Israel joining in). Together with other indications in the narrative, such as the celebration on the correct date, this remark creates the awareness that Josiah's Passover is the fulfillment of a development that had already started with Hezekiah. Although the Hezekiah celebration was an important step along the way, the real fulfillment of the Passover command according to "the Book of the Law" occurred only during Josiah's reign.

A second problem arising from this evaluation is the comparative note "since the days of the prophet Samuel." We read in the Hezekiah account that the Passover had not been celebrated "since the days of Solomon" (30:26). And the source text in 2 Kings 23:22 has "since the days of the judges who led Israel." The present description therefore goes back even beyond the monarchy to the time of Samuel, but not as far back as the judges (see Additional Note on 35:18).

Second Chronicles 35:19, in conclusion, relates the Passover to the **eighteenth year of Josiah's reign** again. This is one of the macrostructural temporal markers.

35:20–36:1 / In the following verses the narrative gives an account of Josiah's death and burial. Although the Chronicler used the source text in 2 Kings 23:28–30, he adapted that version freely (by abbreviating certain information and changing the order of presentation) and expanded it with the reference to the encounter with the Egyptian pharaoh, Neco, at Megiddo (609 B.C.). This last episode in the Josiah account creates some tension with the preceding sections, particularly with Huldah's prophecy that the king would be gathered to his fathers and would be buried in peace (2 Chron. 34:28). That Josiah died in a violent battle is therefore unexpected. However, it is clear that the Chronicler wanted to use this battle account, like so many others encountered before, to promote specific theological ideas.

In 2 Chronicles 35:20 the transition to the last part of the Josiah account is established by means of another temporal indication (after all this), as well as a shift in location (from Jerusalem, which was the setting of the greater part of the previous narrative, to **Megiddo**— which is mentioned by name in 35:22—where Josiah would encounter **Neco king of Egypt** in battle). Both these textual features represent the Chronicler's own construction over against the source text, 2 Kings 23:29 (which has "in his days" [so NRSV but not NIV] as temporal marker). The temporal marker in 2 Chronicles 35:20 is particularly interesting. The full expression is the following: **after all this, when Josiah had set the temple in order** (*kun*). The reference to the temple comes as a surprise, since this episode follows after Josiah's Passover celebrations and not directly after the temple building or restoration. It is important to note, however, that this phrase brings closure to a narrative line already started with David and continued via Solomon and Hezekiah to Josiah. The Passover celebrations of Josiah complete the temple building initiated by Solomon. According to the Chronicler's construction, the whole history of Judah and Israel witnesses to the close relationship between temple and Passover (see Additional Note on 35:14–16 and 35:20). This aspect, when viewed against the sociohistorical background of the time of origin of the Chronicler's work, is quite significant. In the Second Temple period under Persian imperial dominion, it was of the utmost importance for the Chronicler to emphasize the foundation of the postexilic cult, namely, the temple in Jerusalem and the proper celebration of the Passover. The postexilic phase saw the formation of a well-organized cultic community, something that is traced back to Josiah's time in this narrative.

The Chronicler's account continues by reporting in 35:21 (without parallel in Kings) on a message that was sent by Neco to Josiah, who came against him. The message is quoted in Neco's direct speech: **What quarrel is there between you and me, O king of Judah? It is not you I am attacking at this time, but the house with which I am at war. God has told me to hurry; so stop opposing God, who is with me, or he will destroy**

you (35:21). This is one of five direct speeches by foreign monarchs in Chronicles (the others being those by Hiram of Tyre and the queen of Sheba in the Solomon account, Sennacherib in the Hezekiah account, and Cyrus in the conclusion to the book). All these monarchs—except Sennacherib—are portrayed very positively. In this case, Pharaoh Neco speaks on behalf of God. It may, of course, be disputed which God the pharaoh referred to (taking into account that he came from another religious environment), but in the Chronicler's construction the insinuation is that this king is—almost prophetlike—speaking on behalf of the God of Israel (although he is not explicitly named Yahweh). Neco even claims that God is with him and will destroy Josiah if he does not stop opposing God. And the great irony is that the king of All-Israel does not obey: **Josiah, however, would not turn away from him, but disguised himself to engage him in battle. He would not listen to what Neco had said at God's command but went to fight him on the plain of Megiddo** (35:22). Although the king's history is without any blemish and during his reign the cult reached its climax in the proper celebration of Passover, the Chronicler ends this narrative by describing how a foreign monarch exposed Josiah's disobedience to God. The great King Josiah should not be the center of attention, but the focus should rather be on the God who has dominion even over foreign monarchs. This element of the Chronicler's narrative is highly significant within the postexilic situation of Persian dominion (see summary of §4).

Josiah's death is portrayed very differently in Chronicles from the version in Kings. There it is said that "Neco faced him and killed him at Megiddo. Josiah's servants brought his body in a chariot from Megiddo to Jerusalem and buried him in his own tomb" (2 Kgs. 23:29b–30). According to the Chronicler's version, **archers shot King Josiah** (2 Chron. 35:23), but, although heavily wounded, he could still order his officers to take him away in a chariot. Therefore, **they took him out of his chariot, put him in the other chariot he had and brought him to Jerusalem, where he died** (35:24). Since other written extrabiblical witnesses to this event provide even further variations on this story, the death of Josiah has generated much scholarly debate (see Additional Note on 35:22–24). The Chronicler mentions that **he was buried in the tombs of his fathers** (35:24), in contrast to 2 Kings 23:30, which has "in his own tomb."

The Chronicler's burial notice continues by mentioning the mourning for the king after his death (an element that is absent from all other royal narratives): **All Judah and Jerusalem mourned for him. Jeremiah composed laments for Josiah, and to this day all the men and women** singers commemorate Josiah in the laments. These became a tradition in Israel and are written in the Laments (2 Chron. 35:24b–25). This remark has influenced some interpreters to erroneously associate the prophet Jeremiah with a tradition of lament, and particularly with the book of Lamentations (which does not deal with the death of Josiah, but rather with the fall of Jerusalem). The reference to Jeremiah is significant on another level: this is the first of four times that the prophet Jeremiah is mentioned in Chronicles, with all references concentrated toward the end of the book.

The conclusion to Josiah's reign in 35:26–36:1 is an assembly of textual material from 2 Kings 23:28 and 23:30. In the usual reference to other sources, the Chronicler adds that these sources provide more information on **his acts of devotion, according to what is written in the Law of the LORD** (instead of the version in Kings: "all he did"). The Chronicler's emphasis on Josiah's adherence to "the Law of the LORD" is clear.

The people of the land took the lead again and made Jehoahaz, Josiah's son, king in his stead (36:1).

In conclusion, in the wider context of the books of Chronicles, the Josiah account plays an important role in the macrostructure of the Chronicler's narrative. The Chronicler particularly used the Hebrew term *kun* ("to complete/establish/put in order") to bring closure to the narrative about the temple in 35:20. In that way, the reader is brought to the understanding that temple building (under David and Solomon) and Passover celebration (under Hezekiah and Josiah) are closely related in the cognitive environment of the Chronicler. Analogous relationships were developed by the Chronicler between David and Solomon, on the one hand, and Hezekiah and Josiah, on the other hand. David prepared the temple-building process, while his son completed what he intended. The relationship between Hezekiah and Josiah is of a similar kind. The reinstitution of the Passover under Hezekiah was completed and institutionalized under Josiah. The suggestion of the Chronicler's construction is that the development from David to Solomon (which was interrupted by the division of the united monarchy) was taken up by Hezekiah again and that it climaxed during the reign of King Josiah. This relationship can be summarized schematically in the following diagram:

Additional Notes §4.15

34:3–7 / It is difficult to establish to what extent the Deuteronomistic version of Josiah's cultic reform measures served as source text for the Chronicler. The much-abbreviated version in Chronicles shows similarities in some terminology and in general geographic presentation, but the details are very different. Some intensive studies have been done on the Deuteronomistic version of Josiah's reform catalog. Christof Hardmeier, for example, argues that 2 Kgs. 23:16–20, 24a is a stylistically homogeneous textual unit that should be regarded as a late Deuteronomistic rewriting aimed at universalizing the significance of the cultic reform measures of Josiah. He further argues that 2 Kgs. 23:4–15 contains a reworked version of a pre-Deuteronomistic small cultic reform account. The reworking of this pre-Deuteronomistic unit into a big cultic reform account was undertaken by the Deuteronomistic editors in order to emphasize the significance of the Josianic reform measures. This reworking, which makes Josiah the cultic reformer par excellence, then contributes to building the climax of the entire Deuteronomistic History. The terminology used in the Chronicler's version of the reform measures occurs in both the supposed reworked pre-Deuteronomistic part and the late-Deuteronomistic rewriting in the Kings version. One should therefore assume that the Chronicler had a text available in which these two parts had already been merged (C. Hardmeier, "King Josiah in the Climax of the Deuteronomic History [2 Kings 22–23] and the Pre-Deuteronomic Document of a Cult Reform at the Place of Residence [23.4–15]: Criticism of Sources, Reconstruction of Literary Pre-stages and the Theology of History in 2 Kings 22–23," in *Good Kings and Bad Kings* [ed. L. L. Grabbe; London: T&T Clark, 2005]).

34:30 / Mark Leuchter ("'The Prophets' and 'The Levites,'" pp. 31–47) comments on the substitution of "the prophets" in 2 Kgs. 23:2 with **the Levites** in 2 Chron. 34:30. He concludes that the substitution fits a larger pattern whose aim is to incorporate Jeremiah into the narrative of Josiah's reign and to establish him as the "archetypal Levite-prophet" in the Chronicler's historiography. The name's inclusion specifically in the narrative of Josiah's covenant ceremony shows that the Chronicler is aware that "the Levite-prophet typology of the Jeremiah tradition was forged during that king's reign" (p. 44).

35:1–19 / For a comparison of the Chronicler's versions of Hezekiah's and Josiah's Passover celebrations, see Jonker, *Reflections of King Josiah*, chap. 5. Jonker (chap. 6) relates these portrayals of Passover to the Pentateuchal texts about Passover (Exod. 12; Num. 9; Deut. 16).

35:3 / The remark about the carrying of the **ark** by the Levites seems out of place, given that the ark had already been placed in the temple in Solomon's time. Some commentators think that the reference is metaphorical (so S. J. De Vries, *1 and 2 Chronicles* [Forms of Old Testament Literature 11; Grand Rapids: Eerdmans, 1989], p. 414). According to Japhet (*I and II Chronicles* [London: SCM, 1993], p. 1048), some rabbinic and other scholars speculated that the ark either was taken out of the temple during the time of Manasseh and returned by Josiah or that it had been removed to be concealed or even destroyed. In the end Japhet also opts for a metaphorical understanding.

35:13 / The Chronicler indicates the method of preparation of the Passover sacrificial animals in this verse: **they roasted the Passover animals over the fire as prescribed.** The Hebrew verb used here (*bashal*), however, is normally associated with the boiling of something in water. It is the same verb used in the next sentence in the expression **and boiled** (*bashal*) **the holy offerings in pots, caldrons and pans.** This creates a problem, which is already registered in the NIV's attempt to iron out the difficulty by translating the first verb with **roasted.** Pentateuchal prescriptions on the mode of preparation of the Passover animal show interesting differences. Exodus 12:8–9 stipulates that the Passover lamb should not be eaten raw (*na ʾ*) or cooked in water (*ubashel mebushal bammayim*), but should be roasted on a fire (*tseli ʾesh*). Deuteronomy 16:7 stipulates that the meat should be roasted (so the NIV, translating the word *bashal*; the NRSV translation "cook" expresses the specific word better). The combination "boiling over fire" in 2 Chron. 35:13 does not occur anywhere in the legal stipulations of the Pentateuch. One possible explanation for the Chronicler's expression (which is also accepted by many commentaries) is that the Chronicler deliberately intertwined two different Pentateuchal legal traditions in this narrative. The Chronicler thereby illustrated his adherence to both the Priestly tradition (Exod. 12) and the Deuteronomic tradition (Deut. 16).

35:14–16 and 35:20 / Many commentators refer to the important role that the verb *kun* ("to order/prepare") plays in the Passover narrative. A concordance search shows that 42 of the 108 *hiphil* occurrences of this verb occur in Chronicles. It is quite significant that 28 of the 42 occurrences are used in the temple-building narratives of David-Solomon and in the Hezekiah and Josiah narratives. The *niphal* form of the verb also plays a structuring role in this context. In 8:16 it is said that all Solomon's building activities had been completed (with the *niphal* of *kun*). The next occurrence of a *niphal* is in 29:35 at the completion of Hezekiah's restoration of the temple. After that it occurs twice in the Josiah narrative (35:10, 16). Here it frames the narrative of the Passover celebration. The completion of the temple (for the first time, as well as after its restoration) and the celebration of the Passover under King Josiah are linked by means of the *niphal* form of the verb *kun*.

35:18 / By referring to **the days of the prophet Samuel,** the Chronicler goes beyond the celebrations in the days of Hezekiah (**Passover**) and Solomon (**Feast of Unleavened Bread**). Why Samuel? Dillard's opinion should be considered here: "This shift of wording from the parallel account may reflect the Chronicler's desire to introduce a Levitical prophet into the narrative once again (1 Chron. 6:25–28; cf. 1 Sam 1:1)" (R. B. Dillard, *2 Chronicles* [WBC 15; Waco: Word Books, 1987], p. 291). Samuel is indeed an important character in the Chronicles. A concordance search shows that, outside the books of Samuel, the name Samuel occurs only nine times—seven of them in Chronicles (1 Chron. 6:28, 33; 9:22;

11:3; 26:28; 29:29; 2 Chron. 35:18). The combination "Samuel the prophet" in 2 Chron. 35:18 is one of only two occurrences in the Old Testament (the other being in 1 Sam. 3:20; in 1 Chron. 9:22; 26:28; and 29:29 Samuel is called *chozeh*, "seer"). By referring to Samuel, the Chronicler indicates that the historical period is the same as in the Deuteronomistic version ("the days of the judges"), but the list creates the additional important thematic links with (a) the Levitical prophetic tradition (1 Chron. 6:28 and 6:33 explicitly list Samuel in the Levitical genealogies) and (b) the David narrative (the occurrences in 9:22; 26:28; and 29:29 explicitly link Samuel to the David narrative, even calling Samuel, in 29:29, the one who wrote down everything that David did during his reign).

35:22–24 / Differences in depiction of the death of Josiah in various textual witnesses abound. Most scholars accept that the reason behind the various portrayals of Josiah's death is the theological problem of why such an exemplary king died a violent death inflicted by an Egyptian pharaoh's men. Christine Mitchell ("Ironic Death of Josiah," pp. 421–35) develops a literary perspective on the issue. In her view, the Chronicler deliberately patterns the death of Josiah after the death of Ahab in both 1 Kgs. 22 and 2 Chron. 18. That Ahab-Josiah patterning also forges links between Josiah's death and the death of Saul in both 1 Sam. 31 and 1 Chron. 10. Finally, Mitchell finds literary links also between Josiah's death and the deaths of Ahaziah and Amaziah (2 Chron. 22 and 25, respectively). Her literary study leads to the following conclusion: "[Josiah's] death in battle is a foolish death—he thinks that by furthering Hezekiah's work, he would die in peace, even if the exile itself was inevitable. But it is also an ironic death, as he does die in shalom, in a way, by dying in Jerusalem. The Chronicler's depiction of Josiah was not simply an interpretive expansion of the account in 2 Kings 23; it was a rewriting of the account" (pp. 434–35).

§4.16 Jehoahaz, Jehoiakim, Jehoiachin, Zedekiah (2 Chron. 36:2–14)

The accounts of the last four kings of Judah are very brief. Two of them (Jehoahaz and Jehoiachin) ruled for only about three months each, while the other two (Jehoiakim and Zedekiah) each ruled for eleven years. Jehoahaz and Jehoiakim therefore were nothing more than transitional figures bracketing the rule of King Jehoiakim of Judah and leading to the rule of Zedekiah. Although Jehoahaz and Jehoiakim were still successors to the throne of their respective fathers, Jehoiakim and Zedekiah were actually puppet figures put on the throne by the Egyptian and Babylonian kings, respectively (36:4, 10). The Chronicler made use of the Deuteronomistic accounts of these kings' reigns (in 2 Kgs. 23:31–24:20) but abbreviated even further the already short accounts given there.

36:2–4 / We saw in the concluding verse of the Josiah narrative (36:1) that "the people of the land" made **Jehoahaz** king "in Jerusalem in place of his father." The Chronicler omitted two pieces of information given in the source text, namely, the name of the king's mother (but this was also the case in all other royal narratives, starting with Manasseh) and the evaluation of the king (which is unusual). In 2 Kings 23:32 Jehoahaz is evaluated negatively with the words: "He did evil in the eyes of the LORD, just as his fathers had done." Like his father Josiah, Jehoahaz was also in his short reign of three months caught in the international political rivalry between the imperial forces of Egypt and Babylon (which at this stage had already taken over from the Assyrians as the dominant political power to the northeast). The new phase of Babylonian rule brought new attempts at territorial expansion and therefore also required new alliances with smaller nations. According to 2 Chronicles 36:2, King Jehoahaz was a victim of the international politics of the time: **the king of Egypt dethroned him in Jerusalem.** Jehoahaz probably preferred his father's anti-Egyptian policy, and that would explain why Neco removed him after only **three months.** The Egyptian removal of the Judahite king was accompanied by **a levy of a hundred talents of silver and a talent of gold** that was **imposed on Judah,** and thereby Judah became a vassal state of Egypt. We also hear in 36:4 that **Neco took . . . Jehoahaz and carried him off to Egypt.** The Kings version adds "and there he died," information that is not provided in Chronicles. There is no real royal succession here, but rather a replacement of King Jehoahaz. Second Chronicles 36:4 also states: **The king of Egypt made Eliakim, a brother of Jehoahaz, king over Judah and Jerusalem and changed Eliakim's name to Jehoiakim.** This move suggests that internal differences between the two brothers, the sons of Josiah, could have resulted in Egypt's getting a more favorable figure (from the Egyptian perspective) on the throne in Judah. Since Judah forms the land bridge between Egypt and the Mesopotamian empires, a favorable inclination in this part of the world would have been important for Egypt.

36:5–8 / These verses also contain a much-abbreviated version of the royal narrative in the source text in 2 Kings 23:35–24:7. Not only is the information of how **Jehoiakim** taxed his own citizens to pay for the tribute to Egypt omitted (2 Kgs. 23:35), but the customary change of omitting the king's mother's name was also made. The negative evaluation of the king is repeated from the source text, although the words "just as his fathers had done" were omitted, because that would have placed a blemish on Josiah's reputation (something that the Chronicler wanted to avoid). The tussle between Babylon and Egypt also influenced this king's reign (ca. 609/608–598/597 B.C.). The source text (in 2 Kgs. 23:1–4) describes how Jehoiakim was made subservient to Babylon and how he was punished by Nebuchadnezzar for rebelling against Babylon. The Chronicler abbreviates this account to the one phrase: **Nebuchadnezzar king of Babylon attacked him and bound him with bronze shackles to take him to Babylon** (2 Chron. 36:6). With this information following immediately after the words **he did evil in the eyes of the LORD his God** (36:5), the Chronicler insinuates that Jehoiakim's removal from the throne by Nebuchadnezzar serves as a punishment for his not seeking the Lord and instead doing what was right in his own eyes. The additional information provided by the Chronicler, namely, **Nebuchadnezzar also took to Babylon articles from the temple of the LORD and put them in his temple there** (36:7), is not present in the source text in Kings but is reflected in the book of Daniel (which mentions in 1:1 that Jerusalem was besieged by Nebuchadnezzar). It was impossible for the Chronicler to make use of Daniel, since this book originated only much later, so one should therefore assume that some other available sources documented this event. The carrying off of "articles from the temple of the LORD" would certainly mean the tragic defilement of the temple of Solomon and the desecration of the sanctuary. The Jehoiakim account ends with reference to other sources again as well as a note on the king's succession. The information was taken over from the source text in 2 Kings 24:5–6, but the Chronicler added the words **the detestable things he did and all that was found against him** (2 Chron. 36:8) in order to deprecate the king even further. The normal addition is made to the source reference (**the book of the kings of Israel and Judah** instead of the source text's version "the book of the annals of the kings of Judah"), but the Deuteronomist's indication that "Jehoiakim rested with his fathers" was omitted, resulting in no death notice for this king in Chronicles (as in the account of the previous king; see Additional Note on 36:8). In line with the omission of a previous section on the international politics of the time, the Chronicler furthermore omits the information provided in 2 Kings 24:7 about the Egyptians no longer being able to push back the Babylonian influence. It seems that the Chronicler thought: "The less said about this dark hour, the better!"

36:9–10 / The changes made to the introductory information about King **Jehoiachin** in the source text (2 Kgs. 24:8–9) are similar to those effected in the account of the previous king. The mother's name is omitted again, and the negative evaluation **he did evil in the eyes of the LORD** does not include the phrase in Kings "just as his father had done." The age indication is problematic (see Additional Note on 36:9). The lengthy description of the Babylonian campaign against **Jerusalem** in 2 Kings 24:10–17 is abbreviated in Chronicles into one phrase: **in the spring, King Nebuchadnezzar sent for him and brought him to Babylon** (36:10). Again (as in the case of Jehoiakim), the Babylonian king **took articles of value from the temple of the LORD** with him. The section closes with the indication that **King Nebuchadnezzar . . . made Jehoiachin's uncle, Zedekiah, king over Judah and Jerusalem.** Whereas this subsection is the last time we hear about Jehoiachin in Chronicles, the source text in 2 Kings 25:27–30 mentions that he was freed from prison by Evil-Merodach, who was then king of Babylon. In the Deuteronomist's construction, the liberation of Jehoiachin becomes a symbol of hope and restoration. The Chronicler ends his narrative, however, with another symbol of hope and restoration, namely, Cyrus.

36:11–14 / The final ruler over Judah (who ruled approximately 598/597–587/586 B.C.) is **Zedekiah**, Jehoiachin's uncle and therefore another son of Josiah. Although he ruled for **eleven years** (according to both the Kings and Chronicles versions), his rule actually entailed nothing more than taking care of an exiled state. The Chronicler used the source text in 2 Kings 24:18–20 but made some changes with which the reader is familiar by now. The name of the king's mother was omitted, and significant changes were made to the motivation for the negative evaluation of the king. Second Chronicles 36:12 indicates that he **did not humble (***kana'***) himself before Jeremiah the prophet, who spoke the word of the L**ORD**.** He therefore **became stiff-necked and hardened his heart and would not turn to the L**ORD**, the God of Israel** (36:13). The evilness of Zedekiah, in the Chronicler's vision, also had impact on the priests and the people: **all the leaders of the priests and the people became more and more unfaithful** (*ma'al* in a construction that repeats the word twice), **following all the detestable practices of the nations and defiling the temple of the L**ORD**, which he had consecrated (***qadash***) in Jerusalem** (36:14). From the terminology it becomes clear that the Chronicler's reformulation of his source material was intended to emphasize the apostasy involved in the downfall of the kingdom of Judah. This represents not only the fate of history or international politics—at the core of Judah's downfall lies unfaithfulness to Yahweh, the God of their father David. The Chronicler mentions, as does the Kings source text, that the final nail in the coffin of Judah was when Zedekiah **also rebelled against King Nebuchadnezzar** (36:13). The Chronicler adds, however, that Nebuchadnezzar **had made him take an oath in God's name** (cf. Ezek. 17:11–21). Zedekiah's rebellion, therefore, violated the very oath he had sworn "in God's name." With the Zedekiah narrative we come to the end of the Chronicler's royal narratives. The following two subsections describe the fall of Jerusalem and the liberation of the exiles under King Cyrus of Persia.

Additional Notes §4.16

36:2 / There is a text-critical problem with the formulation **the king of Egypt dethroned him in Jerusalem.** The problem cannot be seen so clearly in the NIV (which opted for the translation **dethroned** instead of "removed," the more usual translation for the Hebrew verb used here), but the prepositional indication **in Jerusalem** does not make good sense in the Hebrew (which would read "removed him *in* Jerusalem"). It seems that the Greek translators in the Septuagint had already experienced this difficulty, since they omitted the Greek equivalent of the Hebrew prepositional indication. The Deuteronomist's version in 2 Kgs. 23:33 differs significantly: "Pharaoh Neco put him in chains at Riblah in the land of Hamath so that he might not reign in Jerusalem." The form of the Hebrew text might be the result of a scribal error but might also be an indication that Jerusalem, which once was the seat of the proud Davidic monarchy, now has become the seat of its final destruction.

36:5–8 / More information about King **Jehoiakim** is also provided in various sections of the book of Jeremiah (e.g., Jer. 25:1–3; 36:1–2, 9; 45:1–2; 46:1–2). This prophet was a contemporary of the king, and he prophesied in Judah in the final years before the Babylonian exile started.

36:8 / Different versions of the death of **Jehoiakim** exist. Whereas the Chronicler omits the information given in Kings, namely, "he rested with his fathers," this information is indeed provided in the Septuagint translation of Chronicles.

36:9 / The NIV indicates in a footnote that most Hebrew manuscripts have "eight" as the age of the new king. On account of the parallel text in 2 Kgs. 24:8, as well as of the Septuagint and Syriac readings of the Chronicles text, the NIV has **eighteen years**. McKenzie provides the following explanation, which relates the problem to the issue of the length of the king's reign (**three months and ten days**): "The number should be 'eighteen' as in 2 Kgs 24:8 rather than 'eight.' A scribe attempting to correct the error mistakenly inserted the missing element at a later point in the verse, leading to the addition of ten days to Jehoiachin's reign" (*1–2 Chronicles*, p. 369).

36:12 / The remark that King Zedekiah **did not humble himself before Jeremiah the prophet** seems strange. The normal accusation is that the king or people did not humble themselves before Yahweh. Hermann-Josef Stipp ("Zedekiah in the Book of Jeremiah: On the Formation of a Biblical Character," *CBQ* 58 [1996], pp. 627–48) shows, however, that the same Zedekiah does not get similar harsh treatment in the book of Jeremiah: "The verdict pronounced by the writers of Chronicles typifies an advanced state of a concept that took shape over a long period of time. Stages of this process are attested in the book of Jeremiah itself, where we encounter a remarkable variety of attitudes toward this last Davidic king" (p. 627). The prominence of Jeremiah is discussed in the next section.

§4.17 The Fall of Jerusalem (2 Chron. 36:15–21)

Judah's very sad and violent end at the hands of their Babylonian masters is the theme of the second to last subsection in the book of Chronicles. It is clear from this text that the Chronicler's intention was certainly not to give a factual account of the end of the Judean kingdom but rather to provide a theological interpretation of this event of the past. Second Chronicles 36:21 particularly links what happened in the past to "the word of the LORD" that came to them "spoken by Jeremiah." Judah's destruction and consequent captivity in exile in Babylon are explicitly indicated to be a fulfillment of Jeremiah's prophecy—or at least that is the traditional interpretation. Furthermore, the Chronicler proceeds to interpret the duration of the exile as a period of sabbath rest for the land. The desolation of the land is indicated to be a keeping of the sabbath in order to complete the symbolic period of seventy years. The end of this seventy-year period, according to the Chronicler, coincides with the establishment of the kingdom of Persia.

A comparison with the Deuteronomistic source texts in 2 Kings 24–25 shows that the Chronicler has been very free in his reconstruction of the final phases of Judah's existence. Although the Chronicler also refers to certain events mentioned in 2 Kings, such as the killing of certain youths, the plundering and destruction of the temple in Jerusalem, and the deportation of Judeans to Babylon, these events seem not to be the focus of the Chronicler's reconstruction. The final episode in Judah's existence is introduced by the Chronicler in 36:15–16 as the result of Yahweh's anger not being contained any longer after the people had despised the words of the messengers and scoffed at the prophets who were sent to them by Yahweh. And the episode ends with another indication that Jeremiah's prophecy of doom has now been fulfilled. A comparison with the versions of these final events in Judah's history as reported in the prophetic book of Jeremiah confirms that the Chronicler went his own way in his description. In Jeremiah 39:1–10 and 52:3–30, more or less the same version of these final events is presented compared to that in 2 Kings 24–25.

Why would the Chronicler be more interested in giving a theological appraisal of the exile than a historical account? Scholars are in agreement that Chronicles is not the odd one out in this regard. The other descriptions of the exilic period contained in the Old Testament are also not objective but theological interpretations. Although the Chronicler's version differs remarkably from those of 2 Kings and Jeremiah, the Chronicler simply continued the tradition of interpreting the events from within his own context—a tradition already present in the source texts.

36:15–16 / The information contained in these verses is not represented in one of the source texts and could therefore be from the Chronicler's own hand. It is claimed that the destruction and deportation were the results of God's wrath, which became so great that **there was no remedy** any longer. These verses claim that **the Lord, the God of their fathers, sent word to them through his messengers again and again** on account of his **pity on his people and on his dwelling place** (a reference to the temple). However, **they mocked God's messengers, despised his words and scoffed at his prophets.** The persistence of these deeds is given expression by the participle active forms used in the Hebrew text (and should rather be translated as "kept mocking . . . kept despising . . . kept scoffing"). As a direct result of this situation, **the wrath of the Lord was aroused against his people.**

36:17–19 / Second Chronicles 36:17–19 is a very free summary of information provided in the source texts. Although the source texts do not explicitly link Nebuchadnezzar's campaign with the activity of Yahweh, it is claimed in 36:17 that Yahweh **brought up against them the king of the Babylonians.** This verse therefore links up with the claim made in the previous two verses that the Lord is actually behind the Babylonian destruction of Judah. This subsection furthermore emphasizes the killing of youths **with the sword in the sanctuary** and also that the Babylonians (called by their alternative name, Chaldeans, in the Hebrew text) had no compassion for either young or old. This summary relates to the source texts (particularly 2 Kgs. 25:1–7; Jer. 39:1–7; 52:4–11), which all mention the killing of Zedekiah's son as well as the putting out of Zedekiah's eyes.

Second Chronicles 36:18–19 summarizes the elaborate descriptions in the source texts of the capturing of the temple vessels and palace treasures, as well as the burning down of the **temple** and the **palaces** and the destruction of **the wall of Jerusalem** (2 Kgs. 25:8–10, 13–17; Jer. 52:12–14, 17–23). The order of the information, however, was inverted by the Chronicler, who first mentions the capturing of the temple objects in

36:18 and then the destruction of the temple, wall, and palaces in 36:19. In the source texts (2 Kgs. 25 and Jer. 52) the information is provided in the opposite order. This inversion probably sought to indicate that the temple vessels were not harmed, which might be the conclusion from the source texts, where the destruction comes first.

36:20 / The first part of 36:20 might still be a summary of the information provided in 2 Kings 24:11–12, 18–21 and Jeremiah 39:9–10; 52:15–16, 24–30. No individuals or groups are mentioned in 2 Chronicles 36:20, but those taken into captivity are collectively called **the remnant, who escaped from the sword.** This might be the Chronicler's summary of what is called "the people who remained in the city" in 2 Kings 25:11 and Jeremiah 39:9; 52:15. The Chronicler, however, omits any mention that some vinedressers and tillers of the soil were left in the land (according to the other three versions). On account of this omission, the Chronicler's version is often indicated as supporting the so-called myth of the empty land (see Additional Note on 36:20).

The last few words of 36:20, **until the kingdom of Persia came to power,** introduce a new element (which is probably from the Chronicler's hand), namely, that the exilic period ended with the emergence of the Persian kingdom. This idea is picked up again in the conclusion to the book, in 36:22–23.

36:21 / Second Chronicles 36:21 is certainly the Chronicler's own composition. In this verse, three new elements are introduced: **the land enjoyed its sabbath rests; until the seventy years were completed;** and **in fulfillment of the word of the LORD spoken by Jeremiah.** It is argued by various scholars that the mention of "the seventy years" is a direct reference to Jeremiah 25 and 29. The "seventy years"—which was added to the source texts by the Chronicler—apparently provided the bridge to recall the prophecies of Jeremiah. As Japhet argues, "For the Chronicler . . . 'seventy years' is not a chronological datum which may be explained by various calculations, but a historical and theological concept: a time limit for the duration of the land's desolation, established by a divine word through his prophet" (*I and II Chronicles* [London: SCM, 1993], p. 1076).

We also find in this verse the Chronicler's interesting interpretation of the exile as "sabbath rests" for the land. In this instance, it is clear that the Chronicler recalled certain legal educational material from Leviticus 26:31–35, which threatens the destruction of cities and sanctuaries and the scattering of Israelites among the nations for rebellion. And after that: "Then the land will enjoy its sabbath years all the time that it lies desolate . . . ; then the land will rest and enjoy its sabbaths. All the time that it lies desolate, the land will have the rest it did not have during the sabbaths you lived in it" (Lev. 26:34–35). This idea is continued in Leviticus 26:43: "For the land will be deserted by them and will enjoy its sabbaths while it lies desolate without them." The terminological similarities are again obvious.

The question remains how the Chronicler could interpret the "desolation" and "sabbath rest" of Leviticus positively. Possibly, in his view Judah's exile gave the land its proper restoration, something the people had denied it. Also, the application of "sabbath rest" implies a limited, but necessary, interim period of exile, after which "redemption" (i.e., a return to normal life) comes. The Chronicler's addition of Jeremiah's "seventy years" further enhances his turning of the desolation and sabbath period into an undeniably hopeful description.

Additional Notes §4.17

36:15–16 / Erhard Gerstenberger ("Prophetie in den Chronikbüchern: Jahwes Wort in zweierlei Gestalt?," pp. 351–67) argues that the distinction between **prophets** and **messengers** should probably be traced back to the Persian communication system, in which messengers played a pivotal role. Although one would never be able to know for certain, this could be a good explanation for the Chronicler involving figures in prophetic roles who are not portrayed as such in the Deuteronomistic source texts. The suggestion would then be that figures such as David, Neco, and Cyrus were conveying messages from Yahweh. Particularly the mention of Cyrus would certainly have had a polemical function then. Monarchs (Judahite or foreign) are conveying messages from Yahweh, the God of Israel (see commentary on 36:22–23)!

36:20 / Despite the claims of some biblical texts (the so-called myth of the empty land), there is much evidence that the land was definitely not left empty during the **exile**. The reason is that only the political and religious leadership was deported, but rural communities continued their existence without any catastrophic disturbance.

36:21 / The link between Chronicles and **Jeremiah** should not be surprising. As McKenzie notes (*1–2 Chronicles*, pp. 28–29), since the Chronicler probably lived in Jerusalem, he was intimately acquainted with the temple, its personnel (e.g., the Levites), and its operations. He may even have grown up in those very circles.

§4.18 Liberation under Emperor Cyrus (2 Chron. 36:22–23)

The final subsection in the Chronicler's historiography deals with the pending liberation under Cyrus, the Persian emperor. This information is absent from the Deuteronomist's version in Kings, which leads some scholars to believe that the Deuteronomistic History in broad terms was finalized during the exile, before there were any signs of liberation yet. The Chronicler, writing some two centuries later, of course knew about the emergence of Persia, the return of the exiles, the rebuilding of the temple and Jerusalem, and the restoration of Yahweh's people.

Although 36:22–23 is not to be found in the Deuteronomistic source text, these verses are present in the introduction to the book of Ezra (in Ezra 1:1–3). Scholars debate intensely which one of these versions is the original, but a consensus has emerged that the Chronicler probably copied these verses from the earlier book of Ezra in order to establish a unity of some sort with the historiography contained in Ezra-Nehemiah (which describes the history after the exile). However, the inclusion of these verses, and particularly the figure of Cyrus, at the conclusion of Chronicles not only served a literary function but also concluded the whole history of Israel from a universalist perspective. The book starts with Adam and ends with Cyrus. With those figures bracketing his historiography, the Chronicler put the history of Israel within the context of wider humanity and the nations.

36:22–23 / The previous subsection emphasized that the exile was a fulfillment of the prophecy of Jeremiah, and now 36:22 indicates that also the liberation under Cyrus the Great was **to fulfill the word of the Lord spoken by Jeremiah**. It is explicitly said that **the Lord moved the heart of Cyrus king of Persia to make a proclamation throughout his realm**. It is noteworthy that the covenant name, Yahweh, is used to refer to the deity (whereas in the case of Pharaoh Neco in 2 Chron. 35 it was the generic name God) and that prophetic terms are used here as well. The expression "the Lord moved the heart of X" is very often used in a context where a prophet is commissioned by Yahweh to speak on his behalf. This prophetic impression is strengthened by the introduction to Cyrus's edict in 36:23: **this is what Cyrus king of Persia says.** The expression used here is well known as the so-called prophetic formula that normally introduces oracles in the prophetic literature. Cyrus of Persia is thus portrayed as if he were a prophet of Yahweh, announcing the return and restoration of the captives from Israel and Judah. This is quite significant in terms of what the book of Chronicles intended to communicate to its audience in the late Persian era. The Persian imperial regime is presented here with the insinuation that the providence of Yahweh is embodied in this imperial dispensation.

The direct quotation from Cyrus's written document is introduced with the claim that **the Lord, the God of heaven, has given me all the kingdoms of the earth.** This suggests that the Persian emperor's authority over the nations subservient to the empire was actually an authority received from Yahweh. This view portrays Yahweh as a universal God who not only determines the history of the miserable lands of Judah and Israel but also moves the great empires of the world. Yahweh's power to bring change is not limited to the boundaries of Israel or Judah but spreads out over the mighty Persian Empire.

Cyrus furthermore claims that **the Lord . . . has appointed me to build a temple for him at Jerusalem in Judah.** We know that Cyrus was eventually instrumental in the rebuilding of the Jerusalem temple and city walls. However, this remark not only functions on the level of history; it also functions as a literary bridge to another king who was commissioned by Yahweh to build a temple, namely, Solomon. What has been lost through a whole series of Judahite kings not doing right in the eyes of Yahweh will be regained by Cyrus the Persian. Could one perhaps assume that the Chronicler, by drawing these literary lines, wanted the reader to realize that the eternal Davidic dynasty can be continued even in the Persian ruler? And could one, by reading backward from 36:22–23, assume that the Chronicler's image of Solomon was a disguised polemic directed at the Persian rulers (probably through their governors in Jerusalem, who were appointed from the local population) to suggest to them that good rulership implies that Yahweh be sought?

The book therefore ends with the invitation from Cyrus: **anyone of his people among you—may the Lord his God be with him, and let him go up.** The Chronicler's work ends on the hopeful note of pending return and restoration, something that had already been realized in his own day but that remains necessary to hear in every new era in history!

Additional Note §4.18

36:23 / We know from extrabiblical sources (such as the Cyrus Cylinder) that the Persian Empire under the leadership of **Cyrus** invaded Babylon in 539 B.C. and that an edict was promulgated in 538 B.C. in which permission was given to the captives from Israel and Judah to return to their homeland.

Summary of §4

At the end of the Chronicler's narrative stretching from King Rehoboam's reign to the fall of Jerusalem and the pending liberation, my observations can be summarized in the following points.

a. Although the Chronicler very deliberately chooses to follow the Judahite (Davidic) royal line in his description, his historiography is not Judahite in the strict sense of the word. The Chronicler is presenting the history of All-Israel. All-Israel, in the Chronicler's understanding, had already gone through its prototypical formative period during the reigns of David and Solomon. But the new phase in history, following the death of King Solomon, brought new challenges to the understanding of All-Israel. The political reality, as witnessed in the Deuteronomistic account, was that the united kingdom of David and Solomon split into two, with two monarchical lines and two cultic traditions stemming from that development. There is no doubt that the Chronicler's allegiance was with the southern kingdom, Judah. But this ideological choice did not result in the Chronicler excluding the northern tribes from his understanding of All-Israel. By means of his historiography (particularly through the description of the monarchy in 2 Chron. 10–36) the Chronicler redefines this concept as something that transcends political reality. All-Israel is not constituted and consolidated by means of battles and the gaining of influence in the sociopolitical world. And All-Israel is also not destroyed or annihilated by the realities of regional politics or even imperial subservience. All-Israel is rather defined by Yahweh, the God of the fathers, and the God of David and Solomon, also being the God of All-Israel. This God has chosen to dwell in the temple in Jerusalem, and this God upholds his promise to David of an eternal kingship. Judah and Israel (and even other nations and empires) form part of All-Israel only insofar as they seek this God and humble themselves before this God. All-Israel is defined in terms of a particular understanding of the relationship between Yahweh and his people.

b. That Yahweh is the God of All-Israel becomes evident particularly through his involvement in Judah's battles. The Chronicler's battle accounts are not military histories but rather theological appraisals. There is absolutely no doubt that Yahweh fights the battle on Judah's behalf, provided that the king and people seek Yahweh and rely on him. Then no enemy, irrespective of its military resources, can remain standing before Yahweh. However, Yahweh can also be on the side of the enemy! God can also use Judah's enemies—ranging from the northern kingdom, Israel, to the neighboring nations and even the great empires—to punish Judah for its apostasy and to bring the Judahites to humble themselves again before him.

c. The pattern of immediate retribution (which is identified by many commentators as one of the central themes in Chronicles) also functions within the context mentioned in the previous two points. Immediate retribution is not a theological notion as such that functions independently of the Chronicler's attempt to define All-Israel as a community seeking Yahweh. The Chronicler certainly indicates that Yahweh brings retribution and does not postpone it to subsequent generations. However, accounts of this retribution always stand in service of the Chronicler's undertaking to show that dedication to Yahweh defines the basic attitude of All-Israel toward their deity.

d. The Chronicler employs many literary patterns to drive home this point. He develops, for example, two conglomerates of terminology in his own material and the material selected from his source texts. On the one side of the spectrum are concepts such as "to seek" (*darash* or *biqqesh*) Yahweh, "to rely" (*sha'an*) upon Yahweh, and "to humble oneself" (*kana'*) before Yahweh. An attitude characterized by these inclinations leads to winning battles, having a very able military force, gaining influence and fame, acquiring many wives, and even receiving a proper burial in the City of David together with deceased royalty of the past. The other side of the spectrum is represented by concepts such as "to forsake" (*'azab*) Yahweh and "to be disloyal/apostate" (*ma'al*) to Yahweh. This inclination leads to losing battles, falling ill, dying, and not being buried with the royal fathers. Between these two extremes of the spectrum, there are no alternatives.

e. The seeking of Yahweh is not a generalized category ascribed to certain kings and not to others. The basic religious inclination advocated by the Chronicler is something manifested in the realities of the kings' lives. This is particularly illustrated in the Chronicler keeping to the Deuteronomist's evaluation of the kings but not refraining from altering those depictions. Good kings can go wrong and deviate from being wholeheartedly dedicated to Yahweh (e.g., Asa, Joash, and Uzziah). And bad kings can repent and gain access to Yahweh's gracious presence (e.g., Manasseh).

f. Related to the above-mentioned perspective, the Chronicler sometimes wanted to drive home certain theological understandings typically associated with Deuteronomic theology but not expressed well enough in the Deuteronomistic source texts. It seems then that the Chronicler wanted to be more Deuteronomic than his Deuteronomistic source text (e.g., the Chronicler's portrayal of Jehoshaphat's legal reforms and other examples in the histories of Asa and Hezekiah).

g. The Chronicler draws some literary parallels in his work that—on a macrostructural level—give the reader of the book access into the thought world of the writer and his audience. One prominent parallel relationship is that between David-Solomon, on the one hand, and Hezekiah-Josiah, on the other. The Chronicler's basic construction of All-Israelite history runs through these four figures. However, another parallel relationship is closely associated with these kings. The same development that we see between David and Solomon in terms of temple building is also manifested between Hezekiah and Josiah in terms of the Passover celebration. That the issues of temple building and the Passover celebration are so prominent in the Chronicler's construction is a clear reflection of the importance of temple worship and Passover celebration in the Chronicler's own time. This is how a cultic community establishes itself (*kun*), namely, through temple worship and the Passover. All-Israel, even long after the end of the Judahite monarchy, needs to ensure proper care for the Second Temple in Jerusalem as well as dedicated celebration of the Passover.

h. The sociopolitical context of the Chronicler's time is also in the background of the literary construction. It is noteworthy that all foreign monarchs (except Sennacherib of Assyria, which was no longer in existence as an empire in the Chronicler's time) are portrayed positively. That the climax of the book is reached when a Persian emperor, Cyrus, announces the liberation and restoration of All-Israel in fulfillment of a Yahwistic prophet's words illustrates the Chronicler's attitude toward his own context. He sees Cyrus the

Persian as the one who is fulfilling Yahweh's gracious restoration (as a neo-Solomonic figure). The Chronicler accepts the Persian imperial presence as the context within which Yahwism can flourish and be restored, depending on the wholehearted dedication of the people. Yahwism is therefore not dependent on the existence of the kingdom of Judah but can even be practiced in the context of imperial rule.

i. In the process of defining All-Israel and Yahwism in the Persian imperial context, the Chronicler also engages with the sociopolitical realities. Not only does the reader of Chronicles witness a process of enculturation in the Persian imperial context, but different processes of differentiation also simultaneously emerge. First, we have witnessed in the Chronicler's work a few occasions where the boundaries between Israel (as the northern kingdom) and Judah have been blurred. And these examples contribute to our understanding of All-Israel as formulated by the Chronicler. However, there is absolutely no doubt that the Chronicler wanted to advocate the centrality of Jerusalem and the temple in Jerusalem for the All-Israelite community of the late Persian period. The sociopolitical reality of the Persian province of Samaria to the north (consisting of approximately the same tribal areas of the former kingdom of Israel) certainly influenced the Chronicler to argue for an inclusive understanding of the Yahweh community, but with its base and main sphere of influence in Jerusalem and the province of Yehud. A process of intragroup categorization can be witnessed in the Chronicler's attempt to relate Yehud to, but also to differentiate Yehud from, the northern provincial neighbor, Samaria. Second, the sociopolitical reality of the neighboring provinces of Philistia (Ashdod) to the west, Transjordan to the east, and Idumea with the Arabian areas to the south also had an influence on the Chronicler's construction. It is no coincidence that the Chronicler imported so many new battle accounts into his narrative, involving mostly the nations from these surrounding areas. In those narratives the Chronicler defines All-Israel at its margins. Intergroup categorization takes place when the Chronicler engages with the surrounding provincial reality of his time. But there is also a third level of engagement with the sociopolitical context of the Chronicler's time, namely, the Persian imperial context. In point (h) I indicated that the Chronicler has come to terms with the imperial context and is trying to define All-Israel and Yahwism within that context. However, that does not mean that he does not also engage critically with this context. By presenting Cyrus as a prophetlike figure, the Chronicler polemically states that Yahweh also has dominion over the Persian rulers. They act (and should act) in accordance with what Yahweh commissions them to do. By drawing some literary lines between Solomon and Cyrus and by presenting some examples of good-kings-gone-bad and bad-kings-becoming-repentant, the Chronicler subtly recommends a prototype of kingship to those rulers who have authority over Yehud in his time. In this way the Chronicler engages in another process of intergroup categorization that differentiates All-Israel from the Persian imperial context.

At the end of this commentary one should be reminded of an aspect discussed in the introduction: The Chronicler did not subscribe to a theory of the contingency of history. History, and therefore also the continuation of the past into the present and future, can and should be interpreted theologically. The existence of the Yahweh community and All-Israel is not simply a function of fate. For the Chronicler, and all other believers, there is more than meets the eye in the past, present, and future.

For Further Reading

The list below contains a selection of publications—ranging from technical and specialized/exegetical to pastoral and devotional—that have appeared since 2000. For earlier publications the reader may consult the comprehensive bibliography in Knoppers, *1 Chronicles 1–9*, pp. 141–241.

Commentaries

Allen, L. C. *1 and 2 Chronicles*. The Preacher's Commentary. Nashville: Nelson, 2002.

Barber, C. J. *1 Chronicles*. Focus on the Bible. Ross-shire, UK: Christian Focus, 2004.

———. *2 Chronicles*. Focus on the Bible. Ross-shire, UK: Christian Focus, 2004.

Beentjes, P. *1 Kronieken: Commentaar voor bijbelstudie, onderwijs en prediking*. Verklaring van de Hebreeuwse Bijbel. Kampen: Kok, 2002.

Conti, M. *1/2 Kings, 1/2 Chronicles, Ezra-Nehemiah, Esther*. ACCS. Downers Grove, IL: InterVarsity, 2008.

Corduan, W. *1st and 2nd Chronicles*. Holman Old Testament Commentary. Nashville: Broadman & Holman, 2004.

Dirksen, P. B. *1 Chronicles*. HCOT. Leuven: Peeters, 2005.

Hicks, J. M. *1 and 2 Chronicles*. College Press NIV Commentary. Joplin, MO: College Press, 2001.

Hill, A. E. *1 and 2 Chronicles*. NIVAC. Grand Rapids: Zondervan, 2003.

Hooker, P. K. *First and Second Chronicles*. Westminster Bible Commentary. Louisville: Westminster John Knox, 2001.

Jarick, J. *1 Chronicles*. Readings. London: Sheffield Academic Press, 2002.

———. *2 Chronicles*. Readings. Sheffield, UK: Sheffield Phoenix, 2007.

Klein, R. W. *1 Chronicles: A Commentary*. Hermeneia. Minneapolis: Fortress, 2006.

———. *2 Chronicles: A Commentary*. Hermeneia. Minneapolis: Fortress, 2012.

Knoppers, G. N. *1 Chronicles 1–9*. AB 12. New York: Doubleday, 2003.

———. *1 Chronicles 10–29*. AB 12A. New York: Doubleday, 2004.

McKenzie, S. L. *1–2 Chronicles*. AOTC. Nashville: Abingdon, 2004.

Selman, M. S. *2 Chronicles: An Introduction and a Commentary*. TOTC 11. Downers Grove, IL: InterVarsity Academic, 2008.

Stewart, A. *A House of Prayer: The Message of 2 Chronicles.* Welwyn Commentary Series. Darlington, UK: Evangelical Press, 2002.

Tuell, S. S. *First and Second Chronicles.* Interpretation. Louisville: John Knox, 2001.

General works

Achenbach, R. "Einige Beobachtungen zu der sogenannten 'Jeho'asch-Inschrift'. Eine Schrifttafel aus dem 9. Jh. V.Chr. oder eine Fälschung? Oder: Ueber einen erstaunlichen Internetauftritt." *BN* 117 (2003), pp. 5–14.

Albertz, R. *Israel in Exile: The History and Literature of the Sixth Century B.C.E.* Atlanta: SBL, 2003.

Amit, Y. "The Saul Polemic in the Persian Period." Pages 647–61 in *Judah and the Judeans in the Persian Period.* Edited by O. Lipschits and M. Oeming. Winona Lake, IN: Eisenbrauns, 2006.

Assis, E. "From Adam to Esau and Israel: An Anti-Edomite Ideology in 1 Chronicles 1." *VT* 56/3 (2006), pp. 287–302.

Auld, A. G. "What If the Chronicler Did Use the Deuteronomistic History?" *BibInt* 8/1,2 (2000), pp. 137–50.

Avioz, M. "Nathan's Prophecy in II Sam 7 and in I Chr 17: Text, Context, and Meaning." *ZAW* 116/4 (2004), pp. 542–54.

Barick, B. "Another Shaking of Jehoshaphat's Family Tree: Jehoram and Ahaziah Once Again." *VT* 51/1 (2001), pp. 9–25.

Beentjes, P. C. "Prophets in the Book of Chronicles." Pages 45–53 in *The Elusive Prophet: The Prophet as a Historical Person, Literary Character and Anonymous Artist.* Edited by J. C. De Moor. Leiden: Brill, 2001.

―――. *Tradition and Transformation in the Book of Chronicles.* SSN 52. Leiden: Brill, 2008.

Ben Zvi, E. "The Chronicler as a Historian: Building Texts." Pages 100–116 in *History, Literature and Theology in the Book of Chronicles.* London: Equinox, 2006.

―――. "A House of Treasures: The Account of Amaziah in 2 Chronicles 25— Observations and Implications." *SJOT* 22/1 (2008), pp. 63–85.

―――. "The Secession of the Northern Kingdom in Chronicles: Accepted 'Facts' and New Meanings." Pages 117–43 in *History, Literature and Theology in the Book of Chronicles.* London: Equinox, 2006.

―――. "Shifting the Gaze: Historiographic Constraints in Chronicles and their Implications." Pages 78–99 in *History, Literature and Theology in the Book of Chronicles.* London: Equinox, 2006.

Berquist, J. L. "Constructions of Identity in Postcolonial Yehud." Pages 53–66 in *Judah and the Judeans in the Persian Period.* Edited by O. Lipschits and M. Oeming. Winona Lake, IN: Eisenbrauns, 2006.

Blenkinsopp, J. "'We Pay No Heed to Heavenly Voices': The 'End of Prophecy' and the Formation of the Canon." Pages 192–207 in *Treasures Old and New: Essays in the Theology of the Pentateuch.* Edited by J. Blenkinsopp. Grand Rapids: Eerdmans, 2004.

Blum, E. "Historiographie oder Dichtung? Zur Eigenart alttestamentlicher Geschichtsüberlieferungen." Pages 65–86 in *Das Alte Testament – ein*

Geschichtsbuch? Beiträge des Symposiums "Das Alte Testament und die Kultur der Moderne" anlässlich des 100. Geburtstags Gerhard von Rads (1901–1971) Heidelberg 18.–21. Oktober 2001. Edited by E. Blum and C. Hardmeier. Münster: LIT Verlag, 2005.

Briant, P. *From Cyrus to Alexander: A History of the Persian Empire*. Winona Lake, IN: Eisenbrauns, 2002.

Brooks, S. S. *Saul and the Monarchy: A New Look*. Aldershot, UK: Ashgate, 2005).

Chavel, S. "The Second Passover, Pilgrimage, and the Centralized Cult." *HTR* 102/1 (2009), pp. 1–24.

Doan, W., and T. Giles. "The Song of Asaph: A Performance-Critical Analysis of 1 Chronicles 16:8–36." *CBQ* 70/1 (2008), pp. 29–43.

Duke, R. K. "Recent Research in Chronicles." *CurBS* 8/1 (2009), pp. 10–50.

Edelman, D. "Hezekiah's Alleged Cultic Centralization." *JSOT* 32/4 (2008), pp. 395–434.

Finkelstein, I. "Rehoboam's Fortified Cities (II Chr 11,5–12): A Hasmonean Reality?" *ZAW* 123/1 (2011), pp. 96–107.

Gardner, A. "1 Chronicles 8:28–32; 9:35–38: Complementary or Contrasting Genealogies?" *ABR* 55 (2007), pp. 13–28.

Gerstenberger, E. S. *Israel in der Perserzeit. 5. und 4. Jahrhundert v.Chr.* Stuttgart: Kohlhammer, 2005.

———. "Prophetie in den Chronikbüchern: Jahwes Wort in zweierlei Gestalt?" Pages 351–67 in *Schriftprophetie. FS für Jörg Jeremias zum 65. Geburtstag*. Edited by F. Hartenstein et al. Neukirchen-Vluyn: Neukirchener Verlag, 2004.

Grabbe, L. L. *A History of the Jews and Judaism in the Second Temple Period*. London: T&T Clark, 2004.

Graham, M. P., S. L. McKenzie, and G. N. Knoppers, eds. *The Chronicler as Theologian: Essays in Honor of Ralph W. Klein*. JSOTSup 371. London: T&T Clark, 2003.

Gross, W. "Vorsicht: archäologische Objekte zweifelhafter Herkunft." *TQ* 183 (2003), pp. 177–78.

Haemig, M. J. "Jehoshaphat and His Prayer among Sixteenth Century Lutherans." *CH* 73/3 (2004), pp. 533–35.

Hanspach, A. *Inspirierte Interpreten. Das Prophetenverständnis der Chronikbücher und sein Ort in der Religion und Literatur zur Zeit des zweiten Tempels*. St. Ottilien, Germany: EOS, 2000.

Hentschel, G. *Saul. Schuld, Reue und Tragik eines 'Gesalbten.'* Leipzig: Evangelischer Verlagsanstalt, 2003.

Hom, M. "'To' or 'Against'?: The Interpretation of *yb' 'l* in 2 Chr 28:20." *VT* 60 (2010), pp. 560–64.

Hunt, A. *Missing Priests: The Zadokites in Tradition and History*. New York: T&T Clark, 2006.

Janse van Rensburg, H. "The Attack of Judah in Sennacherib's Third Campaign: An Ideological Study of the Various Texts." *OTE* 17/4 (2004), pp. 560–79.

Jonker, L. C. "Another Look at the Psalm Headings: Observations on the Musical Terminology." *JNSL* 30/1 (2004), pp. 65–85.

————. "The Chronicler and the Prophets: Who Were His Authoritative Sources?" *SJOT* 22/2 (2008), pp. 271–92.

————. "The Chronicler Singing Psalms: Revisiting the Chronicler's Psalm in 1 Chronicles 16." Pages 115–30 in *My Spirit at Rest in the North Country" (Zechariah 6.8): Collected Communications to the XXth Congress of the IOSOT. Helsinki 2010.* Edited by H.-M. Niemann and M. Augustin. Frankfurt: Peter Lang, 2011.

————. "The Chronicler's Portrayal of Solomon as the King of Peace within the Context of the International Peace Discourses of the Persian Era." *OTE* 21/3 (2008), pp. 653–69.

————. "The Cushites in the Chronicler's Version of Asa's Reign: A Secondary Audience in Chronicles?" *OTE* 19/3 (2006), pp. 863–81.

————. "David's Officials according to the Chronicler (1 Chronicles 23–27): A Reflection of Second Temple Self-Categorization?" Pages 65–91 in *Historiography and Identity (Re)formulation in Second Temple Historiographical Literature.* Edited by L. C. Jonker. LHBOTS 534. London: T&T Clark, 2010.

————. "The Disappearing Nehushtan: The Chronicler's Reinterpretation of Hezekiah's Reformation Measures." Pages 116–40 in *From Ebla to Stellenbosch: Syro-Palistinian Religions and the Hebrew Bible.* Edited by I. Cornelius and L. C. Jonker. ADPV 37. Wiesbaden: Harrossowitz, 2008.

————. "Engaging with Different Contexts: A Survey of the Various Levels of Identity Negotiation in Chronicles." Pages 63–94 in *Texts, Contexts and Readings in Postexilic Literature: Explorations into Historiography and Identity Negotiation in Hebrew Bible and Related Texts.* Edited by L. C. Jonker. FAT II/53. Tübingen: Mohr Siebeck, 2011.

————. "The Exile as Sabbath Rest: The Chronicler's Interpretation of the Exile." *OTE* 20/3 (2007), pp. 702–19.

————. "Kronistens etter-eksilske lesning av Pentateukens genealogier." Pages 33–46 in *Jerusalem, Samaria og jordens ender: Bibeltolkninger tilegnet Magnar Kartveit, 65 år, 7. oktober 2011.* Edited by K. Holter and J. Ådna. Trondheim: Tapir Academic Press, 2011.

————. *Reflections of King Josiah in Chronicles: Late Stages of the Josiah Reception in 2 Chr 34f.* TSHB 2. Gütersloh: Gütersloher Verlag, 2003.

————. "Refocusing the Battle Accounts of the Kings: Identity Formation in the Books of Chronicles." Pages 245–74 in *Behutsamens Lesen. Alttestamentliche Exegese im interdisziplinären Methodendiskurs.* Edited by S. Lubs et al. Leipzig: Evangelische Verlagsanstalt, 2007.

————. "Reforming History: The Hermeneutical Significance of the Books of Chronicles." *VT* 57/1 (2007), pp. 21–44.

————. "Revisiting the Psalm Headings: Second Temple Levitical Propaganda?" Pages 102–22 in *Psalms and Liturgy.* Edited by D. J. Human and C. J. A. Vos. London: T&T Clark, 2004.

————. "Revisiting the Saul Narrative in Chronicles: Interacting with the Persian Imperial Context?" *OTE* 23/2 (2010), pp. 283–305.

————. "The Rhetorics of Finding a New Identity in a Multi-cultural and Multi-religious Society." *Verbum et Ecclesia* 24/2 (2004), pp. 396–416.

————. "Textual Identities in the Books of Chronicles: The Case of Jehoram's History." Pages 197–218 in *Community Identity in Judean Historiography. Biblical and Comparative Perspectives.* Edited by G. N. Knoppers and K. Ristau. Winona Lake, IN: Eisenbrauns, 2009.

————. "Who Constitutes Society? Yehud's Self-understanding in the Late Persian Era as Reflected in the Books of Chronicles." *JBL* 127/4 (2008), pp. 707–28.

Kalimi, I. *An Ancient Israelite Historian.* SSN 46. Assen: Van Gorcum, 2005.

————. "The Story about the Murder of the Prophet Zechariah in the Gospels and Its Relation to Chronicles." *RB* 116/2 (2009), pp. 246–61.

————. "The View of Jerusalem in the Ethnographical Introduction of Chronicles (1 Chr 1–9)." *Bib* 83/4 (2002), pp. 556–62.

Kloner, A., and I. Stern. "Idumea in the Late Persian Period (Fourth Century B.C.E.)." Pages 139–44 in *Judah and the Judeans in the Fourth Century B.C.E.* Edited by O. Lipschits, G. N. Knoppers, and R. Albertz. Winona Lake, IN: Eisenbrauns, 2007.

Knauf, E. A. "Jehoash's Improbably Inscription." *BN* 117 (2003), pp. 22–26.

Knoppers, G. N. "Greek Historiography and the Chronicler's History: A Reexamination." *JBL* 122/4 (2003), pp. 627–50.

————. "Intermarriage, Social Complexity, and Ethnic Diversity in the Genealogy of Judah." *JBL* 20/1 (2001), pp. 15–30.

————. "Israel's First King and 'the Kingdom of YHWH in the Hands of the Sons of David.' The Place of the Saulide Monarchy in the Chronicler's Historiography." Pages 187–213 in *Saul in Story and Tradition.* Edited by C. S. Ehrlich and M. C. White. FAT 47. Tübingen: Mohr Siebeck, 2006.

————. "Revisiting the Samarian Question in the Persian Period." Pages 265–89 in *Judah and the Judeans in the Persian Period.* Edited by O. Lipschits and M. Oeming. Winona Lake, IN: Eisenbrauns, 2006.

————. "Shem, Ham and Japheth: The Universal and the Particular in the Genealogy of Nations." Pages 13–31 in *The Chronicler as Theologian: Essays in Honor of Ralph W. Klein.* Edited by M. P. Graham. JSOTSup 371. London: T&T Clark, 2003.

————. "The Synoptic Problem? An Old Testament Perspective." *BBR* 19/1 (2009), pp. 11–34.

Knoppers, G. N., and P. B. Harvey Jr. "Omitted and Remaining Matters: On the Names Given to the Book of Chronicles in Antiquity." *JBL* 121/2 (2002), pp. 227–43.

Kuberski, P. "La Crémation dans la Bible? La Mort de Saül et de ses Fils (1 S 31; 1 Ch 10)." *Revue des sciences religieuses* 83/2 (2009), pp. 185–200.

Labahn, A., and E. Ben Zvi. "Observations on Women in the Genealogies of 1 Chronicles 1–9." *Bib* 84/4 (2003), pp. 457–78.

Leuchter, M. "'The Prophets' and 'The Levites' in Josiah's Covenant Ceremony." *ZAW* 121 (2009), pp. 31–47.

Levin, Y. "From Lists to History: Chronological Aspects of the Chronicler's Genealogies." *JBL* 123/4 (2004), pp. 601–36.

————. "Who Was the Chronicler's Audience? A Hint from His Genealogies." *JBL* 122/2 (2003), pp. 229–45.

Lipschits, O. *The Fall and Rise of Jerusalem.* Winona Lake, IN: Eisenbrauns, 2005.

————. "On Cash-Boxes and Finding or Not Finding Books: Jehoash's and Josiah's Decisions to Repair the Temple." Pages 239–54 in *Essays on Ancient Israel in Its Near Eastern Context: A Tribute to Nadav Na'aman.* Edited by Y. Amit, E. Ben Zvi, I. Finkelstein, and O. Lipschits. Winona Lake, IN: Eisenbrauns, 2006.

Lux, R. "Der zweite Tempel von Jerusalem—ein persisches oder prophetisches Projekt?" Pages 145–72 in *Das Alte Testament—ein Geschichtsbuch?! Geschichtschreibung oder Geschichtsüberlieferung im antiken Israel.* Edited by U. Becker and J. van Oorschot. Leipzig: Evangelische Verlagsanstalt, 2005.

McKenzie, S. L. "The Trouble with King Jehoshaphat." Pages 299–314 in *Reflection and Refraction: Studies in Biblical Historiography in Honour of A. Greame Auld.* Edited by R. Rezetko, T. H. Lim, and W. B. Aucker. Leiden: Brill, 2007.

Mitchell, C. "The Ironic Death of Josiah in Chronicles." *CBQ* 68/3 (2006), pp. 421–35.

————. "Power, *Eros,* and Biblical Genres." *The Bible and Critical Theory* 3/2 (2007), pp. 18.1–11.

Norin, S. "Die sogenannte Joaschinschrift." *BN* 117 (2005), pp. 61–74.

O'Kennedy, D. F. "Twee Weergawes van die Gebed van Salomo (1 Kon. 8 en 2 Kron. 6): 'n Vergelykende Studie." *AcT* 26/2 (2006), pp. 155–77.

Ortiz, S. "Urban City Planning in the Eighth Century: A Case Study of Recent Excavations at Tel Gezer (Reading Between the Lines: Uzziah's Expansion and Tel Gezer)." *RevExp* 106 (2009), pp. 361–81.

Rudman, D. "A Note on the Personal Name Amon [2 Kings 21,19–26 ‖ 2 Chr 33:21–25]." *Bib* 81/3 (2000), pp. 403–5.

Schaper, J. *Priester und Leviten im achämenidischen Juda.* Tübingen: Mohr Siebeck, 2000.

Schmidt, B. B., ed. *The Quest for the Historical Israel: Debating Archaeology and the History of Early Israel.* Leiden: Brill, 2007.

Snyman, G. F. "A Possible World of Text Production for the Genealogy in 1 Chronicles 2.3–4.23." Pages 32–60 in *The Chronicler as Theologian: Essays in Honor of Ralph W. Klein.* Edited by M. P. Graham. JSOTSup 371. London: T&T Clark.

Sparks, J. T. *The Chronicler's Genealogies: Towards an Understanding of 1 Chronicles 1–9.* Leiden: Brill, 2008.

Talshir, Z. "The Reign of Solomon in the Making: Pseudo-Connections between 3 Kingdoms and Chronicles." *VT* 50/2 (2000), pp. 233–49.

Throntveit, M. "Songs in a New Key: The Psalmic Structure of the Chronicler's Hymn (I Chr 16:8–36)." Pages 153–70 in *A God So Near: Essays on Old Testament Theology in Honor of Patrick D. Miller.* Edited by B. A. Strawn and N. R. Bowen. Winona Lake, IN: Eisenbrauns, 2003.

Van den Eynde, S. "Chronicler's Use of the Collocation ארון ברית יהוה." *ZAW* 113 (2001), pp. 422–30.

Van Peursen, W., and E. Talstra. "Computer-Assisted Analysis of Parallel Texts in the Bible: The Case of 2 Kings xviii–xxix and Its Parallels in Isaiah and Chronicles." *VT* 57 (2007), pp. 45–72.

Wagner, D. *Geist und Tora. Studien zur göttlichen Legitimation und Delegitimation von Herrschaft im Alten Testament anhand der Erzählungen über König Saul.* ABG 15. Leipzig: Evangelischer Verlagsanstalt, 2005.

Wiesehöfer, J. *Das antike Persien.* Düsseldorf: Albatros, 2005.

————. *Das frühe Persien. Geschichte eines antiken Weltreichs.* 3d ed. München: C. H. Beck, 2006.

Willi, T. "'Den Herrn aufsuchen . . .' Einsatz und Thema des narrativen Teils der Chronikbücher." Pages 432–44 in *L'Ecrit et l'Esprit: Etudes d'histoire du texte et de théologie biblique en hommage à Adrian Schenker.* Edited by D. Boehler et al. Göttingen: Vandenhoeck & Ruprecht, 2005.

————. "Gibt es in der Chronik eine 'Dynastie Davids'? Ein Beitrag zur Semantik von *byt.*" Pages 393–404 in '. . . *der seine Lust hat am Wort des Herrn!' Festschrift für Ernst Jenni zum 80. Geburtstag.* Edited by J. Luchsinger. Münster: Ugarit-Verlag, 2007.

————. "Inovation aus Tradition. Die chronistischen Bürgerlisten Israel 1Chr 1-9 im Focus von 1Chr 9." Pages 405–18 in *"Sieben Augen auf einem Stein" (Sach 3,9): Studien zur Literatur des Zweiten Tempels; Festschrift für Ina Willi-Plein zum 65. Geburtstag.* Edited by F. Hartenstein. Neukirchen-Vluyn: Neukirchener Verlag, 2007.

————. "Zwei Jahrzehnte Forschung an Chronik und Esra-Nehemia." *Theologische Rundschau* 67 (2002), pp. 61–104.

Williamson, H. G. M. *Studies in Persian Period History and Historiography.* Tübingen: Mohr Siebeck, 2004.

Subject Index

Scripture Index